MACROECONOMICS AND THE REAL WORLD

Volume 1

MACROECONOMICS
and the REAL WORLD

Volume 1
Econometric Techniques and Macroeconomics

Edited by
ROGER E. BACKHOUSE
ANDREA SALANTI

OXFORD
UNIVERSITY PRESS

This book has been printed digitally and produced in a standard specification in order to ensure its continuing availability

OXFORD
UNIVERSITY PRESS

Great Clarendon Street, Oxford OX2 6DP

Oxford University Press is a department of the University of Oxford.
It furthers the University's objective of excellence in research, scholarship,
and education by publishing world-wide in

Oxford New York

Auckland Bangkok Buenos Aires Cape Town Chennai
Dar es Salaam Delhi Hong Kong Istanbul Karachi Kolkata
Kuala Lumpur Madrid Melbourne Mexico City Mumbai Nairobi
São Paulo Shanghai Taipei Tokyo Toronto

Oxford is a registered trade mark of Oxford University Press
in the UK and in certain other countries

Published in the United States
by Oxford University Press Inc., New York

ISBN 978-0-19-924204-7

ACKNOWLEDGEMENTS

The essays and comments collected in these two volumes were originally presented at, or arose out of, a conference on 'Theory and Evidence in Macroeconomics', held at the University of Bergamo on 15–17 October 1998. The editors would like to thank all the participants for their valuable contributions and, last but not least, Ms Laura Capelli and Ms Paola Bortolotti of the secretarial staff of the Department of Economics of the University of Bergamo for their invaluable assistance. Very grateful acknowledgements are also due to the same Department for the financial support which made possible the organization of the conference. Editing these volumes took place whilst Roger Backhouse was holding a British Academy Research Readership and he wishes to thank the British Academy for its support. Five papers from the conference (by McCallum, Vercelli, Smith, Juselius, and Dixon) were included as a symposium in the *Journal of Economic Methodology* (6(2), July 1999). Two of these have been substantially revised and the remaining three are published here with the permission of Routledge.

CONTENTS

1. Introduction to volume 1   1
   Roger E. Backhouse and Andrea Salanti

PART I: BUSINESS CYCLES   21

2. Knowing the cycle   23
   Don Harding and Adrian Pagan

3. Fiscal shocks in an efficiency wage model   43
   Craig Burnside, Martin Eichenbaum, and Jonas D. M. Fisher

4A. The return of business cycles   61
   James E. Hartley

4B. Business cycles: general discussion   69

PART II: MONETARY POLICY   83

5. Does money determine UK inflation over the long run?   85
   David F. Hendry

6. Recent developments in monetary policy analysis:
   the roles of theory and evidence   115
   Bennett T. McCallum

7A. Explanatory strategies for monetary policy analysis   141
   Mary S. Morgan

7B. Monetary policy: general discussion   155

PART III: THE INFLUENCE OF RECENT DEVELOPMENTS
          IN ECONOMETRIC TECHNIQUES   165

8. Models and relations in economics and econometrics   167
   Katarina Juselius

9. Unit roots and all that: the impact of time-series
   methods on macroeconomics   199
   Ron P. Smith

10A. Models all the way down   219
      Kevin D. Hoover

10B. New econometric techniques and macroeconomics   225
      Carlo Favero

10C. Econometric techniques: general discussion   237

PART IV: GROWTH   247

11.   Econometric analysis and the study of economic growth:
      a sceptical perspective   249
      Steven N. Durlauf

12.   Growth models and the explanation of the forces
      behind development processes   263
      Paolo Sylos Labini

13.   Why so much scepticism about growth theory?   275
      Andrea Salanti

1 Introduction to volume 1

ROGER E. BACKHOUSE AND ANDREA SALANTI

1. Introduction

Macroeconomics poses important, and difficult methodological questions, some of which do not arise in microeconomics. These are important for practising macro-economists because there is widespread disagreement in macroeconomics, both over policy and over how data should be analysed. It may be the case that there is more of a consensus over macroeconomic theory than in the days when the 'monetarist–Keynesian' controversy was at its height, with widespread agreement that theories should be based on individual optimization and rational expectations, but differences remain. On top of this are differences over the type of evidence that should be used and how it should be used. What, for example, should be the relationship between the assumption of individual rationality, microeconomic evidence, historical studies, and statistics? Even if we confine our attention to statistical evidence, there remain acute divisions over how such evidence should be used.

Furthermore, macroeconomics has always represented a sort of methodological paradox within economics. On the one hand, if only because of the problem of aggregation, macrotheories and models look less rigorous and theoretically justified than their counterparts in microeconomics. On the other hand, due to its having to deal with 'analysis applied to facts' (Hicks 1979: p. ix) in the shape of either 'commonsense perception' and 'everyday experience' (Solow 1998: 1–3) or 'empirical modelling' (Granger 1999), it should be more easily approachable by means of the conceptual tools of the philosophy of (hard) science, at least those traditionally connected with the empiricist tradition. Somewhat surprisingly, however, the traditional methodological literature (see, for example, Blaug 1992; Caldwell 1993) offers little guidance. Induction versus deduction, confirmation versus falsification, the Duhem–Quine problem, piecemeal theorizing, adhocness, and the tenacity of theories are all issues that have to be faced but in order to say something about them it is necessary to discuss the subject in far more detail than has often been done.[1]

It was to address such problems that we organized a conference on the theme, 'Theory and evidence in macroeconomics', held in the University of Bergamo on 15–17 October 1998. We took the view that, in order to make progress, it was

---

[1] This is not to say that methodological discussions of macroeconomics, and/or (macro)econometrics have been completely absent. Examples include Backhouse (1995, 1997); Darnell and Evans (1990); Dow (1996); Epstein (1987); Granger (1999); Hands (1993); Hoover (1988, 1995); Klein (1994); Mayer (1993); Morgan (1988, 1990); Pagan (1987); Vercelli and Dimitri (1992). Macroeconomics has, however, been comparatively neglected in the recent literature on economic methodology.

necessary to bring together practising macroeconomists and econometricians as well as specialists in economic methodology. We decided on eight topics, and for each of these we commissioned two papers, one from someone more committed to econometric research, the other from someone nearer the theoretical end of the spectrum. Specialists in methodology were selected as discussants. We then allowed considerable time for discussion from the floor, correctly anticipating that this would be one of the most valuable aspects of the conference.

The result of that process (involving, as usual, a few unavoidable deviations from the envisaged ideal) is the papers contained in this and the companion volume. Though the division is to a certain extent arbitrary, the papers fall broadly into two categories. Volume 1 is focused on alternative econometric techniques and the impact these have had, or should have, on macroeconomics, whilst Volume 2 is centred on the closely related questions of Keynesian economics, employment, and policy. However, there is enormous overlap between the two volumes, which should be considered as a whole.

2. Methodological questions in macroeconomics

Macroeconomics would seem a particularly important subject for methodological analysis, for a variety of reasons:

- When critics point to the failure of economics, it is frequently macroeconomics (in particular macroeconomic forecasting) to which they point.
- There is believed to be much greater disagreement amongst economists on macro-economic questions than on microeconomic ones.
- Though the increased availability of micro data sets and suitable computing technology has changed the situation substantially in recent years, econometrics has generally been more prominent in macroeconomics than in microeconomics.
- Macroeconomics raises specific questions about the use of econometrics due to the nature of the data, in particular the time-series properties of much macroeconomic data.
- The agenda for macroeconomics is, to a greater extent than that for micro-economics, determined by factors outside the discipline. Macroeconomics has to provide diagnoses and remedies for problems such as unemployment, inflation, productivity slowdowns, and financial crises, whether or not these are the topics that, from a scientific point of view, are the ones the discipline is best equipped to tackle.

Thus Blanchard and Fisher (1989: p. xii) write:

Working macroeconomists, like doctors treating cancer, cannot wait for all the answers to analyse events and help policy. They have to take guesses and rely on a battery of models that cannot be derived from first principles but have repeatedly proved useful.

In this respect macroeconomics is more like social science as seen by Kuhn (1970: 164):

> The latter [social scientists] often tend, as the former [natural scientists] almost never do, to defend their choice of a research problem—e.g. the effects of racial discrimination or the causes of the business cycle—chiefly in terms of the social importance of achieving a solution.[2]

Even if there are doubts about how far Kuhn's characterization is appropriate for all natural sciences and even if the difference between micro and macro is not a sharp one, there is nonetheless an important difference in emphasis.

The main reason why macroeconomics poses distinctive methodological questions is that it has to look in two directions: towards macroeconomic evidence about the real world and towards microeconomics. These raise different sets of problems and in addition to these, questions arise about how these two types of evidence should be combined and what should be done when they conflict.

2.1. Macroeconomics and macroeconomic evidence

The most familiar form of macroeconomic evidence is statistical: aggregative data such as national income accounts, employment statistics, interest rate and price data, and so on. These are usually taken to refer directly to variables that appear in macroeconomic models, though even this is sometimes problematic. For example, it can be unclear which measure of national income to use and switching from one to another may give different results. More difficult, once it is established what data set to use, there arises the question of how to analyse it and how to confront it with the model. Should testing comprise confirmation or falsification: is it better to find a model that fits the data or to use the data to reject models that are unsatisfactory? Whichever choice is made, the biggest question turns out to be what statistical techniques to employ in order to estimate parameters and decide whether the fit between the model and the data is satisfactory.

Though such issues arise in any discipline where statistical evidence is used, macroeconomics faces particular problems because of distinctive characteristics of macroeconomic data. The data are typically aggregative. There is aggregation over commodities, with data on real variables often being obtained, in practice, by deflating income data with more or less appropriate price indices. Data on stocks, notably capital, are often calculated by perpetual inventory methods—as cumulative sums of net investment. There is also aggregation over time. The macroeconomist typically works with a model specified in continuous time (or based around a time-period of arbitrary length) and has to fit this using monthly, quarterly, or annual data.

These features of macroeconomic data raise methodological problems at two levels. They clearly pose practical questions that must be answered whenever statistical work is undertaken. However, they are also relevant to deeper methodological issues that relate to those discussed in the methodology literature. The most obvious set of

---

[2] Kuhn goes on to ask, 'Which group would one then expect to solve problems at a more rapid rate?'

problems arises in studies based on time-series data sets. Time-series data pose specific statistical problems, with a range of competing methods having been developed to solve them. It is hard to comment on strategies for testing theories, and even on the possibility of confirming or refuting theories, without taking these into account for they raise the question of how far it is in practice possible to test a theory and what would constitute such a conclusive test. Cross-section studies, such as those often used in the growth literature, raise a different set of issues. Neither case, for example, conforms to the type of experimental situation for which classical statistical methods were developed. The difference between the processes by which macroeconomic data are generated and laboratory experiments also create conceptual problems about what constitutes replication.[3]

In addition to statistical data, macroeconomics also uses institutional and historical evidence about the real world. Economists have direct information about central bank operating procedures, about the way in which fiscal decisions are made, legislative changes, and many other things that are believed to be relevant to macroeconomic phenomena.[4] There is also a wealth of historical evidence. This may include statistical information but this is combined with other evidence and, more importantly, relates to specific events. Thus where an econometric study might represent the unique features of the Great Depression or World War II as random shocks, elements of a stochastic process with particular properties, the historian may see more significance in them and reach a conclusion very different from that reached by the econometrician. This raises the question of how these different types of evidence should be reconciled.

2.2. Macroeconomics and microeconomics

The relationship between micro- and macroeconomics raises a different set of methodological questions. The contemporary consensus is that macroeconomic theories should be derived from microeconomic foundations and that these should be based on the assumption of individual rationality. A major problem, however, is that the conditions under which it is possible to aggregate from micro to macro are almost never satisfied. How should economists respond to this? One is to disregard aggregation problems, using devices such as the representative agent, trusting that if this is illegitimate, this will show up when the resulting macromodels are confronted with macroevidence. Another response is that aggregation problems undermine the search for microfoundations and economics should instead be searching for regularities at the macrolevel.

Both these strategies, however, raise further problems of their own. The strategy of seeking regularities can be criticized by arguing that they can never be established by induction, however much data are available and because the processes whereby they are collected and aggregated mean they can never be free of theory. The theoretical

---

[3] See Cartwright (1991); Backhouse (1997: ch. 11).
[4] It is this kind of evidence about the institutional environment which offers, for instance, some insights on how to shape the behaviour of economic policy authorities in a way suitable for game-theoretic analysis.

strategy is always open to the criticism of simply begging the relevant questions in more than one respect. Indeed, even apart from doubts about aggregation conditions, the representative agent fiction ends up by preventing macroeconomics from exploiting all the richness of modern microeconomic theory.

For its part, microeconomic evidence is often contradictory and ambiguous. During the last three decades microeconomists have abandoned the constricting neo-Walrasian idea of general equilibrium analysis as the overarching theoretical framework in order to exploit the wider descriptive flexibility allowed by a range of partial equilibrium approaches. In doing this, however, they have had to incur a cost. Many such models reach interesting results only *because* they are deliberately biased caricatures, in the sense of Gibbard and Varian (1978), that are thought to provide interesting insights into some microeconomic situations. This means that they are inadequate as general microfoundations.[5]

All of these questions relate to issues that methodologists and philosophers of science have discussed. To provide effective answers, however, requires attention to detail—to attend to the practicalities of what can actually be done. This can make things more complicated but equally it may point to solutions. Difficulties that seem significant in the abstract may in practice turn out to be much less important.

3. Microfoundations

It is nowadays widely accepted that macroeconomic models need microfoundations and that these should be based on assumptions of rational expectations and intertemporal utility maximization. This view is best represented in the paper by Burnside, Eichenbaum, and Fisher (1-3). [Note: references of this form denote volume number and chapter.] They model behaviour in terms of a representative household maximizing a discounted sum of expected utility and a perfectly competitive firm maximizing profit. Even though the model is calibrated to fit certain macroeconomic evidence, its properties reflect the values chosen for the parameters that describe microeconomic behaviour. It is, therefore, an attempt to base macroeconomic theory on rigorous microfoundations. This view that macrotheories need microfoundations is shared by Delli Gatti and Tamborini (2-8) and Dixon (2-9). The difference is that they seek to establish different microfoundations involving rationing and imperfect competition.

This view contrasts with the approach taken by Hendry (1-5) and Juselius (1-8) for whom theory does no more than suggest a behavioural relationship and a list of variables that might affect the macroeconomic problem they are tackling. Microfoundations are implicit, in that there are well-known microeconomic theories that will produce money-demand functions of the form that they use but the detail is left in the background. There are several microtheories that could be used. This contrasts with the view that microfoundations should be explicit.

---

[5] For a different opinion on the possibility of exploiting an eclectic mixture of different microfoundations for different aggregate markets, see Stiglitz (1992).

The problem with seeking to base macromodels on explicit, formal, microfoundations is that the conditions required for aggregation are either unknown or are not met. Sims (2-4B) made the point that, given that we know that many markets are oligopolistic, the ideal would be to work with oligopolistic microfoundations. The problem is that we do not know how to aggregate such models, which is why much of the imperfect-competition literature assumes monopolistic competition. However, this is an interesting line of defence, for it seems clear that, even if markets exhibit perfect or monopolistic competition, the conditions required for aggregation are unlikely to be met. Rigorous aggregation in these models is possible only through assuming away aggregation problems, such as by postulating a single representative agent or markets populated by identical firms. Rigour has been purchased at the cost of making assumptions that are contradicted by the evidence or, at least, that introduce some *ad hoc* specifications just in order to obtain the solvability of the model.[6]

This raises the question of how one can justify such an approach. The obvious answer is that the assumptions are justified by the success of the model—which in Burnside, Eichenbaum, and Fisher's case is its ability to mimic the response of the economy to a fiscal shock. If this criterion is met, the implied conclusion is that aggregation problems and departures from competitive, optimizing behaviour are in practice not sufficiently important to matter. Thus Pagan (2-10B) responds to New Keynesian models by saying that he does not see what implications they have for the data, and that some of them output dynamics that are more complicated than anything one does see in the data.

What is probably the most widely held defence of formal microfoundations based on optimizing behaviour was articulated by Eichenbaum (2-4B). It has two strands. The first is that understanding a phenomenon means knowing what it means in terms of agents' motivations. For him, merely fitting equations, or finding regularities, does not constitute understanding. The second is that optimization is a way of being precise so that it is not necessary for people to guess what you mean. His objection to Keynes is not that he was wrong but that it is impossible, even decades later, to work out what he meant. In another session (2-7B) he added a third—that one of the merits of 'optimization-based' models is that they break down the separateness of macro and micro. If the goal is not so much to generate the best theory as to develop conditions under which progress is likely to occur, this may be important if it leads to the exploration of avenues that would otherwise remain closed. The sociological effect of a theory may be significant. This opens up the questions of whether the sociology of the profession (also referred to by Morgan (2-4B)) may merit more attention.

Arguments against this were offered by Hendry. He (1-7B) introduces the idea that behaviour may mimic rationality even though it is not rational. Expectations, he argued, could not possibly be rational because the sort of information that would be

---

[6] Think, for instance, of the widely employed Dixit–Stiglitz assumption that good are symmetrical imperfect substitutes in models of monopolistic competition. Many would agree that this assumption is far from satisfactory in a number of respects but, as noted by Lipsey (2-4A) and Sims (2-4B), it is nonetheless widely employed because of its analytical tractability.

needed is obviously not available. Some behaviour is clearly irrational. However, under some circumstances agents may mimic rationality. During the sample covered by his model, for example, agents could have formed unbiased expectations simply by assuming $\Delta^2 \log P = 0$ and assuming that inflation would be the same as in the previous period. Such a forecasting rule would not be efficient, but one might defend it as boundedly rational in the same way that Dixon (2-10B) points out that cost-plus pricing rules may be boundedly rational. Such rules can imply behaviour that is different from what one would derive from full optimization models—cost-plus pricing, for example, implies price stickiness.

Perhaps the most radical response to the project of seeking formal microfoundations, also offered by Hendry (1-7B), is that macroeconomic models should be about discovering system properties—properties of macroeconomic systems that are not to be found at the level of individual agents. He likens his models, not based on formal microfoundations, to the models used in hydrology.[7]

Hendry, therefore, is arguing that macroeconomics (though it clearly has to be consistent with what we know of microeconomic behaviour) is partly autonomous in that it may uncover relationships that emerge only at the macroeconomic level and that these relationships can provide the basis for explanations. This is in marked contrast with the RBC programme, exemplified by Eichenbaum, which seeks to explain macroeconomic phenomena in terms of behaviour at the microeconomic level. Similar issues are raised by Ferri (2-5) who argues that the Phillips curve should be seen as a system relationship, depending on the operation of the entire economic system. He also raises the possibility that it may be derived from microfoundations other than optimization in perfectly competitive markets.

This choice between theories with rigorous microfoundations and theories that represent purely macroeconomic properties is linked to other methodological issues, notably the virtues of simplicity and the relative weights to attach to theory versus stable statistical relationships. Eichenbaum (1-7B) points out that McCallum's paper (1-6) 'points to some of the tensions in the desire for simplicity when we model and the desire for richness of detail when we actually go to the data'. One reason why Hendry differs from Eichenbaum and McCallum, being much more sceptical about the value of simple models, is that he attaches great weight to the data and he attaches great significance to the enormous number of factors that have to be taken into account in order to explain the historical record.

However, the significance of these issues depends on specific contexts. This is illustrated by the discussion of the labour market. Oswald and Trostel (2-6) share with Burnside, Eichenbaum, and Fisher the view that the microeconomic foundations of macroeconomics are important, but they use statistical, microeconomic evidence to challenge some of the simplifying assumptions that macrotheorists frequently make.

---

[7] 'I think it is simply unimaginable where hydrology would be today if hydrologists had insisted on working out the theory of turbulence from quantum dynamics. They wouldn't have made one iota of a contribution to understanding it because it is a system property and it is enormously complicated how turbulence behaves, how waves behave, how they propagate, etc.' (1-7B, p. 156).

Hendry (2-4B), though sharing their desire to place a high weight on observable statistical regularities, is sceptical about the value of their results. The reason, he argues, why there is so much more consensus amongst labour economists using large-sample cross-section data sets is that they are failing to apply statistical tests that are as rigorous as those used in the analysis of macro time-series data. Hausman made the point that it is hazardous to use any observed relationship in a theory if we do not know why it obtains. However, even if they represent correlations that correspond to no causal relationship, they may nonetheless be phenomena that theorists ought to be trying to explain.

4. Can macroeconomic theories be tested?

A basic tenet of the modern conception of science is that the ultimate criterion for appraising theories is, or should be, they should fit with what happens (or seems to happen) in the real world or in the laboratory. Given the obvious difficulties with conceiving of experiments in macroeconomics, econometrics might therefore appear as the best set of tools at our disposal for testing theories. This requires, of course, that theories are properly designed for testing and that appropriate data and quantitative techniques for their treatment are available. Because these conditions are hard to meet, the problem of testing is never as trivial as one might expect from this commonsense account of scientific research activity.

Macroeconomics (and microeconomics too, for that matter) is no exception. Indeed, economic methodologists have, following philosophers, made much of the Duhem–Quine problem and the impossibility of conclusively testing any scientific theory. Methodology textbooks all point to the auxiliary assumptions and *ceteris paribus* conditions that make it possible to save any theory from refutation. In macroeconomics and econometrics this problem arises in four guises: (i) identification; (ii) model specification; (iii) observational equivalence; and (iv) evaluation of (possibly alternative) models. The papers and discussions brought together in these volumes touch on all four of these, discussing both their implications in practice and how they might be reduced.

Sometimes, in the methodological literature, a distinction is made between 'testing theories' and 'building empirical models' (or similar expressions), as if the respective outcomes would require two quite different *methodological* appraisals.[8] In what follows very little emphasis is placed on this distinction because, in our opinion, it is at most a matter of degree and not one of real substance. 'Measurement without theory' may surely be a neat and impressive label for an academic manifesto but if taken literally it is simply false: what actually happens when people say that they are not trying to test any particular theory it is that they are testing (possibly particular versions of) a theory or a model of their own instead of one provided ready-made by 'theorists'. Admittedly,

---

[8] Cf., e.g. Granger (1999) and Morgan (1988, 1990).

such models may well have been designed according to criteria and priorities very different from those usually endorsed by theorists, but this just means that we are dealing with a different kind of theory (which, is *per se* perfectly legitimate).

4.1. Identification and specification

The traditional view about identification and specification problems is based upon a distinction which sees identification as primarily a statistical matter and specification as something to be approached with reference to some a priori knowledge provided by economic theory. Such a view was repeatedly challenged during the conference— there was close to a consensus that the two issues are strictly intertwined.

On the one hand, for instance, Smith (1-9) argues that identification is an economic problem, not the statistical one that econometrics textbooks sometimes lead readers to assume it to be. It is fundamentally a matter of data interpretation. Textbook discussions of the properties of relevant matrices may be important in helping economists to sort out the statistical properties of their models and hence whether their assumptions are consistent with what the econometrician claims to have identified. In the last resort, however, identification involves making a judgement about the data that takes into account more than simply the structure of the model and the numbers fed into the computer. On the other hand Hendry, in his own contribution (1-5) as well as in a number of scattered observations in general discussions, advocates a more 'data-driven' approach to model specification. Taken together, both these positions undermine the traditional view that identification is a purely statistical problem and model specification is a theoretical issue.

Another source of tension between theoretical representations and properties of data emerges from Harding and Pagan's (1-2) proposal to (re)focus applied research on business cycles on to the time-honoured task of identifying the 'turning points' in economic activity (a perspective that recent theories of business cycle tend to neglect). The subsequent comment by Hartley (1-4A) and general discussion (1-4B) remind us that our perception of facts is theory-laden to the point that even the definition of what constitutes a business cycle is controversial.

For these reasons, among others, identification and model specification can never be completely conclusive and therefore, as McCallum (1-6) points out, single econometric studies are generally not decisive. What happens is rather that evidence has a cumulative effect to the point where the weight of evidence becomes convincing. Evidence from different studies is brought together in an informal, but nonetheless persuasive, way.

Juselius (1-8) approaches the problem of whether economic theories can be tested by posing a challenge to macroeconomic theorists from another perspective. As an econometrician, she argues that the possibilities for confronting models with evidence depend crucially on how they are formulated. The traditional approach involves formulating a deterministic theoretical model to which error terms are added so that inferences can be made concerning parameter values. This, she argues, means that it will never be possible to test models against all the stochastic properties of the data.

To do this, models need to be formulated as stochastic models from the start. In other words, Juselius suggests that economic theories could be constructed so as to be more testable than they are at the moment.[9]

A related point is that in practice the testability of a theory may depend on how one approaches the relationship between theory and data. A common approach is to start from a theoretical model, add stochastic components and then test the model. An alternative approach is to start with a general stochastic model, testing theoretical relationships as restrictions on this. These two approaches can produce very different results. The contrast between these two methods is one way in which the conflict between deduction and induction emerges in practice. It would be going too far to classify either method as deductive or inductive but there is a clear difference of emphasis. Juselius's method, of starting with a general stochastic model, obviously involves theory at the start (for no model can be completely general) but it allows maximum scope for data to influence the final model. This is very much in the spirit of induction. In contrast, the standard approach tests a model the detailed specification of which comes from economic theory.

4.2. Observational equivalence and evaluation

Identification and specification, however, do not exhaust the problem of testability of macroeconomic theories. When theories and their applications are subjected to overall evaluations of their predictive or explanatory power a number of other problems come into the foreground. Two issues, in particular, deserve to be mentioned.

The first arises from theorists' attitudes towards theoretical models which are not suited to empirical testing but which they nonetheless consider useful in other respects.[10] In Vercelli's paper (2-2), for example, the question is raised of whether a successful theory *should* be testable. It is argued that the longevity of the IS–LM model arises not from its success in meeting empirical tests but in its flexibility. This model which, at its minimum, comprises equilibrium loci for the product and money markets, is compatible with numerous assumptions about what lies behind these loci.[11] The IS–LM model is thus not testable, but provides a framework within which testable models can be constructed. Such an argument immediately suggests scope for a Kuhnian or a Lakatosian analysis. For example, we might reconstruct the IS–LM

---

[9] The points made in the previous two paragraphs are related to points made in Backhouse (1997) in the context of replication. There it is suggested that replication is informal, involving a series of studies rather than ones that are individually persuasive, and is a question of how economic theories are formulated.

[10] Such an attitude is by no means confined to macroeconomics. In the introductory chapter of one of the most acclaimed advanced textbooks in microeconomics the author is very explicit: 'What constitutes better understanding? ... The standard acid test is that the theory should be (a) testable and (b) tested empirically, either in the real world or in the lab. But many of the models and theories ... have not been subjected to a rigorous empirical test, and some of them may never be. Yet, I maintain, models untested rigorously may still lead to better understanding, through a process that combines casual empiricism and intuition' (Kreps 1990: 7).

[11] It could be formulated even more generally if, following Tobin (1969), the LM curve is seen as the equilibrium locus for the entire financial sector, which may not even involve a single asset that is designated 'money'.

model itself as a Lakatosian hard core with the microfoundations of the two loci lying in the protective belt. The problem with such an interpretation, however, is that they have no commitment to the IS–LM independently of the assumptions on which the curves are based. They are derived relationships, not something about which economists have commitments. It would therefore be paradoxical if something that is a derived feature of the model, and which is not in itself testable, were something to which economists were committed.[12] Vercelli explores some of the reasons, other than the model's predictive success and mainly related to the adaptability of IS–LM models to changing macroeconomic environments, why the model might have persisted for so long.

Economists' theoretical commitments seem to play an important role in evaluating theories in another respect—in accepting or rejecting particular causal explanations that empirical evidence seems to suggest as the most likely among those contemplated as possibilities within a given class of models. Indeed, one way to characterize the explanatory role of theoretical models is to say, following Rappaport (1998: ch. 8), in his turn referring to Miller (1987), that formal modelling helps to delimit the set of possible (causal) explanations appropriate to specific situations. According to this interpretation, causal explanations emerge from the comparison of rival hypotheses, among which the most plausible should be selected on the basis of the available empirical evidence in any specific circumstance.

What happens, however, is that some hypotheses are regarded as more (or less) plausible than others on a priori grounds, quite independently of the robustness of the available empirical research. A number of general discussions in the two volumes (see, for instance, 1-4B on business cycles; 1-7B on monetary policy; 2-7B on the labour market; 2-10B on new Keynesian economics) provide clear examples of how people of different theoretical persuasions react differently to the same kind of 'evidence'.

5. Do macroeconomic theories change in response to evidence?

McCallum (1-6) argues that though the evolution of macroeconomic theory has in part been driven by theoretical considerations (pre-eminent amongst which is the assumption of rational expectations), theorists have undoubtedly taken account of evidence. Behind this general claim, lies his judgement that the balance between the roles of theory and evidence is about right. Two things are worth noting about this. The first is that he sees the problem as one of a balance between two influences. This is consistent with a view whereby theory and evidence both impact on macroeconomists' views about the world. It is not consistent with the 'conventional view' of the role of evidence as being to test theories—in such a context it does not make sense to speak of

---

[12] This is not to say that it is not possible to offer a Lakatosian interpretation of the evolution of IS–LM models. For example, one might suggest that such research in the 1950s and 1960s could be explained as a programme based on: (i) the analysis of a small number of aggregate relations; (ii) the analysis of market equilibrium conditions; and (iii) the possibility of an equilibrium with less than full employment. But the IS–LM model itself does not form part of such a hard core.

the relative impacts of theory and evidence. The second is that McCallum's is a pragmatic, empirical judgement. Consider, for instance, his views concerning price stickiness as a phenomenon that arises in many macroeconomic models but for which there is no theoretical reason whatsoever. Models can be built to explain price stickiness, but that is a different matter. The main reason why price stickiness is assumed is, McCallum claims, that it is necessary in order to explain the evidence. In a similar vein he argues that contemporary models take the interest rate, not the money supply, as the authorities' monetary policy instrument because this is how monetary authorities are known to operate. One of the significant features of these two examples is that evidence is convincing, if not overwhelming, even though there is no formal econometric test that has been decisive.[13] McCallum even expresses doubts about the limited work that has been done (in particular by Blinder) to test price stickiness directly.

However, although decisive tests are rarely possible, some papers cite one example where such a test occurred: the rejection of the hypothesis that monetary shocks were the cause of the business cycle. This led directly to the emergence of real business cycle theory. McCallum claims simply that 'the upsurge of the RBC movement can be viewed as principally empirical' (McCallum 1-6). Smith goes even further, writing of Nelson and Plosser's work that:

[t]heir results killed the previously fashionable model which explained GDP variations by money-supply surprises; there was no way this could be true since money-supply surprises were white noise by construction and GDP variations were highly persistent. The Lucas supply curve, found in most theoretical models at that time, just could not provide an interpretation of summary statistics of the time-series properties. (Smith 1-9, p. 206)

This is as close to a decisive result as one could reasonably hope for. It is, of course, important to bear in mind, however, that though empirical work did have this effect, it was within the context of a very specific set of theoretical assumptions such as rational expectations and competitive market clearing. In the context of Juselius's claims cited in the previous section it is worth noting that it was only because the stochastic properties of the theoretical model were precisely specified (money-supply shocks are white noise) that the model was testable.

Looking at IS–LM analysis, Vercelli (2-2) argues that macroeconomic theory made major changes directly in response to evidence. These changes took two forms. The major structural change in the economic environment that took place in the 1970s led to a new generation of IS–LM models. These were based on forward-looking expectations and the assumption that the classical dichotomy must hold in the long run. These are theoretical requirements but the motivation of making such modifications was that the models could not otherwise explain the new economic regime. In addition minor changes in the environment produced minor amendments to the model. The simplest IS–LM model, Vercelli claims, was successful in the 1950s because the world fitted the model, with few significant supply shocks. When such

---

[13] This is consistent with the claims made by Summers (1991).

shocks occurred in the 1960s, the model had to be augmented with a Phillips curve. In other words, though the IS–LM model itself survived, evidence was crucial in causing changes in the way the model was used and in the way it was understood. It remains to be established, however, whether or not these changes can be regarded as examples of progressive improvements in macroeconomic theory. More detailed analysis would be necessary to exclude the possibility that in some cases the modifications to which supporters of IS–LM resorted were *ad hoc* (one doubtful case being the addition of the Phillips curve).[14]

Dixon's paper (2-9) also supports the idea that theories may persist despite anomalous evidence. Faced with evidence that Walrasian models could not explain, such as the persistence of unemployment and shocks to output, resort was made to the *ad hoc* assumption of sticky prices. This was *ad hoc* in the sense that it was inconsistent with the assumption of competitive equilibrium. Economists were also prepared to ignore the fact—obvious to most people—that when people become unemployed their welfare falls.

This example raises two further methodological points. The first is that the role of theory and evidence may depend critically on the time-period that is investigated and the stage of development of a theory. The pattern Dixon points out, which is compatible with Kuhn's account of scientific revolutions, is that evidence produces anomalies and *ad hoc* modifications of the theory. There then follows a stage in which the resulting theoretical inconsistencies are removed. In some cases this can be regarded as saving the paradigm. In others it results in the creation of a new paradigm.[15] If we look only at this second stage, theoretical considerations appear decisive. The second point concerns whether or not it is undesirable to rely on *ad hoc* modifications to a theory. McCallum (1986), for example, has argued that when the world is more complicated than any model we could analyse, it cannot be assumed that theories containing *ad hoc* assumptions are necessarily inferior to ones that do not.[16]

There is a further aspect of the relationship between theory and evidence that may encourage the practice of having recourse to *ad hoc* assumptions in macroeconomics. As a number of papers point out, empirical evidence is often far from being decisive. Sometimes it may offer clear suggestions about things that were *less* important than expected together with much less clear insights about the relevant determinants.[17] In other cases, as Durlauf (1-11) maintains, apropos of the econometric evidence provided by the empirical work connected with new growth theory, applied research turns out to be inconclusive because it offers too many different explanatory variables. Finally, it may happen that empirical evidence cannot properly be exploited, simply because theorists are unable (given the theoretical strategies to which they are committed) to build up a theory consistent with it. Oswald and Trostel (2-6, p. 139) are quite explicit

---

[14] For a useful discussion of the various ways in which the term '*ad hoc*' has been used, see Hands (1988).

[15] We leave open the question of whether the new Keynesian imperfect competition approach to macroeconomics amounts to a new paradigm in Kuhn's sense.

[16] The Dixit–Stiglitz assumption of goods that are symmetrical imperfect substitutes in models of monopolistic competition (see n. 6 above) could be regarded as a case in point.

[17] Cf., e.g. Hendry's (1-5) conclusions about what determined UK inflation during the 1960s and 1970s.

on this point. After having presented six alleged regularities in labour-market data (they are modest enough to avoid to call them 'stylized facts'), they conclude that

[t]hese disparate types of evidence suggest that labour markets do not operate in a simple competitive spot-market fashion. The emerging findings will face opposition—because the competitive spot-market paradigm is the dominant way the profession thinks (both formally and informally). ... The profession's modelling strategies will not change quickly. There are significant obstacles. First, and probably most importantly, the appropriate alternative strategy is not clear.

All in all, it seems possible to conclude that empirical evidence drives theoretical changes in macroeconomics when two conditions are satisfied: evidence must be unambiguous (as far as it can be reasonably expected) *and* suited to theoretical rationalization (notably with reference to the problem of aggregation). Otherwise the door remains open for theories grounded on more doubtful and somewhat compromising assumptions.

6. Macroeconomics and policy

The relationship between macroeconomics and government policy raises methodological questions that have implications for the choices economists make between theories. It is usually taken as given that one of the main reasons for doing macroeconomics is to improve the quality of the advice that can be offered to policy-makers. This argument, however, can be taken in several directions. If the main requirement of policy-makers is accurate forecasts, economic theory is relevant only in so far as it leads to this end. If they offer better forecasts, for example, VARs or other time-series models may be all that is required, even if they cannot be interpreted and even if there is no theoretical rationale for the variables that appear in them. The problem with this strategy is that, should the system change, models may cease to forecast well. Macroeconomic theory becomes relevant as a means for finding models that will be more robust. In other words, our belief about the likely robustness of a model may depend not only on its past performance (what statistical analysis can measure) but also on our beliefs about whether or not it corresponds to features of the economy that are likely to remain unchanged in the presence of shocks to the system. This is a theoretical as much as a statistical question.

Policy-makers, however, require more than forecasts. They want to understand why things are happening and how the economy will respond to actions they might take. This is a statement not just about the relationship of macroeconomic models to the real world (whether the models seek to explain rather than just to forecast) but it is also a statement about the relationship of macroeconomic models to the questions policy-makers are asking and what they are able to understand. This issue arises sharply in the discussion of the business cycle. Harding and Pagan (1-2) claim that what concerns policy-makers is fluctuations in output, especially turning points. This leads them to argue that any model that purports to be a model of the business cycle should explain the key features of the classical cycle and they present algorithms that can be used to extract the required information. Pagan (1-4B) therefore argues that before he will take a business-cycle model seriously he wants to know what sort of business cycle it generates. They are critical of Burnside, Eichenbaum, and Fisher (1-3) for not providing this information. Burnside, Eichenbaum, and Fisher (1-4B) respond by arguing that the cycle generated by their model will depend on how the exogenous technology shocks are modelled and so they do not answer this question. They argue that what matters to policy-makers is how a model responds to policy interventions and so they prefer to evaluate their model by seeing how it responds to different shocks.

Whether or not one judges a business-cycle model on the basis of its ability to explain turning points in a variable such as real GDP or in terms of its ability to explain co-movements of various series depends on what one is trying to explain. Harding and Pagan argue that if one is claiming to explain the business cycle, then one should explain turning points in a variable such as real GDP since that is the way in which the business cycle is understood by most policy-makers. Burnside, Eichenbaum, and Fisher, they contend, claim to be offering a business-cycle model, but fail to show whether their model does generate a business cycle as the term is generally understood. This raises the question of whether the question of how one defines the business cycle is a purely semantic issue, of no real importance. Thus Eichenbaum points out that the business cycle is merely a construction we place upon the data: all there really is out there is 'a bunch of decision-makers and a bunch of data' (1-4B). Sims makes a similar point in a different way when he argues that to require every business-cycle model to explain turning points in output is to impose a lexicographic ordering on the criteria by which models are tested and that there is no justification for doing so. One might wish to trade off performance in one dimension in order to obtain better performance in another dimension. Morgan responds by questioning whether it is necessary to have congruence between models, definitions, and concepts in the same piece of applied work. Different answers to the question of what policy-makers are interested in may lead to the use of different models. Given economists' different starting points, it is going to take different things to make different economists have confidence in a model. As Eichenbaum puts it, 'it is not going to be one size fits all' (1-4B).

In the course of this discussion, Eichenbaum questions the extent to which research should be driven by the concerns of policy-makers. First, he suggests that policy-makers are unduly driven by day-to-day considerations and that research ought not to be driven by these. Second, he is concerned not just with operating within existing institutions but with designing different institutions. Macromodels provide laboratories that can be used to test these. Eichenbaum's view on the concerns of policy-makers is reinforced by Mayer's (2-11) reading of the US Federal Open Market Committee's use of academic research, at least in the 1970s. The FOMC's discussions focused on the current state of the economy and on the very immediate effect of minor changes in the federal funds rate, two issues on which the academic literature had little to say. Though it can be argued that academic economists should take more interest in these questions, it is possible that this represents an appropriate division of labour.

Thus although the argument that macroeconomics should be judged by the extent to which it provides useful advice to policy-makers, this must be qualified. The advice that policy-makers find useful at any particular time may not relate to fundamental issues but it may depend on prior beliefs about optimal policies. It may also depend, as was revealed in the Maes's paper (2-12) and the ensuing discussion (2-13B), on the nature of the training received by government officials and hence on the types of arguments they are equipped to understand.

7. Econometric techniques and macroeconomics

The first set of papers addresses the question of how we should address the business cycle. The two papers present contrasting views of how one should evaluate the cycle which relate to their authors's differences on what causes the cycle and even on what the cycle comprises. Harding and Pagan (1-2) argue that the classical cycle is important and argue for an algorithm that measures what they see as its most important features, notably turning points. Burnside, Eichenbaum, and Fisher (1-3) ignore turning points and focus on co-movements, demonstrating this by showing how to appraise a model by seeing how well it predicts the consequences of a fiscal shock. The ensuing discussion shows how beliefs about the cycle and beliefs about what constitute effective econometric methods are intertwined. Econometric evidence does affect beliefs about the cycle but beliefs about the cycle also influence the techniques that economists choose to use and hence the evidence that they find convincing. The notions of what the business cycle is and of what constitutes a good model are difficult to separate from ideas about what are the appropriate econometric techniques to use.

Two different strategies are adopted in the papers on monetary policy. Hendry (1-5) illustrates his methodological views by providing the type of econometric analysis that he sees as necessary to determine whether money does determine UK inflation in the long run. In reaching the conclusion that money is far from being the sole explanation of long-run inflation he emphasizes the enormous range of factors that have to be brought in to explain the historical experience and how difficult it is to find a relationship that is stable in the long run. In contrast, McCallum (1-6) surveys the evolution of thinking on monetary policy over the quarter century from 1973 to 1998 seeking to establish the factors responsible for the changes that have taken place. He points to considerable convergence between central bank and academic thinking and argues that the current state of macroeconomics, including the influence on the subject of both theory and evidence, is more satisfactory than some critics have suggested. The discussion raises several important issues. Morgan (1-7A) draws attention to the contrasting ways in which Hendry and McCallum use models. Hendry wishes to describe the world without doing an injustice to the complexity of the causes that operate in the real world. McCallum uses simpler models to represent theoretical claims about the structure of the economy. They are both representations but serve different functions. She also argues that McCallum's history reveals considerable instability in the way policy-makers have thought about monetary policy—that it is unlike what one would expect if there were a dominant paradigm. The ensuing discussion (1-7B) explores several of the points on which Hendry and McCallum disagree: the significance of rational expectations, the weight that can be placed on stable statistical relationships, and the usefulness of certain statistical tools, in particular the analysis of cointegration and unit-roots.

The following group of papers takes up the theme of what new econometric techniques have been able to contribute to macroeconomics. Juselius (1-8) argues that the problem has been a gap between the approach adopted by theorists, which is to formulate non-stochastic, usually static, models and then add error terms, and the empirical approach, which starts with a stochastic representation of the data. She argues that there is a need for an approach that develops theoretical models of the economy that replicate the stochastic features of real-world data, such as time-dependence, integration, and cointegration effects and short and long-run feedback effects. She then illustrates how this might be achieved through offering an analysis of the demand for money using the cointegrated VAR model. Smith (1-9) offers a more sceptical assessment of what recent econometric techniques have contributed. His argument is that when VARs, Granger causality, and cointegration techniques were introduced, economists expected too much of them and were disappointed. Statistical analysis cannot, he points out, in itself provide interpretation. Thus he sees identification as the key issue.

Hoover (1-10A) opens the discussion by arguing that a theme common to both papers is the search for structure, in the sense of relationships that will be invariant to interventions and shocks. It is not enough to find trends even if all we want is to forecast. We need to know that we have found a relationship that will survive. His solution to the theory–data gap is that we need to take modelling seriously, recognizing that confidence in a model derives not only from its statistical success but also from our prior beliefs about the economy. It is not a matter of testing models against 'pure' data, for even data are the result of models—rather it is a matter of continual criticism and adjustment. Favero (1-10B) agrees with Smith that identification is one of the key issues at stake and points out the different problems involved by short-run and long-run identification. Moreover, the different approaches to macroeconometrics on the two sides of the Atlantic (the so called VAR and LSE approaches) are viewed as reflecting different strategies for dealing with the underlying theory, and/or data. Each strategy encounters its own identification and specification problems, a fact which should prompt more collaborative efforts and communications between econometricians of different persuasions.

The general discussion (1-10C) opens with a strong challenge from Sims, who argues that RBC and identified VAR models provided the integration of theory and econometrics for which Juselius was looking and that cointegration appears attractive only because of a naïve sticking with Neyman–Pearson testing procedures. The correct procedure is to focus on likelihood functions. Subsequent contributions bring out the depth of disagreement on these issues, though some saw evidence of a certain degree of convergence in that RBC models had come increasingly to look more like European models. Much of this discussion is discussed in Section 3 above.

Durlauf's paper (1-11)[18] questions the econometrics that underlie country cross-sections studies of economic growth, arguing that though it has uncovered interesting relationships it has done little to adjudicate between competing explanations of growth. Though the previous group of papers was on time-series analysis, many of the same issues crop up, notably model specification and the difficulty in using statistical results to discriminate between theories. His conclusion is that, to remedy the situation, it is necessary not only to make greater use of modern statistical techniques, but also of more eclectic sources of evidence and to supplement this with greater use of historical studies. Sylos Labini (1-12), in contrast, focuses entirely on theory, pointing out that certain inconsistencies have arisen in the attempt to use static theoretical tools to analyse dynamic processes. His conclusion is that, even if we confine our attention to theoretical problems, we do not even have an adequate dynamic theory of growth. In his discussion, Salanti (1-13) notes that, despite their quite different perspectives, both authors share a good dose of scepticism and dissatisfaction about what new growth theory has to say about causal mechanisms fostering growth. Perhaps this is so because development and growth are matters that involve too many things (as a matter of theory as well as of facts) outside the domain of economics as it is usually perceived.

REFERENCES

Backhouse, R. E. (1995) *Interpreting Macroeconomics: Explorations in the History of Macroeconomic Thought* (London and New York: Routledge).
—— (1997) *Truth and Progress in Economic Knowledge* (Cheltenham and Lyme, NH: Edward Elgar).
Blanchard, O. J. and S. Fisher (1989) *Lectures on Macroeconomics* (Cambridge, Mass. and London: MIT Press).
Blaug, M. (1992) *The Methodology of Economics. Or How Economists Explain*, 2nd edn. (Cambridge and New York: Cambridge University Press).
Caldwell, B. J. (1993) *Beyond Positivism. Economic Methodology in the Twentieth Century*, rev. edn. (London and New York: Routledge).
Cartwright, N. (1991) 'Replicability, reproducibility, and robustness: Comment on Harry Collins', *History of Political Economy* 23: 145–55.
Darnell, A. C. and J. L. Evans (1990) *The Limits of Econometrics* (Aldershot and Brookfield, Vt.: Edward Elgar).
Dow, S. C. (1996) *The Methodology of Macroeconomic Thought. A Conceptual Analysis of Schools of Thought in Economics* (Cheltenham and Brookfield, VT: Edward Elgar).
Epstein, R. (1997) *A History of Econometrics* (Amsterdam: North-Holland).
Gibbard, A. and H. Varian (1978) 'Economic models', *Journal of Philosophy* 75: 664–77.
Granger, W. J. (1999) *Empirical Modelling in Economics. Specification and Evaluation* (Cambridge and New York: Cambridge University Press).

[18] Steven Durlauf was prevented from participating in the conference and sent his promised paper for the volume after it. Paolo Sylos Labini, in his turn, sent for publication a revised version somewhat different from the one he delivered. There is, therefore, no report of the discussion in that session.

Hands, D. W. (1988) 'Ad hocness in economics and the Popperian tradition', in N. de Marchi (ed.), *The Popperian Legacy in Economics* (Cambridge and New York: Cambridge University Press: 121–37).

—— (1993) *Testing, Rationality and Progress. Essays on the Popperian Tradition in Economic Methodology* (Lanham, Md.: Rowman & Littlefield).

Hicks, J. R. (1979) *Causality in Economics* (Oxford: Blackwell).

Hoover, K. D. (1988) *The New Classical Macroeconomics. A Sceptical Inquiry* (Oxford and Cambridge, Mass.: Blackwell).

—— (ed.) (1995) *Macroeconometrics. Developments, Tensions, and Prospects* (Boston and Dortrecht: Kluwer).

Klein, P. A. (ed.) (1994) *The Role of Economic Theory* (Boston and Dortrecht: Kluwer).

Kreps, D. M. (1990) *A Course in Microeconomic Theory* (London: Harvester Wheatsheaf).

Kuhn, T. S. (1970) *The Structure of Scientific Revolutions*, 2nd edn. (Chicago and London: University of Chicago Press).

McCallum, B. T. (1986) 'On "real" and "sticky-price" theories of the business cycle', *Journal of Money, Credit and Banking* 18: 397–414.

Mayer, T. (1993) *Truth Versus Precision in Economics* (Aldershot and Brookfield, VT: Edward Elgar).

Miller, R. (1987) *Fact and Method* (Princeton, NJ: Princeton University Press).

Morgan, M. S. (1988) 'Finding a satisfactory empirical model', in N. de Marchi (ed.), *The Popperian Legacy in Economics* (Cambridge and New York: Cambridge University Press: 199–211).

—— (1990) *The History of Econometric Ideas* (Cambridge and New York: Cambridge University Press).

Pagan, A. (1987) 'Three econometric methodologies: A critical appraisal', *Journal of Economic Surveys* 1: 3–24.

Rappaport, S. (1998) *Models and Reality in Economics* (Cheltenham and Northampton, Mass.: Edward Elgar).

Solow, R. M. (1998) *Monopolistic Competition and Macroeconomic Theory* (Cambridge and New York: Cambridge University Press).

Stiglitz, J. E. (1992) 'Methodological issues and the new Keynesian economics', in A. Vercelli and N. Dimitri (eds.), *Macroeconomics. A Survey of Research Strategies* (Oxford and New York: Oxford University Press: 38–86).

Summers, L. H. (1991) 'The scientific illusion in empirical macroeconomics', *Scandinavian Journal of Economics* 93: 129–48.

Tobin, J. (1969) 'A general equilibrium approach to monetary theory', *Journal of Money, Credit and Banking* 1: 15–29.

Vercelli, A. and N. Dimitri (eds.) (1992) *Macroeconomics: A Survey of Research Strategies* (Oxford and New York: Oxford University Press).

Part I
BUSINESS CYCLES

2 Knowing the cycle

DON HARDING AND ADRIAN PAGAN

1. Introduction

Judged by the number of papers being published today with 'the business cycle' somewhere in their title, we should be starting to have a good understanding of what accounts for that phenomenon. Yet, to paraphrase Christiano and Fitzgerald (1998), the business cycle remains a puzzle. Moreover, if one surveyed policy-makers whose concerns are with the business cycle, it seems unlikely that many would agree that this explosion of academic articles has been of much use to them in their decisions. Given that the stimulus for much research on the cycle is supposedly to improve policy actions directed towards it, the latter state of affairs is rather unusual. What could cause it to happen? One possibility, suggested by Lucas (1981: 18), is that the phenomenon is intrinsically difficult to understand.

The nature of the questions to which we want answers, the level of theorizing at which there seems to be any real hope of obtaining reliable answers, and the equipment at hand for theorizing at this level combine to make genuine progress painfully slow.

There is undoubtedly some truth in this. Macroeconomic phenomena are inherently complex. But, complexity cannot be the whole story. Anyone who has spent time in both the academic and policy communities knows that there is another problem arising from the two groups tending to have a different perspective on, and way of talking about the cycle. A different perspective because the focus of policy-makers is largely upon what has been termed the 'classical cycle' in the levels of economic activity, whereas academic research has increasingly moved towards examining cycles in data which have been subject to a rather complex process of trend removal. Thus the attention of academics is fixed on something that does not enter into the policy-maker's calculus. In this transition, information needed to address questions relating to the classical cycle has been lost and potentially valuable information that might be gained from academic research has been sacrificed. A different way of talking about the cycle emerges from the fact that policy-makers largely follow Burns and Mitchell

The first author is Senior Research Fellow and Assistant Director at the Melbourne Institute at the University of Melbourne. The second author is at the Australian National University and is a Professorial Fellow at the University of Melbourne. Research for this paper was supported by ARC Grant A79802751. We are grateful for the comments of Ern Boehm, Michael Boldin, John Landon-Lane, Jan Jacobs, Lou Maccini, Jim Nason, Graeme Wells, and participants at various seminars where earlier versions of the paper were given: the Theory and Evidence in Macroeconomics Conference held at the University of Bergamo, and seminars at CEMFI, the University of Melbourne, Macquarie University, the Third Australian Macroeconomics Workshop, and the Reserve Bank of New Zealand.

(1946) in paying attention to the *turning points* in economic activity, while academics concentrate upon the *moments* of random variables taken to represent economic activity. Perhaps the contrast just made is too stark. In fact, academics are sometimes a little schizophrenic when talking about the cycle and are not averse to motivating their research by reference to published evidence on turning points even if it is never central to their later investigation, e.g. Christiano and Fitzgerald (1998).

Section 2 sets out our attitude to some of the issues noted above. It deals with the definition of a cycle, and the business cycle in particular. In it we define a cycle in terms of the turning points of a series, this being the methodology set out in Burns and Mitchell (1946), and we argue that the classical cycle is *the* business cycle. Section 3 has three subsections. The first describes methods for locating turning points while the second outlines how such information may be converted into measures that are useful when thinking about the nature of the cycle. The final subsection takes up the issue of defining the cycle in terms of 'co-movements' and discusses how this fits into our schema.

Section 4 constructs some evidence on the cycle that is useful when faced with the need to evaluate theories of the cycle. Some standard theories are examined according to their predictions about such quantities. Theories are stories about the way in which the cycle arises. Many of these stories involve an act of faith, in that they ultimately attribute the cycle to forces that are exogenous to the economic system, and it is natural that new stories are arising which seek to remove such a constraint. We briefly describe some of these and ask how successful they have been in accounting for the evidence.

2. What should we be trying to explain?

Empirical research involves matching phenomena that theory predicts should be found in a population with the sample analog of those phenomena. If many of the phenomena that the theory predicts are ultimately found to be in the sample, then our confidence in the theory is increased. Theories that can explain more of the phenomena in the sample than other theories are generally preferred, although parsimony and rigour of the explanation are also important criteria.

Macroeconomic data show three temporal phenomena that require explanation. The most notable of these is that prosperity and population increase on average, thereby introducing trends into most macroeconomic data. Macroeconomic data also exhibit the somewhat subtler phenomenon of fluctuation. The third and most subtle phenomenon is that macroeconomic series seem to show visual patterns which are referred to as 'cycles'. Actually, although called 'cycles', these patterns are better thought of as recurrences since they involve recurring phases of expansion and contraction that may have no definite periodicity. Ultimately, we seek to jointly explain these three phenomena.

Burns and Mitchell followed a long tradition and defined the cycle in terms of the peaks and troughs in the *level* of variables that measure economic activity, i.e. they studied the 'classical' cycle. However, a discordance arises between what Burns and

Mitchell did, and what much of the academic literature does today, owing to the fact that the emphasis placed upon turning-point calculations by Burns and Mitchell has been discarded in favour of computing moments of the data. Indeed, some see this as a crucial distinction. Jacobs (1998: 2), for example, feels that a study of the business cycle always involves an analysis of turning points, while the academic literature focuses upon what he terms 'economic fluctuations'. The latter is summarized by the moments of the random variables taken to underlie the series representing economic activity. After jettisoning the Burns and Mitchell approach to the business cycle in favour of studying economic fluctuations, academic researchers immediately ran into the difficulty that data on real quantities are almost always non-stationary and moments needed to be computed from data made stationary through some transformation. So the series taken to represent economic activity was transformed and the classical cycle in the levels of activity was lost. Consequently, academic research on fluctuations in the past quarter century has matched theory and evidence using quite a different data set to that which business cycle analysts of much of this century would have used.

Which cycle should we study? Mathematically, three types of cycle might be distinguished. As mentioned earlier the classical cycle pertains to the turning-point patterns seen in the log of the level of economic activity, designated by $y(t)$. Other cycles that might be looked at derive from the turning points of $y(t)$ after removing different types of trends. For example, the turning points could be located in either $z_d(t) = y(t) - T_d(t)$, where $T_d(t)$ is a deterministic trend, or $z_{st}(t) = y(t) - T_d(t) - T_s(t)$, where $T_s(t)$ is a stochastic one. As it is possible to extract these different trends in many ways there will be a myriad of cycles. An extensive literature has demonstrated that fact, e.g. Canova (1994, 1998). To see the differences between the different cycles consider analysing post-World War II US data by varying the nature of how trend is accounted for. The classical cycle corresponds to the NBER definition and, according to their datings, there were eight post-war cycles of average duration of sixty-two months, with expansions absorbing fifty-one of these months. If one detrends using the phase-averaging method, thereby producing NBER-type growth cycles, the period 1948–97 witnessed twelve growth cycles of length forty-six months.[1] Expansions and contractions in this growth cycle are of equal size (FIBCR 1998: 52). Finally, removing both a deterministic and a stochastic trend using the popular HP filter ($\lambda = 1600$) results in cycles of thirty months duration and such cycles also exhibit expansions and contractions of equal length. Consequently, given the disparity in the characteristics of the cycles produced by varying the trend extraction filter it is somewhat extraordinary to read articles in which the validity of work done with trend

---

[1] Impressed by the fact that countries such as Germany did not have a classical recession in the post-World War II period until March 1966, NBER researchers themselves—such as Mintz (1969, 1972)—felt that it was productive to investigate *growth cycles* for such countries. These were cycles in the *level of detrended economic activity*, where the trend was measured with the 'phase-averaging' method. Until recently, this was also the main focus of attention for research on Asian economies. But the growth cycle has rarely been of much interest in most Western countries. With the exception of those countries whose capital stock was destroyed in World War II, Western countries had generally gone through the 'catch-up' phase of high growth many decades before.

adjusted series is justified by reference to classical cycle characteristics.[2] In fact, academic researchers using HP filtered data should be asking whether they are producing a three year cycle, not the six year one that they are familiar with from the NBER data on the classical cycle. In short, which cycle we work with makes a great deal of difference to the business cycle 'facts'. By far the best-documented cycle is the classical version, and it is certainly the one which gathers most attention in policy and media discussion, so one might expect that it would receive most attention by academics.

We see four arguments in favour of judging business cycle research by how well it explains the classical cycle. First, almost all models of the cycle explain the levels of series through their use of forcing processes that have both a deterministic and a stochastic trend. Since these assumptions are an important part of the model, entering into both the calibration procedures and the choices of agents, it does not seem unreasonable to ask whether the output of such models can explain the classical cycle. Second, the classical cycle summarizes the interaction between trend and fluctuations and therefore provides a unique opportunity to assess how well particular theories have captured trend and fluctuation and the interaction between them. Third, apart from questions of relevance, gathering information on the phases—expansions and contractions—of the classical cycle involves fewer subjective decisions than for the growth cycle, in that the former is independent of the method of detrending and thereby of the perspective of the observer. For this reason the classical cycle provides the opportunity to gather statistics that can be unambiguously called business cycle facts. Because of the problem of trend removal the growth cycle does not offer this opportunity. Finally, policy-makers and the business community alike seek information on the classical cycle.

3. Gathering evidence on the business cycle

3.1. Finding turning points

The detection and description of the classical and growth cycles is accomplished by first isolating turning points in the series, after which those dates are used to mark off periods of expansions and contractions. Viewed in this light business cycle analysis involves pattern recognition techniques and this fact goes to the heart of how one learns about the business cycle from $y(t)$ and $z(t)$.

As mentioned earlier business cycle features are documented by recognizing turning points in a series taken as representing aggregate activity. Location of such points can sometimes be done visually. When performing the datings in this way the eye is also very good at filtering out 'false turning points', i.e. movements which are short lived. Translating the ocular judgements into an algorithm has proved to be challenging. At a minimum such an algorithm needs to perform three tasks.

1. Determination of a potential set of turning points, i.e. the peaks and troughs in a series.

---

[2] For example, Christiano and Fitzgerald (1998: 58).

2. A procedure for ensuring that peaks and troughs alternate.
3. A set of rules that recombine the turning points established after steps one and two in order to satisfy predetermined criteria concerning the duration and amplitudes of phases and complete cycles; what we will refer to as 'censoring rules'.

There are a variety of ways to identify a potential set of peaks and troughs. For example, Wecker (1979) uses the rule $\{\Delta y(t) > 0, \Delta y(t+1) < 0, \Delta y(t+2) < 0\}$ to locate a peak.[3] Essentially, these rules attempt to approximate the standard calculus definition that $dy/dt > 0$ to the left of a peak and $dy/dt < 0$ to the right of a peak. Harding (1997) introduces the concepts of expansion terminating sequences (ETS) and contraction terminating sequences (CTS) which are patterns that terminate expansions and contractions respectively. Several candidates for these sequences exist. For example, a rule popularized by Arthur Okun is that a recession involves at least two quarters of negative growth so that ETS $= \{\Delta y(t+1) < 0, \Delta y(t+2) < 0\}$ signals a peak at time t. This rule is widely used in the media and policy circles to signal a classical recession. An extended version of Okun's procedure involves terminating an expansion when two quarters of negative growth are encountered and terminating a contraction when two periods of positive growth are encountered, i.e. the ETS is just that given above while the CTS $= \{\Delta y(t+1) > 0, \Delta y(t+2) > 0\}$. This is the rule that we use for dating purposes in this paper.

All these rules emphasize that, even though the classical cycle refers to the behaviour of the level of a variable, the analysis of its turning points is done with a stationary series viz. transformations of the first differenced series, $\Delta y(t)$, such as $\text{sgn}(\Delta y(t))$.[4] It cannot be stressed too much that the rules above *are not locating a cycle in* $\Delta y(t)$; rather $\Delta y(t)$ is just an input into the dating process of the classical cycle. Moreover, it will be the characteristics of $\Delta y(t)$ which determine the nature of the classical cycle. To expand further on this theme it is useful to consider the case where GDP follows a random walk with drift μ_y, variance σ^2 and normally distributed innovations. In this instance the probability of obtaining one quarter of negative growth is $\Phi(-\mu_y/\sigma)$, where $\Phi(\cdot)$ represents the cumulative normal distribution. Thus the ratio of drift to standard deviation is important for the cycle. The larger is μ_y/σ the fewer the turning points that will be observed in a series.

Having established the fact that the ratio (μ_y/σ) is likely to be important for the classical cycle, it is natural to estimate that quantity for later use when we seek to explain the observed business cycle. Table 2.1 summarizes information on μ_y, σ, and (μ_y/σ) for a variety of US series, using the sample period 1948q1 to 1997q1. A notable feature is that investment is highly volatile relative to trend growth and thus should exhibit a cycle which is very different to that for GDP and consumption.

---

[3] A trough would be defined by $\{\Delta y(t-1) < 0, \Delta y(t) < 0, \Delta y(t+1) > 0\}$. Pagan (1997) uses this rule to compute the average length of a cycle.

[4] When working with growth cycles it is $\Delta z(t)$ which is analysed. As we explain elsewhere, Harding and Pagan (1999), the Bry–Boschan (1971) algorithm for locating turning points involves the sign of 'long differences' $y(t) - y(t-k)$. Of course, these are the sum of first differences.

3.2. Measuring the cycle using turning-point information

Given that turning points have been established how should the dating information be used in conjunction with the series from which the dates were derived? Inspection of comments that are frequently made about the cycle suggests that there are four items of interest:

- The duration of the cycle and its phases
- The amplitude of the cycle and its phases
- Any asymmetric behaviour of the phases
- Cumulative movements within phases.

In thinking about these measures, it is useful to consider a phase as a triangle. Figure 2.1 shows a stylized recession with A being the peak and C the trough. The height of the triangle is the amplitude and the base is the duration. Knowledge of these two elements for any cycle enables one to compute the area of the triangle, and thereby an approximation to (say) the cumulated losses in output from peak to trough, relative to the previous peak. Designating the duration of the ith phase as D_i and the amplitude as A_i, the product $C_{Ti} = 0.5(D_i A_i)$ will be referred to as the '*triangle approximation*' to the cumulative movements. In practice the *actual cumulative movements* (C_i) may differ

TABLE 2.1. *Moments of growth rates in various series*

	μ_y	σ	μ_y/σ
GDP per capita	0.46	1.08	0.42
Consumption per capita	0.49	0.89	0.56
Investment per capita	0.51	5.75	0.09

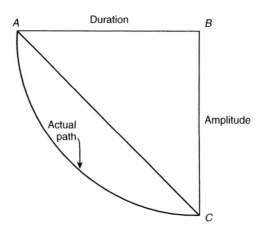

FIG. 2.1. *Stylized recession phase*

from C_{Ti} since the actual path through the phase may not be well approximated by a triangle, and this points to the need for an index of the average *excess cumulative movements*; the natural candidate is $E_i = (C_{Ti} - C_i + 0.5 * A_i)/D_i$. In this formula D_i is the duration of the phase and the term $0.5 * A_i$ removes the bias that arises in using a sum of rectangles (C_i) to approximate a triangle. Although it is C_i which is of fundamental interest to policy-makers and historians, the triangle approximation is still likely to be useful in shedding light upon the ability of business-cycle models to generate realistic cycles.

3.3. *Another view of the cycle*

There is no doubt that Burns and Mitchell used a wide range of series to come up with a single reference cycle.[5] This fact has led to an impression in the academic literature that what was important in discussing the business cycle were the interrelationships (or co-movements) between the specific series used to construct the reference information. For example, Cooley and Prescott (1995: 26) summarize what they feel the implications of Burns and Mitchell's work was in the following way:

the one very regular feature of these fluctuations is the way variables move together. It is the co-movements of variables that Burns and Mitchell worked so hard to document and that Robert Lucas emphasized as the defining features of the business cycle.

Lucas's statements just invoked are:

Technically, movements about trend in gross national product in any country can be well described by a stochastically disturbed difference equation of very low order. These movements do not exhibit uniformity of either period or amplitude.... Those regularities which are observed are in the co-movements among different aggregative time series. (1981: 217)

The central finding, of course, was the similarity of all peacetime cycles with one another, once variation in duration was controlled for, in the sense that each cycle exhibits about the same pattern of co-movements among variables as do the others. (ibid. 274)

What is strange here is the transformation in the motivation for considering many series. In Burns and Mitchell's case it was simply an instrument used to define *the* business cycle, through the way in which turning points in many series clustered together; in much of the modern literature it has become an end unto itself. In fact the latter's obsession with co-movements between series seems to miss the point of why we are interested in the business cycle. It is an extraordinary feature of much of the modern academic literature that one can find papers which provide extensive accounts of the co-movements of consumption, investment etc. but which make little or no reference to the temporal characteristics of the series that might be taken to be aggregate economic activity, namely output. 'Hamlet without the Prince' is the phrase that comes to mind when reading such papers.

---

[5] Epstein (1999) argues that Burns and Mitchell probably valued the specific cycle information as highly as that contained in the reference cycle, i.e. the dispersion of the turning points in the specific series around the 'central tendency' of the reference cycle was important to them.

Apart from the fact that the modern literature departs from the older one for no apparent reason, what should be of equal concern is the fact that some of the statements quoted in defence of the movement have had a remarkable impact despite being close to contradictory. How exactly could Lucas conclude that there is no uniformity in temporal movements in output and yet be confident that there are uniform co-movements? It is certainly true that it is possible to conclude that individual cycles in activity differ in both duration and depth, through an analysis of their turning points, but then one should apply the same test to the question of co-movements, leading one to enquire into the evidence that such co-movements are stable across individual cycles. As mentioned above, the academic literature has mostly identified co-movements with covariances, and then estimated the latter with a sample period which includes many cycles. Hence, it is *assumed* that the co-movements are the same across cycles.[6] One cannot claim an empirical regularity from an assumption. Indeed, although rarely done, one might try to address the issue of whether the covariances are stable across cycles. An exercise in which an F test is performed to test the hypothesis that the slope coefficient of a regression of HP-detrended consumption upon HP-detrended output ($\lambda = 1600$) is constant across the eight classical cycles identified in US data is resoundingly rejected (a p value of less than 0.000).[7]

Nevertheless, even if we are fundamentally interested in explaining the cycle in economic activity, it may be very hard to discriminate between theories simply on the basis of their predictions for this univariate series. Because most theories make predictions about the behaviour of sub-aggregates such as consumption and investment, it makes sense to study the cycles in these variables as well. Each variable selected for investigation would have a set of cycle characteristics obtained by applying the dating rules discussed in the preceding section to each of the individual series. Later we use such information to shed light on the ability of models to replicate an actual economy.

4. Theory, evidence, and the cycle

Textbooks are the obvious places to look in for distilled economic knowledge of the business cycle. A comprehensive text book discussion of the business cycle would involve a description of the cycle, an account of frameworks for analysing the cycle and identification of the most important shocks. Although there may be more, we found four texts that meet these criteria: Sachs and Larrain (1993), Auerbach and Kotlikoff (1995), Romer (1996), and Blanchard and Fischer (1989). All of these texts use statistics from the NBER dating methodology to describe features of the cycle. The added value of such statistics is very evident on reading these texts.

---

[6] Kim *et al.* (1994) and Fisher *et al.* (1996) examine the stability of covariances across time.

[7] It might be argued that it is the signs of the covariances which are stable across cycles but it still remains true that one cannot ascertain this by pooling all cycles together as the complete sample does. Moreover, one might wonder about the value of economic research which assures us that consumption and income are positively correlated.

The search for a theoretical explanation of economic phenomena is an enduring one. Theory endows an analyst with a framework for thinking about an issue; a common language to describe either what has happened or might have happened as a result of an action; the possibility of making quantitative statements about the latter; and the allocation of 'names' to the driving forces underlying macroeconomic events. For much of the history of macroeconomics it was the first of these benefits that was perceived of as being paramount and the role of evidence was in fact quite limited. Today, the last two have come into their own. Macroeconomics has an air of precision about it which was not there over much of the past century. Joyful descriptions of the new era, such as the following—taken from Usabiaga-Ibánez's (1999) interview with Larry Christiano—abound:

It was exciting and it helped to put an end to the embarrassment that macroeconomists suffered at the hands of other economists who laughed at their primitive ways of doing economics.

Triumphalism like this inevitably breeds strong statements about the ability of the theory to explain macroeconomic phenomena such as the cycle and these too have abounded.[8] In regards to the latter, it is perhaps no accident that the sense of satisfaction expressed about the achievements of this new 'quantitative theory' stem from its having paid more attention to the evidence than has been customary with the theories of the past and, indeed, even some of those of the present.

As evident from Christiano's comment above many believe that an important feature of the modern approach to analysing economic fluctuations is that it shares the same framework as other areas of economics. In fact, the argument could even be strengthened by noting that most policy institutes use models that have as their core a set of principles that Christiano would probably deem to be an important legacy of the modern approach. These include the notions that shocks are the driving forces of the macroeconomy and that the economy should be viewed as growing along a balanced growth path with forward-looking agents making optimal decisions. These principles have become widely accepted, have been adopted in the conversations of those who follow the cycle, and are embodied in many policy models, e.g. the MULTIMOD model used at the IMF (Laxton *et al.* 1998). However, these common elements only produce a skeletal framework; filling in the details leads to heterogeneity, with many different choices being made about the way in which dynamics should be introduced, the naming of the shocks, etc.

So we have seen a move towards parametric models featuring stochastic shocks as a primary vehicle for talking about the business cycle. However, accompanying this shift has been an increasing tendency in academia for the business cycle to be spoken of in terms of the parameters of these models, rather than the turning points of the series that they would generate, and this underpins the necessity to tease out the business cycle implications of the models in this alternative dimension. It is important to adopt a

---

[8] Although it is fair to say that Christiano is more reserved in such judgements. In the same interview that the quotation is taken from he sees the developments as important more for their methodological implications than for the knowledge gleaned from them about specific issues such as the cycle.

turning point perspective as the resulting business cycle statistics combine together the parameters of underlying theoretical models in a natural way. For example, while the knowledge that a model prediction about growth rate volatility differs from its counterpart in the data tells us something about the adequacy of that model in replicating that data, it does not tell us much about the importance of the discrepancy for the nature of the cycle. Producing statistics that directly address the ability of a model to replicate business cycle characteristics is an important objective of our work.

Ideally, we would like to map the parameters of any given model into quantities that are more informative about the cycle. To do that, we return to our basic contention that an understanding of the classical cycle derives from a description of what governs the temporal behaviour of $\Delta y(t)$, and examine what theoretical work has to say about the latter. One immediately encounters the obstacle that few modern theories of the cycle provide quantitative evidence on this variable. Rather, the information provided is upon the characteristics of $z_{st}(t)$, and these do not readily map into those of $\Delta y(t)$. A simple illustration of the difficulties encountered in effecting the mapping is to be had by making $y(t)$ a pure random walk and constructing $z_{st}(t)$ from it with the HP filter. The serial correlation properties of $z_{st}(t)$ are extremely complex, in that there are negative serial correlation coefficients of very high order, and these serve to produce a spectral density of $z_{st}(t)$ with a peak, something which is certainly not descriptive of $\Delta y(t)$.[9] It is only if $z_d(t)$ is used in place of $z_{st}(t)$ that one might recover the classical cycle properties reasonably easily.[10]

We start with a benchmark model for $\Delta y(t)$ of the form

$$\Delta y(t) = \mu + \sigma e(t). \tag{1}$$

Using values of μ and σ found from US data on per capita GDP over the period 1948q1–1997q1, and assuming that $e(t)$ is n.i.d. $(0, 1)$, we simulate business cycle statistics from (1) and compare them to the data. The first column of Table 2.2 has the latter while the second column contains the former. A simple extension of this model would be to consider what happens if there is serial correlation in growth rates i.e. the model has the form

$$\Delta y(t) = \mu_1 + \rho\,\Delta y(t-1) + \sigma_1 e(t). \tag{2}$$

In (1) and (2) the shocks are permanent. Instead one might treat them as only being persistent i.e. the data comes from a model that is stationary around trend. Defining $z(t) = y(t) - a - bt$ such a model might be

$$z(t) = \rho_z z(t-1) + \sigma_z \varepsilon(t). \tag{3}$$

---

[9] After applying the 'Okun' rule to simulated data which has been passed through the HP filter, a cycle of around 30 months emerges, illustrating once again that the information generated from $z_{st}(t)$ is neither about the classical cycle nor the growth cycle appearing in (say) FIBCR publications.

[10] As an aside, even if one thought that the growth cycle was the most important cycle to study, and we do not, it would be $\Delta z(t)$ which one needs information upon.

TABLE 2.2. *Actual and simulated business cycle characteristics*

	Data	RW equation (1)	RW equation (2)	DT ($\rho_z = 0.97$)	DT ($\rho_z = 0.9$)
Mean duration (quarters)					
PT	4.4	3.7	4.2	4.0	4.5
TP	13.9	11.8	10.3	9.8	7.5**
Mean amplitude (per cent)					
PT	−3.4	−1.8**	−2.6	−2.00**	−4.1
TP	12.4	8.9	9.2	6.8**	8.3**
Cumulation (per cent)					
PT	−8.0	−4.3	−7.8	−5.0	−11.3**
TP	153	91	83	52	44.2**
Excess					
PT	−0.0	−0.1	−0.1	−0.1	−0.2
TP	1.4	0.1**	0.1**	0.1**	0.2**

**Indicates that less than 5 per cent of simulations were further out in the tail relative to the data estimate.

One can estimate the parameters of (2) and (3) from the data as well. Doing so, the third column of Table 2.2 contains simulated statistics pertaining to (2) and the remaining columns—designated as DT—relate to (3), parameterized with two sets of values for ρ_z and σ_z. One of these is from the data, $\rho_z = 0.97$; the other has a smaller value of $\rho_z = 0.9$. To make these two parameterizations comparable we keep $\text{std}(z(t))$ constant, where $\text{std}(z(t)) = \sigma_z/\sqrt{(1 - \rho_z^2)}$, by varying σ_z. Thus the objective of the last two simulations is to study the effects of persistence without changing the volatility of $z(t)$.

In Table 2.2 contractions are designated as PT and expansions as TP. With the exception of duration statistics, all measurements are made in terms of percentage changes. There are some striking results in the table. First the random walk model does an excellent job of matching classical cycle statistics on most dimensions. Its deficiencies are twofold. It fails to produce contractions that are deep and the shape of an average expansion is much closer to a triangle than that in reality. Rapid recovery in the early part of an expansion has been documented in Sichel (1994) and this is most likely the origin of the magnitude of the 'excess' computations for expansions in Table 2.2.[11]

Adding in serial correlation to growth rates tends to improve the explanation of the cycle on some dimensions and worsen it on others. Attempts to replicate this feature are the motivating force in many studies of US GDP, e.g. Ramey and Watson (1997). Comparing the results of columns two and three shows that the presence of positive serial correlation in growth rates makes for shorter cycles. The origin of this result is most clearly understood by thinking about the Okun rule. When there is positive serial

---

[11] Note that the excess measure in the tables is found by averaging the E_i over all cycles rather than constructing it from the average values of C_i and C_{Ti}.

correlation between adjacent growth rates the probability of getting two negative outcomes is greater than when they were independent, and this should have the effect of producing more turning points and a shorter cycle; just what is observed. Column four shows that one can do quite well with a model of output that does not have a stochastic trend but whose shocks are still quite persistent, while column five indicates that the degree of persistence is very important in getting the duration of the cycle and the length of expansions correct. Generally, a model without very persistent shocks will fail to match many of the characteristics.

As a companion to the statistical models simulated in Table 2.2 we present equivalent simulations of some popular theoretical models in Table 2.3. A difficulty one faces in moving to theoretical models is that such models ensure a steady state growth path of per capita output through a deterministic trend term within the forcing processes. Because the magnitude of this trend is unknown it is chosen to be that which replicates the observed deterministic trend in per capita output. Accordingly, we also force the simulated output to agree with the data on this dimension by adding on a trend term to ensure that all variables grow at the 0.456 per cent per quarter observed over 1948–97. That rate is a little higher than the 0.4 per cent used in King *et al.* (1998). There are then four models to be investigated. First, there is the basic real business cycle (RBC) model set out in King *et al.* (1988), where technology is a unit root process. This configuration is termed RBC1. RBC2 is a variant of RBC1 wherein the standard deviation of the shocks to technology is set to 1.19 per cent per quarter versus the 1.48 per cent of RBC1; the latter was the level needed to reproduce the observed standard deviation of per capita quarterly GDP growth of 1.08 per cent. It is interesting to observe that, with the unit root in technology, the variance of technology shocks needs

TABLE 2.3. *Actual and simulated business cycle characteristics*

	Data	RBC1	RBC2	RBC3	ENDO
Mean duration (quarters)					
PT	4.4	3.9	3.6	3.8	3.9
TP	13.9	11.6	13.7	11.2	11.0
Mean amplitude (per cent)					
PT	−3.4	−1.9**	−1.4**	−2.0**	−2.7
TP	12.4	9.0	9.2	8.9	11.3
Cumulation (per cent)					
PT	−8.0	−5.0	−3.1**	−5.0	−6.8
TP	153	95	117	86	103
Excess					
PT	−0.0	−0.1	−0.1	−0.1	−0.1
TP	1.4	0.1**	0.1**	0.1**	0.1**

**Indicates that less than 5 per cent of simulations were further out in the tail relative to the data.

to be larger than that for the growth in GDP. RBC3 is the model of Christiano and Eichenbaum (1992), as interpreted by Cogley and Nason (1995); this has a unit root in technology and a stationary government expenditure process. Finally, the last model, ENDO, is the endogenous growth model set out and calibrated in Collard (1999).

Table 2.3 shows that all models generate cycles that roughly accord with the data, although none can reproduce the shape of expansions. RBC2 manages to get the cumulated gains in output during the average expansion closest to reality but does so by having expansions that last too long. In many ways the endogenous growth model does best, albeit it understates the duration of expansions. Comparing RBC1 and RBC3 there is clearly little to be gained by adding in government expenditure shocks.

The business cycle characteristics just found for various statistical and theoretical models can serve as the foundation for investigating how theoretical models would generate a classical cycle. A perusal of the results from Table 2.3 points to the need for theories of the cycle to provide accounts of the origin of the following three elements:

(i) Trend growth of the right magnitude.
(ii) Persistent shocks.
(iii) Volatility in growth rates of the right magnitude.

How do theoretical models incorporate these features? Generally (i) has been handled with words somewhat like those used by Schmitt-Grohe (1998) 'I follow the literature by assuming that the drift in the technology process . . . is equal to 1.6 per cent per year', and we have already adopted the strategy in the simulations of Table 2.3 of equating it to what is seen in the data. Trend growth is very important to cycle outcomes and is the source of the 'business cycle asymmetry' often referred to. Since drift in the technology process is the only source of trend growth in the majority of theoretical models it is clear that a major determinant of the classical cycle is thereby made exogenous. As the 'new paradigm' debate of the past few years in the USA has emphasized, being unable to explain the determinants of trend growth is a major limitation when it comes to eliciting the business cycle implications of any such developments. From our earlier analysis, it is clear that a rise in trend growth, with the volatility of output growth being held constant, will lead to a rise in both the length of the cycle and the duration of its expansions, thereby providing a possible explanation for the length of the current classical expansion in the USA.[12]

How is persistence of shocks to be introduced? The three RBC models in Table 2.3 have it as being the concomitant of exogenous processes that are highly persistent, e.g. as Cogley and Nason (1995) show, most RBC type models tend to preserve the nature of the process that has been specified for technology shocks. Three methods of endogenously generating persistence seem to have had some success. One is through allowing for endogenous growth, e.g. Collard (1999). Such models produce a unit root in output, independently of whether the technology process has a stochastic trend, and the ability to generate persistence endogenously is a point in its favour. It is also the case that it produces some serial correlation in growth rates—see Collard

---

[12] Another explanation derives from the argument that σ has fallen, see McConnell and Quiros (1998).

(1999: 479)—and, as the simulations of an ARIMA(1,1,0) model in Table 2.2 (equation (2)) showed, this tends to reduce the length of the cycle. Clearly, it does not produce the same amount of serial correlation as the ARIMA model does, so the cycle is not as short.[13]

The second method of inducing persistence is through 'belief shocks'. Belief shocks stem from indeterminancies in models which allow the addition of such shocks to the Euler equation describing consumption choices. Schmitt-Grohe (1998) investigates the ability of such shocks to produce serial correlation in $\Delta y(t)$ and finds that the models in which they are embedded are more successful on this dimension than are RBC models featuring only technology shocks. What is not directly answered in her work is whether such shocks can make $y(t)$ a process that is persistent enough. Simulations of her calibrated 'belief shocks only' model suggests that not enough persistence eventuates in those circumstances, since the average durations are 8.2/8.3 quarters, making for expansions that are much too short and contractions that are too long.

The last approach involves price and wage rigidities. These seem to provide a promising alternative mechanism, although there is little quantitative evidence on their effectiveness. Work by Chari *et al.* (1996) suggested that, in an optimizing model, it was hard to get much persistence of demand shocks from price rigidities, but Huang and Liu (1998) note that this would not be true of models with staggered wage contracts. Effectively, this result makes the slope of the Phillips curve the key parameter; if it is low then output will tend to have a unit root. Kiley (1999) shows that the way in which one models sticky prices is very important to any conclusions on persistence. He demonstrates that partial adjustment models of prices tend to have much more persistence over a range of values of the elasticity of labour supply than does the staggered price model investigated by Chari *et al.* (1996). Each of these models effectively involve a price–cost cycle; a mechanism that has had a long history in empirical business cycle work, see Pagan (1997).

The final item in the trio of issues listed above involves how one produces volatility in growth rates that matches the data. In many instances the parameters of exogenous forcing processes have been selected to produce this outcome.[14] In other cases Solow residual type computations are used to estimate the volatility of productivity shocks for use in a model. This is a little closer to being an independent measure of volatility, although it is not entirely satisfactory, since it uses a series, output, that one is seeking to explain—see Hartley *et al.* (1997).

---

[13] In the notation of Collard's paper $\gamma = 0.117$ is selected as this seems to be his preferred value (1999: 477). He notes later (ibid. 479) that $\gamma = 0.5$ would be needed to get the correct serial correlation in growth rates.

[14] There seems to be an emerging trend in this vein e.g. Schmitt-Grohe (1998) and Christiano and Harrison (1998). No defence of the practice is given but it seems to be rooted in the idea that the business cycle is about co-movements and so it does not matter if σ is set so as to match the data on output. One might also point out that estimation of parameters is often done in a GMM framework in which the second moment of output is one of those used to define the estimator. If the number of moments and parameters were identical, then one has simply re-parameterized the problem, and the volatility of output would be perfectly reproduced, regardless of the validity of the theoretical model. Even if the number of moments exceeds the number of parameters the number that are effectively used in the construction of the estimator may be the same, i.e. the weights attached to the excess moments by GMM may be very small.

Now let us look at the models according to how they account for the trio of issues just raised. Model RBC1 of Table 2.3 satisfies all of the requirements by construction; both trend growth in output and the volatility of growth rates are fixed at what is observed, and the stochastic trend in output derives from the assumptions on technological change. Given that it is known that RBC1 generates little serial correlation in output growth rates, it is scarcely surprising that its statistics are essentially those of the random walk with drift model in Table 2.2. Consequently, although it does produce a realistic cycle, it does so because the crucial elements in the explanation have been *assumed* and very little, if anything, derives from the economics underlying RBC theory. The RBC2 simulations illustrate just how important it is to get the volatility in growth rates right. As we observed earlier, having a unit root in the technology process in the RBC1 model leads to the volatility of output growth being below that of technology, unlike the situation when technology is an AR(1). Ideally one wants a small volatility in technology in order to avoid 'technological regress'. Consequently, if the standard deviation of technology shocks was set to a realistic value, the output cycles would be unrealistic. This can be seen from the RBC2 simulations in which that parameter has been reduced by 20 per cent. Recent work by King and Rebelo (1998), in the situation where technology is a stationary process, has managed to amplify technology shocks by allowing for the impact of variable capacity utilization, and this seems a step in the right direction. The same set of problems arises in regard to RBC3, since Cogley and Nason (1995) calibrated the variance of both of the shocks in that model to reproduce the variance of output. Nevertheless, in this situation the standard deviation of technology shocks could be set at a much lower value than in RBC1; effectively 'amplification' comes about due to the presence of a second shock. To summarize, getting a standard deviation for output growth of the right magnitude from standard RBC models has been quite a challenge.

In gauging the success of any theoretical model it is obviously unwise to restrict one's attention to the output cycle, even if this is the business cycle, particularly if the first two moments of output growth predicted by theoretical models are largely designed to match the data. An important insight of the DSGE literature is that one needs to look at other implications of a model when judging theories. Accordingly, an analysis of specific cycles is useful in this task. One advantage of proceeding in this way is that one needs to be confident that the cycle in aggregate economic activity is not being reproduced at the expense of inducing implausible cycles in some other macroeconomic series. The endogenous growth model provides a good illustration of this point. In Collard's (1999) version the levels of consumption and investment are a fixed ratio to output and so the turning points must be exactly the same as for output, something which is incompatible with the data.

A more subtle demonstration of the value of specific cycle information is available from the RBC1 model. Table 2.4 records specific cycles in consumption and investment from the actual data as well as artificial series simulated from that model. It is apparent that the model does not perform as well in terms of capturing specific cycles as it does the business cycle. Concentrating first on consumption, and thinking in terms of our earlier analysis, a possible reason for the discrepancy between the predicted

TABLE 2.4. *Actual and simulated specific cycle characteristics*

	Consumption		Investment	
	Data	RBC1	Data	RBC1
Mean duration (quarters)				
PT	3.7	3.4	5.1	4.7
TP	21.3	24.5	7.7	7.8
Mean amplitude (per cent)				
PT	−2.2	−0.8**	−19.1	−5.4**
TP	14.2	13.6	26.3	11.0**
Cumulated (per cent)				
PT	4.2	−1.9	−46.6	−16.7**
TP	262	394	161.2	65**
Excess				
PT	0.2	−0.0**	1.0	−0.2**
TP	0.6	0.1	2.9	0.2**

**Indicates that less than 5 per cent of simulations were further out in the tail relative to the data estimate.

and actual durations of an expansion is that the predicted volatility of consumption growth is incorrect. This conjecture is borne out by the data: volatility of consumption growth implied by RBC1 is 0.56 per cent per quarter, while the data has a value of 0.89 per cent. The smaller volatility acts to produce a longer cycle in consumption. Investment has a quite different difficulty. Durations are well matched but the amplitudes are problematic. To explore this further we simulated data from a random walk with the same mean and variance for investment growth as in the data. The resulting statistics were quite close to those from RBC1 in Table 2.4. Thus the failure to match the amplitudes of expansions and contractions may point to a problem with models driven solely by technology in explaining the specific cycle in that series.[15] One factor which is accorded importance in much public discussion of investment movements is 'sentiment'. Studies of asset price fluctuations have introduced fluctuations in sentiment by making the risk aversion coefficient in the CRRA utility function be realizations of a two state Markov process—see Gordon and St-Amour (1998)—and this may be useful for explanations of the investment cycle as well.

---

[15] The conclusion we reach about the ability of the basic RBC model to explain the specific cycles for investment and consumption differs from that in King and Plosser (1994). The difference seems to stem from two sources. First, King and Plosser did not look at specific cycles but 'cycle relatives' i.e. measurements of the amplitude of a specific cycle were done in relation to the turning points of the reference cycle and not the specific cycle. Second, the volatility of investment in the RBC1 model is about 2/3 of what it is in the model used by King and Plosser, which had technology following an AR(1) process with parameter 0.95. The parameters we use for RBC1 are taken directly from King *et al.* (1988).

All of the above has been predicated upon the idea that it is the evidence on the average cycle which theories should be confronted with. Using the framework outlined earlier, computer simulations reveal something about the nature of the shocks which are needed to realize realistic cycles and the types of models that will produce the latter. For example, it seems fair to conclude that linear models are more than capable of accounting for the cycle. But perhaps the emphasis upon averages misses something. It is possible that items like monetary shocks are important to specific contractions but may appear very unimportant when averaged over many expansions and contractions. This was the experience in Dungey and Pagan (1997) when accounting for movements in $z_d(t)$ in Australia. Moreover, there can be no denying that many policy makers are very influenced by particular cycles, and lessons are drawn from them that are often meant to apply to the average cycle. A very good example of the latter phenomenon is the cycle of the early 1990s, which did seem to depart significantly from the average cycle on some dimensions, at least in countries such as the UK and Australia. Specifically, the contraction phase was of lengthy duration and, accordingly, this resulted in very large cumulated output losses. Since the cycle was also accompanied by strong asset price movements it has been argued that investment was inhibited through constraints on the amount of collateral that firms could provide to the banking sector for loans. Some models have emerged to capture such feedbacks, e.g. Kiyotaki and Moore (1997), although it is currently unclear whether in accounting for a particular cycle they have produced a model of output dynamics that fails to reproduce the average cycle. It may be in accounting for particular cycles that non-linearities become important, with the simple dynamics characterizing output being temporarily modified to quite complex ones depending on whether (say) some threshold is exceeded. When looked at over many cycles, it is unlikely that this threshold would have been attained very often, so that estimated equations would reveal only simple dynamics.

The final element in textbooks is the naming of the important shocks. A long list of these is generally entertained and sometimes they are located out of the realm of economics, e.g. Sachs and Larrain (1993: 530) give credence to policy shocks designed for political outcomes as a factor driving the cycle with their claim:

Thus, when Democrats are elected president, monetary policy is generally eased, while when Republican presidents are elected, monetary policy is generally tightened. As a result, Democratic presidents tend to have booms early in their tenure, while Republican presidents tend to preside over recessions in the first half of a new term.[16]

After providing a list of shocks, textbook discussion frequently founders on the question of the relative importance of the listed shocks in explaining the cycle. It would seem that we are better at agreeing on the statistical nature of the important shocks, as exemplified by their persistence and volatility, than we are at agreeing over what we should call them. To some extent this reflects the fact that much of our information about such questions has traditionally come from VAR models in which the definition

---

[16] Table 17.4 of Sachs and Larrain provides growth rates in GDP for each year of the presidency from 1948 to 1984 in support of this contention.

of the shocks relies on very little theory. That has to change. Only then can we really begin to sort out the relative contribution of a nominated list of shocks, and only then will we know the cycle.

REFERENCES

Auerbach, A. and L. Kotlikoff (1995) *Macroeconomics: An Integrated Approach* (South-Western College Publishing, Cincinnati, Ohio).

Blanchard, O. and S. Fischer (1989) *Lectures on Macroeconomics* (Cambridge, Mass.: MIT Press).

Bry, G. and C. Boschan (1971) *Cyclical Analysis of Time Series: Selected Procedures and Computer Programs* (New York: NBER).

Burns, A. F. and W. C. Mitchell (1946) *Measuring Business Cycles* (New York: NBER).

Canova, F. (1994) 'Detrending and Turning Points', *European Economic Review* 38: 614–23.

—— (1998) 'Detrending and Business Cycle Facts', *Journal of Monetary Economics* 41: 475–512.

Chari, V. V., P. J. Kehoe, and E. R. McGrattan (1996) 'Sticky Price Models of the Business Cycle: Can the Contract Multiplier Solve the Persistence Problem', NBER Working Paper 5809.

Christiano, L. and M. Eichenbaum (1992) 'Current Real Business Cycle Theories and Aggregate Labor Market Fluctuations', *American Economic Review* 82: 430–50.

—— and T. FitzGerald (1998) 'The Business Cycle: It's Still a Puzzle', *Economic Perspectives* 1998(4): 56–83.

—— and S. Harrison (1998) 'Chaos, Sunspots and Automatic Stabilizers' (mimeo, Northwestern University).

Cogley, T. and J. Nason (1995) 'Output Dynamics in Real-Business-Cycle-Models', *American Economic Review* 85: 492–511.

Collard, F. (1999) 'Spectral and Persistence Properties of Cyclical Growth', *Journal of Economic Dynamics and Control*, 23: 463–88.

Cooley, T. F. and E. C. Prescott (1995) 'Economic Growth and Business Cycles', ch. 1 of T. F. Cooley and E. C. Prescott (eds.), *Frontiers of Business Cycle Research* (Princeton, NJ: Princeton University Press).

Dungey, M. and A. R. Pagan (1997) 'Towards a Structural VAR Model of the Australian Economy', *Working Papers in Economics and Econometrics*, Australian National University, 319.

Epstein, P. (1999) 'Wesley Mitchell's Grand Design and its Critics', *Journal of Economic Issues*, 33: 525–53.

FIBCR (1998) *International Economic Indicators—A Monthly Outlook* 21(1–2).

Fisher, L., G. Otto, and G. M. Voss (1996) 'Australian Business Cycle Facts', *Australian Economic Papers* 35: 202–22.

Gordon, S. and P. St-Amour (1998) 'Asset Prices with Contingent Risk Preferences', Paper given at the Summer Meetings of the Econometric Society, Montreal.

Harding, D. (1997) 'The Definition, Dating and Duration of Cycles', Paper presented to the Melbourne Institute conference on Business Cycles: Policy and Analysis.

—— and A. R. Pagan (1999) 'Dissecting the Cycle' (mimeo, University of Melbourne).

Hartley, J. E., K. D. Hoover, and K. D. Salyer (1997) 'The Limits of Business Cycle Research: Assessing the Real Business Cycle Model', *Oxford Review of Economic Policy* 13: 34–54.

Huang, K. X. D. and Z. Liu (1998) 'Staggered Contracts and Business Cycle Persistence', Discussion Paper 127 (Institute for Empirical Macroeconomics, Federal Reserve Bank of Minneapolis).

Jacobs, J. (1998) *Econometric Business Cycle Research* (Boston: Kluwer Academic Publishers).

Kiley, M. (1999) 'Partial Adjustment and Staggered Price Setting', Discussion Paper 1999–1, Division of Research and Statistics, Federal Reserve Board.

Kim, K. H., R. A. Buckle, and V. Hall (1994) 'Key Features of New Zealand Business Cycles', *Economic Record* 70: 56–72.

King, R. G. and C. I. Plosser (1994) 'Real Business Cycles and the Test of the Adelmans', *Journal of Monetary Economics* 33: 405–38.

——, ——, and S. T. Rebelo (1988) 'Production, Growth and Business Cycles II: New Directions', *Journal of Monetary Economics* 21: 309–41.

—— and S. Rebelo (1999) 'Resuscitating Real Business Cycles', in M. Woodford and J. Taylor (eds.), *Handbook of Macroeconomics* (North-Holland: Elsevier).

Kiyotaki, N. and J. Moore (1997) 'Credit Cycles', *Journal of Political Economy* 105: 211–48.

Laxton, D., P. Isard, H. Faruqee, E. Prasad, and B. Turtelboom (1998) *MULTIMOD Mark III: The Core Dynamic and Steady-State Models*, Occasional Paper 164 (Washington, DC: International Monetary Fund).

Lucas, R. E. (1981) 'Methods and Problems in Business Cycle Theory', in R. E. Lucas, *Studies in Business Cycle Theory* (Cambridge, Mass.: MIT Press).

McConnell, M. and G. P. Quiros (1998) 'Output Fluctuations in the United States: What Has Changed Since the Early 1980s', Staff Report 41 (New York: Federal Reserve Bank of New York).

Mintz, I. (1969) 'Dating Postwar Business Cycles, Methods and Their Application to Western Germany, 1950–1967', NBER Occasional Paper 107 (New York: NBER).

—— (1972) 'Dating American Growth Cycles', in V. Zarnowitz (ed.), *The Business Cycle Today* (New York: NBER): 39–88.

—— (1974) 'Dating United States Growth Cycles', in *Explorations in Economic Research*, NBER Occasional Paper 1(1): 1–113.

Pagan, A. R. (1997) 'Policy, Theory and the Cycle', *Oxford Review of Economic Policy* 13: 19–33.

Ramey, G. and J. Watson (1997) 'Contractual Fragility, Job Destruction and Business Cycles', *Quarterly Journal of Economics* 112: 873–911.

Romer, D. (1996) *Advanced Macroeconomics* (New York: McGraw-Hill).

Sachs, J. and F. Larrain (1993) *Macroeconomics in the Global Economy* (Hemel Hempstead: Harvester Wheatsheaf).

Schmitt-Grohe, S. (1998) 'Endogenous Business Cycles and the Dynamics of Output, Hours and Consumption' (mimeo, Board of Governors of the Federal Reserve System).

Sichel, D. E. (1994) 'Inventories and the Three Phases of the Business Cycle', *Journal of Business and Economic Statistics* 12: 269–77.

Simkins, S. P. (1994) 'Do Real Business Cycle Models Really Exhibit Business Cycle Behavior', *Journal of Monetary Economics* 33: 381–404.

Temin, P. (1998) 'The Causes of American Business Cycles: An Essay in Economic Historiography', Working Paper 6692 (New York: NBER).

Tinbergen, J. (1939) *Statistical Testing of Business Cycle Theories*, 2 vols (Geneva: League of Nations).

Usabiaga-Ibáñez, C. (1999) 'Interview with Larry Christiano', in C. Usabiaga-Ibáñez (ed.), *The Current State of Macroeconomics: Methodology, Theory and Economic Policy: Conversations with Leading Macro Economists* (Macmillan).

Wecker, W. (1979) 'Predicting the Turning Points of a Time Series', *Journal of Business* 52: 35–50.

3 Fiscal shocks in an efficiency wage model

CRAIG BURNSIDE, MARTIN EICHENBAUM, AND
JONAS D. M. FISHER

1. Introduction

This paper illustrates a particular limited information strategy for assessing the empirical plausibility of alternative quantitative general equilibrium business-cycle models. The basic strategy is to test whether a model economy can account for the response of the actual economy to an exogenous shock. To be useful, this strategy requires that we know how the actual economy responds to the shock in question and that different models generate different predictions for that response. Here, we concentrate on the response of aggregate hours worked and real wages to a fiscal policy shock.[1] The fiscal policy shock is identified with the dynamic response of government purchases and average marginal income tax rates to an exogenous increase in military purchases.

Burnside *et al.* (1999) (BEF) show that standard real business cycle (RBC) models can account for the salient features of how hours worked and after-tax real wages respond to a fiscal policy shock, but only if it is assumed that marginal tax rates are constant. When this counterfactual assumption is abandoned, RBC models cannot account for the response of the economy to a fiscal policy shock. For example, high labour supply elasticity versions of these models counterfactually predict that after a fiscal policy shock, government purchases are negatively correlated with hours worked. In reality, after a fiscal policy shock, government purchases and hours worked are strongly positively correlated. Low labour supply elasticity versions of these models greatly understate the conditional volatility of hours worked. So regardless of what is assumed about the elasticity of labour supply, the model cannot account for the facts. Ramey and Shapiro (1998) show that various two-sector versions of the RBC model generate predictions for aggregate hours worked and real wages that are very similar to those of the one-sector model. So presumably these models too would fail our diagnostic test. Rotemberg and Woodford (1992) and Devereux *et al.* (1996) study the effects of changes in government purchases in stochastic general equilibrium models which incorporate increasing returns and oligopolistic pricing. Since their models imply that a positive shock to government purchases raises real wages, they would fail our test.

The views expressed in this paper do not necessarily represent the views of the Federal Reserve Bank of Chicago, the Federal Reserve System or the World Bank. Martin Eichenbaum gratefully acknowledges the financial support of a grant from the National Science Foundation to the National Bureau of Economic Research.

[1] See Christiano *et al.* (1998) for a similar approach to evaluating alternative models of the monetary transmission mechanism.

In this paper, we examine a variant of Alexopoulos's (1998) model of efficiency wages. We find that, like the other models discussed above, the efficiency wage model cannot account for the quantitative responses of hours worked and of real wages to a fiscal policy shock. In particular it shares the strengths and weaknesses of high labour supply elasticity RBC models. So the model can account for the conditional volatility of real wages and hours worked. But it cannot account for the temporal pattern of how these variables respond to a fiscal policy shock and generates a counterfactual negative conditional correlation between government purchases and hours worked. Integrating over the results we have obtained with the different models, we conclude there is a puzzle. Measurement is ahead of theory.

To identify *exogenous* changes to government purchases and tax rates we build on the approach used by Ramey and Shapiro (1998) who focus on exogenous movements in defence spending. To isolate such movements, they identify three political events that led to large military build-ups which were arguably unrelated to developments in the domestic US economy. We refer to these events as 'Ramey–Shapiro episodes'. Controlling for other shocks, we explore how the US economy behaved after the onset of the Ramey–Shapiro episodes and use the results in two ways. First, we use it to construct the basic experiment that is conducted in the model. Specifically we confront agents in the model with a sequence of changes in total government purchases and marginal income tax rates that coincide with the estimated dynamic response of those variables to a Ramey and Shapiro episode. Second, we use the estimated dynamic response paths of aggregate hours worked and after-tax real wages as the standard against which we assess our model's performance.

The remainder of this paper is organized as follows. Section 2 summarizes our evidence regarding the dynamic effects of a fiscal shock. Section 3 discusses our procedure for results to assess the empirical plausibility of competing business-cycle models. Section 4 presents a version of Alexopoulos's (1998) efficiency wage model, modified to allow for fiscal shocks. Section 5 assesses the quantitative properties of the model. Finally, Section 6 contains concluding remarks.

2. Evidence on the effects of a shock to fiscal policy

In this section we accomplish two tasks. First, we describe our strategy for estimating the effects of an exogenous shock to fiscal policy. Second, we present the results of implementing this strategy.[2]

2.1. Identifying the effects of a fiscal policy shock

Ramey and Shapiro (1998) use a 'narrative approach' to isolate three arguably exogenous events that led to large military build-ups and total government purchases: the beginning of the Korean War (1950: 3), the beginning of major US involvement

---

[2] This section is a condensed version of a similar section in BEF.

in the Vietnam War (1965: 1), and the beginning of the Carter–Reagan defence build-up (1980: 1).

To estimate the exogenous movements in government purchases, G_t, and average marginal tax rates, τ_t, induced by the onset of a Ramey–Shapiro episode, and the corresponding movements in other variables, we use the following procedure. Define the set of dummy variables D_t, where $D_t = 1$ if $t = \{1950: 3, 1965: 1, 1980: 1\}$ and zero otherwise. We include D_t as an explanatory variable in a vector autoregression (VAR). Suppose that the $k \times 1$ vector stochastic process Z_t has the representation:

$$Z_t = A_0 + A_1(L)Z_{t-1} + A_2(L)D_t + u_t,\tag{2.1}$$

where $A_1(L)$ and $A_2(L)$ are finite ordered matrix polynomials in non-negative powers of the lag operator, $Eu_t = 0$,

$$Eu'_t u_{t-s} = \begin{cases} 0 & \text{for all } s \neq 0, \\ \Sigma & \text{for } s = 0, \end{cases}$$

and Σ is a positive definite $k \times k$ matrix. The A_i can be consistently estimated using least squares. The response of Z_{it+k}, the ith element of Z_{t+k}, to the onset of a Ramey–Shapiro episode at date t, is given by the coefficient on L^k in the expansion of $[I - A_1(L)L]^{-1} A_2(L)$. Note that this procedure assumes that the Ramey–Shapiro episodes are of equal intensity.[3]

2.2. Empirical results

In this subsection we present the results of implementing the procedure discussed above. Unless otherwise noted, the vector Z_t contains the log level of time t real *GDP*, the three-month Treasury bill rate, the log of the producer price index of crude fuel, the log level of a measure of the average marginal income tax rate, the log level of real government purchases, and either the log level of real wages or the log of aggregate hours worked.[4] Our measure of the tax rate, taken from Stephenson (1998), is an updated version of the average marginal statutory tax rate constructed by Barro and Sahasakul (1983). It is a weighted average of statutory marginal tax rates, where the weights are the shares of adjusted gross income subject to each statutory rate.[5] In all cases we included six lagged values of all variables in the VAR. All estimates are based on quarterly data from 1947: 1 to 1994: 4.

Figure 3.1 reports the responses of real government purchases and the tax rate to the onset of a Ramey–Shapiro episode. The solid lines display point estimates of the

[3] BEF modify this procedure to allow the different episodes to have different intensities. They show that the qualitative nature of the estimated impulse response functions does not depend on whether one imposes the equal intensity assumption or not.

[4] An appendix available from us describes the data in more detail.

[5] See Stephenson (1998) for refinements to the Barro–Sahasakul measure. We found that our results were insensitive to ignoring these refinements, and to using another tax rate measure suggested by Seater (1985).

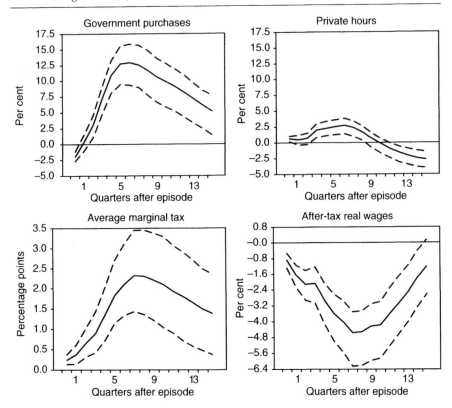

FIG. 3.1. *Responses of real government purchases, tax rate, aggregate hours worked in private sector, and after-tax real wages in the manufacturing sector to the onset of a Ramey–Shapiro episode*

coefficients of the dynamic response functions.[6] The dashed lines are 68 per cent confidence intervals.[7] Consistent with results in Ramey and Shapiro (1998) and Edelberg, Eichenbaum, and Fisher (1999), the onset of a Ramey–Shapiro episode leads to a large, persistent, hump-shaped rise in government purchases, with a peak response of 13 per cent roughly six quarters after the shock. In addition, the tax rate rises in a hump-shaped pattern, mirroring the hump-shaped dynamic response function of government purchases. The peak response of 2.3 percentage points occurs roughly seven quarters after the onset of a Ramey–Shapiro episode. This represents a rise of roughly 13 per cent in the tax rate relative to its value in 1949.

---

[6] The impulse response function of the tax rate is reported in percentage points. The other impulse response functions are reported in percentage deviations from each variable's unshocked path.

[7] See BEF for details of the construction of these confidence bands. These confidence bands assume that the dates marking the onset of the Ramey–Shapiro episodes are known with certainty. We have conducted experiments to quantify the importance of 'date uncertainty'. Specifically we take into account the possibility that the exact Ramey–Shapiro dates might be off by up to three quarters each. We find our results to be robust to these experiments.

Figure 3.1 also displays the responses of aggregate hours worked in the private sector and the after-tax real wages in the manufacturing sector to the onset of a Ramey–Shapiro episode. Two key results emerge here. First, hours worked has a delayed, hump-shaped response with a peak response of over 2 per cent occurring roughly six periods after the fiscal shock. Second, the after-tax real wage falls after the fiscal policy shock.[8]

3. A limited information diagnostic procedure

The previous section displayed our estimates of the dynamic consequences of a fiscal policy shock to government purchases, average marginal tax rates, hours worked, and real wages. In this section we provide a short discussion, taken from BEF, of a limited information procedure for using these results to assess the empirical plausibility of competing models.

We partition Z_t as

$$Z_t = \begin{pmatrix} \bar{Z}_t \\ F_t \end{pmatrix},$$

where $F_t = (G_t \, \tau_t)'$ and $\bar{Z}_t$ is a $(k - 2) \times 1$ vector of the other variables. For the class of models that we consider the equilibrium law of motion for Z_t takes the form of a system of linear difference equations:

$$B_0 Z_t = \kappa + B_1(L) Z_{t-1} + B_2(L) D_t + \varepsilon_t. \tag{3.1}$$

Here $B_1(L)$ is a finite-ordered matrix polynomial in the lag operator, $B_2(L) = [0'_{k-2} \ M(L)']'$, 0_{k-2} is a $k - 2$ vector of zeros, and the elements of $\varepsilon_t = (\varepsilon'_{\bar{z}t} \ \varepsilon'_{Ft})'$ are uncorrelated with each other, with D_t and with lagged values of Z_t. The last two rows of (3.1) are the policy rule for the fiscal variables, F_t. With this specification the only variables that are directly affected by D_t are those in F_t. The onset of a Ramey–Shapiro episode $(D_t = 1)$ sets off a chain of exogenous movements in F_t which leads to movements in $\bar{Z}_t$ through the mechanisms embedded in the particular model under consideration.

Our theoretical model (3.1), and a VAR of the form (2.1) are equivalent when

$$A_0 = B_0^{-1} \kappa, \quad A_1(L) = B_0^{-1} B_1(L), \quad A_2(L) = B_0^{-1} B_2(L), \quad u_t = B_0^{-1} \varepsilon_t. \tag{3.2}$$

To characterize impulse response functions we use the moving average representation (MAR) corresponding to (3.1) given by

$$Z_t = \Pi_0 + \Pi(L) \varepsilon_t + H(L) D_t. \tag{3.3}$$

By assumption, $\{\Pi_i\}$ and $\{H_i\}$ form square summable sequences. Note that $H(L)$ completely characterizes the dynamic response path of the vector Z_t to the time t

---

[8] In BEF we find qualitatively similar results for other measures of hours worked and real wages.

realization of D_t. In particular, the response of Z_{t+j} is given by the coefficient on L^j in $H(L)$.

It is useful to write the last two rows of (3.3) as

$$F_t = \Pi_0^2 + \Pi^2(L)\varepsilon_t + H^2(L)D_t. \tag{3.4}$$

We do not identify the elements of ε_t in our empirical analysis. However, under our assumptions, D_t is orthogonal to ε_t. So we can study the effects of a change in D_t abstracting from movements in ε_t. This is equivalent to working with the exogenous variable policy rule

$$F_t = \Pi_0^2 + H^2(L)D_t. \tag{3.5}$$

To assess the empirical plausibility of a model's implications for an exogenous shock to fiscal policy we can proceed as follows:

1. Estimate the VAR given by (2.1) using US data. This yields estimates $\hat{A}_0$, $\hat{A}_1(L)$, and $\hat{A}_2(L)$.
2. Use the estimates $\hat{A}_0$, $\hat{A}_1(L)$, and $\hat{A}_2(L)$ to obtain a moving average representation for Z_t that is equivalent to (3.3):

$$Z_t = \left[I - \hat{A}_1(1)\right]^{-1}\hat{A}_0 + \left[I - \hat{A}_1(L)L\right]^{-1}\hat{A}_2(L)D_t + \left[I - \hat{A}_1(L)L\right]^{-1}u_t$$
$$= \Pi_{d0} + H_d(L)D_t + \tilde{\Pi}_d(L)u_t.$$

Notice that $H_d^1(L)$, the first $(k-2) \times 1$ sub-block of $H_d(L)$, characterizes the dynamic responses of the non-fiscal variables, $\bar{Z}_t$, to the onset of a Ramey–Shapiro episode.

3. Use $H_d^2(L)$, the last 2×1 sub-block of $H_d(L)$, to characterize the exogenous variable fiscal policy rule in the theoretical model given by (3.5).
4. Using this rule, and calibrating the remaining model parameters, study the theoretical model's implications for the dynamic responses of the non-fiscal variables to the onset of the Ramey–Shapiro episode. Denote the polynomial in the lag operator that characterizes these responses as $H_m^1(L)$.
5. Compare these responses, obtained using the theoretical model, to their empirical counterparts, estimated in the second step. Abstracting from sampling uncertainty and the linearity assumptions implicit in the VAR analysis, the two sets of response functions should be the same, i.e. it should be the case that $H_m^1(L) = H_d^1(L)$.[9]

Results in Burnside and Eichenbaum (1996) suggest that uncertainty about the structural parameters of the model describing preferences and technology are unlikely

---

[9] As discussed in BEF the previous conclusion depends on the following simplification regarding agents' views about the law of motion for D_t: agents expect $D_t = 0$ for all t. In addition, a realization of $D_t = 1$ does not affect agents' future expectations of D_t, i.e. they continue to expect that future values of D_t will equal zero. So from their perspective, a realization of $D_t = 1$ is just like the realization of an iid exogenous shock to F_t. But once such a shock occurs, the expected response of F_{t+j} is given by the coefficient on L^j in the polynomial $H^2(L)$.

to significantly affect inference for the models we consider. Hence, we ignore this source of uncertainty. We do take into account sampling uncertainty pertaining to the estimated response of the US economy to a fiscal policy shock. Sampling uncertainty about the $\hat{A}_i$ from our VAR generates uncertainty about our data-based estimates of the impulse responses $H^1(L)$, $H_d^1(L)$, and our data-based estimates of $H^2(L)$, $H_d^2(L)$. In addition sampling uncertainty in $H_d^2(L)$ feeds into uncertainty about our model-based estimates of $H^1(L)$, $H_m^1(L)$.

BEF show how to account for these sources of sampling uncertainty when assessing the ability of the model to account for various conditional moments of the data, i.e. moments pertaining to the behaviour of the economy conditional on a fiscal shock having occurred. One way to estimate such a moment is to use a point estimate, $\hat{\theta}_H$, of the vector of coefficients, θ_H, characterizing $H(L)$, in a way that does not involve the use of an economic model. We let $d(\hat{\theta}_H)$ denote the point estimate of a conditional moment obtained in this way. A different way to estimate the conditional moment is to use an economic model along with values for the parameters describing agents' preferences and technology and an estimate of the coefficients characterizing the exogenous variable policy rule, θ_H^2. Note that θ_H^2 is a subset of θ_H. We denote by $m(\hat{\theta}_H^2)$ the point estimate of the conditional moment in question derived from the economic model.

Let

$$s(\theta_H) = d(\theta_H) - m(\theta_H^2).$$

We are interested in testing hypotheses of the form:

$$H_0: \ s(\theta_H) = 0.$$

An implication of results in Eichenbaum *et al.* (1988) and Newey and West (1987) is that the test statistic

$$\mathcal{J} = s(\hat{\theta}_H)'\widehat{\mathrm{var}}\left[s(\hat{\theta}_H)\right]^{-1}s(\hat{\theta}_H), \tag{3.6}$$

is asymptotically distributed as a chi-squared distribution with 1 degree of freedom, where $\widehat{\mathrm{var}}[s(\hat{\theta}_H)]$ is a consistent estimator of $\mathrm{var}[s(\hat{\theta}_H)]$.[10] Below we use this test statistic to formally assess the ability of an efficiency wage model to account for various conditional moments of the data.

---

[10] To generate an estimate of $\mathrm{var}[s(\hat{\theta}_H)]$ we use the same bootstrap procedure employed to compute confidence intervals for the impulse response functions estimated in the data. Specifically, let θ_{Hi} be the point estimate of the moving average coefficients of Z_t implied by the VAR coefficients generated by the ith bootstrap draw, $i = 1, \ldots, N$, where $N = 500$. Then

$$\widehat{\mathrm{var}}\left[s(\hat{\theta}_H)\right] = \frac{1}{N-1}\sum_{i=1}^{N}\left(s(\theta_{Hi}) - \bar{s}(\theta_{Hi})\right)^2,$$

where $\bar{s}(\theta_{Hi}) = (1/N)\sum_{i=1}^{N} s(\theta_{Hi})$, is a consistent estimate of $\mathrm{var}[s(\hat{\theta}_H)]$.

4. A general equilibrium efficiency wage model

In this section we describe a version of Alexopoulos's (1998) efficiency wage model, modified to allow for distortionary income taxes. The basic structure of the model is similar to a standard RBC model with the exception of the labour market. In contrast to RBC models, we assume that a worker's effort is imperfectly observable by firms. Competitive firms offer contracts that induce workers not to shirk on the job. These contracts specify a real wage, an effort level, and a specification that a worker will be dismissed and paid only a fraction of the wage if he is caught shirking on the job. Given a no-bonding constraint, the supply for labour will in general exceed the demand for labour, resulting in unemployment. Whether the *ex-post* utility of employed workers exceeds the utility of unemployed individuals depends on the nature of risk-sharing among members of the household. In the version of Alexopoulos's model discussed below, risk-sharing is imperfect (by assumption) and unemployed workers are worse off, *ex-post*, than employed workers.[11]

4.1. The government

The government faces the flow budget constraint

$$G_t \leq \tau_t(r_t - \delta)K_t + \tau_t W_t n_t h + \Phi_t,$$

where G_t is real government purchases, τ_t is the marginal tax rate, r_t is the rental rate of capital, $0 < \delta < 1$ is the depreciation rate, W_t is the real wage rate, n_t is employment, and Φ_t is lump-sum taxes. By assumption h, hours worked per worker, is constant so that hours and employment move in proportion to one another. The fiscal policy rule is of the form given by the last two rows of (3.1).

4.2. Households

The representative household owns the stock of capital, makes all capital related decisions, and pays both capital income taxes and lump-sum taxes. The household consists of a unit measure continuum of individuals. If individuals earn labour income, they must pay taxes on it. Employed members of the household partly insure the income of unemployed members of the household.

The household accumulates capital according to

$$K_{t+1} = (1 - \delta)K_t + I_t, \tag{4.1}$$

where K_t is the beginning of period t capital stock and I_t is time t investment. The household rents capital to firms at the competitively determined rate r_t, and rental income, net of depreciation, is taxed at the margin. The household uses its rental

---

[11] Alexopolous (1998) shows that in her model, with complete risk-sharing, unemployed workers are *ex-post* better off than employed workers. This version of her model is observationally equivalent to Hansen's (1985) RBC model with indivisible labour supply. See Woodford (1994) for a similar argument.

income net of these taxes and any lump-sum taxes that it pays to buy new capital. It distributes any remaining funds equally among the individual members of the household. We denote this common income as

$$C_t^h = (1 - \tau_t)(r_t - \delta)K_t - \Phi_t - (K_{t+1} - K_t). \tag{4.2}$$

Members of the household derive their remaining income from selling labour services to firms or from partial unemployment insurance provided by the household.[12] They are assumed to take both the terms of labour contracts and firms' demand for labour parametrically. In addition, from the perspective of firms, all individuals look alike. So we can think of the employment outcome for any individual as being determined completely randomly. Some individuals will be employed, while others will be unemployed. Under our assumptions, no individual would choose to be unemployed, because the *ex-post* utility of such an individual will be less than or equal to that of an employed individual.

Employed workers will either work and exert the level of effort required by the labour contract, denoted e_t, or they will shirk. The labour contract stipulates that if workers are caught shirking, they will be fired and receive only a fraction s of their wages. The technology for detecting shirkers is imperfect, so that a shirker is only caught with probability d.

The household only observes the initial employment status of its members, not whether they shirked or were fired. Each employed member of the household transfers Ψ_t units of income to a pool which is distributed equally among the unemployed members of the household. By assumption, the household chooses the level of the transfer so that unemployed members of the household will be at least as well off as any shirker caught by the firm would be.[13] Finally, we assume that labour income is taxed. Members of the household who pay the insurance transfer receive no tax credit for it, while recipients of transfers do not pay taxes on that type of income.

Our assumptions imply that the consumption of an employed individual who does not shirk is constrained by

$$C_t \leq C_t^h + (1 - \tau_t)W_t h - \Psi_t. \tag{4.3}$$

An employed individual who shirks but does not get caught faces the same constraint. An employed individual who shirks and is caught only receives the fraction s of his contractual wages. Hence, his consumption, C_t^s, is constrained by

$$C_t^s \leq C_t^h + (1 - \tau_t)sW_t h - \Psi_t. \tag{4.4}$$

Suppose that n_t members of the household are employed while $1 - n_t$ are unemployed. This implies that the transfer received by each unemployed person is

---

[12] It is straightforward to reformulate the model so that a self-financing unemployment insurance programme is provided by the government rather than the household.

[13] Alexopoulos (1998) also considers the case in which there is perfect insurance across members of the family.

$n_t \Psi_t / (1 - n_t)$. Hence, the consumption of an unemployed individual, C_t^u, is constrained by

$$C_t^u \leq C_t^h + \frac{n_t}{1 - n_t} \Psi_t. \tag{4.5}$$

The instantaneous utility of an individual with consumption level C, and a positive level of effort e, is given by

$$\log(C) + \eta \log(T - \xi - he)$$

while the instantaneous utility of an individual with consumption level C who exerts no work effort is given by

$$\log(C) + \eta \ln(T),$$

where $\eta > 0$, T is the time endowment, and ξ is the fixed cost of exerting non-zero effort.

Thus, an employed worker who does not shirk has utility

$$\log(C_t) + \eta \ln(T - \xi - he_t),$$

where e_t is determined by the contract offered by the firm.

An employed worker who shirks but is not caught has utility

$$\log(C_t) + \eta \ln(T)$$

while a shirker who is caught has utility

$$\log(C_t^s) + \eta \ln(T).$$

Finally, an unemployed individual has utility

$$\log(C_t^u) + \eta \ln(T).$$

Let n_t^s be the number of shirkers and let d be the probability of a shirker being caught. Since there is a continuum of individuals, this implies that dn_t^s is the number of shirkers caught and $(1 - d)n_t^s$ is the number of shirkers not caught.

Notice that the effective leisure time of caught shirkers and unemployed individuals is the same. If the family sets the transfer so that their consumption and utility levels are the same, this will imply that

$$\Psi_t = (1 - n_t)(1 - \tau_t)sW_t h. \tag{4.6}$$

The household takes the effort level and wage rate as given in the contracts offered by the firm. The household also takes firms' labour demand as given. The only decisions the household makes are those regarding capital and the level of common income, in order to maximize the expected utility of an individual household member:

$$\max_{\{C_t, K_{t+1}\}_{t=0}^{\infty}} E_0 \sum_{t=0}^{\infty} \beta^t \{(n_t - n_t^s)[\log(C_t) + \eta \log(T - \xi - he_t)]$$
$$+ n_t^s[(1 - d)\log(C_t) + d \log(C_t^s) + \eta \log(T)]$$
$$+ (1 - n_t)[\log(C_t^u) + \eta \ln(T)]\}$$

subject to (4.2)–(4.6).

4.3. The firm

A perfectly competitive firm produces output using the technology

$$Y_t = K_t^\alpha (n_t he_t X_t)^{1-\alpha},$$

where n_t is the number of workers it hires. It maximizes its profits

$$\max_{W_t, n_t, K_t, e_t} K_t^\alpha (n_t he_t X_t)^{1-\alpha} - W_t n_t h - r_t K_t$$

subject to the 'no shirking' condition:

$$\log(C_t) + \eta \log(T - \xi - he_t) \geq (1 - d)\log(C_t) + d\log(C_t^s) + \eta \ln(T). \quad (4.7)$$

According to (4.7) the expected utility of an employee who does not shirk is at least as great as the expected utility of an employee who shirks. Here we assume that all employed workers are monitored and the exogenous probability of being caught shirking is d. In equilibrium there is no shirking. Given a wage rate, W_t, we can think of (4.7) as indicating a maximal level of effort the firm will be able to extract from workers. Rearranging the constraint we see that

$$e_t \leq e(W_t) = \frac{T - \xi}{h} - \frac{T}{h} \left(\frac{C_t^s}{C_t}\right)^{d/\eta}.$$

The firm takes the level of the intra-household transfer Ψ_t parametrically. This is what allows us to write the expression on the right-hand side as a function, from the firm's point of view, only of its choice regarding W_t.

Alexopoulos (1998) shows that the first–order conditions for the firm, along with the expression for $e(W_t)$ imply that C_t/C_t^s is a constant given by χ where χ satisfies

$$Td(1 - s\chi)(\chi - 1) = \eta(1 - s)\left[(T - \xi)\chi^{1+d/\eta} - T\chi\right]. \quad (4.8)$$

This is a non-linear equation in χ that can be solved numerically.

The level of employment, n_t, which characterizes the solution to the firm's problem will not in general coincide with the number of workers who wish to work at the contract characterized by $(W_t, e(W_t))$. As long as the demand for workers is less than the supply of workers, (4.7) will hold with equality and there will be equilibrium unemployment. We confine ourselves to calibrated versions of the model in which this is the case and in which all of the inequality constraints above hold with equality.

We use the log linearization procedure described by Christiano (1998) to solve for the competitive equilibrium of this economy.

5. Quantitative properties of the model

This section assesses the quantitative properties of our model. We proceed in three steps. First, we discuss how we calibrate the model's parameters. Second, we discuss how the model responds over time to a fiscal shock. Third, we formally assess the ability of the model to account for various conditional moments of the data.

5.1. Model calibration

Alexopoulos (1998) estimates and analyses the lump-sum version of the model above using the Generalized Method of Moments procedures discussed in Christiano and Eichenbaum (1992). Here we simply calibrate the model by choosing parameters to match a number of features of postwar US data. We assume that the time endowment is $T = 1369$ which corresponds to a quarter consisting of 15 hours per day. We assume that the fixed cost of providing non-zero effort is given by $\xi = 16$. We parameterize χ to imply that being unemployed lowers a worker's consumption by about 22 per cent (see Gruber 1997). This requires $\chi = 1.285$. We set $\beta = 1.03^{-1/4}$, $\gamma = 1.004$, $\alpha = 0.34$, and $\delta = 0.021$ (see Christiano and Eichenbaum 1992). We chose $s = 0.72$ so that the steady state value of n would be equal to its sample average, 0.93. Finally, (4.8) can be used to solve for d/η as a function of parameters whose values we have already specified. This results in a value of d/η equal to about 0.062.

5.2. Impulse response functions

Figure 3.2 displays the dynamic response functions of hours worked, investment, before and after-tax real wages, household transfers of consumption (C_t^h), as well as the marginal tax rate to a fiscal policy shock. Notice that hours worked $(n_t h)$ initially rises roughly 5 per cent in the impact period of the shock (time 0) and then declines, reaching its pre-shock level after about three quarters. Thereafter $n_t h$ continues to fall, reaching a maximal decline of about 7 per cent around period 8, roughly the same time as the maximal rise in government purchases and the marginal tax rate. So, as in the case of the one-sector model RBC analysed in BEF, hours worked decline when income tax rates and government purchases are high.[14] The behaviour of the before-tax real wage mirrors the movements in $n_t h$, initially declining and then rising above its

---

[14] This result is reminiscent of the balanced budget case in Baxter and King (1993).

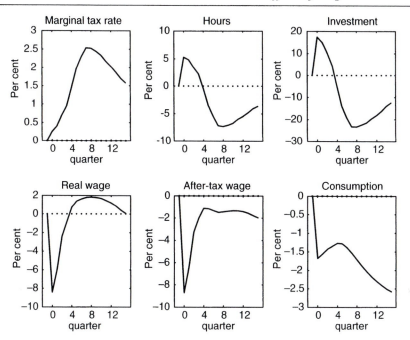

FIG. 3.2. *Response of model economy to a fiscal shock: time-varying distortionary tax rate*

pre-shock level roughly three periods after the shock. In contrast the after-tax real wage remains below its pre-shock level for over twelve periods. Finally notice that the response of investment is qualitatively very similar to that of $n_t h$, while C_t^h moves in the opposite manner, falling when $n_t h$ rises, and climbing when $n_t h$ falls.

To see the intuition behind the forces at work in the model, note that equations (4.3) and (4.4), evaluated at equality, imply

$$\frac{C_t}{C_t^s} = \frac{C_t^h + (1 - \tau_t)W_t h - \Psi_t}{C_t^h + (1 - \tau_t)sW_t h - \Psi_t}. \tag{5.1}$$

It follows that, other things equal, the ratio of an employed worker's consumption to that of a fired worker's consumption, (C_t/C_t^s) is a decreasing function of C_t^h.

Suppose that all taxes are lump-sum. Then (4.2) can be written as

$$C_t^h = (r_t - \delta)K_t - \Phi_t - (K_{t+1} - K_t). \tag{5.2}$$

With this specification, increases in government purchases are financed by increases in Φ_t. So, other things equal, an increase in G_t causes C_t^h to fall and (C_t/C_t^s) to rise. But in equilibrium (C_t/C_t^s) must be equal to the constant χ. So some other factor in (5.1) must adjust. In equilibrium workers are indifferent between shirking and not shirking. So a rise in (C_t/C_t^s) would cause workers to strictly prefer not to shirk. In such a situation, firms could cut real wages without inducing shirking behaviour. Equations (4.6) and (5.1) can be used to show that a decline in W_t will move C_t/C_t^s back down towards its constant value χ. The net result then of a fiscal shock is a decline in the real wage and an increase in employment.[15]

When the rise in government purchases is persistent there will be a significant rise in the present value of the household's taxes. As in the neoclassical model, this rise induces the household to increase investment. From (5.2) we see that a rise in $(K_{t+1} - K_t)$ acts like a rise in Φ_t. This reinforces the effects discussed above, exerting upward pressure on employment and downward pressure on real wages. For reference Figure 3.3 presents the dynamic response functions for the model economy under the assumption that the rise in government purchases induced by a fiscal policy shock is entirely financed by lump-sum taxes. Consistent with this intuition we see from Figure 3.3 that in the lump-sum tax case, the fiscal policy shock leads to a hump-shaped, persistent rise in n_t, and investment, as well as a persistent, hump-shaped fall in before and after-tax real wage rates.

To understand the impact of distortionary taxes on the model, recall that in their presence, C_t^h is given by

$$C_t^h = (1 - \tau_t)(r_t - \delta)K_t - \Phi_t - (K_{t+1} - K_t).$$

A rise in τ_t has two effects: (i) it directly reduces C_t^h via the term $(1 - \tau_t)(r_t - \delta)K_t$, and (ii) it indirectly affects C_t^h via its effect on $K_{t+1} - K_t$. The first effect acts much like the increase in Φ_t described above. Other things equal then, the rise in τ_t tends to magnify the initial fall in real wages and the rise in n_t. The second effect works through the household's incentive to invest in capital. Other things equal, a higher future value of τ_{t+1} reduces the time t return to capital and the incentive to invest at time t. We refer to this as the one-period-ahead tax effect. In addition there is an intertemporal effect associated with movements in τ_t which induces the household to shift investment towards periods in which τ_t is relatively low.

Recall that according to our estimates, τ_t responds in a hump-shaped manner to a fiscal period shock, rising by relatively small amounts in the first few periods. So the one-period-ahead tax effect initially has a relatively small dampening effect on investment. But the intertemporal tax effects are quite large. Agents have an incentive to invest to pay off their higher tax bills and they may as well do so in periods in which τ_t is relatively small. Consistent with this, we see from Figures 3.2 and 3.3 that initially investment rises by more in the distortionary tax case than in the lump-sum tax case. Other things equal this means that C_t^h falls by more and (C_t/C_t^s) rises by more in the distortionary tax case. So firms must lower real wages by relatively more in the distortionary case to prevent shirking, which in turn leads to relatively larger initial rises in n_t.

As marginal tax rates begin to rise significantly, the one-period-ahead tax effect becomes quantitatively important. By period 3 investment falls to its pre-shock level

---

[15] The rise in n_t is determined by the firm's demand for labour.

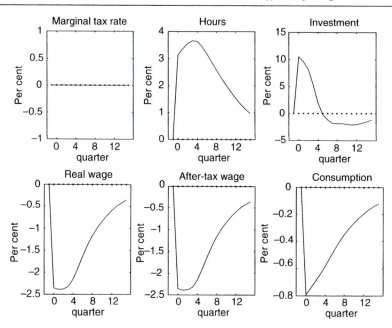

FIG. 3.3. *Response of model economy to a fiscal shock: constant distortionary tax rate*

and continues to fall, reaching a maximal decline of roughly 25 per cent in period 8, the period in which τ_t peaks. Other things equal, the decline in investment causes C_t^h to rise and (C_t/C_t^s) to fall. To restore (C_t/C_t^s) to its equilibrium value of χ, real wages rise which induces a fall in n_t. This explains the sharp decline in hours worked and investment after period 3 in Figure 3.3. It also accounts for the fact that they are at their lowest levels when government purchases and taxes are at their highest levels.

5.3. Test statistics

We conclude this subsection by reporting the results of formally testing the models' ability to account for various conditional moments of the data using the J-statistic defined in (3.6). We begin by discussing four moments pertaining to hours worked. The first two moments relate to the maximal response of hours worked in the aftermath of a Ramey–Shapiro episode: $R_1(n)$ and $R_2(n)$ are the peak rise in $n_t h$ and the average response of $n_t h$ in periods 4 through 7 after a fiscal policy shock. The values of these moments for the model and the data, $R_i^m(n)$ and $R_i^d(n)$, $i = 1, 2$, respectively, were calculated using estimates of the relevant dynamic response functions. The third moment is the correlation between g_t and $n_t h$, $\rho(g, n)$, induced by a fiscal policy shock. We let $\rho^m(g, n)$ and $\rho^d(g, n)$ denote the values of this moment implied by the model and the data, respectively. The final moment, σ_n, is the standard deviation of hours worked induced by the onset of a Ramey–Shapiro shock. Below, σ_n^m and σ_n^d denote the values of this moment implied by the model and the data, respectively.[16]

Column 1 of Table 3.1 reports the results of testing the individual hypotheses: $R_i^d(n) - R_i^m(n) = 0$, $i = 1, 2$, $\rho^d(g, n) - \rho^m(g, n) = 0$, and $\sigma_n^d - \sigma_n^m = 0$. Note that we cannot reject the hypothesis that $R_1^d(n) - R_1^m(n) = 0$ at conventional significance levels, nor can we reject the hypothesis that $\sigma_n^d - \sigma_n^m = 0$. However, while the model can match the overall volatility of σ_n and the peak response of $n_t h$, it does so in a way that is inconsistent with the *timing* of the actual movements in $n_t h$. Consistent with our discussion above, the model predicts that $n_t h$ is strongly negatively correlated with g_t with $\rho^m(g, n)$ equal to -0.80. But in the data g_t and $n_t h$ are strongly positively correlated, with $\rho^d(g, n) = 0.69$. Not surprisingly, we can reject the hypothesis that $\rho^d(g, n) - \rho^m(g, n) = 0$ at the 1 per cent significance level. Consistent with the notion that model mispredicts the timing of the response of $n_t h$, we can also reject the hypothesis that $R_2^d(n) - R_2^m(n) = 0$. This reflects that the maximal response of $n_t h$ in the model occurs before period 4 while in the data they occur after period 4.

Column 2 of Table 3.1 provides the results of formally testing the analog hypotheses for real wages. Specifically, the first two moments pertain to the maximal response of after-tax real wages in the aftermath of a Ramey–Shapiro episode: $R_1[(1 - \tau)W]$ and $R_2[(1 - \tau)W]$ denote the maximal declines in $(1 - \tau_t)W_t$ and the average response of $(1 - \tau_t)W_t$ in periods 4 through 7 after a fiscal policy shock. The third moment which we consider is the correlation between g_t and $(1 - \tau_t)W_t$, $\rho[g, (1 - \tau)W]$, induced by a fiscal policy shock. The final moment, $\sigma_{(1-\tau)W}$, is the standard deviation of the after-tax real wage induced by the onset of a Ramey–Shapiro episode.

Notice that we cannot reject the hypotheses that the model accounts for the peak declines in real wages and the conditional volatility in real wages. But as with $n_t h$, the model does so in a way that is inconsistent with the *timing* of the actual movements in W_t. In the data after-tax wages and government purchases are strongly negatively correlated with $\rho[g, (1 - \tau)W]$ equal to -0.90. In the model these variables are less strongly correlated (-0.32). As result we can reject the hypothesis that the model can account for the correlation between after-tax real wages and government purchases at the 1 per cent significance level. We can also easily reject the hypothesis that the average response of real wages during periods in 4 through 7 is the same in the model and in the data.

---

[16] We calculated the last two moments as follows. Let the actual and model implied dynamic response function of a variable x_t to a fiscal policy shock be given by $H_x(L)D_t$ and $\tilde{H}_x(L)D_t$, respectively, $x_t = \{n_t, g_t\}$. The value of σ_x implied by the model and in the data is given by $\sigma_x^m = \{\sum_{i=0}^{\infty}[\tilde{H}_x(i)]^2\}^{1/2}$ and $\sigma_x^d = \{\sum_{i=0}^{\infty}[H_x(i)]^2\}^{1/2}$, respectively. Here $H_x(i)$ and $\tilde{H}_x(i)$ denote the ith coefficient in the polynomial lag operator $H_x(L)$ and $\tilde{H}_x(L)$. The value of $\rho(g_t, n_t)$ implied by the model and in the data is given by $\rho^m(g, n) = \{\sum_{i=0}^{\infty}\tilde{H}_n(i)H_g(i)\}/\sigma_n^m\sigma_g^d$ and $\rho^d(g, n) = \{\sum_{i=0}^{\infty}H_n(i)H_g(i)\}/\sigma_n^d\sigma_g^d$, respectively. Note that the value of σ_g in the model is equal to σ_g^d by construction. In practice we calculated σ_n^m, σ_n^d, $\rho^m(g, n)$, $\rho^d(g, n)$, and σ_g^d using the first twelve coefficients of the relevant dynamic response functions.

TABLE 3.1. *Testing individual hypotheses*

Moment	Hours worked	After-tax real wage
Peak		
Data	2.78	−4.55
Model	5.27	−8.71
J-statistic	1.76	0.00
P-value	0.19	0.99
Average of periods 4–7		
Data	2.51	−3.77
Model	−4.17	−1.28
J-statistic	3.63	5.29
P-value	0.06	0.02
Correlation with government purchases		
Data	0.81	−0.97
Model	−0.77	−0.32
J-statistic	13.0	16.3
P-value	0.00	0.00
Standard deviation		
Data	5.92	11.8
Model	18.6	12.1
J-statistic	2.28	0.00
P-value	0.13	1.00

6. Conclusion

This paper implements a particular limited information strategy for assessing the empirical plausibility of competing business-cycle models. The basic strategy is to confront models with experiments that we claim to have isolated in the data and whose effects on the actual economy we know. The experiment that we focus on is an exogenous fiscal shock that leads to persistent movements in government purchases and average marginal tax rates. We analysed the ability of a particular general equilibrium efficiency wage model to account for the actual responses of hours worked and of real wages to a fiscal policy shock. Our key finding is that the model cannot do so unless we make the counterfactual assumption that marginal tax rates are constant. This failure reflects, to a large extent, the response of investment to the fiscal policy shock. We anticipate addressing this shortcoming in future work.

REFERENCES

Alexopoulos, M. (1998) 'Efficiency Wages, Unemployment and the Business Cycle', MS, Northwestern University.

Barro, R. J. and C. Sahasakul (1983) 'Measuring the Average Marginal Tax Rate from the Individual Income Tax', *Journal of Business* 56: 419–52.

Baxter, M. and R. G. King (1993) 'Fiscal Policy in General Equilibrium', *American Economic Review* 83: 315–34.

Burnside, C. and M. Eichenbaum (1996) 'Factor Hoarding and the Propagation of Business Cycle Shocks', *American Economic Review* 86: 1154–74.

—— and J. Fisher (1999) 'Assessing the Effects of Fiscal Shocks', MS, Northwestern University.

Christiano, L. J. (1998) 'Solving Dynamic Equilibrium Models by a Method of Undetermined Coefficients', NBER Technical Working Paper 225.

—— and M. Eichenbaum (1992) 'Current Real Business Cycle Theories and Aggregate Labor Market Fluctuations', *American Economic Review* 82: 430–50.

—— and C. Evans (1998) 'Modelling Money', NBER Working Paper 6371.

Devereux, M. B., Head, A. C., and M. Lapham (1996) 'Monopolistic Competition, Increasing Returns, and the Effects of Government Spending', *Journal of Money, Credit and Banking* 28(2): 233–54.

Edelberg, W. Eichenbaum, M., and Fisher, J. (1999) 'Understanding the Effects of Shocks to Government Purchases', *Review of Economics Dynamics* 2: 166–206.

Eichenbaum, M., Hansen, L. P., and Singleton, K. J. (1988) 'A Time Series Analysis of Representative Agent Models of Consumption and Leisure under Uncertainty', *Quarterly Journal of Economics* 103(1): 51–78.

Gruber, J. (1997) 'The Consumption Smoothing Benefits of Unemployment Insurance', *American Economic Review* 87: 192–205.

Hansen, G. (1985) 'Indivisible Labor and the Business Cycle', *Journal of Monetary Economics* 16(3): 309–28.

Newey, W. and K. West (1987) 'A Simple, Positive Semi-Definite Heteroskedasticity and Autocorrelation Consistent Covariance Matrix', *Econometrica* 55: 703–8.

Ramey, V. and M. D. Shapiro (1998) 'Costly Capital Reallocation and the Effects of Government Spending', *Carnegie-Rochester Conference Series on Public Policy* 48: 145–94.

Rotemberg, J. and M. Woodford (1992) 'Oligopolistic Pricing and the Effects of Aggregate Demand on Economic Activity', *Journal of Political Economy* 100: 1153–297.

Seater, J. (1985) 'On the Construction of Marginal Federal Personal and Social Security Tax Rates in the US', *Journal of Monetary Economics* 15: 121–35.

Stephenson, E. F. (1998) 'Average Marginal Tax Rates Revisited', *Journal of Monetary Economics* 41: 389–409.

Woodford, M. (1994) 'Notes on Dynamic Efficiency Wage Models', MS, Princeton University.

4A   The return of business cycles

JAMES E. HARTLEY

So, what is a business cycle, anyway? It seems like an odd question to ask this late in the study of business cycles. Surely, we should know by now. Yet, the profession seems unable to agree upon an answer. Part of the reason for this state of affairs is that there are two questions getting confused in much of the literature: (i) is 'the' cycle a classical cycle or a growth cycle? and (ii) is 'the' cycle movements in an aggregate variable or co-movements among several aggregates? The questions get conflated because, historically, Burns and Mitchell studied classical cycles and movements of aggregates, while recent research, particularly real business-cycle research, has studied growth cycles by looking at co-movements. But, there is no necessary connection between the answers to these two questions.

First, think about the growth cycle. Why do economists want to study cycles in growth? The modern interest in the growth cycle began in the late 1960s, when economists looked around and noticed that the business cycle was, in the word of the day, 'obsolete' (Bronfenbrenner 1969). After all, the US economy had not had a good, old-fashioned recession in a long time, and Germany did not have its first post-war recession until 1966. Since nobody wants to study something that is obsolete, economists started to study growth cycles. The idea at the time was simply to apply the methods of studying the classical cycle to detrended data (Klein 1976).

Thirty years later, it seems worthwhile to re-examine this question. For the last thirty years, we have been declaring the classical cycle and, in particular, the classical recession to be dead, but they have had a nasty way of being resurrected. It seems fair to say that the classical cycle is not dead. So why do economists not look at it? Harding and Pagan argue that it is only economists who care about the growth cycle, that normal people care only about the classical cycle. But, they overstate the case a bit. Listen to how Stock and Watson motivate their study of cycles for the *Handbook of Macroeconomics*:

Also evident in [the plot of an industrial production index] are the prolonged periods of increases and decreases that constitute the American business cycle. These fluctuations coincide with some of the signal events of the US economy over the century: the Great Depression of the 1930s; the subsequent recovery and growth during World War II; the sustained boom of the 1960s, associated in part with spending on the war in Vietnam; the recession of 1973–5, associated with the first OPEC price increases; the disinflationary twin recessions of the early 1980s; the recession of 1990, associated with the invasion of Kuwait by Iraq; and the long expansions of the 1980s and the early 1990s. (Stock and Watson 1999: 5)

This catalogue of the major events in the classical cycle comes just before they declare that from here on out, they will talk only of growth cycles. Rhetorically, we care about the classical cycle; but we study the growth cycle. Rhetorically, even economists care about classical recessions, but we study growth recessions. Is there a connection? Harding and Pagan provide much evidence that there are big differences and conclude 'No', but there is one interesting connection. In a growing economy, a classical recession must be a growth recession. Now, if Stock and Watson are right about what are generally accepted to be the causes of the big classical recessions—two money shocks, two oil shocks—then our stories about the growth cycles need to include such things. But oddly they generally do not.

Why not? It is because of the other big change: Lucas (1977) did not just reinforce the profession's drift toward studying growth cycles, he also made a big break with the profession by declaring it was the co-movements which we should care about. When you are looking at co-movements, you are never faced with the problem of explaining why output turned down at a particular point. In this, as Harding and Pagan note, Lucas was misreading the reason Burns and Mitchell looked at co-movements.[1] But, the result was a paper that in many ways became the touchstone of business-cycle research. Henceforth, people would cite Lucas (1977) as the rationale for studying the co-movements of aggregate series (e.g. Prescott 1986: 10).

What are the interesting business-cycle facts, these co-movements which we should be building a model to explain? It's hard to know. Lucas lists seven of them. Twenty years later, Cooley and Prescott (1995) have ten business cycle facts—but only *one* of Lucas's seven facts makes that list of ten facts. So, which fact has consistently been on the list? 'Production of producer and consumer durables exhibits much greater amplitude than does production of non-durables.' Indeed, this fact has been the constant refrain of the business-cycle literature in the last twenty years. And a rather dull refrain it is. It is hardly a distinguishing feature of business cycles that consumption of non-durables is relatively smooth—that is one of the most obvious implications of the life-cycle hypothesis after all. Replicating that fact does not make for a uniquely interesting model.

So, what of the other 'facts'? Are all cycles alike in co-movements? How do we know? As Harding and Pagan note, we do not.[2] Moreover, as both Canova (1998) and Pagan (1997) have shown, the 'facts' of a detrended set of aggregate data depend a lot on how one detrends the data. Kydland and Prescott (1996: 76–7n) are, however, unimpressed. They write: 'The resulting deviations from trend are nothing more than well-defined statistics. We emphasize that given the way the theory has developed,

---

[1] Morgan (1990: 22–56) is a good discussion of the aims of Burns and Mitchell. On the present matter, she notes, 'Correlation of one time series with another (with or without lagging) was another popular tool of data analysis in the 1920s. Correlation techniques were not rejected outright, but Mitchell distrusted the technique because he believed correlations could easily be manipulated' (ibid.: 50). Similarly, we can note Mitchell's (1927: 468) own definition of what he was studying: '[W]e indicate both the generic features and the distinguishing characteristics of business cycles by saying that they are recurrences of rise and decline in activity, affecting most of the economic processes of communities with well-developed business organization, not divisible into waves of amplitudes nearly equal to their own, and averaging in communities at different stages of development from about three to about six or seven years in duration.'

[2] What evidence there is on the subject suggests that the co-movements do vary across cycles. For example, Merz (1999) documents changes in the cyclicality of unemployment outflows over time; Hartley (1999) shows that the co-movement of real wages and GDP is different in the 1970s than at other times.

these statistics measure nothing.' Note that last phrase: 'these statistics measure nothing.' Kydland and Prescott have moved beyond Burns and Mitchell's 'Measurement without Theory' (Koopmans 1947) into the brave new world of pseudo-measurement without theory: we're not really measuring anything, so it's OK that we don't have a theory to explain what we are not doing.

And, thus, the standard real business-cycle test of matching co-movements of data detrended by using the Hodrick–Prescott filter with lambda set to exactly 1600 seems to have run out of steam. And it is not immediately clear where to turn. When real business-cycle models themselves are subjected to other tests, they almost always fail, and fail conclusively. To take one example, chosen practically at random, Canova, Finn, and Pagan (1994) test the restrictions on the VAR implied by a particular real business-cycle model and find that the model fails the test. To add insult to injury, they compare a rather simple old-style Keynesian macromodel to a modern real business-cycle model along these grounds, and the Keynesian model does at least as well, if not better. Now, for our purposes here, it is well worth noting that the real business-cycle model chosen as a foil by Canova, Finn, and Pagan was not some paltry insignificant real business-cycle model, but rather one developed by Burnside, Eichenbaum, and Rebelo (1993).

In the paper included here, Burnside, Eichenbaum, and Fisher (BEF) move from these sorts of results to the logical next step. They abandon the study of the cycle altogether. BEF have written a paper for a session entitled 'Business Cycles' and thus ostensibly on the subject of business cycles. But, the most remarkable thing about their paper is that other than when they note that they are looking at 'business-cycle models', the words 'business cycle' do not appear in the paper even once. There is simply no business cycle anywhere in this paper. As Harding and Pagan put it, 'Hamlet without the Prince' indeed.

Instead, BEF resurrect one of the old-style Keynesian tests—the event study. They ask the question: can a given model explain the behaviour of the economy in the face of a particular real world shock, namely a positive US defence spending shock? I find this movement both fascinating and encouraging, because in moving away from models intending to match co-movements over time and towards models intending to explore historical events, we are moving back towards a world in which we can talk about classical cycles and the events which cause them. Indeed, the second of BEF's three defence spending shocks is one of the major events listed by Stock and Watson in their quick list of important business cycle events.

So how does their event study work? BEF exploit the idea that similar shocks should have similar effects on the economy. But, to do this, it is important that the set of shocks being labelled 'similar' are in fact similar. Thus, for example, there are strong theoretical reasons to suspect that the economy may behave differently after a permanent shock to government spending from how it would after a temporary shock.[3] If we look at a plot of real defence spending over time, we do see that in all three of

---

[3] The importance of not mixing permanent and temporary shocks is emphasized in Burnside *et al.* (1999).

cases used by BEF, defence spending rises, hits a peak, and then falls. But in the Korean War case, it settles down at a much higher level than that at which it started out; in the other two cases, it falls all the way back down. In the first case it looks as if there is a permanent component to the shock; in the other two cases, it looks temporary. The study cries out for an 'event robustness' test. Now, while I am loath to suggest that the authors go from three to two data observations, that is the whole idea behind an event study—if there really were only two temporary shocks to defence spending, then that's all there were.

Proceeding to the tests, BEF first note that the standard real business-cycle model cannot account for the behaviour of the economy after a fiscal policy shock. So, instead, they examine an efficiency wage model originally developed by Alexopoulos (1998), finding that it too fails to replicate the temporal pattern of the economy after a fiscal policy shock.

But, despite its failure to mimic the economy, BEF's decision to examine this model in detail at all is noteworthy because of how the model differs from the standard RBC model. Taking this model as an indicator of the types of model now being examined by business-cycle theorists in the wake of growing disillusionment with the standard RBC model is interesting for the light it sheds on what such theorists believe needs to be incorporated into a model.

The model starts off in a rather interesting fashion: with the maximization of the utility of a representative household. But this household is unlike any household with which we are acquainted; it has a continuum of members. The closest real-world approximation to a group with an infinite number of members is a macroeconomy. And, indeed, as we dig into the model a bit, we find that this is in fact exactly what BEF have created.

Consider the idea of the maximization problem. The whole point of a representative agent model is to ground the problem in the deep taste and technology parameters of the individual actually making the decision. As Sargent (1982: 383) most clearly described it, the goal is to model 'the objective functions that agents are maximizing and the constraints they are facing, and which lead them to choose the decision rules that they do.'[4] Now, let us take this direction seriously, and imagine the present model in the light cast by Sargent. How exactly does a household with infinitely many members work? Who exactly is doing the maximizing? Who gets to pick the taste parameters? Is it some sort of collaborative effort? A dictatorship? A benevolent family planner?

The curiosities of this family arrangement show up clearly in the transfer between the members who work and those who do not. Who decides how big this transfer should be? Oddly, it is not the members of the household who decide; they are not asked to choose the optimal level of transfers, but rather the level is imposed by assumption. The reason why they are not asked is apparent—they would choose the wrong level; presumably they would pick an income-smoothing transfer and this is what BEF want to prohibit because such a level of transfers leads directly to the result

---

[4] A full discussion of the goals of representative agent models is provided in Hartley (1997).

that the unemployed are better off than the employed. So the transfer is set suboptimally from the perspective of every single member of the household. How can this be done? How is it enforced? Well, there must be something above the individuals—some aggregate restriction which emerges from somewhere other than the choice of the individual agent.

And, indeed, in footnote 12, BEF suggest that just such an outside imposition may be occurring. They note, 'It is straightforward to re-formulate the model so that a self-financing unemployment insurance programme is provided by the government rather than the household.' Now as a mathematical matter, this statement is surely correct. But what about as a matter of economics? If it is the government setting the level of the transfer, why did it pick that level? Is there any reason to assume that the *government* would 'choose the level of the transfer so that the unemployed members of the household will be at least as well off as any shirker caught by the firm would be'? This *deus ex machina* happening to pick exactly the level of transfers preferred by BEF is more reminiscent of something that would show up in an old-style Keynesian macro-model than in a Sargent-style, microfounded representative agent model.

The difficulty in making sense of the way this transfer works in the model is compounded when we look at the parameterization of the model. When calibrating, BEF set χ at a level which means that 'being unemployed lowers a worker's consumption by about 22 per cent.' Now the parameter χ is actually the ratio of the consumption of the employed to that of the shirkers who are caught and fired (equation (4.8)), but since, by assumption the level of transfers to the unemployed are set to give them the same consumption as they would get if they shirked and were fired, the same ratio serves the purpose which BEF state.

But, why 22 per cent? BEF give Gruber as the source of the figure. When we turn there we read, 'In the absence of UI [unemployment insurance], I estimate that the consumption of the unemployed would fall by 22 per cent—over three times the average fall in the presence of this public program' (Gruber 1997: 203). So, the calibration of this model assumes that the family is setting the transfer to ensure that the unemployed have 22 per cent less consumption, which is the level that Gruber estimates they would have without government insurance. But, when the actual government does insure, the consumption loss is only one-third of that amount. In other words, BEF's source for their 22 per cent figure explicitly notes that when the actual government picks the level of the transfer, it does *not* pick the level which results in a 22 per cent loss in consumption. Gruber's paper is arguing that the actual government behaves differently from the 'family' in this model. So, again, it is hard to figure out who in the model used by BEF is deciding on the level of the transfer; if it is the individuals who are deciding, why do they not get to pick the utility-maximizing level, and if it is the government who is deciding, why does it use the 22 per cent figure instead of the lower figure Gruber finds that the government actually uses?

Or, similarly, consider the maximization problem itself. BEF introduce it by saying it is the maximization of the utility of a representative individual of the representative household. But, if we read the problem in this way, then it is rather odd. Our representative family member is not allowed to decide whether or not he wants to shirk. It is simply not a choice variable. However, the percentage of times the worker shirks does show up in the constraint the agent faces. If we take Sargent seriously and read this problem as 'the objective functions that agents are maximizing and the constraints they are facing, and which lead them to choose the decision rules that they do', then we are faced with an agent who is maximizing a problem in which he, through no choice of his own, expects to shirk in a pre-determined percentage of time-periods.

Now, this is in no way a problem in solving the model. We, those of us outside the model, know that the firm is picking the wage level to ensure that the agent never shirks. And indeed, it is because the firm thinks the agent might shirk that it sets the wage at the non-market clearing level. Thus, in the solution to the model, the agents *never* shirk and if we were to give them the choice to shirk, they would optimally choose not to do so. We know this. The agents in the model, however, do not. If we imagine being the representative agent, which is exactly the thought experiment which justifies the whole approach of representative agent modelling, then this objective function coupled with this constraint is very strange. The problem reads as if there is some sort of random shirking disease that strikes the population, forcing our hapless agents to expect to shirk as often as said disease hits.

When we start to put all these things together, we begin to notice a pattern. If we take the model seriously as a representative agent model, then we begin to notice that either the world these agents live in is very strange or there are restrictions coming from somewhere beyond the agent, that this is not, in fact, the objective function the agent is actually maximizing nor the constraints he is actually facing. The set-up of the model asks us to imagine a family which decides to make transfers to the unemployed members of the family, but then the model does not let them pick the level of the transfer. It is not sensible to tell agents they can make a choice about the level of transfer but not let them choose the optimal level, but it is sensible to write down a problem with a given level of transfers if we believe there are some aggregate restrictions on how transfers can be implemented. Similarly, the set-up of the model asks us to imagine workers who have to decide whether or not to shirk, but the objective function used does not have shirking as a choice variable. It's not sensible for an individual making that choice to be told a priori how many time-periods he should expect to shirk. But, it is sensible to write a problem in which a given percentage of the time there will be shirking, if the problem is for an aggregate entity who cannot force the agents to exert effort.

When we start putting together the oddities of this model, we notice that they are all there for a reason, and a very good reason from my way of thinking. The model is crafted in a manner to guarantee that the aggregate economy will *not* behave as if it were one giant individual. The model is crafted in a way to guarantee that there will be macroeconomic phenomena like involuntary unemployment. BEF have rediscovered macroeconomics.

So, what do we make of all this? Let me state the conclusion boldly, since I know that the discussion period to follow will afford ample opportunity for others to correct my immoderation. Theory and evidence in business-cycle research are pointing to the same conclusion. Theory is showing us that the representative agent, equilibrium real business-cycle model is unable to explain aggregate dynamics, that we need some sort of aggregate model. BEF exemplify this movement by using a model with aggregate restrictions simply imposed. Evidence is showing us that the co-movements of aggregates are not very interesting, that it is the episodes of crisis, the classical cycle, that are the interesting parts of business cycles. Harding and Pagan exemplify this movement by taking seriously the question of measuring the cycle. Together, they lead to the inescapable conclusion: real business-cycle theory is dead; long live the study of the business cycle.

REFERENCES

Alexopoulos, M. (1998) 'Efficiency Wages, Unemployment and the Business Cycle', MS, Northwestern University.

Bronfenbrenner, M. (ed.) (1969) *Is the Business Cycle Obsolete?* (New York: Wiley-Interscience).

Burnside, C., M. Eichenbaum, and J. D. M. Fisher (1999) 'Assessing the Effects of Fiscal Shocks' MS, Northwestern University.

——, ——, and S. Rebelo (1993) 'Labor Hoarding and the Business Cycle', *Journal of Political Economy* 48: 253–77.

Canova, F. (1998) 'Detrending and Business Cycle Facts', *Journal of Monetary Economics* 41: 475–512.

——, M. Finn, and A. R. Pagan (1994) 'Evaluating a Real Business Cycle Model', in C. Hargreaves (ed.), *Nonstationary Time Series Analysis and Cointegration* (Oxford: Oxford University Press): 225–55.

Cooley, T. F. and E. C. Prescott (1995) 'Economic Growth and Business Cycles', in T. F. Cooley (ed.), *Frontiers of Business Cycle Research* (Princeton, NJ: Princeton University Press): 1–38.

Gruber, J. (1997) 'The Consumption Smoothing Benefits of Unemployment Insurance', *American Economic Review* 87: 192–205.

Hartley, J. E. (1997) *The Representative Agent in Macroeconomics* (London: Routledge).

—— (1999) 'Real Myths and a Monetary Fact', *Applied Economics* 31: 1325–9.

Klein, F. A. (1976) *Business Cycles in the Postwar World: Some Reflections on Recent Research* (Washington, DC: American Enterprise Institute for Public Policy Research).

Koopmans, T. C. (1947) 'Measurement without Theory', *Review of Economics and Statistics* 29: 161–72.

Kydland, F. E. and E. C. Prescott (1996) 'The Computational Experiment: An Econometric Tool', *Journal of Economic Perspectives* 10: 69–85.

Lucas, R. E. Jr. (1977) 'Understanding Business Cycles', in K. Brunner and A. H. Meltzer (eds.), *Stabilization of the Domestic and International Economy*, Carnegie–Rochester Conference Series in Public Policy (Amsterdam: North-Holland): 7–29.

Merz, M. (1999) 'Time Series Evidence of Unemployment Flows: The Sample Period Matters', *Journal of Business and Economic Statistics* 17: 324–34.

Mitchell, W. C. (1927) *Business Cycles: The Problem and Its Setting* (New York: National Bureau of Economic Research).

Morgan, M. S. (1990) *The History of Econometric Ideas* (Cambridge: Cambridge University Press).

4B Business cycles: general discussion

Martin Eichenbaum: I believe it is a technical misreading of the paper to say that shirking is not a choice problem. The whole incentive compatibility constraint the firm faces when designing its contracts is the awareness that any worker that they hire, at each point in time, chooses whether to supply effort or not. So it is not the case that there is this exogenous probability of shirking or not. The only thing that is exogenous is whether you are caught, which is a simplification.

The issue of optimal risk-sharing and the continuum of the family—again there is a sense in which it is a technical issue and a sense in which it is not. Let me proceed by analogy. The Hansen (1985) and Rogerson (1988) model can be thought of as follows. There is a guy with a utility function that is linear in leisure and you can imagine this as emerging from various kinds of model—one with a family with a continuum of size in which there is perfect risk-sharing; the other as an explicit Arrow–Debreu market of the sort that Burnside and I describe in our *AER* article (1996). So the shortest answer is that we can certainly abandon the shorthand of a continuum of individuals in the family and go to a much richer market structure of the sort that we describe in the *AER* article.

Bennett McCallum: I liked a lot of the Harding and Pagan paper. Everything seemed to follow nicely once their definition of the business cycle was accepted, but I am little uneasy about that because it suggests that policy-makers in the USA would not be unhappy if output were to grow at a fourth of 1 per cent per year or something like that. I just don't understand how that would be the case. You say as long as output is growing, people are happy and the policy-makers are not concerned with the way in which output relative to some sort of reference value is growing but just whether output itself is growing. So I would like a response on this.

My other comment has to do with the point about whether there is a discussion of cycles in the Burnside, Eichenbaum, and Fisher paper. I don't ever hear the policy-makers I talk to, who are mostly Fed people, ever use the word 'cycle'. They don't talk about cycles at all so I am not sure that this is a weakness in the paper.

Tom Mayer: I very much liked the idea of using case studies and I applaud Burnside, Eichenbaum, and Fisher's paper for that. However, what you have done is not like a traditional case study, the way they used to be done, because you don't pay much attention to the history and you go right into the econometrics of it. The paper covers several war episodes and I think those differ. The reason that is important is because one of those episodes, the Korean War, was a much bigger change in defence expenditure than the others. If you look at your chart 1 and think of squaring the deviations from the mean, I wouldn't be surprised if the Korean War dominates the whole story. The Korean War was different from the other ones. Not only were there much larger effects on defence expenditures, but also there was something else going on. In December 1950, when the Chinese troops came in there was a bit of a panic. There was concern that this would turn into World War III, that there would be rationing and consumer goods would be scarce. There was a big bump up in consumer expenditures which may explain some of the results you find on purchases of consumer durables. People bought durables because they thought this might be their last chance to do it. Then during the Korean War you also had credit rationing. There were restrictions on purchases of automobiles and other durables. That may have affected expenditure. Whether this effect was large or not has been debated, but there was that restriction. I don't remember offhand whether there was also a restriction on residential construction but I think there was. Some of the results you get for residential construction and consumer durables may be due to this institutional factor of credit restrictions.

Huw Dixon: This typical definition of a recession being two quarters of negative growth may make sense in the UK or the USA where the average growth rate is $2\frac{1}{2}$ per cent, but if you are looking at economies where you have 5 per cent average growth rates this does not make as much sense perhaps and you ought to adjust that to having a positive constant as the magic figure. It is related to changes in unemployment, something that is not mentioned.

Eichenbaum's $X(t)$ vector excludes nominal variables. We take that as given because it is an RBC-type model, but why should we take that as given? If you look at all the three episodes you are talking about, certainly the Vietnam War and the Korean War, from what I remember, there were quite big nominal changes going on. I would be interested to know why you think it is a good thing to do that.

Eichenbaum: There is another paper, by Edelberg *et al.* (1999), that documents these things about inflation and the inclusion of nominal variables does not change the pattern of results that we were describing.

David Hendry: First, a response to Pagan on stationarity. A simple example of a series with zeros and ones that is non-stationary is to toss a coin with a head and a tail and half-way through the experiment change it to a coin with a head on both sides. It is clearly a non-stationary process. Nothing guarantees the stationarity of any of the data at which we look.

The rest of my concerns are with the Burnside, Eichenbaum, and Fisher paper. For someone like myself, everything that I want to see in the paper is missing. There is no evidence that the VAR fits the data, there is no evidence that it is constant. As Mayer said a moment ago, the size of the dummy variable coefficients could be dramatically different between the episodes. They don't even report how big they were and looking at the timing of dummies versus the actual change in the data it would be very surprising if they reflected, correctly, what had actually happened in the period. That is all independent of whether they are in fact exogenous, which I think I would go along with.

Ericsson and I have a paper coming out in the next issue of *Empirical Economics* (1999) entitled, 'Successive corroboration entails refutation' that shows that if you take a series of things that you think corroborate your model one by one, then put them together, they can frequently refute the model. I have this worry about this work for, while it is great to see it moving more and more towards reality compared to the earlier versions of these models, so that many of the things that one would hope to see in a model are beginning to become present, it is still the case that I suspect that very few firms in the USA cut nominal wages at the times of any of these wars and the fall in real wages is coming about because of the price shocks that all wars suffer because of the shortage of real commodities, goods, etc. The huge explosion that you pick up in your fuel data was probably occurring in other essential raw materials. We know from Rob Engle's work (discussion paper version of Engle 1982) that this was the biggest inflation in this sequence in the USA and I think real wages fell because prices went up and because there was a delay in contract re-negotiation. Your model explains this fact and has regular contract re-negotiation. So if you put those together it refutes the model.

Craig Burnside: I just want to say a couple of things about the previous discussion and about Harding and Pagan's paper. It seems to me that this question is clearly a semantic one. Lots of different people have different definitions of what a business cycle is and we could fight about it all day without reaching a single accepted definition. So I am willing to accept Pagan's definition if he will accept mine. I will accept anybody's. As to which one is more important, it seems to me that nothing Pagan has said shows that his definition is more important than any other. That would have to be settled any other way and I haven't seen, in any of the papers that I have read, mystery about how we should consider business cycles. As to the issue of co-movements, it seems to me that co-movements are basically everything. If I took this argument that co-movements weren't important, I would just write down this model and we could all go home. Pagan has basically argued that ΔY_t is a random walk with drift. In the USA there is a little more serial correlation, but that is not that important. So that is basically it. Of course, we want to know what that epsilon is. Well, I could tell you what the epsilon is and I might say that it is this kind of shock and that makes output respond in this way. I could write down a model saying that there are G shocks driving the cycle. Output should respond to G shocks in this way because they seem to in the data. Similarly, we could write down models with monetary policy shocks and we could lump them all into epsilon. The question is, do other variables respond to those shocks in the right ways and without looking at co-movements you are not going to know that. So we write down models where we include different types of shocks, we see whether output goes up or down, we see whether real wages go up or down, we see whether consumption goes up or down, we check whether consumption is smoother than output, we do all of those things and we compare those things with what goes on in the data. That seems exactly the right way to try to understand whether the model we are using is one that makes sense, because it makes sense in lots of different dimensions, not just the one whether output goes up or down.

Christopher Sims: I would like to point out that Harding and Pagan have been too modest. Their analysis can actually be extended to fields other than economics. For example, in medicine, much modern medical research has got away from the essence of the problem which is defining sickness. The ordinary person cares whether he is sick or not. You can look at the modern medical literature and find no mention of sickness at all in many of the papers that are written. It is all about co-movements of symptoms, about how rashes and fever and blood chemistry move together or do not move together, and in fact it often distinguishes different kinds of episodes of co-movements that are all to the ordinary person just sickness. In fact it sometimes even claims that it is interesting to study episodes in which a person has certain co-movements of bacterial counts and so on that don't keep him from going to work and in which he wouldn't claim he was sick and that something can be learned from such episodes. One might argue that medicine has got away from its roots and that it would be good for doctors to have a conference in which they discussed what sickness really is.

Now there are a couple of things in the paper that I like. It is nice to see another confirmation that non-linear mechanisms, though you can find a little evidence for them sometimes, are not a first-order phenomenon for the most part in the study of business cycles. I also agree that the Hodrik–Prescott filter is basically a blight on our discipline and that we ought to get rid of it, though it seems very difficult to do so. But I think that on the whole the paper is on the wrong track, going backwards and internally contradictory.

This notion of averages versus episodes, co-movements and study of causal mechanisms, versus study of particular episodes and the debate over it goes back to Klein and Goldberger (1955). The Adelmans (1959) took Klein's model to task for not producing enough cyclical movement and, back at that time, when people were first doing big Keynesian models, there were objections that this was getting away from studying historical episodes. The conflict is really the conflict between those who are trying to do what Harding and Pagan point to at the end of the paper as the future—system modelling—versus those who wish that the study of economics could remain simpler and who want to keep us focused on individual historical episodes and who distrust what happens when we start looking at large systems and start focusing on causal mechanisms rather than particular episodes. I don't disagree with the idea that it is a good idea to force system modellers to come back and look at episodes. A good system model has implicit in it a story about every episode in the data and we probably do too little of that, though probably not as little as the discussion seems to suggest. I have a recent paper (1999) that studies the Great Depression using identified VARs and I think there ought to be more of that kind of work. The paper as a whole is a strange mixture, at the beginning calling for a return to old-fashioned style, one-variable-at-a-time, let's-identify-the-cycle sorts of approaches, and then at the end saying the future is with system modelling which is exactly the opposite of this sort of approach.

Katarina Juselius: I would also like to comment on Harding and Pagan's definition of the cycle and say that I fear that you cannot learn from just looking at one series. I think what would be useful here is to say that there are in the economy the concepts of what I will call a sustainable long-run steady state in the sense that if the economy moves away from it some structural adjustment is usually required. If you think of these concepts and of the deviation from the sustainable long-run steady-state relation as a long-run cycle, then I think it usually has the properties you have found in your data. The important point here is that if you define the steady-state and the deviation from the long-run steady-state as a cycle, then you also know something about, say, whether you are now moving in a direction which is not sustainable (for example into a position where the economy is clearly overheating). Even if the economy grows and activity is high, there is reason for concern if it is too high. You need to know, when you start going down, when you have passed the steady-state and are going into a recession. To know that, I think you need the concept of a steady-state and then you need more than one variable. I agree here with Sims that you need to look at this question in a systems framework. You need to be able to distinguish between what is the really long run, what is the medium long run (which is sustainable in a much shorter perspective) and I guess that the growth cycles are more or less deviations from the medium-run steady-state relation.

Roger Backhouse: The question I want to raise is the relationship of our concept of the cycle to broader issues of the way macroeconomics is conceived. Is there any link, and I am not sure of the answer here, between the way we think of the cycle, the classical cycle versus the growth cycle, and the way we conceive of employment and unemployment. I would have thought that if you asked most people what they thought of as the business cycle (I am not thinking here of specialist macroeconomists) they would think of fluctuations in unemployment, or perhaps fluctuations in capacity utilization or something like that. Now if you deal with an equilibrium model where everything is equilibrium, there is not a clear concept of full employment, the level of employment responds to factor prices and so on, then perhaps that leads to a different concept of the business cycle. Think of the old-fashioned Keynesian models where you had a horizontal supply curve up to full employment and then it became vertical. There you can think of a business cycle in terms of capacity utilization or unemployment and it is very straightforward. When you change your theoretical structure, maybe your whole idea of the cycle has to change. That makes me wonder whether it is right to focus just on GNP. This is the same point as others have made, but from a slightly different perspective.

Adrian Pagan: This is related to Hendry's and Mayer's question. When are these shocks, these wars, really the same thing? It is important not only that they can be different magnitudes but also whether the responses of the economy to them are going to be the same. Presumably a large fraction of expenditure on the Vietnam War and the Korean War was spent on wages and salaries that went overseas and some of that expenditure would have been treated as imports. American troops in Vietnam, spending money on rest and recreation, would actually be treated as imports coming into America in order to get the national accounts to add up. However, in the Reagan–Carter build-up it doesn't seem to me that it is the same type of thing at all. There you have purely domestic expenditures which you would expect to be reflected in domestic outcomes, not in imported outcomes. When you talk about these things, I don't know what the nature of the shock is. How much of it is equipment? How much is wages and salaries, etc.? It seems to me that the Gulf War would have been a better example of a third shock than the Carter–Reagan build-up and I was a little puzzled about why that was not part of the set.

Eichenbaum: Ramey and Shapiro (1998) did a very nice job of reading historical method and trying to come to grips with this notion that what's really crucial from the perspective of the model is when agents knew that there was going to be an increase in government purchases, not when those purchases actually increased. That is what led us away from initially structural VARs. Since then we have done a variety of robustness things and tried to identify these VARs in other ways. The issue that Pagan raises is a good one, and that has to do with linearity and stationarity. It is clearly a maintained hypothesis of our empirical methods that these are linear systems and that the only difference between these shocks was in magnitude. That is obviously not literally true. There were some differences in the composition of government purchases in these episodes, but we are assuming these are second-order things, which may or may not be misleading. We are assuming it is a linear, stationary system.

Pagan: It was not a question of linearity. The point is that the impulse–response of, say, consumption would be different in one of the shocks from in the other.

Eichenbaum: I don't think there is anything in the data that enables one to say that these shocks are obviously very different.

Pagan: Turning to McCallum, I think it is true that the policy-makers don't only worry about the level of output—they do worry about growth rates below trend. When we give this definition of the change in the level of activity I would not be unhappy with someone studying the level of activity less some potential growth rate because people frequently talk about growth being below potential. So a study of ΔZ_t is not something I am really opposed to. The problem comes that this potential growth rate is being measured by a Hodrik–Prescott type of filter which takes out of it almost all of the action that you need to generate the cycle. So whether it is ΔY_t or ΔZ_t is not something I care about.

McCallum: I agree with you on that. I am saying that you need to measure output in relation to some reference path, and we need to have a better concept of what that reference path is. Instead of Hodrik–Prescott or a linear trend, we want to have a measure of something like market clearing output.

Pagan: What we say in the paper is that most of this literature focuses on NBER dates and they talk about the cycle in NBER terms. This is the classical cycle. If you then analyse the classical cycle, we try to show that the way to think about it is as a sequence of changes in output—this is the way to determine the dating.

Regarding the definition of a recession as two quarters of negative growth, that is actually not the one we use. The definition that we use essentially just looks at the graph and determines a turning point. If you were looking at an Asian economy, you would have wanted to take out 6 or 7 per cent per year and study what is left over. I should say, though, that the growth cycle is a study of ΔZ_t (the growth rate of detrended output)—it is not a study of Z_t—and that is one of my problems. I would be more than happy if the whole literature by people who build business–cycle models gave me statistics that told me whether they could explain the change in this detrended quantity. But they do not tell me that, and yet that is the essence of turning points. If you want to talk about business cycles, you need to define a turning point. We looked at the Schmidt-Grohe (1998) model and took the output from that because she is one of the few people who gives you the information that enables you to do that sort of assessment. Very rarely do you see that type of thing.

I don't disagree with what Hendry says. Structural change clearly makes things non-stationary. What I was thinking about in this context was that most people use these techniques to evaluate models. On Burnside's point, I don't think this definition of a business cycle is a semantic one. This is what I have been hearing for a long time, but you have to ask what we use these things for. I read papers like his and they don't talk to me about anything I am interested in. I want to know what causes the cycle. I don't want to know whether consumption co-varies with income. That may be an interesting question for them, but it is not an interesting question for most policy people. Surely that is what we are doing this stuff for. When Eichenbaum goes out and talks to banks, people don't talk like this. They talk in the normal way you see in the *Wall St Journal*. But if you can first demonstrate with your models that you produce the right sort of cycle in output, then I am more than happy for people to go out and start examining co-movements. I am not opposed to co-movements, but this is a secondary characteristic. The first thing is to produce a model that reproduces the cycle we see, and a lot of these models won't produce the cycle you see unless it is imposed exogenously from technology.

To Sims, I am not opposed to system modelling, but first you have got to get the definitions right. How are we going to evaluate systems? There are obviously cycles in lots of different series—unemployment, consumption, output—and I don't mind producing a complete set of statistics on those things. We just focus on a particular individual series because most of the attention paid in the press and in policy discussion is to output. The paper makes the point that, if you are going to evaluate a model, there are lots of characteristics you may want to look at, but this paper is about what you can learn about the business cycle from these models. If I want to read the literature and know what a particular model says about the cycle, I want a way to summarize it.

To Dixon, I would say that output is what I am most comfortable with. Real wages and other things affect unemployment.

Eichenbaum: If I can briefly take up this issue of policy-makers, it is true that I occasionally speak to policy-makers, but that leaves me with mixed emotions. I am very hesitant about letting them set my intellectual agenda. My experience with policy-makers is that they are driven by day-to-day considerations and our research ought not to be driven by these. But it does raise the issue of why are we writing down these models. I think it is not necessarily to give day-to-day guidance, though I think some people would clearly disagree with that. For me it is, in part, that we want to design interesting institutions, that we want to have interesting laboratories for interesting alternative rules, and there are some very interesting things going on in that context in monetary policy in the States. The point is that to get an answer from a model you have to have some confidence in the model. You know the model is wrong and so the question is how much confidence should you have in it. Some people are going to look at the cycle, others at the co-movements. But I think that to decide what it is that will make everyone have confidence in these models—it is not going to be one size fits all.

Pagan: Do the models that you write down generate business cycles?

Eichenbaum: We didn't want to show that. We think we can learn something about labour markets from confronting the model with a very specific experiment.

Pagan: That's fine, but if I sit there I want to know when I see a so-called business-cycle model, what sort of business cycle it generates, and that is what I don't find in those papers.

Burnside: It depends on what you model the exogenous processes as being. You said it is a function of the exogenous technology shock that is fed through most real business-cycle models—they can match the cyclical facts. If I make the model dif-ferent, I add lots of differerent shocks to it, it is still going to depend on how I model the exogenous shocks. It will always do so. So I don't understand that particular point. Presumably the way to reject the real business-cycle model driven by technology shocks is not by whether it can replicate that one business–cycle fact or not. It is by looking along lots of different dimensions and saying, 'This model is crazy because it has lots and lots of false predictions even though this person has somehow made it match the data on business–cycle facts'. It seems to be that this is always the way to reject the models.

Pagan: Take the paper by Schmidt-Grohe with belief shocks. The claim in this paper is that belief shocks can generate the persistence that we need. Now the fact is that this is not true when I go and look at the business cycles implied by the paper. I am more than happy for you to decide whether it is a good model or a bad model of activity after I have established whether it generates a cycle that I see in reality. I don't often get the information to do this. Instead I get given detrended, Hodrick–Prescott filtered data which are just rubbish because they don't relate to the cycle we see.

Eichenbaum: As a literature fact, lets be careful before we go too crazy on the RBC guys. There are a variety of papers in various journals that report things both ways, both with growth rates of output and not H-P filtered. Now maybe there is not enough, but it seems to be again that you want to do diagnostics and there are lots of different ways of looking at the data. What is the H-P filter? It is another bunch of second moments. I am not going to attach any religious significance to the particular second moments that it produces, but it is one way of getting an interesting insight into the dimensions along which you are doing well or are not.

James Hartley: The issue here is that you are asking different questions in some sense. The good way to phrase it is, 'Does a good model explain the business cycle?' It depends on whether the model was designed to explain the business cycle or not, and that is why I find your response that the point of the paper you presented was to talk about labour market efficiency strange. Was the paper meant to explain the business cycle or not? If it was, then where is the business cycle?

Eichenbaum: Again, what this paper tries to do is to say we are going to have to build models which are 'reasonable'. The question is how we diagnose models that are reasonable. One way, not the only way, is to confront them with particular experiments and the idea is that this will provide useful information to the next round where someone wants to do a business-cycle model. But it may provide information to someone who wants to do a growth model. I am not wedded to the idea that every paper I do has to have the title business cycle in it. It is a model.

Mary Morgan: We seem to be moving around various problems here, and maybe there is something obvious that needs to be said. The point that I take from Pagan's paper is that if you are going to talk about business cycles then you want to have a congruence between the model and your concepts and definitions and what you are trying to answer. I think a lot of the discussion has been between different groups, who have different concepts and want different definitions and want different measurements and approach it with different models. I think the issue is congruence between all those levels in one piece of applied work, and this cannot be separate from what the question is. If the question is what is driving you, as I think it is with Pagan's 'What policy-makers are interested in', that has to fit with what kind of measurements you use. These need to be thought about as a package.

Another point about the collective amnesia which Sims mentioned, going back to Klein. A lot of these issues about detrending and so on go back much further, to 1917–18 discussions, through the 1920s, and I think it is unfortunate that a lot of that memory has got lost. I think one of the things that happens is that it is assumed that Mitchell would have used GNP figures as the best or an adequate representation of the business-cycle concept if he had had them. I think that is just wrong. His concept, right back through his research programme, is that business cycles were the co-movements: there were these congeries of cyclical movements that move together, so in a way he was a systems thinker without being a modeller. I think he just wasn't a modeller.

Pagan: I still don't believe Mitchell was a co-movement fan. When he and Burns were together I am sure they weren't, because there is no point in a reference cycle and a specific cycle distinction unless you really think in two different ways. The reference cycle is certainly an average of lots of different things, but it is really an attempt to get the common factor out and only after that does the question arise of how they all relate to one another.

Actually, the Adelmans (1959) did find that the Klein–Goldberger model (I think this is too well known to need a reference) generated cycles along Burns and Mitchell lines. That was what surprised King and Plosser (1994)—when they ran a real business-cycle model it also reproduced the Burns and Mitchell results and they couldn't understand how you could have such vastly different models producing the same thing. The answer was, of course, that they all produced a random walk and it is pretty easy to produce one.

Sims: Even if you want to explain the business cycle, I don't think it is right to go in a lexicographic way as Pagan seems to suggest—that the first test is how well the model reproduces the business cycle. If we want to explain the business cycle, we mean that we want to use the model to do something about the business cycle—to think about institutional changes that would modify from a welfare point of view, to make policy interventions. Any of those uses of the model will start to make us ask whether the model's descriptions of the interrelations amongst variables are right, and there is no way to evaluate that without going beyond asking whether we have reproduced the one-dimensional business-cycle facts, and in a world of imperfect models we may want to use one that is not quite perfect in matching one-dimensional business-cycle facts, but seems to have done a good job in capturing the critical cross-variable relationships that are related to the evaluation of policy interventions.

Hartley: I think that is the point. Does a good macroeconomic model have to explain the business cycle? Is it possible to learn something about the macroeconomy in a model that tells us nothing about the business cycle?

Eichenbaum: Which RBC model says nothing about the business cycle? I thought the key problem about RBC models was that you stuck in a unit root, technology shocks, and it nails what the growth rate of output is. That was known ten years ago. That was easy. What Kydland and Prescott did was say that Z_t, the technology shock, was $Z_{t-1} + \varepsilon_t$. Then ΔY_t was equal to ε_t. So they completely explained the business cycle, precisely from your perspective and yet people went on and said, 'Let's think about this a little more carefully.' And it was precisely the co-movement stuff that led people to become increasingly sceptical. But those guys nailed the business cycle by this definition.

Pagan: There is a huge number of papers to say they didn't.

Burnside: The persistence we were talking about is persistence that you say is not important—it is where x is a moving average component of the growth rate of GDP in the USA. Most RBC models are set up to get the $\mu + \varepsilon$ part right, and they nail it. Other people said no, this other extra persistence in output is important. What we and the RBC literature are talking about is that little extra hump-shape in the spectrum.

Pagan: There is no hump-shape in the spectrum. That's another misconception. If you calculate that spectral density, it all comes from some serial correlations between 10 and 14. The peak occurs at a three-year frequency, which is what you get with the Hodrick–Prescott filter. You do not need peaks in a spectral density to produce cycles like we see. They add absolutely nothing to it.

Eichenbaum: The literature criticized RBC models not because they couldn't get $\Delta Y_t = \varepsilon_t$, but they couldn't get ΔY_t to be serially correlated.

Hartley: If I could come back to my question, 'Does a good model have to explain the business cycle?' The answer is 'No'. Good models can completely miss the business cycle. Getting the business cycle right does not mean it is a good model. If you are not making claims about the business cycle, you can justify the model on lots of other grounds.

Eichenbaum: To relay what Sims said, a good macromodel ought not to do a terrible job of tracking Y_t. Beyond that, I am not sure it is worth worrying about the semantics.

Eichenbaum: Returning to Morgan's point, the question is 'What do you want to do with this thing?' I might be willing to tolerate deterioration along one dimension for improvements in other dimensions. I just can't see a lexicographic ordering over moments as a decision-maker.

Backhouse: Is the issue that is dividing you that when you get your model which produces variations in output, those variations in output are not perfect? They are never going to be perfect. The issue is where are your criteria coming from to decide whether those failures of your model are significant. Surely there is no way you can find that just by looking at the statistical properties of the output series, or can you? Do you have to go beyond that?

Eichenbaum: I thought one of the major breakthroughs in macro was trying to be very careful about the response of many variables to a given shock. Multivariate analysis. It is interesting that if you go to an economic fluctuations meeting in the States, and 'new Keynesians' are there, the language is really very similar to the language of the RBC guys or whatever, which is 'I don't like your model, because it predicts, given this shock, this variable is moving this way and we don't think it moves in that way.' Those are the nature of the arguments with people adding lots of counterfactual predictions along a variety of dimensions. Because we all think it is easy to get $\Delta Y_t = \varepsilon_t$. It was done ten years ago. So we shouldn't be arguing about that.

Pagan: You say that we have some fact, and one model explains it but another doesn't. What I am asking is, what is the significance of that fact for the business cycle? It is true that it may be interesting, but it may be irrelevant to the cycle.

Eichenbaum: I want to go back to Sims's point about whether it is an interesting fact from the perspective of a decision-maker, not from the perspective of the business cycle. I don't think that there is any object out there that is the business cycle. There is a bunch of decision-makers and a bunch of data. Anything after that is something we are going to make up.

Andrew Oswald: What would count as a test that would allow you to say which side was right? What could you agree on that would constitute a persuasive test?

Burnside: I think those on the other side of the argument are saying that if you mention business cycle in your paper, then you should produce a bunch of statistics about the business cycle along the lines of what Pagan has in his paper.

Pagan: It is a suggestion.

Sims: The test is keeping policy-makers happy. You could write two versions of the paper, one with statistics on the cycle and one without, and see which makes policy-makers happy.

Pagan: Alan Blinder at the FOMC got to the stage of saying, 'Don't send me any more papers on real business cycles.' Perhaps that settles it!

REFERENCES

Adelman, I. and Adelman, F. L. (1959) 'The Dynamic Properties of the Klein–Goldberger Model', *Econometrica* 27: 596–625.
Burnside, C. and Eichenbaum. M. (1996) 'Factor hoarding and the propagation of business cycle shocks', *American Economic Review* 86: 1154–74.
Edelberg, W., Eichenbaum, M., and Fisher, J. (1999) 'Understanding the effects of shocks to government purchases', *Review of Economic Dynamics* 2: 166–206.
Engle, R. F. (1982) 'Autoregressive conditional heteroscedasticity, with estimates of the variance of United Kingdom inflation', *Econometrica* 50: 987–1007.
Ericsson, N. and Hendry, D. F. (1999) 'Encompassing and rational expectations: how sequential corroboration can imply refutation', *Empirical Economics* 24: 1–21.
Hansen, G. (1985) 'Indivisible labor and the business cycle', *Journal of Monetary Economics* 16(3): 309–28.
King, R. G. and Plosser, C. I. (1994) 'Real business cycles and the test of the Adelmans', *Journal of Monetary Economics* 33: 405–38.
Klein, L. R. and Goldberger, A. S. (1955) *An Econometric Model of the United States, 1929–1952* (Amsterdam: North-Holland).

Ramey, V. and Shapiro, M. D. (1998) 'Costly capital reallocation and the effects of government spending', *Carnegie-Rochester Conference Series on Public Policy* 48: 145–94.

Rogerson, R. (1988) 'Indivisible labor, lotteries and equilibrium', *Journal of Monetary Economics* 21(1): 3–16.

Schmidt-Grohe, S. (1998) 'Endogenous business cycles and the dynamics of output, hours and consumption' (mimeo, Board of Governors of the Federal Reserve System).

Sims, C. (1999) 'The role of interest rate policy in the generation and propagation of business cycles: what has changed since the 30s?', in *Proceedings of the 1998 Annual Research Conference* (Federal Reserve Bank of Boston).

Part II
MONETARY POLICY

5 Does money determine UK inflation over the long run?

DAVID F. HENDRY

1. Introduction

Inflation has long been the focus of theoretical, empirical, and policy debates, yet despite a huge literature, there are few eclectic studies of long runs of data. Most analyses have adopted specific perspectives or objectives, such as testing the impact of money growth on inflation, or building a model of price determination from costs and mark-ups. When other determinants may matter, little confidence can be placed in the outcomes of partial analyses. Here, we contrast a model of UK inflation over the last century and a quarter—where most extant theories of inflation are given the opportunity to matter, so that no 'single cause' explanation is imposed from the outset—with a model based on an inverted money-demand equation (from Ericsson *et al.* 1998).

To model the 'long run'—both in the sense of an extended sample over time, and when seeking sustained relationships between the levels of economic variables—necessitates handling the many non-stationarities manifest in economic data. The three forms most pertinent to annual observations are cumulation of past shocks leading to integrated data, deterministic shifts inducing structural breaks, and changes to the measurement system. We briefly comment on each of these in turn. On the first, the theory of testing for unit roots is now well developed (see e.g. Dickey and Fuller 1979, 1981; Phillips and Perron 1988), and the related construct of cointegration is the subject of extensive treatments in Banerjee and Hendry (1992), Hamilton (1994), Hendry (1995a), Johansen (1995), and Hatanaka (1996) among others (see Hendry 1997, for a historical review). Consequently, unit-root non-stationarities can be handled relatively well. However, less attention has been paid to modelling deterministic shifts and other forms of structural breaks. The research in Clements and Hendry (1998) and Hendry and Doornik (1997) establishes the primacy of deterministic shifts in inducing predictive failure, so we discuss these in Section 2. The third problem is the least analysed, with no studies to my knowledge of the substantial alterations over time to the methods by which aggregate data are collected and processed. These difficulties are compounded in empirical modelling by the need to *simultaneously* select from non-stationary data the relevant variables, appropriate measures thereof, their lags, and functional forms.

Financial support from the UK Economic and Social Research Council under grant R000237500 is gratefully acknowledged. I am also grateful to a seminar at the University of Dundee, and participants at the Bergamo Conference for helpful suggestions, and to Gavin Cameron and John Muellbauer for additional data and insightful discussions.

On the one hand, a long sample period in historical time is needed to establish cointegration as a genuine long-run relation, rather than a convenient local approximation. On the other hand, the longer the data period, the more both evolutionary and structural changes can intrude to confound modelling. Since the economy is a nonstationary process, the entity about which knowledge is acquired changes over time. A data period from 1874 to 1993 includes many major policy regime changes (including rationing and price controls; the creation and partial destruction of the welfare state; nationalization and privatization; financial innovation and deregulation, etc.), perhaps two technological revolutions, world wars and oil crises, together with changes from the gold standard through Bretton Woods fixed exchange rates and currency pegs with exchange controls, to floating rates, as well as witnessing a reversal of the relative positions in world power of the UK and the USA. While such factors pose serious challenges to empirical models, they also suggest that abstract theories will exclude much of the policy-relevant environment—and anyway, theories have themselves evolved over time.

The problems of empirical modelling seem likely to persist, irrespective of developments in economic theory and econometric technology. The possible solution discussed in Hendry (1993) is to use general-to-specific modelling methods within studies, and encompassing checks between, seeking a progressive accumulation of knowledge and understanding of economic systems complementary to, and interacting with, economic analyses. The former aspect has recently received considerable support from the Monte Carlo study in Hoover and Perez (1999), who find that general-to-specific works well as a model-selection approach. Here, the initial general model included variables representative of all the main theories noted below, and allowed zero–one indicator variables for all turbulent years (such as major wars, oil crises, etc., and their aftermaths). Such dummies serve approximately the same role as omitting the corresponding observations (see Salkever 1976), so can be viewed as a check on 'data homogeneity'. Since unrestricted indicators ensure a perfect fit for observations where they take unit value, strong restrictions were placed on them, leading to two indicators overall, so almost all residuals are non-zero. While the initial indicators were selected on the basis of the known economic history, the restrictions were data based, involving a 'large'- and a 'medium'-sized shock, although the peak inflation episodes involve both. These indicators summarize salient deviations unaccounted for by the economic variables. The simplification analysis was then conducted conditional on these indicators, although some may represent endogenous responses to perceived inflation problems. This approach was used with reasonable success in Hendry (1999), even though Doornik *et al.* (1998) show that indicators can distort the determination of cointegration rank (see Section 2.1). We also report the performance of the selected model when the dummies are excluded, to evaluate the extent to which the data can be explained by the economic variables alone.

Thus, in line with the analysis in Hendry (1995*a*), the emphasis is on a progressive research strategy, not an attempt to find 'economic laws'. One cannot expect too much of simple, near-linear, constant-parameter models in describing dramatic historical events. For example, the effects on inflation of any excess demands may depend on the states of all the others, requiring so many interaction terms that the available data would be saturated by a sufficiently general initial model. Conversely, between studies, using the notion of extended constancy defined and explored in Hendry (1996) and Ericsson *et al.* (1998), suggests that empirical progress is feasible: see the series of studies leading to the final specification of the latter's model of broad money demand over the same time period as analysed here.

The structure of this chapter is as follows. Section 2 considers structural breaks and their modelling by indicator variables. Section 3 discusses the data series to be analysed, and notes some of the main measurement issues, followed in Section 4 by preliminary data descriptions. Next, Section 5 reviews the economic analysis background, and the role of the cointegration relations. Section 6 then discusses the empirical model of UK annual inflation from Hendry (1998), and Section 7 compares these results to a model using a monetary explanation. Finally, Section 8 draws some implications and concludes.

2. Structural breaks

In their studies of the impact of structural breaks on the forecast performance of econometric equations, Hendry and Doornik (1997), Clements and Hendry (1999), and Hendry (2000) highlight the key role played by shifts in deterministic factors, especially in unconditional means and trends. Such shifts may reflect changes in omitted variables, but the important feature is the extent to which the unconditional expectations of the $I(0)$ components alter: these are the equilibrium means around which the cointegration relations 'equilibrium correct'. Specifically, in Monte Carlo experiments, parameter changes which leave unconditional expectations unaltered are isomorphic to changes in models with zero means, and so are often undetectable. Thus, we focus on shifts in unconditional expectations.

Presently, there is a dearth of econometric methods for modelling intercept shifts, beyond the ubiquitous indicator variable. Under co-breaking (see Hendry 1995*b*), dummies would not be needed by definition, as shifts in the regressors would account for those in the regressand. When modelling inflation, there are several reasons why co-breaking may not occur. First, the information set is incomplete here, as commodity prices are absent: in periods like wars, and during the oil crises, such prices are likely to change considerably, with dummies acting as proxies for the missing variables. If any variables subject to deterministic shifts are erroneously included or falsely excluded, predictive failure will result, equivalent to a shift within the equation under consideration. Although a single-equation analysis is used here, the ultimate aim is a system model of the aggregate UK economy, and in a system context, adding commodity-price data would simply push the problem one layer down: the dummies would occur in the commodity-price equations, rather than in the aggregate-price equation (unless their shift factors were modelled in turn), so we decided to use dummies in the price equation directly.

Secondly, price controls and rationing were implemented during World War II, and again it is difficult to model the complicated effects of this intervention beyond using dummies to reflect their effectiveness relative to the excess demands prevalent at the time.

Thirdly, many risks rise sharply during wars, and hence there may be important departures from the usual equilibrium relations operating: for example, Ericsson *et al.* (1998) find demand for money is about 3.5 per cent higher in wartime than explained by the regressors. Dummies are needed to partial out such effects, since the increased money stock is presumably precautionary, and hence should not exert the same demand pressure as an equivalent increase might do during a less risky period. Equally, a state of emergency may lead wage pressures to be lower *ceteris paribus* conditional on any excess goods and factor demands. Consequently, we will initially 'saturate' the turbulent years by zero–one indicators for each observation, then restrict these so far as possible, taking account of the economic history. An obvious implication is that the residuals in empirical models should not be confounded with any 'shocks' to the behavioural equations: for example, if the dummies were not included, an important component of the residuals would be the shocks to other equations that these dummies partial out—as well as the measurement errors.[1]

2.1. Indicator variables

Since deterministic step shifts in levels become 'blips' or 'outliers' in differenced data, the latter are the focus of this subsection.[2] Indicator variables are often added to empirical models to remove the impacts of 'outliers', and thereby obtain a better estimate of innovation variances: however, the effectiveness of doing so is different in a static regression, a stationary dynamic model, and a cointegrated process, as we now show.

First, consider a bivariate linear regression as the data generation process (DGP):

$$y_t = \beta_0 + \beta_1 z_t + v_t, \quad \text{where } v_t \sim \mathsf{IN}[0, \sigma_v^2],$$

when $z_t = 1_{\{t=T_b\}}$ is a zero–one indicator ($1_{\{t=T_b\}} = 0$ except for $t = T_b$) so:

$$\begin{pmatrix} \hat{\beta}_0 \\ \hat{\beta}_1 \end{pmatrix} = \begin{pmatrix} T & 1 \\ 1 & 1 \end{pmatrix}^{-1} \begin{pmatrix} \sum y_t \\ y_{T_b} \end{pmatrix} = \begin{pmatrix} \beta_0 \\ \beta_1 \end{pmatrix} + \frac{1}{T-1} \begin{pmatrix} \sum v_t - v_{T_b} \\ -\sum v_t + T v_{T_b} \end{pmatrix}.$$

Letting $\bar{v}_{\{T_b\}} = (T-1)^{-1} \sum_{j \neq T_b} v_t$, then:

$$\begin{pmatrix} \sqrt{T}(\hat{\beta}_0 - \beta_0) \\ (\hat{\beta}_1 - \beta_1) \end{pmatrix} = \begin{pmatrix} \sqrt{T}\bar{v}_{\{T_b\}} \\ (v_{T_b} - \bar{v}_{\{T_b\}}) \end{pmatrix} \xrightarrow{\mathcal{D}} \mathsf{N}_2[0, \sigma_v^2 \mathbf{I}]. \tag{1}$$

---

[1] As yet, I have not experimented with wage–price freeze dummies.
[2] 'Outliers' are defined as residuals larger than 3σ in absolute value.

Thus, different scalings are needed to obtain a non-degenerate limiting distribution even in this simplest case. While $\hat{\beta}_1$ is unbiased for β_1, it is inconsistent. The limiting distribution of $\sqrt{T}(\hat{\beta}_0 - \beta_0)$ is unaffected by the presence of the dummy, and is invariant to the value of β_1; indeed, the result is precisely equivalent to dropping the T_b^{th} observation (if $T_b = T$, $z_{T+1} = 1$ is an intercept correction 'setting the model back on track', so the forecast-error variance is double the fitted variance).

When the impulse is large in terms of the error relative to the available sample, as occurs in our empirical example, we approximate its effect by $\beta_1 = \sqrt{T}\delta$, with $y_t = \beta_0 + \delta\sqrt{T}z_t + v_t$, so (1) becomes:

$$\begin{pmatrix} \sqrt{T}(\hat{\beta}_0 - \beta_0) \\ \sqrt{T}(\hat{\beta}_1 - \delta) \end{pmatrix} = \begin{pmatrix} \sqrt{T}\bar{v}_{\{T_b\}} \\ (v_{T_b} - \bar{v}_{\{T_b\}}) \end{pmatrix} \xrightarrow{\mathcal{D}} \mathsf{N}_2[\mathbf{0}, \sigma_v^2\mathbf{I}].$$

Thus, a $\sqrt{T}$ scaling is needed for $\hat{\beta}_1 - \delta$, but the limiting distribution of $\hat{\beta}_0 - \beta_0$ is the same as before. The impact of the outlier is completely removed by including z_t, whereas its effect remains if an indicator is not included, in which case, $\hat{\sigma}_v^2$ is upwards biased.

Now consider a stationary AR(1) DGP:

$$y_t = \rho y_{t-1} + \psi z_t + v_t, \quad \text{where } v_t \sim \mathsf{IN}[0, \sigma_v^2], \tag{2}$$

when $|\rho| < 1$, and $y_0 \sim \mathsf{N}[0, \sigma_u^2]$, where $\sigma_u^2 = \sigma_v^2/(1 - \rho^2)$, so:

$$T^{-1}\sum_{t=1}^{T} \mathsf{E}[y_t^2] \simeq \sigma_u^2 + \frac{T^{-1}\psi^2}{1 - \rho^2}. \tag{3}$$

When ψ is a fixed number, its effect on (3) is negligible for large T, and hence it has no influence on the limiting distribution. Least-squares estimation of (2) yields:

$$\begin{pmatrix} \sqrt{T}(\hat{\rho} - \rho) \\ \hat{\psi} - \psi \end{pmatrix} \xrightarrow{\mathcal{D}} \mathsf{N}_2\left[\mathbf{0}, \begin{pmatrix} 1 - \rho^2 & 0 \\ 0 & \sigma_v^2 \end{pmatrix}\right].$$

The limiting distribution of $\sqrt{T}(\hat{\rho} - \rho)$ does not depend on the value of ψ, so is unaffected by either the outlier, or the inclusion of the dummy. The residual variance remains a consistent estimator of σ_v^2. As before, different scalings are needed on the two estimators to obtain non-degenerate limiting distributions, and $\hat{\psi}$ is inconsistent for ψ. Omitting the indicator from the estimated model does not affect the limiting distribution, but would bias estimators of ρ and σ_v^2 in finite samples. This is close to the static outcome.

However, when the impulse is 'large', namely $\psi = \sqrt{T}\delta\sigma_v$, then:

$$T^{-1}\sum_{t=1}^{T} \mathsf{E}[y_t^2] \simeq \sigma_u^2(1 + \delta^2). \tag{4}$$

As y_{T_b-1} occurs before the 'blip', it does not depend on ψ, so:

$$\begin{pmatrix} \hat{\rho} - \rho \\ \hat{\delta} - \delta \end{pmatrix} \widetilde{app} \, N_2 \left[0, T^{-1} \begin{pmatrix} (1 - \rho^2)(1 + \delta^2)^{-1} & 0 \\ 0 & 1 \end{pmatrix} \right]. \tag{5}$$

Thus, the approximate distribution of $\hat{\rho}$ in (5) is now affected by the size of the break, but is little affected by the inclusion or exclusion of the dummy, unlike the static model. Again, $\hat{\sigma}_v^2$ is unbiased, but is biased if z_t is omitted. Finally, the appropriately-scaled dummy δ has a variance of $O(T^{-1})$: for example, if $\sigma_v = 0.01$ (1 per cent) and $T = 100$, then $\psi = 0.075$ corresponds to $\delta = 0.75(\text{SE} = 0.1)$, which would be a huge effect. Data-based dummies for outliers could downwards bias $\hat{\sigma}$ if they removed genuine shocks rather than deterministic shifts.

Introducing dummy variables into cointegration analyses raises further issues, even when their existence is based on good historical grounds: see Doornik *et al.* (1998). Despite the existence of useful tests for breaks (see e.g. Perron (1989), Banerjee *et al.* (1992), Andrews (1993), Andrews and Ploberger (1994), and Chu *et al.* (1996)) it is difficult to establish the extent of cointegration when the timing and sizes of many breaks are unknown. In the empirical model, the dummies are non-zero for approximately twenty out of about 120 observations, and zero otherwise. Since the process has a unit root, we consider their cumulative effect, which is roughly 0.4 (the absolute effect is 1.15). The first indicator has a coefficient that is approximately thirty times the standard deviation of the innovations (which is about 0.01), so is roughly $3\sqrt{T}$. Such a huge dummy alters the distribution of the likelihood-ratio test for a unit root, which now depends on the nuisance parameter δ. For example, if the dummy were restricted to the cointegration space, the eigenvalue would converge to a non-zero distribution under the null, so the size of the test would converge to unity. Thus, care is required in the use of indicators in cointegration analyses.

3. Data series

The data for the UK over 1872–1975 comprise broad money (M), net national income (Y), its price deflator (P_{uk}), interest rates (Treasury-bill rate Rs_{uk}, consul rate Rl_{uk}, and the opportunity-cost R_n from Ericsson *et al.* 1998) and population (L), from Friedman and Schwartz (1982). Attfield *et al.* (1995) extended this data to 1993. We also use some US data over 1872–1975 from Friedman and Schwartz (1982), namely prices (P_{us}) and the \$/£ exchange rate (E). Data on the national debt (N) were provided by the Bank of England. Based on Phillips (1958), Shadman-Mehta (1995) updated UK labour-market data to 1991, comprising unemployment (U_{uk}), wages (W_{uk}), a second measure of prices (P_{amp}), and productivity (η). Finally, an annual-average effective exchange rate (eer) is used after 1955, with the external price level that corresponds (P_{w}), scaled to match P_{us} in 1955: from 1955 to 1970, the two exchange rate series matched closely, but P_{us} and P_{w} have different time-series behaviour thereafter. Below, it must be remembered that $P_{w} = P_{us}$ till 1955. Capital letters denote the original variables, and lower-case letters the corresponding logarithms (so $m = \log M$).[3]

The measurement, and even the meaning, of many of these variables has altered greatly over the data period here. The composition of total output today differs greatly from that of the 1860s, and although Divisia price indices could provide a continuous link over time, few of these time-series have that form. Huge changes have occurred in the scales of the data, especially nominal output and money (approximately 600-fold), with prices up about fiftyfold and real variables around twelve (in aggregate, somewhat less per capita). Moreover, the money series is spliced *ex-post* from M2, M3, and M4 as the financial system developed. Even when variables were accurately recorded, such as *Rs* and *e*, their roles have altered greatly: own interest rates were near zero initially, but almost equal to the outside rate by the end of the sample, affecting measures of excess money demand (see e.g. Ericsson *et al.* 1998), and international trade changed greatly, with several radically different exchange-rate regimes.[4] Consequently, legitimate doubt could be cast on every selection used here.

4. Describing UK inflation

All the (log-) levels data seem likely to be integrated (at least $I(1)$), particularly the nominal series. However, they may be measured with $I(1)$ deviations from their theoretical concepts, so inflation could be $I(0)$, but measured with an $I(0)$ error (as with revisions to post-war quarterly inflation: see Hendry 1995*a*: ch. 14). Hendry (1998) shows that the two price indices, $p_{uk,t}$ and $p_{awp,t}$, are not cointegrated, although their measures of inflation are generally close, probably differing by timing (based on centre year or end year) as well as composition and weights: here we only consider the former. Figures 5.1a and b record the levels and differences of that series and world prices since 1872, as well as two other series discussed below.[5]

Several features of p_{uk} are instantly manifest in Figure 5.1: the apparent era of no, or even negative, inflation in many years pre-World War I; the rapid rise in prices during World War I, with approximately 20 per cent changes, then the sharp fall around 1920–1; the slow decline in prices during the interwar period, followed by a fast rise till the late 1960s, then a veritable explosion till 1980; but a distinctly slower rise since. The overall range is impressive: a factor of more than fiftyfold over the century and a quarter (fourfold in logs): a modern £ is worth just under 5 old pence at the start of the sample.

World prices (matched for means in Figure 5.1a) show a similar overall profile to UK, but with lower inflation, particularly after World War II. The vertical difference

---

[3] Gavin Cameron and John Muellbauer kindly provided trade-weighted quarterly data on *eer* from 1955, with the corresponding purchasing-power parity (*ppp*) values.

[4] Money-demand instability was attributed by Hendry and Ericsson (1991) and Baba *et al.* (1992) to mismeasurement of the opportunity cost: when changes in legislation allow new assets to be created, opportunity cost needs to be remeasured to account for the financial innovation and retain unchanged parameters and fit. This is the notion of extended constancy in Hendry (1996).

[5] All the analyses and graphics use PcGive (see Hendry and Doornik 1996*a*).

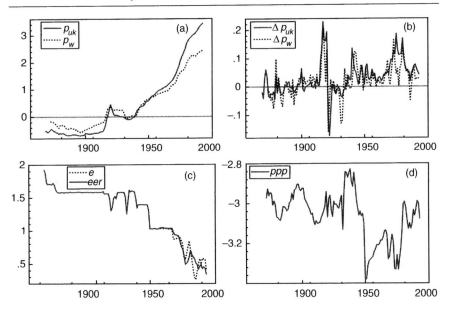

Fig. 5.1. *UK and world price levels, inflation rates, exchange rates, and ppp*

between the two lines is the relative price $p_{uk,w} = p_{uk} - p_w$, a natural variable for economic analysis, albeit depending on the exchange rate. The exchange rate, in units of $ per £, has fallen considerably (roughly 75 per cent), along a similar time path to $p_{uk,w}$.[6] Figure 5.1c records the levels of the exchange rates ($/£ rate and the effective trade-weighted index) and shows their clear divergence from the 1970s onwards. There is much less movement in the underlying real exchange rate, or purchasing-power parity, $ppp = p_{uk,w} + eer$, with a range of about 0.6 (i.e. 60 per cent), and at the end of the century, ppp is close to the value in 1872. This huge reduction in the variability is consistent with cointegration, and with some economic theories of real exchange rate behaviour. Even so, viewed as the real exchange rate, substantial and persistent deviations are clear, going 20 per cent above and almost 40 per cent below the initial value. An inflationary shock, from whatever source, seems to worsen competitiveness, drives down the nominal exchange rate to restore the trade balance, raises prices, and so permanently locks in the past inflation.

Returning to UK and world inflation rates, Δp_{uk} and Δp_w, the UK had relatively more inflation at the start of both world wars (indeed, the USA entered both much later than the UK), but suffered much less deflation in the early 1930s, with more inflation since then, increasingly so later in the sample. Otherwise, the two had similar inflation experiences till the 1960s, and their inflation rate differential fluctuated around zero for most of the sample, only becoming persistently positive after the oil

---

[6] As shown, the two measures of the exchange rate ($/£ rate and the effective trade-weighted index) behave differently after 1970.

crises. Given their different environments, economic policies, and endowments, their inflation track records till the mid-1970s are surprisingly similar, particularly since the UK is viewed as 'inflation prone'. Presumably, the gold standard and Bretton Woods helped ensure that match. After 1970, as Figure 5.1b shows, there is a lower correlation between Δp_{uk} and Δp_w consistent with different policy responses to the oil crises, although the fall in world prices in 1986 seems dubious.

Relative interest-rate levels affect output, and international interest-rate differentials affect capital movements, and hence both could influence e. The level of the short-run interest rate, Rs_{uk} in Figure 5.2a, fluctuated around 3 per cent till after World War I, then fell to 0.5 per cent where it stayed till 1950, then rose to unprecedented levels of 15 per cent in the inflations of the 1970s, before reverting to more 'normal' levels in the early 1990s. The epoch also began with $Rs_{us} > Rs_{uk}$ but ended with the reverse (again shown in Figure 5.2a). When the UK inflated faster than the USA, the interest differential moved against it from favourable in the 1880s to unfavourable by the 1990s. There is much less evidence of cointegration for these interest rates, even though one would be surprised by systematic long-run departures when adjusted for exchange-rate risk: perhaps there is fertile ground for assessing the risk perceptions of the agents who arbitraged between the underlying assets.

Comparably, UK long and short rates look more cointegrated in Figure 5.2b. Even so, there is a prolonged departure from the late 1920s to the mid-1950s, with long rates considerably higher than short: up till then, Rl_{uk} looks like a moving average of Rs_{uk}. This phenomenon of a large differential between long and short may be related to the analysis of the 'liquidity trap' in Keynes (1936). There is a large rise in both with the

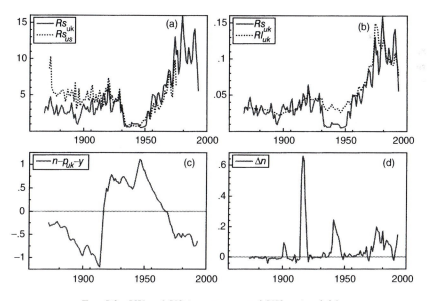

FIG. 5.2. *UK and US interest rates and UK national debt*

epoch of high inflation. There seems little connection between the behaviour of either of these and national debt as Figures 5.2c and d show for the ratio of debt to income $(n - p_{uk} - y)$, and the change in nominal debt, respectively (Δn). The end point of the former is close to its value at the start of the period, despite enormous movements in between. That aspect loosely favours cointegration between debt and income; the contrary evidence is the systematic and prolonged nature of the departures from a constant ratio. Despite governments running deficits since 1945, n/py has fallen steadily in the post-war period due to the high level of inflation: as discussed in Hendry (1980), the government actually ran a large real surplus if measured by the change in its net real wealth, with concomitant large shifts in wealth ownership. The huge impact of 1914–18 is manifest in Δn, and dwarfs any later increase, although those for World War II, the late 1970s, and the Major government at the end of the sample are marked: even the Boer War expenditures seem visible.[7]

Given the likely role of excess demand for goods and services in determining inflation, we now consider national output. This has trended over the sample (Figure 5.3a), with a sharp fall in 1918–19 not recouped till post-World War II. The trend rate of growth has been relatively constant, possibly with a shift in the mean around 1920. The deviations $(d = y - 0.017t)$ from the linear trend are interesting—see Figure 5.3b—suggesting a large 'disequilibrium' in the 1920s and 1930s, only removed late in the sample. Given the severity of the post-World War I shock to

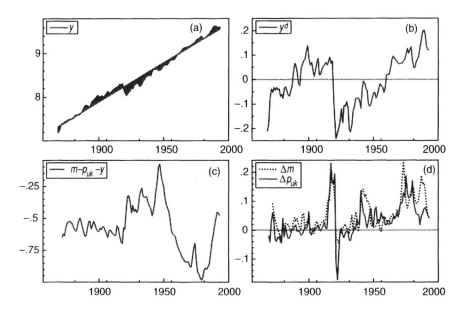

Fig. 5.3. *UK output, trend deviation, and money*

---

[7] The earliest date for the ratio of debt to income is 1833, at which time the log value equalled 0.75, so the Napoleonic Wars seemed to have been relatively as expensive as World War I to the UK government.

output and prices, it is unclear if the deviation series is I(0) or not (it is certainly not stationary), but we will treat it as I(0), and check that assumption on the final inferences. As is well known (see e.g. Perron (1989) and Hendry and Neale (1991)) structural breaks can have a marked effect on unit-root inferences, so wars need careful treatment.

Money variables have behaved in a similar manner to debt, as Figure 5.3c shows for the log inverse velocity of broad money $(v = m - p_{uk} - y)$. There was a large rise in money per unit income in the 1920s, and a fall in the 1960s returning to near the ratio of the 1870s. The main difference from debt is the large increase in money relative to income in the 1980s, associated with the financial innovation of that period, particularly the increasing level of own interest rates, and the percentage of money that earned interest. The measure of opportunity cost (denoted R_n) is taken from Ericsson *et al.* (1998). Much of the observed behaviour seems to be portfolio adjustment, and severs any putative link of 'money causing inflation'. Indeed, we can see from Figure 5.3d, that the link is nowhere very strong: there was large negative inflation in the early 1920s with no corresponding drop in money growth; and large money growth in the 1980s without much inflation. A cross-plot confirms that the relation is neither close nor proportional (the regression line lies well below 45°). Finally, alternative measures of money have behaved differently: the ratio of broad to 'high powered' (the monetary base) has more than doubled.

Wages and prices have grown in line over the century as well (Figure 5.4a), the former faster than the latter. Nevertheless their inflation behaviour has been similar: see Figure 5.4b. Real wages $(w_{uk} - p_{awp})$ have risen by almost tenfold—roughly

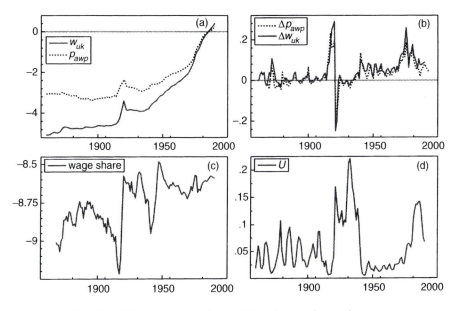

FIG. 5.4. *UK wages, wage inflation, labour share, and unemployment*

proportionately to productivity—such that productivity-adjusted real wages (the share of labour income in total income) have been more nearly constant (Figure 5.4c). We have not adjusted for participation changes, holidays, or hours of work, which may explain the trend. Finally, unemployment has cycled greatly (Figure 5.4d), with the interwar period being a major aberration even compared to the high levels of the 1970s and 1980s.

Taking these graphs as a group, the huge variations in the levels of all the basic time-series are greatly reduced by working with linear combinations of logarithms, ending with near-constant ratios, perturbed by the major historical shocks.

5. Framework for analysing inflation

Important contributions to analysing UK inflation include Phillips (1958), Dicks-Mireaux and Dow (1959), Phillips (1962), Sargan (1964, 1980), Nickell (1990), and Layard *et al.* (1991).[8] However, most explanations are either mono-causal (e.g. Friedman's claim: 'inflation is always and everywhere a monetary phenomenon'), or mono-sectoral (as in 'labour-market' explanations). Frisch (1933) distinguished the source from the mechanism of propagation, and we will focus on the former here for inflation.

Historically, excess demands for goods and services from the private sector was the first designated 'culprit', as discussed by Hume (1752), inducing final-demand prices to rise in order to allocate goods to those most willing to pay. Money might be a source of that excess demand (gold discoveries), though other sources were feasible (a fall in the savings propensity, or improved investment opportunities), and the mechanism assumed the economy was near full employment of resources. Excess demands for factors of production would operate in a similar way, bidding up wages and the prices of capital goods, perhaps via 'cost-push': see e.g. Godley and Nordhaus (1972). Excess money holdings might be spent, enforcing the first source, as suggested by variants of 'quantity theory' (see Friedman 1956), but it will transpire that money creation is not the sole and only cause of inflation in the modern UK economy, whatever may have been the case in the fifteenth to eighteenth centuries under commodity money or early fiat money experiments. Since broad money is demanded primarily as a portfolio asset (albeit the counterpart to credit), it can increase or fall considerably relative to income without much impact on inflation: see Ericsson *et al.* (1998). External shocks affect exchange rates, and hence the prices and quantities of imports and exports as well as the real values of overseas assets. Thus, deviations from *ppp* could precipitate inflation, and such ideas have existed for several centuries, as has that of 'imported inflation', and the inflationary consequences of devaluations. Similarly, government deficits are often viewed as a culprit causing inflation, especially if financed by printing money: see e.g. Metin (1995) for a recent example. Finally, special factors such as wars,

---

[8] This list is not a bibliography, which would be massive, and omits an even larger research effort on other countries.

worldwide commodity price shocks, and price controls can have large effects, albeit that they are also potentially members of the other categories. Empirical treatments of this last group are often rather rudimentary, either 'modelling' by indicator variables to remove their influence, or omitting the associated historical data period even though the turbulent periods can be highly informative. This study is no exception, as discussed above, retaining the relevant sample periods, but using many indicators.

In summary, therefore, forces capable of changing the price level include:

(a) excess demands for goods and services from the private sector;
(b) excess demands for factors of production;
(c) excess money holdings that stimulate excess demand;
(d) external shocks, affecting exchange rates, imports, and exports;
(e) excess government demands (deficits);
(f) special factors such as wars, worldwide commodity price shocks, price controls, etc.

The factors just described fall into two broad categories: 'pass through' effects that change prices while leaving mark-ups (profit margins) relatively constant, and changes in equilibrium aggregate mark-ups. Crudely expressed:

$$\Delta p_{uk} = \Delta \pi_{uk} + \omega_1 \Delta w_{uk} + (1 - \omega_1)[\Delta p_m - \Delta eer],$$

where π_{uk} denotes the mark-up, ω_1 relative cost shares, and all variables are measured 'per unit of output'. Mark-up changes are part of the propagation mechanism, so (a), (c), and (e) may precipitate inflation (or deflation), which then feeds into the 'pass through' determination process for other producers. Conversely, (b) and (d) directly change costs (w_{uk} and p_m in £), although the latter can also affect mark-ups via international competition, and (f) combines both initially, then mainly operates via the former category. Factors such as technical progress or productivity change operate by raising output relative to inputs, so are represented by (a) and (c). Consequently:

$$\Delta p_{uk} = f(y^d - y, l^d - l, k^d - k, m^d - m, ppp, n^d - n, s), \tag{6}$$

where $k^d - k$ denotes the excess demand for capital, and s the special factors. In equilibrium, all the excess demands are zero.

By treating the price level as the cumulation of all past inflationary and deflationary shocks, our analysis entails that prices are an integrated outcome deriving from (a) to (f), where the disequilibrium influences are modelled as deviations from cointegration relations. Banerjee *et al.* (1998) find that prices are $I(2)$, so inflation and the mark-up are both $I(1)$, but the long time-series here suggest that inflation is better approximated by $I(0)$ once the other non-stationarities are modelled. Thus, the factors in (6) are modelled as $I(0)$ deviations from cointegration relations, or proxies thereto (especially in the case of capital), described below.

The underlying model of inflation is based on Hendry (1998), following Hendry and Doornik (1996*b*) and Hendry and Ericsson (1986) who built on Frisch (1949), but using the (then) recent developments in the theory of equilibrium correction (for an overview, see Banerjee *et al.* 1993). It also draws on the approach in Johansen and Juselius (1992), and the formulations in Juselius (1992) and Metin (1995). Inflation is deemed to be the resultant of all the forces of excess demand in the various markets noted above, and the empirical evidence below accords a role to many of the potential effects. In particular, the evidence explicitly excludes any single factor being the sole explanation, be it money, cost push, demand pull, devaluation, or profligate governments. Instead, the deviations of: output from trend, purchasing-power parity, and the ratio of national debt to income, as well as money growth, wage inflation, world inflation, and both long-run and short-run interest rates all matter to some degree, as do lagged rates of change in several of the variables. Excess demand for money, for labour, and the unemployment rate were less important. We have assumed a constant effect from each source, but in practice, the system may operate more like a steam engine, where the valve under most pressure releases first, inducing non-linear effects. Further, a number of episodes are not explained by the model, especially the high rate of inflation in World War I, the collapse in 1920–1, rapid inflation in 1940, and the high inflation during the two oil crises of the 1970s. Dummy variables to remove the large residuals of these periods reveal that there was more than 6 per cent additional inflation during 1915–19, and in 1975 and 1980, as well as at the start of World War II; and roughly the same reduction when price controls came in during 1941–2. Conversely, other than world prices and *ppp* interactions with changes in the exchange rate, all variables enter with a lag of at least one year. Thus, we are modelling the first equation of a large VAR conditional on world prices.

The actual cointegration relationships used in the model are shown in Figures 5.5a–c and visually these appear relatively non-trending and low variance compared to the original variables.

The precise definitions of the (mean-adjusted) cointegration relations are as follows:

$$m^d = m - p_{uk} - y + 0.345 + 6.29R_n,$$

$$y^d = y - 7.21 - 0.017t,$$

$$ppp = eer - p_w + p_{uk} + 3.06,$$

$$U^d = U - 1.54 - 0.17(w_{uk} - p_{uk} - y + l),$$

$$n^d = n - p_{uk} - y + 0.1.$$

6. An empirical model of UK inflation

The sample period is 1875–1993, and the initial indicator variables were included in the general model as $(0, 1)$ dummies for individual observations over 1900, 1914–22, and 1939–46 for the main wars and their after-effects; and 1973–5, and 1979–80 for the two oil crises. These were then simplified and combined as far as possible, using data-based restrictions that were not rejected at the 5 per cent level. The resulting dummies were complex but reasonably consistent with the historical record. First, no effect was

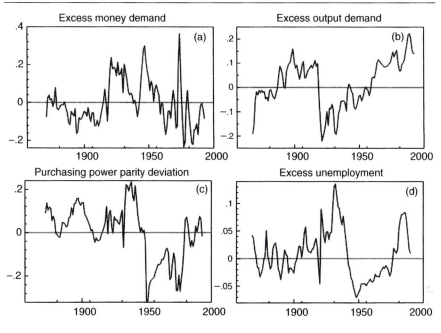

FIG. 5.5. *UK cointegration relations*

found for 1914, whereas the additional impact was relatively constant for 1915–20, with an additional effect in 1917 (the worst year of the war), and a little less in 1918. The post-war crash of 1921 was twice the size of 1915, followed by a further fall in 1922. World War II proved very different from the first, and from the findings for money demand, where the two wars had a very similar effect. After no impact in 1939, the effect for 1940 was the same as 1917, followed by a much smaller impact in 1941. Then price controls and rationing start to bite in 1942, such that a similar-sized negative effect to 1941 holds from 1943 till 1945, so the net effect over the war is close to zero. Finally, dummies for 1900, 1975, and 1980 were needed, the first similar to that for 1941, and other two to 1915. Imposing all these restrictions left the error variance almost unaltered. Thus we ended with:

$$I_1 = \begin{cases} 1 & \text{for } 1915\text{--}17, 1919\text{--}20, 1940, 1975, 1980, \\ -2 & \text{for } 1921, \\ -1 & \text{for } 1922, \\ 0 & \text{otherwise,} \end{cases}$$

and

$$I_2 = \begin{cases} 1 & \text{for } 1900, 1917\text{--}18, 1940\text{--}1, \\ -1 & \text{for } 1943\text{--}5, \\ -\frac{1}{2} & \text{for } 1942, \\ 0 & \text{otherwise.} \end{cases}$$

Perhaps the worst problem with such dummies, when all other explanatory variables have been allowed a free role, is to reveal that the largest shifts are unexplained by any regressor suggested by economic theory—other than the omitted commodity-price variables which are likely to have played a significant, perhaps endogenous, role. Nevertheless, we will re-examine the role of the indicators in Section 6.2 below (see Figure 5.9).

The initial model then allowed for $\Delta p_{w,t}$, and one and two lagged values of it, y^d, m^d, n^d, U^d, ppp, $(Rs_{uk} - Rl_{uk})$, Δp_{uk}, Δp_w, Δw_{uk}, Δm, ΔRs_{uk}, and two ppp interaction terms, measured by $\Delta eer_t ppp_{t-j}$ and $\Delta eer_t ppp^2_{t-j}$ for $j = 1, 2$. The pre-assigned significance level for individual tests in the sequence was 1 per cent. The unrestricted model yielded $\hat{\sigma} = 1.12$ per cent for 53 variables $(SC = -7.43)$, and the first reduction was to restrict the dummies as above, yielding $F_{red}(21, 64) = 1.02$.[9] Then variables with small t-values $(|t| < 1)$ or uninterpretable signs were eliminated: that yielded $F_{red}(12, 85) = 1.01$. The model then had 'representatives' of all the main theories:

$$\Delta p_{uk,t} = \underset{(0.03)}{0.31}\, \Delta p_{w,t} - \underset{(0.011)}{0.063}\, ppp_{t-1} + \underset{(0.03)}{0.12}\, y^d_{t-1} + \underset{(0.003)}{0.006}\, n^d_{t-2}$$

$$+ \underset{(0.03)}{0.14}\, \Delta m_{t-1} + \underset{(0.05)}{0.13}\, \Delta p_{uk,t-1} - \underset{(0.05)}{0.11}\, \Delta U_{t-1} + \underset{(0.04)}{0.14}\, \Delta w_{uk,t-1}$$

$$+ \underset{(0.015)}{0.025}\, m^d_{t-2} - \underset{(0.09)}{0.41}\, (Rs_{uk,t-1} - Rl_{uk,t-1}) - \underset{(0.20)}{0.75}\, \Delta eer_t ppp_{t-1}$$

$$- \underset{(0.9)}{3.2}\, \Delta eee_t ppp^2_{t-1} + \underset{(0.004)}{0.063}\, I_{1,t} + \underset{(0.005)}{0.038}\, I_{2,t} - \underset{(0.002)}{0.001}, \tag{7}$$

$$T = 1875 - 1991, \quad R^2 = 0.969, \quad \hat{\sigma} = 1.13\%, \quad SC = -8.48,$$

$$\chi^2_{nd}(2) = 6.38^*, \quad F_{ar}(4, 98) = 0.55, \quad F_{arch}(1, 100) = 1.9, \quad F_{reset}(1, 101) = 0.16,$$

$$\mathcal{J}t = 2.22, \quad V = 0.24, \quad F_{het}(28, 73) = 0.57, \quad F_{Chow}(12, 90) = 1.11.$$

R^2 is the squared multiple correlation, and $(\cdot)$ denote standard errors. Since the intercept, m^d_{t-2}, and ΔU_{t-1} were not significant at 1 per cent, they were deleted, with $F_{red}(3, 102) = 2.24$. After that sequential simplification, the finally selected model was (overall $F_{red}(41, 64) = 1.16$):

$$\Delta p_{uk,t} = \underset{(0.03)}{0.32}\, \Delta p_{w,t} + \underset{(0.04)}{0.14}\, \Delta w_{uk,t-1} - \underset{(0.011)}{0.055}\, ppp_{t-1} + \underset{(0.02)}{0.12}\, y^d_{t-1} + \underset{(0.003)}{0.010}n^d_{t-2}$$

$$+ \underset{(0.03)}{0.25}\, \Delta p_{uk,t-1} + \underset{(0.03)}{0.11}\, \Delta m_{t-1} - \underset{(0.09)}{0.39}\, (Rs_{uk,t-1} - Rl_{uk,t-1})$$

$$- \underset{(0.18)}{0.54}\, \Delta eer_t ppp_{t-1} - \underset{(0.9)}{3.1}\, \Delta eer_t ppp^2_{t-1} + \underset{(0.004)}{0.066}\, I_{1,t} + \underset{(0.004)}{0.038}\, I_{2,t}, \tag{8}$$

$$T = 1875 - 1991, \quad R^2 = 0.967, \quad \hat{\sigma} = 1.15\%, \quad SC = -8.51,$$

$$\chi^2_{nd}(2) = 6.51^*, \quad F_{ar}(4, 101) = 0.32, \quad F_{arch}(1, 103) = 7.6^{**}, \quad F_{reset}(1, 104) = 0.12,$$

$$\mathcal{J}t = 2.15, \quad V = 0.28, \quad F_{het}(24, 80) = 0.67, \quad F_{Chow}(12, 93) = 0.99.$$

---

[9] When no dummies are included, $\hat{\sigma} = 2.06\%$.

The diagnostic tests are of the form $F_j(k, T - l)$ which denotes an F-test against the alternative hypothesis j for: fourth-order serial correlation (F_{ar}: see Godfrey 1978), first-order autoregressive conditional heteroscedasticity (F_{arch}: see Engle 1982), heteroscedasticity (F_{het}: see White 1980); the RESET test (F_{reset}: see Ramsey 1969); and a chi-square test for normality ($\chi^2_{nd}(2)$: see Doornik and Hansen 1994): * and ** denote significance at the 5 per cent and 1 per cent levels respectively. $\mathcal{J}t$ and V are the variance-change and the joint parameter-constancy tests from Hansen (1992).

All the unconditional diagnostic and constancy tests are insignificant—other than normality—though a significant ARCH effect has appeared, suggesting a volatility term might be useful in long-run inflation modelling (see e.g. Engle 1982). The residual standard error is 1.15 per cent, ignoring the effects of restricting the dummies (1.23 per cent otherwise), so the fit is significantly better than (say) a second-order autoregression in $\Delta p_{uk,t}$ with $I_{1,t}$ and $I_{2,t}$ when $\hat{\sigma} = 1.92$ per cent.

An important advantage of (8) over the earlier models is the absence of an intercept (although all reported R^2s allow for the mean), so there is no autonomous steady-state inflation. Further, lagged domestic inflation plays a relatively small role, so little of the explanation is inertial either. About one-third of contemporaneous 'world inflation' has an impact on the UK, but no lagged effects were significant. ppp deviations are highly significant in this model, having been the mainstay of Hendry and Ericsson (1986), although the adjustment speed is slow. The interaction terms between the change in the exchange rate and the level and squared ppp deviations are both significant, suggesting a larger and asymmetric impact from devaluations the greater the ppp disequilibrium, particularly overvaluations. Excess demand for goods and services has an effect of 12 per cent on inflation; and government debt just 1 per cent after a two-period lag. Changes in nominal (or real) money have an effect of about 11 per cent. Also, 'cost push' has an effect of 14 per cent, and there is loss in both fit and constancy to dropping $\Delta w_{uk,t-1}$. Finally, the long–short interest-rate spread also has a marked effect, leading to higher inflation when long rates exceed short, and lower when $Rs_{uk,t-1} > Rl_{uk,t-1}$: this may reflect a policy response in which the monetary authorities control the short rate, whereas the private sector determines the long rate by their willingness to hold the stock of long-dated bonds (the terms in the national debt and spread cannot be combined, since demand for the former depends positively on the latter). Overall, the majority of the potential explanatory influences are represented in (8).

From a potential policy perspective, the effects that are absent from (8) are equally important. Both the excess money and excess unemployment relations were insignificant, and generally had unexpected signs or small magnitudes. Changes in unemployment played a small role in (7), but little was lost econometrically when this variable was dropped, although ARCH got somewhat worse.

Figure 5.6 shows the fitted and actual values, the scaled residuals and the 'forecasts' over the twelve years 1980–91, with the residual density and histogram. The tracking is close, and almost all the one-step forecasts lie within ± 2 forecast standard errors.

Next, the recursive coefficient estimates are plotted in Figure 5.7, and the tests thereof in Figure 5.8: the last show no evidence of model non-constancy, given

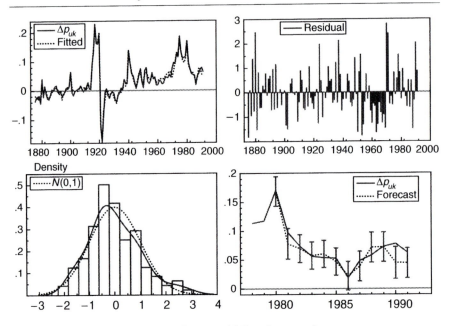

FIG. 5.6. *UK inflation model fit and one-step forecasts*

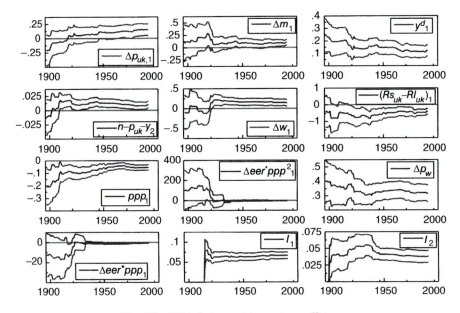

FIG. 5.7. *UK inflation model recursive coefficients*

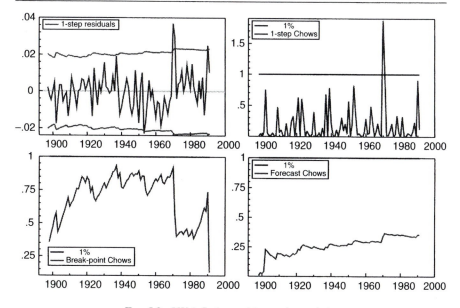

FIG. 5.8. *UK inflation model recursive statistics*

the full-sample specification, though the large blip in 1970–71 probably merits investigation perhaps associated with 'competition and credit control' changes.

6.1. Long-run solution

A steady-state solution of (8) can be derived for a situation where exchange-rate depreciation and the dummies are set equal to zero, real money growth to that of nominal GNP (from $m^d = p_{uk} + y - 0.345 - 6.29R_n$ using real output growth of 1.7 per cent per annum implicit in y^d), with wage inflation equal to UK price inflation plus 1.7 per cent (since wage inflation could consistently exceed price inflation by that amount). Doing so yields:

$$\dot{p}_{uk} = 0.32\dot{p}_w + 0.14(\dot{p}_{uk} + 0.017) + 0.25\dot{p}_{uk} + 0.11(\dot{p}_{uk} + 0.017)$$
$$- 0.055(eer - p_w + p_{uk} + 3.06) + 0.12(y - 7.21 - 0.017t)$$
$$+ 0.010(n - p_{uk} - y + 0.1) - 0.39(Rs_{uk} - Rl_{uk}). \tag{9}$$

When the cointegrating relations persist, with all their parameters constant, then their individual equilibria are zero, and so do not affect steady-state inflation. The historical mean value of $Rl_{uk} - Rs_{uk} = r$ is 0.65 per cent, entailing a steady-state inflation rate of:

$$\dot{p}_{uk} = \frac{0.32\dot{p}_w + 0.0042 + 0.39r}{0.50} = 0.64\dot{p}_w + \frac{0.0068}{0.50} \approx 0.64\dot{p}_w + 1.3\%. \tag{10}$$

When world price inflation $\dot{p}_w$ is equal to its historic mean of 2.2 per cent:

$$\dot{p}_{uk} \approx 2.7\%, \tag{11}$$

as the solution, as against a sample average for $\dot{p}_{uk}$ of 3.2 per cent. The additional 0.5 per cent is accounted for by the special effects, which have a mean value of 0.3 per cent per annum over the sample as a whole, adding 0.3 per cent/$0.5 \approx 0.6$ per cent to the solved values in (10) or (11). Roughly, therefore, the non-war steady-state UK inflation rate has solved at about 2.5 per cent per annum, so historically $\dot{p}_{uk} > \dot{p}_w$. To deviate from that outcome given (8), governments must influence the equilibrium means of the cointegration relations, or the interest rate differential.

Interpreting the equilibrium-correction terms is more difficult, as they specify $I(0)$ relations between $I(1)$ variates without any implication about causal directions. Consequently, an increase in the stock of debt might, but need not, induce an increase in the price level depending on whether or not it was consistent with the remaining terms in the relation. It is not valid to 'invert' the equation on any component, and thereby express the price level as a function of the debt stock, in the belief that then debt determines prices; the same could be done for the ppp relation to show that world prices in £ were the 'main' cause, or even the real-income deviation from trend by relating the price level to nominal income: if the money-demand or unemployment cointegration relations had mattered, then money or wages would do the trick.

Perhaps the biggest surprise to advocates of 'excess money causes inflation' will be the absence of the m^d deviations; and to NAIRU believers, that neither U^d nor ΔU really seems to matter.

6.2. Dropping the dummies

The model in (8) was also estimated excluding the two constructed dummies, which yielded:

$$\Delta p_{uk,t} = \underset{(0.05)}{0.55}\,\Delta p_{w,t} + \underset{(0.05)}{0.11}\,y^d_{t-1} + \underset{(0.06)}{0.06}\,\Delta m_{t-1} + \underset{(0.09)}{0.12}\,\Delta w_{uk,t-1}$$

$$+ \underset{(0.10)}{0.17}\,\Delta p_{uk,t-1} - \underset{(0.022)}{0.068}\,ppp_{t-1} - \underset{(0.006)}{0.0004}\,n^d_{t-2}$$

$$- \underset{(0.35)}{1.78}\,\Delta eer_t ppp_{t-1} - \underset{(1.9)}{7.7}\,\Delta eer_t ppp^2_{t-1} - \underset{(0.18)}{0.37}(Rs_{uk,t-1} - Rl_{uk,t-1}), \tag{12}$$

$$T = 1875\text{--}1991, \quad R^2 = 0.85, \quad \hat{\sigma} = 2.45\%, \quad SC = -7.10,$$

$$\chi^2_{nd}(2) = 15.4^{**}, \quad F_{ar}(4,103) = 1.2, \quad F_{arch}(1,105) = 1.04, \quad F_{reset}(1,106) = 0.67.$$

$$\mathcal{J}t = 1.67, \quad V = 0.28, \quad F_{het}(20,86) = 3.54^{**}, \quad F_{Chow}(12,95) = 0.5.$$

Thus, the dummies explain a great deal of the excess variation by reducing $\hat{\sigma}$ to 1.15 per cent.[10] The unconditional standard deviation of $\Delta p_{uk,t}$ is 6 per cent; and the

---

[10] Measurement errors, both practical and conceptual, are likely to comprise a non-negligible component of that remaining variation.

residual standard deviation from a second-order autoregression is 4.1 per cent. Indeed, the best reduction from the initial model without any dummies yielded $\hat{\sigma} = 2.4$ per cent. However, $R^2 = 0.85$ in (12), so the model still explains most of the main swings even without the dummies; and the relatively unchanged estimates show that the dummies are nearly orthogonal to most regressors other than n^d_{t-2}, which changed greatly during the two wars. Moreover, the model remains constant and still forecasts reasonably well, despite the sharp deterioration in fit, and the many rejections on the diagnostic statistics. Conversely, the advantage of including the dummies is to more clearly reveal the signals hidden in the welter of 'noise' deriving from the largest shocks. Conditional on no war or oil crisis, (8) is likely to provide the better estimate of the forecast-error uncertainty deriving from 'routine' perturbations.

Figure 5.9 shows the fitted and actual values from (12), their cross-plot, the scaled residuals (with the effects of the dummies from (8) superimposed), and the forecasts over the twelve years 1980–91. The aim of Figure 5.9c is to highlight the impact of the dummies on the largest outliers that would otherwise occur: even so, two episodes of misfit remain in the 1930s and 1970s.

6.3. Plate-stacking

An earlier form of representation of the components of an explanation, often used by Tinbergen (see e.g. Tinbergen 1940), which he called 'plate stacking', was to

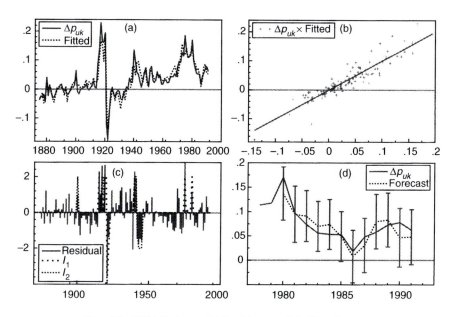

FIG. 5.9. *UK inflation model fit without special-effects dummies*

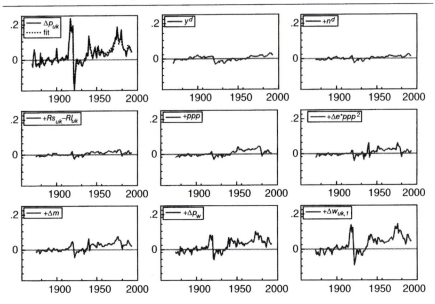

FIG. 5.10. *Cumulative explanation by the regressors*

successively cumulate $\hat{\beta}_i x_{i,t}$ terms, carefully ordered to facilitate visual appearance. Figure 5.10 records the present author's attempt to highlight how much the 'economics' contributes, and how much the indicators. The panels share a common scale, commencing from the final fitted and actual in the top-left panel, and then in rows, from left to right, showing the cumulative terms: $0.12y^d_{t-1}$; $0.12y^d_{t-1} + 0.01n^d_{t-2}$; etc., ending with all the economics variables explanations added in the lower-right panel. The order of such graph is obviously arbitrary, but it serves to reveal that in fact, to a considerable extent, the behaviour of $\Delta p_{uk,t}$ is accounted for without the dummies, which mainly serve to 'remove' the war years.

6.4. Caveats

Perhaps the four main caveats are the data accuracy, the linearity of (8), other than the *ppp* interactions, the large number of data-based dummies, and the conditioning on contemporaneous values for $\Delta p_{w,t}$ and Δeer_t. Concerning the last of these, the parameter constancy is consistent with valid conditioning, and linearity, given the large changes observed over the sample, and indeed with increasing data accuracy (which should improve the fit, so may camouflage other flaws). Also, dropping the interaction terms involving Δeer_t does not matter greatly to fit, diagnostics, or forecasting, so serious misspecifications are unlikely on their account. Dropping $\Delta p_{w,t}$ does matter, and an entirely different reduction would be needed. We have already discussed the role of the dummies.

7. Model comparison

As noted in Section 5, there are many extant theories of inflation, and here we compare the 'eclectic' model in (8) to an equation based on money demand. The money-demand model in Ericsson *et al.* (1998) offers a constant-parameter description of the demand for broad money over the same historical epoch 1878–1993:

$$
\Delta(m - p_{uk})_t = \underset{(0.06)}{0.49} \, \Delta(m - p_{uk})_{t-1} - \underset{(0.04)}{0.10} \, \Delta^2(m - p_{uk})_{t-2} - \underset{(0.04)}{0.62} \, \Delta p_{uk,t}
$$

$$
+ \underset{(0.05)}{0.41} \, \Delta p_{uk,t-1} - \underset{(0.006)}{0.020} \, \Delta r_{n,t} - \underset{(0.016)}{0.040} \, \Delta_2 r l_{uk,t}
$$

$$
- \underset{(0.48)}{2.13}(\bar{u}_{t-1} - \underset{(0.11)}{0.13})\bar{u}_{t-1}^2 + \underset{(0.6)}{3.7}(D_1 + D_3)_t
$$

$$
+ \underset{(0.008)}{0.054} \, D_{c,t} + \underset{(0.028)}{0.090} \, D_{4,t}\Delta r s_{uk,t} + \underset{(0.002)}{0.005} , \tag{13}
$$

$$
T = 116, \quad R^2 = 0.87, \quad \hat{\sigma} = 1.62\%, \quad \chi^2_{nd} = 0.1,
$$

$$
F_{ar}(2,100) = 2.8, \quad F_{arch}(1,100) = 0.06, \quad F_{het}(22,79) = 1.06,
$$

where:

$$
\bar{u}_t = (m - p_{uk} - y)_t + \underset{(0.043)}{0.302} + \underset{(0.39)}{6.89} \, R_{n,t}. \tag{14}
$$

In (13), D_1 and D_3 are indicators for World Wars I and II; D_4 is zero other than unity over 1971–5 (to capture the deregulation following Competition and Credit Control in 1971); D_c extends D_4 to include 1986–9 (for the loosening of credit rationing following the 1986 Building Societies Act of Parliament: see Muellbauer 1994); and (14) is the long-run demand for money, which enters as a non-linear equilibrium correction. Since (13) is conditional on $\Delta p_{uk,t}$, it can be 'inverted' to obtain an inflation equation, although there is no justification for such a practice (see e.g. Engle and Hendry 1993). However, the absence in (8) of the credit derationing dummies, but their key role in (13), suggests a test may be worthwhile. Here, re-estimation yields ($m_{t-1}^{d*} = (\bar{u}_{t-1} - 0.13)\bar{u}_{t-1}^2$):

$$
\Delta p_{uk,t} = \underset{(0.08)}{0.34} \, \Delta p_{uk,t-1} + \underset{(0.07)}{0.14} \, \Delta^2(m - p_{uk})_{t-2} + \underset{(0.13)}{1.20} \, \Delta m_t
$$

$$
- \underset{(0.11)}{0.44} \, \Delta m_{t-1} + \underset{(0.010)}{0.041} \, \Delta r_{n,t} + \underset{(0.029)}{0.081} \, \Delta_2 r l_{uk,t} + \underset{(0.63)}{2.68} \, m_{t-1}^{d*}
$$

$$
- \underset{(1.1)}{3.3}(D_1 + D_3)_t - \underset{(0.014)}{0.052} \, D_{ct} - \underset{(0.046)}{0.17} \, D_{4t}\Delta r s_{uk,t} - \underset{(0.004)}{0.005} , \tag{15}
$$

$$
T = 116, \quad R^2 = 0.81, \quad \hat{\sigma} = 2.77\%, \quad F_{ar}(4,102) = 1.75, \quad F_{reset}(1,105) = 0.4
$$

$$
\chi^2_{nd}(2) = 8.5^*, \quad F_{arch}(1,104) = 1.91, \quad F_{het}(18,87) = 3.05^{**}, \quad V = 0.1, \quad \mathcal{J}t = 1.5
$$

The complete failure of (15) should not be underrated, despite the near-unit long-run and short-run effects of Δm on Δp_{uk}: its standard error is not only more than twice that of (8), it is larger than that of a second-order autoregression of $\Delta p_{uk,t}$ on the indicator variables from (8)—which were not needed in (13). However, over the last twelve data points, $F_{Chow}(12, 93) = 1.1$, so it is relatively constant recently (but fails over the last twenty-one years). Adding the two composite indicators to (15) reduces $\hat{\sigma}$ to 1.92 per cent, which is still heavily variance-dominated by (8). Clearly, therefore, the determinants of inflation are far more than those contained in the inverse money-demand equation (adding m_{t-1}^{d*} to (8) delivers a t of 0.7).

8. Implications and conclusion

The approach of using cointegration to determine equilibria, with the deviations representing disequilibria that influence inflation, captures many of the economic analytical ideas about inflation, as well as providing a useful data description. Moreover, it yields several policy implications.

First, money was not the main cause of inflation in the 1960s and 1970s, and was far from a major influence throughout the entire period. Although the lagged growth in money was significant, the excess demand was not. This finding is consistent with companion studies of money demand which have shown the validity of conditioning on P, and the invalidity of 'inverting' such equations on P, as the result is generally non-constant: Section 7 confirmed that result here.

Secondly, excess demand for goods and services has been an important determinant of inflation throughout, possibly suggesting a major policy role for interest rates to dampen demand, and thereby inflation. In a related model of Δy, with y^d as its feedback, ΔRs_{uk} has a significant negative effect (-0.4). Models with intermittent, discrete, price jumps to reflect mark-ups responding to competitive pressures, or the lack thereof, would be consistent with such an effect from excess demand.

Thirdly, the world inflation rate is highly significant, so a non-negligible part of UK inflation may be 'imported', suggesting that policy might aim at matching world levels rather than achieving fixed targets such as 2.5 per cent p.a. Models of 'pricing to market', rather than by domestic costs, seem consistent here.

Equally, a significant variable is the growth in nominal wages, which might support models of 'cost push', and hence favour policies aimed at labour-market reform and minimizing trade union power. Alternatively, last year's wage inflation may reflect unmodelled influences, so it acts as a proxy rather than a causal factor. Of course, dampening goods demand has factor-demand consequences, so again interest rates would operate, although in both cases, direct tax changes may be powerful by operating on private-sector demands. Most of these are system results, and so far only a subset has been modelled. Nevertheless, excess demand for labour, on the crude measure used here, did not matter, nor did changes in unemployment.[11]

The major role of the real exchange rate has been noted, both the levels disequilibrium effect that ppp has on inflation, and the larger impacts of devaluations out

---

[11] I also found no evidence that levels of unemployment played a role.

of equilibrium. There is direct evidence that such an effect is asymmetric: for example, when the UK left the ERM in September 1992, the resulting devaluation was sharp, but little inflation resulted as sterling was overvalued previously, and the economy was in a state of negative excess demand. This outcome is consistent with the results reported by Hendry and Ericsson (1986), and such an implication was noted at the time. However, the *ppp* swings are slow, and so the disequilibria are very persistent. International interest-rate differentials probably operate quickly on exchange rates, whereas Rs_{uk} operates slowly on inflation and demand, as does the main effect of *ppp*, so will again only slowly alter inflation.

The significance of the long–short spread may reflect capital costs increasing inflation. Controlling Δp_{uk} by Rs_{uk} therefore becomes less clear-cut: if Rl_{uk} responded more, the direct effect could be in the wrong direction. This has been noted previously for the initial impact of deflationary policies, which often raise unit costs in a counter-productive direction.

While the residual standard error of 1.15 per cent is small for a variable that has changed fiftyfold over the sample, the one-year ahead 95 per cent forecast confidence interval is ± 2.3 per cent, which is large relative to the present target of 2.5 per cent for the level of annual inflation. Since inflation variance is likely to increase with the level, the model may overstate the uncertainty at low inflation levels, consistent with the significant ARCH test. Conversely, the target may be too ambitious relative to our measurement system and models.

Both forms of non-stationarity from integrated data (unit roots) and deterministic shifts must be modelled in any long run of data. Cointegration provides a general solution to the former when the latter does not intrude, but large breaks have occurred historically and need to be modelled. While co-breaking offers a promising avenue to the latter (see Hendry 1995*b*), as yet there are no estimation procedures—and there are good reasons to anticipate shifts that do not co-break for a process like inflation. Other approaches need to be developed, although the short analytical section above revealed that even using indicator variables for large innovations did not eliminate their effects on the underlying distributions in dynamic models, and could distort inference in cointegrated processes.

Most extant theories of inflation transpired to be part of the empirical explanation, yielding useful insights into the determinants of inflation. The most significant proximate determinants were excess demand for goods and services, world price inflation, *ppp* deviations, and UK wage inflation. Nominal money growth and financial asset demands also mattered, but excess money and factor demands did not. Special effects were needed for many observations despite commencing with a very unrestricted model which allowed for all the theoretically suggested factors. Possible explanations include the omission of commodity prices (pushing the analysis one layer down, but needing explanations in turn) and better data measures. The prolonged 'stagflation' of the 1970s and early 1980s requires dummies to account for it, notwithstanding so many potential economic variables: perhaps the profession's view of that period needs re-examination.

Equations such as (8) only model proximate determinants, and are part of an interacting system, much of which remains to be modelled in detail before 'deeper' answers to policy questions can be offered. While the results remain tentative, and further progress seems eminently possible, the evidence here is strongly against single-factor explanations, and supports the basic framework that inflation is the resultant of the many excess demands and supplies in the economy. The policy implications suggest that the new monetary arrangements in the UK for controlling inflation will not be easy to operate.

APPENDIX: INDICATOR OPERATORS IN I(1) SYSTEMS

The basic indicator is $1_{\{t=\tau\}}$, a zero-one dummy such that $1_{\{t=\tau\}} = 1$ at time τ, and is zero otherwise $(t \neq \tau)$. Cumulating such indicators delivers a step shift. Generally, let $1_{\{t \geq \tau\}}$ denote an indicator which is unity from τ onwards and zero otherwise. Hence:

$$1_{\{t \geq \tau\}} = \sum_{t=\tau}^{\infty} 1_{\{t=\tau\}} = \frac{1_{\{t=\tau\}}}{1 - L} = \frac{1_{\{t=\tau\}}}{\Delta}.$$

Consequently, in integrated processes, $1_{\{t=\tau\}}$ affects a 'permanent' level change that persists until a corresponding negative impulse occurs.

As an illustration, consider the bivariate I(1) cointegrated system:

$$\Delta x_t = \alpha \beta' x_{t-1} + \delta 1_{\{t=\tau\}} + \epsilon_t$$

or

$$\begin{pmatrix} \Delta y_t \\ \Delta z_t \end{pmatrix} = \begin{pmatrix} \alpha_1 \\ \alpha_2 \end{pmatrix} (y_{t-1} - \beta z_{t-1}) + \begin{pmatrix} \delta_1 \\ \delta_2 \end{pmatrix} 1_{\{t=\tau\}} + \begin{pmatrix} \epsilon_{1,t} \\ \epsilon_{2,t} \end{pmatrix}, \qquad (16)$$

where the levels autoregressive representation has the form:

$$\begin{pmatrix} y_t \\ z_t \end{pmatrix} = \begin{pmatrix} 1 + \alpha_1 & -\alpha_1 \beta \\ \alpha_2 & 1 - \alpha_2 \beta \end{pmatrix} \begin{pmatrix} y_{t-1} \\ z_{t-1} \end{pmatrix} + \begin{pmatrix} \delta_1 \\ \delta_2 \end{pmatrix} 1_{\{t=\tau\}} + \begin{pmatrix} \epsilon_{1,t} \\ \epsilon_{2,t} \end{pmatrix}, \qquad (17)$$

or $A(L)x_t = \delta 1_{\{\tau\}} + \epsilon_t$, with long-run equilibrium matrix:

$$A(1) = \begin{pmatrix} \alpha_1 \\ \alpha_2 \end{pmatrix} (1 : -\beta) = \begin{pmatrix} \alpha_1 & -\alpha_1 \beta \\ \alpha_2 & -\alpha_2 \beta \end{pmatrix}.$$

From (17), the system can be written as

$$(\Delta I_2 - A(1)L)x_t = \delta 1_{\{t=\tau\}} + \epsilon_t,$$

so that:

$$\Delta x_t = \left(I_2 - \frac{A(1)L}{\Delta} \right)^{-1} (\delta 1_{\{t=\tau\}} + \epsilon_t) = C(L)(\delta 1_{\{t=\tau\}} + \epsilon_t),$$

which is the moving-average representation, with $C(L) = \sum_{j=0}^{\infty} C_j L^j$ when $C_0 = I_2$. Letting $C(L) = C(1) + C(\Delta)$ where $C(1) = \sum_{j=0}^{\infty} C_j$:

$$\Delta x_t = C(1)(\delta 1_{\{t=\tau\}} + \epsilon_t) + C(\Delta)(\delta 1_{\{t=\tau\}} + \epsilon_t).$$

On integrating to recover the levels x_t, the first component is the cumulative, or 'permanent', effect, and the second component is $I(0)$:

$$x_t = C(1)\left(\delta 1_{\{t \geq \tau\}} + \sum_{i=0}^{t} \epsilon_i\right) + \sum_{i=0}^{\infty} C_i(\delta 1_{\{t+i=\tau+i\}} + \epsilon_{t-i}). \tag{18}$$

The two distinct effects are apparent in (18): the cumulative influence through $C(1)$, and the distributed lag with coefficients C_i.[12] However, since $(1 : -\beta)x_t$ is also $I(0)$:

$$(1 : -\beta)C(1) = 0.$$

Also, $C(1)\alpha = 0$, where $\alpha'_{\perp}\alpha = 0$ as:

$$\alpha'_{\perp}\Delta x_t = \alpha'_{\perp}\delta 1_{\{t=\tau\}} + \alpha'_{\perp}\epsilon_t,$$

so $C(1)$ has the form $\beta_{\perp} H \alpha'_{\perp}$ where $\beta'_{\perp}\beta = 0$.

When $\delta = \alpha\mu$ (say) the cumulative influence vanishes, and the impulses do not have permanent effects, since (16) becomes:

$$\Delta x_t = \alpha(\beta' x_{t-1} + \mu 1_{\{t=\tau\}}) + \epsilon_t,$$

entailing that system growth is unaffected, but the long-run equilibrium experiences a blip at time τ. Otherwise, let $\delta = \alpha\mu + \gamma$, then:

$$\Delta x_t = \alpha(\beta' x_{t-1} + \mu 1_{\{t=\tau\}}) + \gamma 1_{\{t=\tau\}} + \epsilon_t,$$

so Δx_t has a blip, leading to a permanent level shift. While such hypotheses can only be investigated in a system context, $\gamma = 0$ requires that the indicators enter every equation where the cointegration vectors have non-zero effects, and corresponds to drift co-breaking ($\alpha'_{\perp}\delta = 0$).

REFERENCES

Andrews, D. W. K. (1993) 'Tests for parameter instability and structural change with unknown change point', *Econometrica* 61: 821–56.

---

[12] Notice that the lag operator L induces a lead in the indicator arguments, $L1_{\{t=\tau\}} = 1_{\{t+1=\tau+1\}}$, since the lagged indicator commences one period later: this is not optimal notation, although lagging y_t also shifts it forward.

Andrews, D. W. K. and Ploberger, W. (1994) 'Optimal tests when a nuisance parameter is present only under the alternative', *Econometrica* 62: 1383–414.

Attfield, C. L. F., Demery, D., and Duck, N. W. (1995) 'Estimating the UK demand for money function: A test of two approaches', mimeo, Economics Department, University of Bristol.

Baba, Y., Hendry, D. F., and Starr, R. M. (1992) 'The demand for M1 in the USA, 1960–1988', *Review of Economic Studies* 59: 25–61.

Banerjee, A., Cockerell, L., and Russell, B. (1998) 'An I(2) analysis of inflation and the markup', Discussion paper 98/27, European University Institute, Florence.

——, Dolado, J. J., Galbraith, J. W., and Hendry, D. F. (1993) *Co-integration, Error Correction and the Econometric Analysis of Non-Stationary Data* (Oxford: Oxford University Press).

—— and Hendry, D. F. (1992) 'Testing integration and cointegration: An overview', *Oxford Bulletin of Economics and Statistics* 54: 225–55.

——, Lumsdaine, R. L., and Stock, J. H. (1992) 'Recursive and sequential tests of the unit root and trend break hypothesis', *Journal of Business and Economic Statistics* 10: 271–88.

Chu, C. S., Stinchcombe, M., and White, H. (1996) 'Monitoring structural change', *Econometrica* 64: 1045–65.

Clements, M. P., and Hendry, D. F. (1998) *Forecasting Economic Time Series: The Marshall Lectures on Economic Forecasting* (Cambridge: Cambridge University Press).

—— and Hendry, D. F. (1999) *Forecasting Non-stationary Economic Time Series: The Zeuthen Lectures on Economic Forecasting* (Cambridge, Mass.: MIT Press).

Dickey, D. A. and Fuller, W. A. (1979) 'Distribution of the estimators for autoregressive time series with a unit root', *Journal of the American Statistical Association* 74: 427–31.

—— and Fuller, W. A. (1981) 'Likelihood ratio statistics for autoregressive time series with a unit root', *Econometrica* 49: 1057–72.

Dicks-Mireaux, L. A. and Dow, J. C. R. (1959) 'The determinants of wage inflation: United Kingdom, 1946–1956', *Journal of the Royal Statistical Society* A, 122: 145–84.

Doornik, J. A., and Hansen, H. (1994) 'A practical test for univariate and multivariate normality', Discussion paper, Nuffield College.

——, Hendry, D. F., and Nielsen, B. (1998) 'Inference in cointegrated models: UK M1 revisited', *Journal of Economic Surveys* 12: 533–72.

Engle, R. F. (1982) 'Autoregressive conditional heteroscedasticity, with estimates of the variance of United Kingdom inflations', *Econometrica* 50: 987–1007.

—— and Hendry, D. F. (1993) 'Testing super exogeneity and invariance in regression models', *Journal of Econometrics* 56: 119–39. Reprinted in N. R. Ericsson and J. S. Irons (eds.), *Testing Exogeneity* (Oxford: Oxford University Press, 1994).

Ericsson, N. R., Hendry, D. F., and Prestwich, K. M. (1998) 'The demand for broad money in the United Kingdom, 1878–1993', *Scandinavian Journal of Economics* 100: 289–324.

Friedman, M. (ed.) (1956) *Studies in the Quantity Theory of Money* (Chicago: University of Chicago Press).

—— and Schwartz, A. J. (1982) *Monetary Trends in the United States and the United Kingdom: Their Relation to Income, Prices, and Interest Rates, 1867–1975* (Chicago: University of Chicago Press).

Frisch, R. (1933) 'Propagation problems and impulse problems in dynamic economics', in *Economic Essays in Honour of Gustav Cassel* (London: Allen and Unwin), 171–205. Reprinted as pp. 155–85 in *A.E.A. Readings in Business Cycle Research* (Homewood, Ill).

—— (1949) 'Prolegomena to a pressure-analysis of economic phenomena', *Metroeconomica* 1: 135–60.

Godfrey, L. G. (1978) 'Testing for higher order serial correlation in regression equations when the regressors include lagged dependent variables', *Econometrica* 46: 1303–13.

Godley, W. A. H. and Nordhaus, W. D. (1972) 'Pricing in the trade cycle', *Economic Journal* 82: 853–82.

Hamilton, J. D. (1994) *Time Series Analysis* (Princeton: Princeton University Press).

Hansen, B. E. (1992) 'Testing for parameter instability in linear models', *Journal of Policy Modeling* 14: 517–33.

Hatanaka, M. (1996) *Time-Series-Based Econometrics: Unit Roots and Cointegration* (Oxford: Oxford University Press).

Hendry, D. F. (1980) 'Econometrics: Alchemy or science?' *Economica* 47: 387–406. Reprinted in D. F. Hendry (1993) *Econometrics: Alchemy or Science?* (Oxford: Blackwell).

—— (1993) 'The roles of economic theory and econometrics in time-series economics', Invited address, European Econometric Society, Uppsala.

—— (1995*a*) *Dynamic Econometrics* (Oxford: Oxford University Press).

—— (1995*b*) 'A theory of co-breaking' mimeo, Nuffield College, University of Oxford.

—— (1996) 'On the constancy of time-series econometric equations', *Economic and Social Review* 27: 401–22.

—— (1997) 'Cointegration analysis: An international enterprise', in H. Jeppesen and E. Starup-Jensen (eds.), *University of Copenhagen: Centre of Excellence* (Copenhagen: University of Copenhagen).

—— (1998) 'Modelling UK inflation over the long run', mimeo, Nuffield College, University of Oxford.

—— (1999) 'An econometric analysis of US food expenditure, 1931–1989' in J. R. Magnus and M. S. Morgan (eds.), *Methodology and Tacit Knowledge: Two Experiments in Econometrics* (Chichester/New York: John Wiley & Sons): 341–61.

—— (2000) 'On detectable and non-detectable structural change', *Structural Change and Economic Dynamics*, Anniversary Issue. Forthcoming.

—— and Doornik, J. A. (1996*a*) *Empirical Econometric Modelling using PcGive for Windows* (London: Timberlake Consultants Press).

—— (1996*b*) 'A window on econometrics', *Cyprus Journal of Economics* 8: 77–104.

—— (1997) 'The implications for econometric modelling of forecast failure', *Scottish Journal of Political Economy* 44: 437–61. Special Issue.

—— and Ericsson, N. R. (1986) 'Prolegomenon to a reconstruction: Further econometric appraisal of "*Monetary Trends in ... the United Kingdom*"' by Milton Friedman and Anna J. Schwartz. Discussion paper, Board of Governors of the Federal Reserve System, Washington, DC.

—— (1991) 'Modeling the demand for narrow money in the United Kingdom and the United States', *European Economic Review* 35: 833–86.

—— and Neale, A. J. (1991) 'A Monte Carlo study of the effects of structural breaks on tests for unit roots' in P. Hackl and A. H. Westlund (eds.), *Economic Structural Change, Analysis and Forecasting* (Berlin: Springer-Verlag): 95–119.

Hoover, K. D. and Perez, S. J. (1999) 'Data mining reconsidered: Encompassing and the general-to-specific approach to specification search', *Econometrics Journal* 2: 1–25.

Hume, D. (1752) *Political Discourses* (Edinburgh).

Johansen, S. (1995). *Likelihood-based Inference in Cointegrated Vector Autoregressive Models* (Oxford: Oxford University Press).

—— and Juselius, K. (1992) 'Testing structural hypotheses in a multivariate cointegration analysis of the PPP and the UIP for UK', *Journal of Econometrics* 53: 211–44.

Juselius, K. (1992) 'Domestic and foreign effects on prices in an open economy: The case of Denmark', *Journal of Policy Modeling* 14: 401–28.

Keynes, J. M. (1936) *The General Theory of Employment, Interest and Money* (London: Macmillan).

Layard, R., Nickell, S. J., and Jackman, R. (1991) *Unemployment, Macroeconomic Performance and the Labour Market* (Oxford: Oxford University Press).

Metin, K. (1995) 'An integrated analysis of Turkish inflation', *Oxford Bulletin of Economics and Statistics* 57: 513–31.

Muellbauer, J. N. J. (1994) 'The assessment: Consumer expenditure', *Oxford Review of Economic Policy* 10: 1–41.

Nickell, S. J. (1990) 'Inflation and the UK labour market', *Oxford Review of Economic Policy* 6: 26–35.

Perron, P. (1989) 'The Great Crash, the oil price shock and the unit root hypothesis', *Econometrica* 57: 1361–401.

Phillips, A. W. H. (1958) 'The relation between unemployment and the rate of change of money wage rates in the United Kingdom, 1861–1957', *Economica* 25: 283–99.

—— (1962) *Employment, Inflation and Growth. An Inaugural Lecture* (London: G. Bell & Sons Ltd.).

Phillips, P. C. B. and Perron, P. (1988) 'Testing for a unit root in time series regression', *Biometrika* 75: 335–46.

Ramsey, J. B. (1969) 'Tests for specification errors in classical linear least squares regression analysis', *Journal of the Royal Statistical Society B* 31: 350–71.

Salkever, D. S. (1976) 'The use of dummy variables to compute predictions, prediction errors and confidence intervals', *Journal of Econometrics* 4: 393–97.

Sargan, J. D. (1964) 'Wages and prices in the United Kingdom: A study in econometric methodology' (with discussion) in P. E. Hart, G. Mills, and J. K. Whitaker (eds.), *Econometric Analysis for National Economic Planning*, vol. 16 of *Colston Papers*: 25–63 (London: Butterworth Co.). Reprinted as pp. 275–314 in D. F. Hendry and K. F. Wallis (eds.) (1984). *Econometrics and Quantitative Economics* (Oxford: Blackwell), and as pp. 124–69 in J. D. Sargan (1988) *Contributions to Econometrics*, i (Cambridge: Cambridge University Press).

—— (1980) 'A model of wage-price inflation', *Review of Economic Studies* 47: 979–1012. Reprinted as pp. 170–90 in J. D. Sargan (1988) *Contributions to Econometrics*, i (Cambridge: Cambridge University Press).

Shadman-Mehta, F. (1995) 'An empirical study of the determinants of real wages and employment: The Phillips curve revisited', Unpublished thesis, Université Catholique de Louvain, Belgium.

Tinbergen, J. (1940) *Statistical Testing of Business-Cycle Theories* i: A Method and its application to Investment Activity (Geneva: League of Nations).

White, H. (1980) 'A heteroskedastic-consistent covariance matrix estimator and a direct test for heteroskedasticity', *Econometrica* 48: 817–38.

6 Recent developments in monetary policy analysis: the roles of theory and evidence

BENNETT T. McCALLUM

1. Introduction

Academic thinking about monetary economics—as well as macroeconomics more generally—has altered drastically since 1971–3 and so has the practice of monetary policy. The former has passed through the rational expectations and real-business-cycle revolutions into today's 'new neoclassical synthesis' whereas policymaking has rebounded, after a bad decade following the breakdown of the Bretton Woods system, into an era of low inflation that emphasizes the concepts of central bank independence, transparency, and accountability while exhibiting substantial interest in the consideration of alternative rules for the conduct of monetary policy.[1]

My assignment in this paper is to consider the roles of economic theory and empirical evidence in bringing about these changes—in particular, changes in policy formulation. Have they been driven primarily by theoretical reasoning or by accumulated evidence? As a related matter, has the evolution reflected health or sickness in the macro-monetary branch of economic science?

In discussing actual monetary policymaking, there is a difficulty stemming from the possibility that in practice policy choices are dominated by responses to current political pressures, with economic reasoning of any form playing a strictly subordinate role in the thought processes of voting members of policymaking bodies such as the United States Federal Open Market Committee. There is reason to believe, however, that economic analysis has been playing an increasing role in monetary policy considerations and, in any event, there would be little for economists to discuss if we were to conclude that actual policy is independent of such analysis. Consequently, most of the discussion below will take writings of central bank economists, together with official publications such as inflation reports, as providing some indication of actual monetary policy practices.

Also, it should be admitted at the outset that evaluation of the relative contributions of theory and evidence is extremely difficult. In fact, a proper quantitative evaluation is probably impossible, since economic science evolves by way of a

This paper was prepared for the conference 'Theory and Evidence in Macro-economics', held 15–17 October 1998, in Bergamo, Italy. For helpful suggestions and criticism, I am indebted to Marvin Goodfriend, Jim Hartley, Bob Hetzel, Bob King, Mary Morgan, Edward Nelson, and Harald Uhlig.

[1] A different (but not incompatible) account of post-Bretton Woods developments in monetary analysis is provided by Goodfriend and King (1997), who coined the term 'new neoclassical synthesis'.

complicated back-and-forth interaction of theoretical and empirical considerations. Moreover, these considerations are often combined in the work of a single analyst; for example, most of the researchers listed below in Table 6.1 rely on such a combination in their own work. Consequently, some of this back-and-forth takes place within the minds of individual researchers and thus may not show up at all in the exposition of papers written to report results. Under such circumstances, it is clear that measurement of the relative contributions of theory and evidence must be highly problematic, at best. Accordingly, what is presented in this paper might be regarded more as a number of observations relevant to the issue, rather than as an actual evaluation. My hope is that these observations will shed some light on the evolution of monetary analysis while establishing that both theory and evidence have played important roles.

The outline of the paper is as follows. In Section 2, general analytic trends in macroeconomics will be briefly outlined as a background. Then Section 3 takes up the evolution of monetary policymaking in practice and Section 4 does the same for the formal analysis of monetary policy. Section 5 treats a special topic and Section 6 concludes.

2. Trends in macroeconomics, 1973–98

The years 1971–3 make a good starting point for our discussion because they mark sharp breaks in both macroeconomic thinking and in institutional arrangements relevant to the conduct of monetary policy. In terms of institutions, of course, I have in mind the breakdown of the Bretton Woods exchange rate system, which was catalyzed by the United States's decision of August 1971 not to supply gold to other nations' central banks at $35 per ounce. This abandonment of the system's nominal anchor naturally led other nations to be unwilling to continue to peg their currency values to the (overvalued) US dollar, so the par value exchange-rate agreements disintegrated. New par values were painfully established in the December 1971 meeting at the Smithsonian Institution, but after a new crisis in February 1973 the par-value system crumbled in March 1973 and has not been reassembled as of 1998.[2]

In terms of macroeconomics, the years 1971–3 featured the publication of six papers that initiated the rational expectations revolution. The most celebrated of these, certainly, is Lucas's (1972a) 'Expectations and the neutrality of money', but his (1972b) and (1973) were also extremely influential as were Sargent's (1971) and (1973). Curiously, however, the first publication to use rational expectations in a macro-monetary analysis was none of these but rather Walters (1971), which has apparently had almost no influence.[3]

---

[2] A very brief analysis of the source of the collapse is given below in Section 3.

[3] One reason, perhaps, is that Walters used a different term, namely, 'consistent expectations'. His paper's first footnote states in part: 'What I call *consistent* expectations is formally similar to Richard Muth's rational expectations.' Actually, of course, Richard F. Muth—at the time a leading scholar in the field of housing economics—is the brother of John F. Muth.

TABLE 6.1 *Programmes for NBER and Riksbank–IIES Conferences*

A NBER Conference, 15–17 January 1998

1 Bennett McCallum and Edward Nelson, Carnegie Mellon Univ., 'Performance of operational policy rules in an estimated semi-classical structural model.'
Discussant: Mark Gertler, New York Univ.

2 Julio Rotemberg, Harvard University, and Michael Woodford, Princeton Univ., 'Interest rate rules in an estimated sticky-price model.'
Discussant: Martin Feldstein, Harvard Univ.

3 Laurence Ball, Johns Hopkins Univ., 'Policy rules for open economies.'
Discussant: Thomas Sargent, Stanford Univ.

4 Andrew Haldane and Nicoletta Batini, Bank of England, 'Forward looking rules for monetary policy.'
Discussant: Donald Kohn, Federal Reserve Board

5 Glenn Rudebusch, FRB of San Francisco, and Lars Svensson, Institute for International Economic Studies, 'Policy rules for inflation targeting.'
Discussant: James Stock, Harvard Univ.

6 Andrew Levin, Volcker Wieland, and John Williams, Federal Reserve Board, 'Are simple monetary rules robust to model uncertainty?'
Discussant: Lawrence Christiano, Northwestern Univ.

7 John Taylor, Stanford Univ., 'An historical analysis of monetary policy rules.'
Discussant: Richard Clarida, Columbia Univ.

8 Robert King, University of Virginia, and Alexander Wolman, FRB of Richmond, 'What should monetary policy do when prices are sticky?'
Discussant: Benjamin Friedman, Harvard Univ.

9 Arturo Estrella, FRB of New York, and Frederic Mishkin, Columbia Univ., 'The role of NAIRU in monetary policy: implications of uncertainty and model selection.'
Discussant: Robert Hall, Stanford Univ.

B Riksbank–IIES Conference, 12–13 June 1998

1 Frederic Mishkin, Columbia Univ., 'International experiences with different monetary policy regimes.'
Discussant: Charles Goodhart, London School of Economics and Bank of England

2 John Taylor, Stanford Univ., 'The robustness and efficiency of monetary policy rules as guidelines for interest rate setting by the European Central Bank.'
Discussant: Leonardo Leiderman, Bank of Israel

3 Jürgen von Hagen, Mannheim Univ., 'Money growth targeting.'
Discussant: Stephen Cecchetti, FRB of New York

4 Bennett McCallum and Edward Nelson, Carnegie Mellon Univ., 'Nominal income targeting in an open-economy optimizing model.'
Discussant: Glenn Rudebusch, FRB of San Francisco

5 Dale Henderson with Christopher Erceg and Andrew Levin, Federal Reserve Board, 'Output-gap and price inflation volatilities: reaffirming tradeoffs in an optimizing model.'
Discussant: Stefan Gerlach, Bank for International Settlements

6 Lars Svensson, IIES, 'Inflation targeting as a monetary policy rule.'
Discussant: Alan Blinder, Princeton Univ.

7 Claes Berg, Sveriges Riksbank, and Lars Jonung, Stockholm School of Economics, 'Pioneering price level targeting: the Swedish experience 1931–37.'
Discussant: Mervyn King, Bank of England

8 Panel Discussion
Alan Blinder, Princeton Univ.; Donald Brash, Reserve Bank of New Zealand; Otmar Issing, European Central Bank; Mervyn King, Bank of England; and Guido Tabellini, Bocconi Univ.

At first there was much resistance to the hypothesis of rational expectations, partly because in macroeconomics it was initially associated rather strongly with the policy-ineffectiveness proposition.[4] There were also several other misconceptions, one of which continues today in the argument that it is implausible that all of an economy's agents would believe in the particular model of the economy being used by the analyst.[5] Actually, that is not the assumption required for rational expectations. The latter presumes instead that agents form expectations so as to avoid systematic expectational errors in actuality, which implies that they behave as if they knew the structure of the actual economy. Then expectations will agree with the analyst's model of the economy, but the reason is that this model is by construction the analyst's best attempt to depict the true structure of the economy (otherwise, he/she would use a different model).

Be that as it may, the hypothesis of rational expectations (RE) gradually swept the field in both macroeconomics and microeconomics, a major reason being that it is almost certainly unwise for policy to be conducted under the presumption that any particular pattern of expectational errors will prevail in the future—and ruling out all such patterns implies that expectational errors are orthogonal to information sets (i.e. implies rational expectations). During the late 1970s there was much interest in alternative specifications of price adjustment behavior, since with RE some but not all forms of price adjustment behavior will lead to policy ineffectiveness. Around 1980, however, such research virtually ceased (which is not to say that work with models including slow price adjustments—e.g. Taylor (1989)—ceased). Other topics involving consumption/saving and labor supply behavior became popular for a while, notable contributions including Hall (1978), Hansen and Singleton (1982), and Mankiw *et al.* (1985).

Then shortly following the appearance of Kydland and Prescott (1982), the era of real-business-cycle (RBC) analysis began.[6] For the next dozen years, a large fraction of all research by leading macroeconomic analysts involved RBC reasoning or issues in one way or another, pro or con.[7] In standard RBC analysis it is assumed that price adjustments take place very quickly so that, for practical purposes, there is continuous market clearing for all commodities—including labor—in which case monetary policy actions will in most models have little or no effect on real macroeconomic variables at cyclical frequencies. Typically, moreover, the RBC models imply that cyclical fluctuations that are observed in real variables are the consequence of technology shocks,

---

[4] On the latter, see McCallum (1980).

[5] A variant is the claim that it is implausible that all agents would believe in the same model of the economy. But, first, this is an objection to macroeconomics, not rational expectations, and second, there are some rational expectations models in which agents' expectations are not all alike.

[6] This statement oversimplifies greatly, in several respects. First, Kydland and Prescott (1982) was clearly previewed by Kydland and Prescott (1980). Second, there were important early contributions by other RBC analysts, including King, Long, Plosser, and Rebelo—and, as stated below, RBC analysis developed out of earlier work by Lucas, Barro, Sargent, and others. Third, the rise of RBC analysis was somewhat more gradual than the exposition in the text indicates.

[7] A partial exception was work involving unit-root or cointegration analysis, which was quite popular. But this work lay more in the domain of econometrics than macroeconomics, and besides there were prominent issues concerning this topic's relation to RBC analysis—see, e.g. Nelson and Plosser (1982).

not real shocks to preferences or government fiscal variables. Now, of course this has been a highly controversial hypothesis and I am on record as finding it quite dubious (McCallum 1986, 1989). But it would be wrong to be altogether negative about RBC analysis because much of it has been devoted to the development of new tools of theoretical and empirical analysis, tools that can be employed without any necessary adherence to the RBC hypothesis about the source of cyclical fluctuations.

In recent years, moreover, these tools have been applied in precisely this fashion. Thus a major movement has been under way to construct, estimate, and simulate models in which agents are depicted as solving dynamic optimization problems and interacting on competitive—or, more often, monopolistically competitive—markets, but with some elements of nominal price or wage 'stickiness' built into the structure. The match between these models and actual data is then investigated, often by quasi-RBC procedures, for both real and nominal variables and their interaction. Thus the objective of this line of work is to combine the theoretical discipline of RBC analysis with the greater empirical veracity made possible by the assumption that nominal prices do not adjust instantaneously.[8] Basically, the attempt is to develop a model that is truly structural, and therefore immune to the Lucas (1976) critique of econometric policy analysis.

The mere description of these developments in macroeconomics makes it apparent that they have been driven by a combination of theoretical and empirical impulses. The rational expectations onslaught was primarily theoretical in origin, building upon recognition of the fact that all other expectational hypotheses permit systematic (hence correctable) expectational errors. But the logical basis for the upsurge of the RBC movement can be viewed as principally empirical.[9] Here the point is that RBC models are in essence equilibrium business-cycle models of the type promoted by Lucas (1972a, 1975) but with the monetary shocks eliminated and technology shocks emphasized. And this change in emphasis came about, it can be argued, largely because empirical analysis of various types suggested that the cyclical real effects of monetary policy shocks were in fact very small in relation to the overall variability of output and employment. Some crucial studies providing such evidence were Sims (1980), Litterman and Weiss (1989), Eichenbaum and Singleton (1986), and Nelson and Plosser (1982).[10]

Then there came the more recent movement to incorporate gradual price adjustment—'sticky prices'—into optimizing macromodels. By its very nature, the impetus

---

[8] The first of these papers of which I am aware is King (1990). Other notable efforts with publication dates prior to 1997 include Benassy (1995), Cho (1993), Cho and Cooley (1995), Cooley and Hansen (1995), Hairault and Portier (1993), Kimball (1995), King and Watson (1996), Rotemberg (1996), Ohanian *et al.* (1995), and Yun (1996). For references and a useful review, see Nelson (1998). Some more recent studies will be mentioned below.

[9] This statement has been disputed by several readers, and I must confess that the following argument is not entirely straightforward. But I continue to believe that the leaders of the RBC movement were not Keynesians who were won over by arguments for theoretical purity, but instead were adherents of the Lucas–Barro equilibrium approach who discovered that it was very difficult empirically to assign much importance to monetary shocks.

[10] This is not to imply that these studies are immune to criticism; in fact I have quarrelled with some of them myself. But the point is that, rightly or wrongly, they were influential.

for this movement must have been mainly empirical. For there is no body of theory that tells us that price behavior is sticky; to the contrary it is rather difficult to incorporate sticky prices in a model that stresses optimizing general equilibrium theory.[11]

Thus it has to be the force of evidence that has brought about this important change. Moreover, I think it is only fair to recognize that the RBC movement has itself been strongly concerned with empirical veracity, even though in that regard its preferred measures have been quite different from those used in orthodox time-series econometrics.

With respect to these measures a few brief words may be appropriate before we move on. The 'standard' set of RBC measures was established in the famous Kydland–Prescott (1982) paper, which focused on three sets of second moments for variables that had been 'detrended'. These were: (i) variances of important real variables including output, labor input, average labor productivity, consumption, investment, and capital; (ii) correlations with output of the other variables listed in (i); and (iii) autocorrelations and, to a lesser extent, lead and lag correlations with output.[12] Thus the RBC empirical verification program has been to assess the conformity of these measures as generated by RBC models with actual values pertaining to quarterly data for the US and other economies.

It has been argued by many analysts that these measures provide an inadequate basis for judging the veracity of a macroeconomic model. One problem is that a model may match the data nicely according to the second-moment measures (i), (ii), and (iii) and yet fail dramatically to fit the data in other respects, as illustrated by Altug (1989) and Watson (1993). In this regard there now exists a sizeable literature on the topic of 'calibration vs. estimation'.[13] A different type of concern is that the production function residuals (e.g. Prescott 1986), on which the RBC analysis relies, may not be measures of technology shocks at all, but may instead reflect primarily phenomena of an entirely different origin. Some evidence pointing rather strongly in that direction has been presented by Evans (1992), Basu (1996), and Gali (1997). Also, Cogley and Nason (1995) and others have shown that the dynamic properties of typical RBC models come almost entirely from the properties of the stochastic process assumed to generate the technology shocks, rather than from the modeled behavior of agents.

3. Developments in monetary policy

The 1971–3 collapse of the Bretton Woods system created, for the first time in history, a situation in which the world's leading central banks were responsible for conducting monetary policy without an externally imposed monetary standard (often termed a 'nominal anchor'). Previously, central banks had normally operated under the

---

[11] One reader has suggested that it is illogical for me to cite 'evidence' as providing stimulus for the rise and also the decline of RBC analysis. But I contend that this is not illogical, for different types of evidence were predominant during the two phases of intellectual development.

[12] Actually, the lead and lag correlations appeared somewhat later, in Kydland and Prescott (1986).

[13] See e.g. Hoover (1995) and the symposium, with articles by Kydland and Prescott, Hansen and Heckman, and Sims, in the Winter 1996 issue of the *Journal of Economic Perspectives*.

constraint of some metallic standard (e.g. a gold or silver standard), with wartime departures being understood to be temporary, i.e. of limited duration. Some readers might not think of the Bretton Woods system as one incorporating a metallic standard, but by design it certainly was, since the values of all other currencies were pegged to the US dollar and the latter was pegged to gold at $35 per ounce.[14] In practice, US officials—Treasury and Federal Reserve—did not treat the $35/oz standard as if it were a constraint. This was possible initially because the large devaluation of the dollar relative to gold in 1933–4 had left the dollar undervalued, so several years of postwar inflation could therefore take place before the dollar became overvalued relative to gold, i.e. until the free-market dollar price of gold began to significantly exceed $35/oz. But the effects of these years of mild inflation did gradually accumulate and by 1961 the market price of gold had risen (the value of the dollar had fallen) to about $35/oz. Various patch-up attempts were made to permit the USA to continue to conduct policy without conforming to the requirements of the official standard, but another 10 years of slow but steady US inflation generated an unsustainable position— so the system collapsed.

Faced with the responsibility of establishing a monetary standard of their own design, the world's central banks did not perform well at first and inflation reached levels that were unprecedented for a sustained period without any widespread war. Germany and Japan began to get inflation under control by the middle 1970s but it remained high in the other G-7 nations. In the US and the UK there was a tendency for central banks to deny that their own behavior was an essential ingredient to the inflation process[15] and considerable importance was attached by central banks to employment, output, and other real macroeconomic objectives. The exact nature of central bank thinking during these years is a matter of dispute,[16] but I am myself inclined to share the judgment of Taylor (1996), who depicts central bankers as acting under the influence of 1960s academic ideas that posited the existence of a long-run and exploitable Phillips-type tradeoff between inflation and unemployment rates.[17]

During the 1970s, there was considerable discussion of policy regimes featuring money growth targets. In Germany, the Bundesbank adopted a monetary targeting strategy that has, with some modifications, been officially employed ever since. The other large-nation central bank that was most successful in avoiding inflation in the late 1970s and 1980s, the Bank of Japan, also apparently gave some emphasis to monetary targets (although in this case the extent of dedication to this strategy was apparently smaller). In the United States, monetary growth targets were given official

---

[14] The other nations at Bretton Woods would never have agreed to a system based on a paper dollar standard.

[15] An interesting document in this regard is Burns (1979), a speech given in 1975.

[16] One account that is more detailed but basically consistent with the one given here is Goodfriend (1997).

[17] In my opinion it is entirely clear that the above-optimal inflation of the 1970s cannot plausibly be attributed to the time-inconsistency motivation depicted in the famous analysis of Barro and Gordon (1983); for this model requires that central bankers believe that the public forms its expectations rationally. In fact, central bank policymakers and economists both exhibited considerable hostility to the hypothesis of rational expectations until the middle 1980s.

status by the Humphrey–Hawkins Act of 1975, but evidently played a rather small role in actual policymaking until October 1979.[18] Then on 6 October the Fed began its so-called 'monetarist experiment', i.e. the period (ending in July 1982) during which M1 targets were actively pursued by means of a new operating procedure that featured a non-borrowed reserves instrument. Interest rates quickly rose dramatically, but the effort foundered during 1980 as a result of the selective credit controls that were imposed and then quickly removed. Finally, a period of genuine monetary stringency was begun at the end of 1980 and maintained until the middle of 1982. In response, inflation fell quite rapidly—as did output and employment.[19]

From 1983 until 1990, US inflation fluctuated gently around a midpoint of about 4 or 4.5 per cent per year. A monetary tightening during 1989 interacted with the Persian Gulf oil crisis of 1990 to begin another recession that was mild but lengthy. By late 1992, US inflation had declined further to the 2–3 per cent range that has persisted since. Whether the Fed was deliberately seeking a reduction in the trend inflation rate during 1989–90 is a matter of some dispute.

In terms of operating procedures, the Fed gradually reverted after August 1982 to a scheme that centers on the Federal funds rate as its instrument (or 'operating target'). In addition, interest rates have come to receive more attention—via the term structure but also long-term rates in an unaugmented state—as indicators of monetary conditions. Thus monetary aggregate growth rates have been downgraded in policymaking significance to the point that the biannual congressional hearings, because they legislatively require reference to these figures, always include a few minutes of distinct awkwardness in the Fed's testimony.

Outside the USA, a major development has been the emergence of the European Monetary Union. Partly because of the so-called convergence criteria needed to qualify for participation in the single-currency Euro scheme, to be guided by the ECB (European Central Bank), inflation rates across Europe have fallen remarkably, averaging close to 1.0 per cent for the most recent years (1996–8).

Also highly noteworthy has been the arrival of inflation targeting as a new framework for the conduct of monetary policy. Actually, most central banks, among those that are not constrained by formal exchange-rate commitments, do not adhere to any clear-cut and announced procedures in conducting monetary policy. But of those that have adopted explicit policy frameworks, virtually all have opted for targets expressed in terms of inflation rates, not money stock or nominal income growth rates.[20] Most notable, probably, is the arrangement in New Zealand, which came first and which stipulates that the central bank governor can be removed if the agreed-upon 0–2 per cent inflation target band is not met.[21]

[18] Targets were announced for several money stock measures, which often gave conflicting signals, and target misses were treated as irrelevant bygones during the 1970s.

[19] For additional discussion of the 1979–82 period, including a tabulation of the adjusted M1 growth rates that the Federal open market committee was using at the time (which reveal the tightening during 1981 more clearly than unadjusted values), see Broaddus and Goodfriend (1984).

[20] Among the reviews of inflation targeting are Haldane (1995), Leiderman and Svensson (1995), and Bernanke and Mishkin (1997).

[21] Since the election of 1996, the target band has been widened to 0–3 per cent.

Overall, the most fundamental change since the 1970s has been the assumption of responsibility by central banks for performance in terms of inflation rates. In 1998, it would be extremely surprising to run across a central bank statement that discussed medium-term inflation prospects in a manner suggesting that these are unaffected by monetary policy behavior. So, even though we are here discussing practice and not analysis, one could ask whether theory or evidence has been more responsible for the change in opinion. In this regard there is a 'multicollinearity problem' because, as it happens, both theory and evidence have pointed strongly in the same direction, i.e. toward the proposition that there is no permanent stimulus to real variables from monetary leniency so that sustained easy conditions will produce just inflation, without any lasting boost to output or employment. There is of course some formal econometric evidence in this regard,[22] but even more influential to policymakers, probably, was the informal perception of the 1970s as a decade of experience with high inflation accompanied by no enhancement in terms of output and employment. Thus we have theory, formal evidence, and informal 'experimental' evidence all pointing in the same direction—toward the idea that from a long-term perspective monetary policy's main influence is on growth of the price level with little or no lasting effect on real output's level or growth rate. From this conception it is a natural step to view inflation prevention as the main macroeconomic duty of a modern central bank, with a secondary objective of dampening cyclical fluctuations, and today's general policy climate falls into place.

4. Monetary policy analysis

We now turn to the topic of central concern in this paper, analysis of monetary policy arrangements by economists, i.e. by monetary economics specialists in universities, central banks, and other analytical organizations.[23] In that regard it is quite gratifying to report that in recent years there has been a large amount of interaction between central bank and academic analysts, so that today (August 1998) one would be hard-pressed to tell, for many research papers, whether a particular one had been written by members of one group or the other.[24] To illustrate that point, as well as others to be made below, it will be useful to refer to two major conferences held in the first half of 1998. The first of these is an NBER conference on 'Monetary Policy Rules' held on 15–17 January in Islamorada, Florida, and the second is a Riksbank–IIES conference 'Monetary Policy Rules' held on 12–13 June in Stockholm. Since the conference titles are the same, they will be referred to below as the NBER and Riksbank conferences. The former was organized by John B. Taylor (Stanford University), the latter by Claes Berg (Sveriges Riksbank) and Lars E.O. Svensson (Institute for International Economic Studies, Stockholm University).

[22] See e.g. King and Watson (1994).
[23] Such as the IMF or the economic policy institutes of (e.g.) Germany.
[24] This is a slight exaggeration, since reference to simulation results obtained with Fed models will signal a Federal Reserve author, etc. But the methods and the general characteristics of the models used are extremely similar.

should be remembered that Lucas's critique itself was not new, but merely a (brilliantly persuasive) application of Marschak's (1953) fundamental insight that policy analysis requires a structural (as opposed to reduced-form) model.

There have recently been a few attempts to argue that, whatever the theoretical attractions of rational expectations, evidence suggests that the Lucas critique is of little or no consequence empirically. The most extensive and prominent such argument is perhaps that of Hendry and Ericsson (1991) and Ericsson and Irons (1995), who document that an estimated model of money demand shows no symptoms of parameter change (due to coefficient changes in forecasting equations) across periods with different monetary policy rules in effect. A detailed analysis of these studies is beyond the scope of the present paper, but a basic objection to the Hendry–Ericsson–Irons argument can be presented very briefly. It is simply that money demand relations provide an inappropriate laboratory for the study of Lucas critique effects. The reason is that standard theoretical analysis of money demand behavior, as represented by, e.g. McCallum and Goodfriend (1987), Lucas (1988), Woodford (1995), Walsh (1998: ch. 3), and many others, indicates that forecasting (i.e. expectational) relations are not involved in the optimality conditions (Euler equations) that are typically termed 'money demand functions'.[32] In other words, these relations are ones that are not predicted to shift with policy changes, under Lucas critique reasoning. Thus a failure to shift with policy changes is irrelevant to the issue. A much better laboratory for consideration of this issue would be Phillips-curve relationships, in which expectational variables are prominent.[33]

A related but somewhat different empirical criticism of rational expectations analysis has recently been put forth by Fuhrer (1997). In an analysis based upon a price adjustment (Phillips curve) relation that is formulated so as to nest expectational (forward-looking), inertial (backward-looking), and mixed specifications, Fuhrer finds that the expectational terms provide statistically insignificant explanatory power: 'I find that expectations of future prices are empirically unimportant in explaining price and inflation behavior' (Fuhrer 1997: 349). This would appear to strike a significant blow to the hypothesis of rational expectations, suggesting that expectations are instead formed as fixed-weight distributed lags of past values. My own response to this argument may not be widely accepted, but it has been held for many years (see McCallum 1980: 718).[34] It is that the incorporation of the rational expectations hypothesis is much more important for policy evaluation than at the estimation stage of the research project. It is fairly plausible that systematic expectational errors can be found in data for past years,

---

[32] More precisely, these conditions that relate real money balances to a transaction quantity variable and an opportunity cost variable are obtained by combining first-order optimality conditions with respect to current consumption and money holdings. There is another construct that could more properly be termed a 'money demand function', but it would include an infinite sequence of expected future values of all variables taken parametrically by the household, so has a very different specification. On all this, see McCallum and Goodfriend (1987).

[33] Using the Phillips curve as a laboratory, Alogoskoufis and Smith (1991) find dramatic confirmation of Lucas critique effects.

[34] Another response is that model misspecifications are likely to yield results spuriously suggesting the importance of lagged variables.

distant or recent. But it would be unwise—as mentioned above—to expect any given pattern of expectational errors to prevail in the future, especially if policy is designed to exploit this error pattern. But to conduct policy analysis without assuming rational expectations is to design policy in a manner that attempts to do precisely that, i.e. to exploit a particular pattern. Thus it is desirable to design policy under the assumption of rational expectations even if one has utilized some other expectational hypothesis in estimating the model utilized. Interestingly, Fuhrer himself often uses rational expectations models in his own policy-analysis studies (e.g. Fuhrer 1995).

Another apparent change in monetary policy analysis since 1971–3 is that such analysis is now typically conducted in terms of a choice between alternative policy rules, as contrasted with the choice of policy actions to be taken in a particular episode. But this change is basically a necessary concomitant of the rational expectations assumption and therefore needs no separate discussion.

Rational expectations does not itself imply the absence of a long-run tradeoff between inflation and unemployment. But analysts, like the policymakers mentioned above, moved during the 1970s to near-unanimous acceptance of the Friedman–Phelps–Lucas view that there is no exploitable long-run tradeoff between inflation and output or employment (measured relative to capacity). Undoubtedly, this move was influenced by the same brute experiences as those seen by policymakers, but for analysts there was also some formal econometric work that probably played a role. Thus it was the case that Solow (1969), Tobin (1969), Gordon (1970), and others began quickly to conduct standard tests based on time-series regression estimates very promptly after receiving the challenge of Friedman (1966, 1968) and Phelps (1967). These first studies suggested, as veterans of the period will recall, that long-run tradeoffs, did exist—that the long-run Phillips curve was not vertical. But after Sargent (1971) and Lucas (1972*b*) pointed out the logical flaw that invalidates these studies if expectations are rational, other tests conducted in more appropriate ways by Sargent (1973), McCallum (1976), and Barro (1977) indicated that long-run tradeoffs were not present—a position subscribed to in subsequent studies by Gordon (1975). Thus empirical evidence (of various types) was probably dominant in bringing about a crucial change in analytical views.

The foregoing should not be taken to imply that there are no remaining disagreements concerning long-run relationships between real and monetary variables. Indeed, there are major differences implied by various types of price adjustment models that are currently in use. For example, the type of price adjustment scheme most frequently discussed in practical policymaking circles is that of NAIRU models, where the name is an acronym for non-accelerating-inflation rate of unemployment. In non-technical publications—even including a symposium in the *Journal of Economic Perspectives* (Winter 1997)—models of the NAIRU type are often discussed as if they reflected the property known as the 'natural rate hypothesis' (NRH). But the latter, as formulated by Lucas (1972*b*), asserts that there is no time path of the price level (or the money stock) that would (if maintained) keep output permanently away from its market-clearing natural-rate path. Thus if y_t denotes the log of output and $\bar{y}_t$ is its market-clearing or natural-rate value, the NRH asserts that the unconditional expectation $E(y_t - \bar{y}_t)$ will be unaffected by the selection among monetary policy regimes. Not only will a high inflation rate fail to keep $E(y_t - \bar{y}_t)$ above zero, but so will an increasing (often termed 'accelerating') inflation rate or one with an increasing second (or nth!) difference in p_t, the log of the price level. By contrast, models of the NAIRU type typically possess the implication that a maintained increase in the inflation rate, such as $\Delta p_t = \Delta p_{t-1} + \delta$ for $\delta > 0$, *will* keep $E(y_t - \bar{y}_t) > 0$. Indeed, the very name NAIRU suggests this property, for it suggests a stable relationship between the increase in inflation and $y_t - \bar{y}_t$. But that implies that a properly chosen Δp_t pattern can keep $y_t - \bar{y}_t$ above zero permanently, in contradiction to the NRH.[35]

Another prominent class of price adjustment model is the staggered contracts class typified by Calvo (1983), Rotemberg (1982), and Taylor (1980). These also fail to possess the NRH property, but in the opposite direction: they imply that an ever-increasing inflation rate will tend to keep output permanently low! While I personally consider this violation to be a mark against these models, one that suggests the presence of some dynamic mis-specification, the implications are not nearly so dangerous from a policy perspective as those of the NAIRU class. One price adjustment model that does satisfy the NRH is the '*P*-bar model' used by McCallum and Nelson (1999*b*). Its main weakness is that it fails to produce strong positive serial correlation in inflation rates—i.e. sticky inflation—which seems to be a feature of quarterly data in the US and elsewhere. However, the only compact model known to me that does tend to generate inflation persistence is that of Fuhrer and Moore (1995), which fails to satisfy the NRH (although it fails by less than the others mentioned above).

A striking feature of the typical models in the NBER and Riksbank conferences is that they include no money-demand equations or sectors. That none is necessary can be understood by reference to the following simple three-equation system:

$$y_t = \alpha_0 + \alpha_1 E_t y_{t+1} + \alpha_2 (R_t - E_t \Delta p_{t+1}) + \alpha_3 (g_t - E_t g_{t+1}) + v_t \tag{1}$$

$$\Delta p_t = E_t \Delta p_{t+1} + \alpha_4 (y_t - \bar{y}_t) + u_t \tag{2}$$

$$R_t = \mu_0 + \mu_1 (\Delta p_t - \Delta p^*) + \mu_2 (y_t - \bar{y}_t) + e_t \tag{3}$$

Here equations (1)–(3) represent an expectational IS equation, a price-adjustment relationship, and a Taylor-style monetary-policy rule, respectively. The basic variables are $y_t = $ log of output, $p_t = $ log of price level, and $R_t = $ nominal one-period interest rate, so Δp_t represents inflation, $R_t - E_t \Delta p_{t+1}$ is the real interest rate, and $y_t - \bar{y}_t \equiv \tilde{y}_t$ is the fractional output gap (output relative to its capacity or natural rate value, whose log is $\bar{y}_t$). Also, g_t represents the log of government purchases, which for present purposes we take to be exogenous. In this system, E_t denotes the expectations operator conditional on information available at time t, so $E_t \Delta p_{t+1}$ is the rational expectation formed at t of Δp_{t+1}, the inflation rate one period in the future.

The basic point at hand is that with g_t and $\bar{y}_t$ exogenous, and expectations formed rationally, the three equations (1)–(3) are sufficient in number to fully determine the

---

[35] It should be mentioned, perhaps, that a failure to satisfy the NRH is not the same thing as the absence of monetary superneutrality.

time paths of the model's three endogenous variables, namely, y_t (or $\tilde{y}_t$), Δp_t and R_t. Thus there is no need for a money-demand equation.[36] If nevertheless one such as

$$m_t - p_t = \gamma_0 + \gamma_1 y_t + \gamma_2 R_t + \varepsilon_t \tag{4}$$

were appended to the system, it would not be inconsistent with (1)–(3) but would be irrelevant in the sense that it would play no role in determining the behavior of y_t, Δp_t, or R_t. Its role would be merely to determine the amount of money (m_t, in log terms) that would be demanded and which would therefore necessarily be supplied by the central bank in the process of setting interest rates in conformity with the policy rule (3).

It can be seen that the absence of any money-demand function—or any money-stock variable!—in the prototype system (1)–(3) reflects two properties of the latter. These are that no 'real balance' term $m_t - p_t$ appears in the IS relation (1) and that the interest rate R_t is used as the policy instrument. So we ask, what are the methodological precepts that lead to those two aspects of (1)–(3)?

In the case of the second aspect, that R_t is specified as the instrument variable, the rationale is almost entirely empirical. The fact is that actual central banks in industrial countries conduct monetary policy in a manner that is much more accurately depicted by writing R_t rather than m_t (even if interpreted as the monetary base) as the instrument or operating-target variable. Thus, such policy rules are studied even by economists who might be regarded as possessing 'monetarist' tendencies and possibly even believing that policy might be improved if central banks used m_t as their instrument (e.g. McCallum and Nelson 1999*b*).

The first aspect of the system (1)–(3), that no 'money' term appears in the IS function (1), is by contrast of an a priori origin. Traditionally, of course, it has been usually presumed in analysis of an IS–LM style that IS functions do not include real balance terms.[37] But in recent work, the IS relationship has often been of the expectational variety that includes $E_t y_{t+1}$ as in Kerr and King (1996), McCallum and Nelson (1999*a*) and Rotemberg and Woodford (1997). Such relations are obtained from explicit optimization analysis of the dynamic choice problems faced by individual agents, so they have arguably greater claim to theoretical validity than traditional specifications. But in such analyses, the absence of any monetary real-balance variable depends upon the common assumption that separability obtains in the indirect utility function that reflects the transaction-facilitating properties of the medium of exchange (i.e. money). There is, however, no compelling theoretical basis for that assumption, which is presumably made for analytical convenience. Indeed, it could be argued that separability is not very plausible. Accordingly, the absence of any real-balance term in (1), and the omission of monetary variables from model (1)–(3), hinges on the presumption that non-separabilities of the relevant type are quantitatively

---

[36] Indeed, the Fed's major new quarterly econometric model was constructed without any money demand function or any reference to any monetary aggregate—see Brayton *et al.* (1997).

[37] More accurately, it has been assumed that real balance terms should be included in principle but are of negligible importance practically; the classic reference on this is Patinkin (1965).

unimportant, i.e. that the marginal utility of consumption is (for a given rate of consumption) virtually independent of the level of real money balances. The justification for that presumption has not been explicitly discussed in the studies cited.

It has been mentioned that the NBER and Riksbank conferences featured considerable agreement among participants concerning research strategy. Furthermore, Taylor (1999: 657) argues that there exists a fair amount of *substantive* agreement; specifically that model simulations at the NBER conference 'show that simple policy rules work remarkably well in a variety of situations; they seem to be surprisingly good approximations to fully optimal policies' and 'simple policy rules are more robust than complex rules across a variety of models.' Also, 'introducing information lags as long as a quarter does not affect the performance of the policy rules by very much.' In addition, Taylor mentions other issues about which these studies do not reflect agreement, including: the value of interest-rate 'smoothing' terms in the rules; whether responses should be geared to expected feature values rather than currently observed values; and about measurement of potential or natural-rate output.

One area of disagreement among researchers concerns the distinction between 'optimal control' and 'robustness' approaches for the design of monetary policy rules. For some analysts, the task of policy-rule design is to develop an appropriate macroeconomic model of the economy and then conduct an optimal control exercise to determine what the best policy rule would be for the economy in question. Neither step is trivial, but both represent rather straightforward scientific problems. There would remain the task of convincing actual policymakers to implement this rule, of course, but that is a matter of persuasion rather than scientific investigation. Notable examples of this approach are Feldstein and Stock (1994) and Svensson (1997). To other economists, by contrast, a crucial feature of the policymaking process is the lack of professional agreement concerning the appropriate specification of a model suitable for monetary policy issues. Various members of this group would emphasize different portions of a macromodel,[38] but to all in this group it seems hard to avoid the conclusion that agreement upon model specification is predominately absent—and that different models give rise to different alleged implications for policy. Thus these latter economists believe that in practice the optimal control strategy collapses in

---

[38] My own candidate for the weakest component in a macroeconomic model is the price-adjustment (Phillips curve) sector. In McCallum (1999: n. 14) the argument is stated as follows.

It is not just that the economics profession does not have a well-tested quantitative model of the quarter-to-quarter dynamics, the situation is much worse than that: we do not even have any basic agreement about the qualitative nature of the mechanism. This point can be made by mentioning some of the leading theoretical categories, which include: real business cycle models; monetary misperception models; semi-classical price adjustment models; models with overlapping nominal contracts of the Taylor variety or the Fischer variety or the Calvo-Rotemberg type; models with nominal contracts set as in the recent work of Fuhrer and Moore; NAIRU models; Lucas supply function models; MPS-style markup pricing models; and so on. Not only do we have all of these basic modelling approaches, but to be made operational each of them has to be combined with some measure of capacity output a step that itself involves competing approaches—and with several critical assumptions regarding the nature of different types of unobservable shocks and the time series processes generating them. Thus there are dozens or perhaps hundreds of competing specifications regarding the precise nature of the connection between monetary policy actions and their real short-term consequences. And there is little empirical basis for much narrowing of the range of contenders.

response to the question, 'What is the appropriate model specification?' As a consequence, the approach favored by these analysts is to search for a policy rule that possesses robustness in the sense of yielding reasonably desirable outcomes in policy simulation experiments conducted with a wide variety of models.[39] It is not necessary that the collection of models all be designed and simulated by a single researcher or research team; the work of Bryant *et al.* (1993) and Taylor (1999) represent studies by over a half-dozen research teams each.

In evaluating candidate policy rules, it would clearly be desirable to have at hand an established specification of the appropriate ultimate *goals* of monetary policy. In that regard there are several important issues, including whether a central bank (CB) should keep actual inflation or expected inflation close to some normative value; what that normative value should be (or should it change over time?); and how heavily the variability of output—or is it output relative to capacity (measured how?) or consumption?—should be weighted in relation to the inflation criterion. Of course in optimizing models that are specified at the level of individuals' utility and production functions, the answers to such questions are implicit to the solution to the optimal control problem. But again the fundamental difficulty mentioned above intrudes in a crucial manner, for these answers must depend significantly upon the model's specification. Thus the absence of agreement regarding model specification implies that there can be at present no consensus as to the precise goals that are appropriate. In practice, nevertheless, there seems currently to be a substantial amount of agreement about *actual* CB objectives; namely that most CBs desire to keep realized inflation close to zero (allowing for measurement error) and to keep output (or employment) close to a capacity or natural-rate value that grows with the capital stock, the labor force, and technical progress. As a matter of logic it cannot be rigorously established that these objectives are optimal (from the perspective of individuals' preferences), but it seems a reasonable judgment that they probably provide an appropriate specification of CB macroeconomic goals.

A related research-design issue that has attracted some attention involves the distinction between 'instrument rules' and 'target rules', in the language of Svensson (1997). Rules of the former type, exemplified by Taylor (1993) and presumed in my foregoing comments, specify period-by-period settings of a controllable instrument variable as in equation (3) above. The second type of rules, by contrast, specify target values for some variable or combination of variables that the CB can influence but not directly control, with these values obtained (at least in the work of Svensson) by optimal control exercises on the basis of a designated model and objective function. Thus the specification of a target rule amounts logically to the selection by the analyst of a model and an objective function, whereas an instrument rule reflects the analyst's hypothesis that the CB would (whatever its model and objectives) achieve satisfactory results if it were to implement the rule.[40]

---

[39] Some representatives are Bryant *et al.* (1993), McCallum (1999), and Taylor (1998).

[40] There is also a major controversy as to whether a CB can implement a rule of the 'committed' or 'non-discretionary' type. Since my own affirmative position on this issue (e.g. McCallum 1999) is somewhat unorthodox, I propose not to discuss it in the present paper.

It has been emphasized that models represented by the system (1)–(3) specify slowly adjusting price levels. Thus central-bank policy actions, represented by changes in R_t, typically have effects on real output, y_t. It is of some importance to ask, then, what is the scientific justification for models of this type in preference to ones (including RBC models) in which monetary policy actions have no systematic effects on real variables. Is it theory or empirical evidence that indicates that prices are sticky and monetary policy able to influence output?[41]

Here the argument is much the same as that of Section 2 above—the answer must be empirical evidence since neoclassical theory certainly does not entail price stickiness. But then the question becomes, what *type* of evidence has indicated strongly and clearly that sticky prices and monetary effects on real variables are a feature of actual economies? For it is unclear how to look for the former, empirically, and there is no shortage of empirical studies that fail to find major effects of the latter type (e.g. Eichenbaum and Singleton 1986). Regarding sticky prices *per se* there is some survey evidence provided by Blinder (1994) and studies of particular commodities by others but it is my impression that most analysts have judged these to be non-compelling. More influential, I believe, has been the perception that sharp major changes in monetary policy conditions (e.g. in the USA during 1981) have in fact had major real effects in the same direction, together with the belief that price stickiness provides the most satisfactory means of rationalizing that fact. Ironically, the empirical study that has probably attracted the most support for this viewpoint is Romer and Romer (1989), a study that, like Hoover and Perez (1994), I find rather unsatisfactory.[42]

One source of difficulty in formal empirical studies of monetary policy effects on real variables has been the common practice of focusing attention on real responses to policy innovations—i.e. unexpected components—in vector autoregression (VAR) studies. Although Christiano, Eichenbaum, and Evans (1998) have reported effects of this type in an extensive study, they are not quantitatively large in many VAR studies. But the VAR approach seems inherently to miss the major effects, because the measured innovation component of policy-variable fluctuations is extremely small relative to the systematic component in terms of variability. Thus, for example, the systematic component's variability is about sixteen times as large as for the innovation component in an estimated interest-rate policy rule for the US, 1955–96 (quarterly data). One way of making the relevant point is by consideration of an extreme case. Suppose that a central bank's policy rule is activist but entirely systematic, i.e. is devoid of random

---

[41] There is a small but significant school of thought that attributes real effects of policy to financing constraints in flexible-price models, e.g. Christiano and Eichenbaum (1995). Discussion of this position is beyond the scope of the present paper.

[42] It is obvious that the Romer and Romer (R&R) dummy variable is not exogenous, for it reflects actions taken in response to recently prevailing macroeconomic conditions. Thus my own summary statement (McCallum 1994: 334) is that their study differs from previous attempts to measure monetary policy effects primarily as follows: 'the R&R dummy reflects changes in only one direction, does not reflect the intensity of policy actions, and is based on statements rather than actions. Thus one is led to wonder how use of this dummy, instead of a traditional measure, constitutes an improvement over prior practice.'

components. Then a well-designed VAR study would attribute no importance to monetary policy in affecting output—or inflation!—although it could be that the systematic component of policy was in fact very important.

A related point concerns the way in which empirical evidence works in persuading specialists in monetary economics (and, probably, other areas). In that regard it is almost never the case that an analyst's view on some important hypothesis is crucially dependent upon the results of a formal econometric study—no single study is decisive. This is in part because conclusions about crucial properties of macroeconomic systems almost always require identification of structural parameters in a well-specified model, yet both identification and 'correct specification' are exceedingly difficult to achieve in the macroeconomic context, for there is usually some highly dubious feature of any manageable model. Instead, it is the cumulative effect of several econometric studies, and/or various bits of evidence obtained in more informal ways, all taken together, that is usually persuasive to an analyst.

This section has argued that monetary policy analysis, like macroeconomics more generally and the practice of monetary policy, has been significantly influenced over the last twenty-five years by both theoretical and empirical developments. That such is the case is certainly desirable, I would think. Indeed, there is an important sense in which significant scientific progress inevitably requires both theoretical and empirical inputs. Evidence is necessary, obviously, because theories with content may be construction be untrue, i.e. grossly inconsistent with relevant facts. But theory too is necessary, for one can only make sense of facts and measurements within the disciplining context of a theoretical structure that gives these facts some coherence and delineates what is and is not relevant, etc.

5. Cointegration and monetary analysis

In this section, I would like to take up an issue that is highly pertinent to this paper's theme although it failed to find a place in the above evolutionary discussion. This issue concerns a claim, which appears occasionally in the literature, to the effect that a failure of real money balances, real income, and nominal interest rates to be *cointegrated* implies the absence of any long-run relationship of the type that is necessary for the validity of traditional monetary economics. Cuthbertson and Taylor (1990: 295), for example, have expressed the claim as follows: 'If the concept of a stable, long-run money demand function is to have any empirical content whatsoever, then m_t [i.e. log money] ... must be cointegrated with log prices, log income, and interest rates.' Engle and Granger (1987) presented evidence contrary to the cointegration hypothesis; several other researchers have reached the opposite conclusion but only after accepting the presumption that cointegration is necessary for standard monetary analysis.

My objective here is to argue that this presumption is basically mistaken. Of course there is a technical sense in which it is correct: if $m_t - p_t$, y_t and R_t are all integrated (difference-stationary) of order one[43] but not cointegrated, then the disturbance entering any linear relation between them must by definition be non-stationary, so $m_t - p_t$ and any linear combination of y_t and R_t can drift apart as time passes. But it is highly misleading to conclude that in any practical sense a long-run relationship is therefore non-existent. The following argument is entirely interpretative; it includes no suggestion of *technical* error in the literature discussed. But that does not diminish its importance.

To develop the argument, let us consider again the example of a traditional money-demand function of the form (4). Suppose that $m_t - p_t$, y_t and R_t are all $I(1)$ variables and that each has been processed by the removal of a deterministic trend. Then the cointegration status of relationship (4) depends upon the properties of the disturbance term ε_t: if its process is of the difference-stationary type that includes a unit AR root, then the variables in (4) will not be cointegrated.

But the traditional view of money-demand theory, as represented by the studies cited above, provides no reason for believing that ε_t would instead be trend-stationary (i.e. would possess no AR unit root component). Indeed, it would seem almost to suggest the opposite—for the theoretical rationale for (4) is built upon the transaction-facilitating function of money, but the technology for effecting transactions is constantly evolving. And since technical progress cannot be directly measured by available variables, the effects of technical change (not captured by a deterministic trend) show up in the disturbance term, ε_t. But the nature of technological progress is such that changes (shocks) are typically not reversed. Thus one would expect a priori there to be an important permanent component to the ε_t process, making it one of the integrated type—and thereby making $m_t - p_t$ not cointegrated with y_t and R_t.

In such a case, however, the 'long-run' messages of traditional monetary analysis could easily continue to apply. Provided that the magnitude of the variance of the innovation in ε_t is not large in relation to potential magnitudes of Δm_t values, it will still be true that inflation rates will be principally determined, over long periods of time, by money growth rates. And even without that proviso, long-run monetary neutrality may still prevail, superneutrality may be approximately but not precisely valid, etc. That the disturbance ε_t is of the difference-stationary class is simply not a source of embarrassment or special concern for supporters of the traditional theory of money demand, some of whom have estimated money-demand relations like (4) after *assuming* that ε_t is a pure random walk![44]

---

[43] A time-series variable is integrated of order one, written $I(1)$, if it must be differenced once to obtain a variable that is covariance-stationary. This will be the case for an ARMA variable if its autoregressive parameter has a unit root.

[44] More generally, I would a priori expect cointegration among basic variables—ones that enter utility or production functions, not their differences—to be quite rare, for behavioral relations typically include disturbance terms that represent unobservable (and thus omitted) variables, which include shocks to preferences and technology. But these shocks would seem likely to include significant random-walk components, as argued above. Thus disturbance terms in behavioral relations should, according to this argument, typically possess unit-root components.

6. Conclusion

The picture painted in the preceding discussion is one that attributes major changes in the analysis and practice of monetary policy over the years 1973–98 to a combination of theoretical and empirical influences. This is not a very dramatic conclusion; indeed, one might say that it is almost empty. It would be possible to add a bit of debatable content, by asserting that the mixture of influences has been reasonably appropriate— about the right amount of theory and empirics—but I would not feel comfortable in doing so. Partly that is because I would have preferred that models with complete price flexibility had not been quite so dominant during the years (say) 1982–92, although the surge of work with sticky-price models in recent years may have largely made up for their previous neglect. But an equally important reason stems from the question: what type of evidence could be presented in support of a 'reasonably appropriate' contention? Unfortunately, I know of no satisfactory way of making such a determination, especially since most influential studies involve a blend of theory and evidence. For example, the rather abstract theoretical analysis of Lucas (1972a) was not actually devoid of empirical content in the sense that its theorizing was specifically designed to rationalize a set of broad facts that were (and are) of genuine, fundamental importance. Consequently, I am left with the rather limp conclusion with which this paragraph began.

In conclusion, then, it may be appropriate to add the opinion that the current state of monetary economics is not as highly unsatisfactory as has been claimed over the past decade or so by various commentators at conferences and seminars. The type of claim that I have in mind does not often make it into print, so I cannot provide citations, but I am confident that many readers can supply examples from their own experiences. In any event, the state of monetary economics seems to me to be about as healthy as that of economic analysis in general. The contrary opinion is rather widely held for three reasons, I would suggest, none of which is sound. First, much of the negative opinion has been put forth by economists who are themselves proponents of an entirely unsatisfactory theory of money demand, one involving overlapping generations models in which the asset termed 'money' plays no role as a (transaction-facilitating) medium of exchange. Since this role provides the defining characteristic of money, as distinct from other assets, it is not surprising that proponents of such a theory would find it unsatisfactory. Second, rather inconsequential differences among proponents of the transaction-facilitating approach to money-demand theory—e.g. cash-in-advance, money-in-utility function, shopping time, or transaction-cost-in-budget constraint models—have tended to obscure the fundamental similarity of principles and implications among the variants of this approach. Third, the profession's poor level of understanding of the precise nature of the dynamic connection between monetary and real variables—i.e. of price adjustment relations—has tended to reflect discredit upon monetary economics, although this relation belongs to the realm of macroeconomics more broadly. In that regard, moreover, it is an illusion to believe that macroeconomics is itself in poor condition in relation to microeconomics, an illusion generated by the fact that applied macro features a much more ambitious agenda than applied micro—the understanding of quarter-to-quarter dynamic movements in variables rather than just steady-state values. Correcting for that difference, the extent of disagreement seems about the same in the two sub-disciplines.

REFERENCES

Alogoskoufis, G. L. and Smith, R. (1991) 'The Phillips curve, the persistence of inflation, and the Lucas critique', *American Economic Review* 81: 1254–75.

Altug, S. (1989) 'Time-to-build and aggregate fluctuations', *International Economic Review* 30: 889–920.

Axilrod, S. H. (1983) 'A comment on Brunner and Meltzer', *Carnegie–Rochester Conference Series* 18: 105–12.

Barro, R. J. (1977) 'Unanticipated money growth and unemployment in the United States', *American Economic Review* 67: 101–15.

—— and Gordon, D. B. (1983) 'A positive theory of monetary policy in a natural rate model', *Journal of Political Economy* 91: 589–610.

Basu, S. (1996) 'Procyclical productivity: increasing returns or cyclical utilization', *Quarterly Journal of Economics* 111: 719–51.

Bernanke, B. S. and Mishkin, F. S. (1997) 'Inflation targeting: a new framework for monetary policy?' *Journal of Economic Perspectives* 11: 97–116.

Blinder, A. S. (1994) 'On sticky prices: academic theories meet the real world', *Monetary Policy*, ed. N. G. Mankiw (Chicago: University of Chicago Press).

Brayton, F., Levin, A., Tryon, R. and Williams, J. C. (1997) 'The evolution of macro models at the Federal Reserve Board', *Carnegie–Rochester Conference Series on Public Policy* 47: 43–81.

Broaddus, A. and Goodfriend, M. (1984) 'Base drift and the longer-run growth of M1: experience from a decade of monetary targeting', Federal Reserve Bank of Richmond, *Economic Review* 70 (Nov./Dec.): 3–14.

Brunner, K. and Meltzer, A. H. (1983) 'Strategies and tactics for monetary control', *Carnegie–Rochester Conference Series* 18: 59–104.

Bryant, R. C., Hooper, P. and Mann, C. L. (1993) *Evaluating Policy Regimes: New Research in Empirical Macroeconomics* (Washington: Brookings Institution).

Burns, A. (1979) 'The real issues of inflation and unemployment', *Federal Reserve Readings on Inflation* (Federal Reserve Bank of New York).

Calvo, G. A. (1983) 'Staggered prices in a utility maximizing framework', *Journal of Monetary Economics* 12: 383–98.

Christiano, L. J. and Eichenbaum, M. (1995) 'Liquidity effects, monetary policy, and the business cycle', *Journal of Money, Credit, and Banking* 27: 1113–36.

——, Eichenbaum, M. and Evans, C.L. (1998) 'Monetary policy shocks: what have we learned and to what end?', NBER Working paper 6400. Forthcoming in *Handbook of Macroeconomics*, ed. J. B. Taylor and M. Woodford (Amsterdam: North-Holland).

Cogley, T. and Nason, J. M. (1995) 'Output dynamics in real-business cycle models', *American Economic Review* 85: 492–511.

Cuthbertson, K. and Taylor, M. P. (1990) 'Money demand, expectations, and the forward-looking model', *Journal of Policy Modeling* 12: 289–315.

Eichenbaum, M. and Singleton, K. J. (1986) 'Do equilibrium real business cycle theories explain postwar US business cycles?', *NBER Macroeconomic Annual 1986*. (Cambridge, Mass.: MIT Press).

Engle, R. F. and Granger, C. W. J. (1987) 'Co-integration and error correction: representation, estimation, and testing', *Econometrica* 55: 251–76.

Ericsson, N. and Irons, J. (1995) 'The Lucas critique in practice: theory without measurement', in *Macroeconometrics: Developments, Tensions, and Prospects*, ed. by K. D. Hoover (Boston: Kluwer Academic Press): 263–312.

Evans, C. L. (1992) 'Productivity shocks and real business cycles', *Journal of Monetary Economics* 29: 191–208.

Feldstein, M. and Stock, J. H. (1994) 'The use of a monetary aggregate to target nominal GDP', in *Monetary Policy*, ed. N. G. Mankiw (Chicago: University of Chicago Press).

Friedman, M. (1966) 'Comments', in *Guidelines, Informal Controls, and the Market-place*, ed. G. P. Schultz and R. Z. Aliber (Chicago: University of Chicago Press).

—— (1968) 'The role of monetary policy', *American Economic Review* 58: 1–17.

Fuhrer, J. C. (1995) 'The persistence of inflation and the cost of disinflation', *New England Economic Review* Jan/Feb: 3–16.

—— (1997) 'The (un)importance of forward-looking behavior in price specifications', *Journal of Money, Credit, and Banking* 29: 338–50.

—— and Moore, G. R. (1995) 'Inflation persistence', *Quarterly Journal of Economics* 109: 127–59.

Gali, J. (1997) 'Technology, employment, and the business cycle: do technology shocks explain aggregate fluctuations?', NBER Working Paper 5721.

Goodfriend, M. (1997) 'Monetary policy comes of age: a 20th century odyssey', Federal Reserve Bank of Richmond, *Economic Quarterly* 83 (Winter): 1–22.

—— and King, R. E. (1997) 'The new neoclassical synthesis and the role of monetary policy', *NBER Macroeconomics Annual 1997*: 231–82.

Gordon, R. J. (1970) 'The recent acceleration of inflation and its lessons for the future', *Brookings Papers on Economic Activity* 1: 8–41.

—— (1975) 'The impact of aggregate demand on prices', *Brookings Papers on Economic Activity* 3: 613–62.

Haldane, A. G. (ed.) (1995) *Targeting Inflation* (London: Bank of England).

Hall, R. E. (1978) 'Stochastic implications of the life-cycle-permanent income hypothesis: theory and evidence', *Journal of Political Economy* 86: 971–87.

Hansen, L. P. and Singleton, K. J. (1982) 'Generalized instrumental variables estimation of nonlinear rational expectations models', *Econometrica* 50: 1269–86.

Hendry, D. F. and Ericsson, N. R. (1991) 'Modeling the demand for narrow money in the United Kingdom and the United States', *European Economic Review* 35: 833–86.

Hoover, K. D. (1995) 'Facts and artifacts: calibration and the empirical assessment of real business cycle models', *Oxford Economic Papers* 47: 24–44.

—— and Perez, S. J. (1994) 'Money may matter, but how could you know?', *Journal of Monetary Economics* 34: 89–100.

Kerr, W. and King, R. G. (1996) 'Limits on interest rate rules in the IS–LM model', Federal Reserve Bank of Richmond, *Economic Quarterly* 82 (Spring): 47–75.

King, R. E. (1990) 'Money and business cycles', Working Paper. Forthcoming in *Journal of Monetary Economics*.

—— and Watson, M. W. (1994) 'The post-war US Phillips curve: a revisionist econometric history', *Carnegie–Rochester Conference Series* 41: 157–219.

Kydland, F. E. and Prescott, E. C. (1980) 'A competitive theory of fluctuations and the feasibility of stabilization policy', in *Rational Expectations and Economic Policy*, ed. S. Fischer (Chicago: University of Chicago Press).

—— (1982) 'Time to build and aggregate fluctuations', *Econometrica* 50: 1345–70.

—— (1986) 'The workweek of capital and its cyclical implications', Working paper.

Leiderman, L. and Svensson, L. E. O. (eds.) (1995) *Inflation Targets* (London: Centre for Economic Policy Research).

Litterman, R. B. and Weiss, L. (1989) 'Money, real interest rates, and output: a reinterpretation of postwar US data', *Econometrica* 53: 129–56.

Lucas, R. E., Jr (1972*a*) 'Expectations and the neutrality of money', *Journal of Economic Theory* 4: 103–24.

—— (1972*b*) 'Econometric testing of the natural-rate hypothesis', *The Econometrics of Price Determination*, ed. O. Eckstein (Washington, DC: Board of Governors of the Federal Reserve System).

—— (1973) 'Some international evidence on output–inflation tradeoffs', *American Economic Review* 63: 326–34.

—— (1975) 'An equilibrium model of the business cycle', *Journal of Political Economy* 83: 1113–44.

—— (1976) 'Econometric policy evaluation: a critique', *Carnegie–Rochester Conference Series* 1, 19–46.

—— (1988) 'Money demand in the United States: a quantitative review', *Carnegie–Rochester Conference Series* 29: 137–67.

Mankiw, N. G., Rotemberg, J. J. and Summers, L. (1985) 'Intertemporal substitution in macroeconomics', *Quarterly Journal of Economics* 100: 225–51.

Marschak, J. (1953) 'Economic measurements for policy and prediction', *Studies in Econometric Method*, ed. W. C. Hood and T. J. Koopmans (New York: John Wiley).

McCallum, B. T. (1976) 'Rational expectations and the natural rate hypothesis: some consistent estimates', *Econometrica* 44: 43–52.

—— (1980) 'Rational expectations and macroeconomic stabilization policy', *Journal of Money, Credit, and Banking* 12: 716–46.

—— (1986) 'On "real" and "sticky-price" theories of the business cycle', *Journal of Money, Credit, and Banking* 18: 397–414.

—— (1989) 'Real business cycle models', *Modern Business Cycle Theory*, ed. R. J. Barro (Cambridge, Mass.: Harvard University Press).

—— (1994) 'Comment on "Federal Reserve Policy: Cause and Effect" by M. D. Shapiro', *Monetary Policy*, ed. N. G. Mankiw (Chicago: University of Chicago Press for NBER).

—— (1999) 'Issues in the design of monetary policy rules', *Handbook of Macroeconomics*, ed. J. B. Taylor and M. Woodford (Amsterdam: North-Holland).

—— and Goodfriend, M. S. (1987) 'Demand for money: theoretical studies', *The New Palgrave*, ed. J. Eatwell, M. Milgate and P. Newman (New York: Stockton Press).

—— and Nelson, E. (1999*a*) 'An optimizing IS–LM specification for monetary policy and business cycle analysis', *Journal of Money, Credit, and Banking* 31: 296–316.

—— (1999*b*) 'Nominal income targeting in an open-economy maximizing model', *Journal of Monetary Economics* 43: 553–78.

Nelson, C. R. and Plosser, C. I. (1982) 'Trends and random walks in macroeconomic time series', *Journal of Monetary Economics* 10: 139–62.

Nelson, E. (1998) 'Sluggish inflation and optimizing models of the business cycle', *Journal of Monetary Economics* 42: 303–22.

Patinkin, D. (1965) *Money, Interest, and Prices*, 2nd edn. (New York: Harper & Row).

Phelps, E. S. (1967) 'Phillips curves, expectations of inflation, and optimal unemployment over time', *Economica* 34: 254–81.

Prescott, E. S. (1986) 'Theory ahead of business cycle measurement', *Carnegie–Rochester Conference Series* 25: 11–44.

Romer, C. D. and Romer, D. (1989) 'Does monetary policy matter? A new test in the spirit of Friedman and Schwartz', *NBER Macroeconomics Annual 1989*: 121–70.

Rotemberg, J. J. (1982) 'Monopolistic price adjustment and aggregate output', *Review of Economic Studies* 44: 517–31.

—— and Woodford, M. (1997) 'An optimization based econometric framework for the evaluation of monetary policy', *NBER Macroeconomics Annual 1997*: 297–345.

Sargent, T. J. (1971) 'A note on the accelerationist controversy', *Journal of Money, Credit, and Banking* 3: 50–60.

——(1973) 'Rational expectations, the real rate of interest, and the natural rate of unemployment', *Brookings Papers on Economic Activity* 2: 429–72.

—— and Wallace, N. (1975) '"Rational" expectations, the optimal monetary instrument, and the optimal money supply role', *Journal of Political Economy* 83: 241–54.

Sims, C. A. (1980) 'A comparison of interwar and postwar business cycles: monetarism reconsidered', *American Economic Review Papers and Proceedings* 70: 250–7.

Solow, R. M. (1969) *Price Expectations and the Behavior of the Price Level* (Manchester: Manchester University Press).

Svensson, L. E. O. (1997) 'Inflation forecast targeting: implementing and monitoring inflation targets', *European Economic Review* 41: 1111–46.

Taylor, J. B. (1980) 'Aggregate dynamics and staggered contracts', *Journal of Political Economy* 88: 1–23.

——(1989) 'Monetary policy and the stability of macroeconomic relationships', *Journal of Applied Econometrics* 4: S161–78.

——(1993) 'Discretion versus policy rules in practice', *Carnegie–Rochester Conference Series* 39: 195–214.

——(1996) 'How should monetary policy respond to shocks while maintaining long-run price stability – conceptual issues', *Achieving Price Stability* (Federal Reserve Bank of Kansas City).

——(1999) 'The robustness and efficiency of monetary policy rules as guidelines for interest rate setting by the European Central Bank', *Journal of Monetary Economics* 43: 655–79.

Tobin, J. (1969) 'Discussion', *Inflation: Its Causes, Consequences, and Control*, ed. S. W. Rousseas (New York: New York University).

Walsh, C. E. (1998) *Monetary Theory and Policy* (Cambridge, Mass.: MIT Press).

Walters, A. A. (1971) 'Consistent expectations, distributed lags, and the quantity theory', *Economic Journal* 81: 273–81.

Watson, M. W. (1993) 'Measures of fit for calibrated models', *Journal of Political Economy* 101: 1011–41.

Woodford, M. (1995) 'Price-level determinacy without control of a monetary aggregate', *Carnegie–Rochester Conference Series* 43: 1–46.

7A   Explanatory strategies for monetary policy analysis

MARY S. MORGAN

'Theories' and 'evidence' combine in several different explanatory strategies in these two papers. Ben McCallum's paper uses the categories to explain the history of the changing ideas about monetary policy analysis over the last three decades. In so doing, he reveals something of the way theory and evidence are used in models for making monetary policy. David Hendry uses the categories in providing an econometric analysis of inflation to cover the long-run history. But this description gives no sense of just how differently these two papers use the resources of theory, evidence, and history.

1. Mill's sciences of history and political economy

To discuss these differences, and provide a context for my remarks on these papers, I go back to John Stuart Mill's views on the role of evidence and general laws in history compared to political economy. Mill understood that applying abstract science to the particular case was like history, where many individual circumstances had to be taken into account in explaining events. In a recent discussion of Mill's early struggles to define a science of history, Neil De Marchi (1998)[1] suggests that Mill took from Bentham's discussion of juridical evidence the notion that all the elements which made up the specific circumstances of an event could equally be thought of as *contributing* causes. Later, in his 1836 essay, Mill outlined a method for economic science which focused on a single main cause and viewed all the other explanatory circumstances as *disturbing* causes—to be stripped away in theorizing and then to be gradually added back in empirical work in such a way that we might perhaps hope to measure their combined impact in specific cases. Mill never really delivered on the latter empirical work, but did deliver on the former theorizing with his picture of *homo economicus* (1836). In this move, Mill pictured economic man as being driven by one overriding motivation, with two 'perpetual countermotives' which needed to be stripped away (along with all the other occasional motivations) to get at the true abstraction.

In the philosophy of science, the notion of 'disturbing causes' is often exemplified with the study of planetary motion, where the paths of planets are subject to disturbing

---

[1] My account of Mill's early views on history are gleaned from Neil De Marchi's stimulating paper on the topic. I thank him for this help, but needless to say, he bears no responsibility for any misinterpretation of his arguments about Mill.

influences which are considered not important, that is, not causes that really count as part of explanation, not elements required in describing the true laws of planetary motion. It is in this tradition, the same tradition as that of Mill's *homo economicus* example, that the practice of monetary policy modelling discussed by McCallum lies. Indeed, I suggest that a legitimate characterization of the modern method of modelling as practised in economic theorizing today is to understand it as a direct descendant of that methodological move made by Mill in the 1830s.

By contrast, in Mill's early view of a science of history, the circumstances which determine an event were not to be stripped away, for they were contributing causes in determining the event. Here the problem for Mill was assessing the degree of similarity of circumstances over many events in order to compile similar cases and so provide general historical explanations. Mill did think, at one point in his life, that with such analogical reasoning, you could follow a science of history—though as De Marchi points out, he did not get very far with this project. If we take Mill's science of history (rather than of his political economy), and the importance of taking account of all circumstances while at the same time trying to provide a general account, then it is in this tradition that Ben McCallum's historical sketch explaining why monetary economics has changed over the last thirty years lies.

Taking Mill's project for a science of history together with Mill's full prescription for an empirical science of political economy gives us a way to place David Hendry's paper in the methodology of econometrics: applying the science of political economy to the specific case, like doing history, requires taking account of all the causes or circumstances. The disturbing causes must be understood again as contributing causes. It is important to note that in placing his work in these lines, I do not characterize it as is empiricism, in the way that Wesley Clair Mitchell's statistical business-cycle programme, for example, might be understood. Why not? Because Hendry's programme is essentially a modelling programme.[2] But of what kind and what is the importance of this? It seems to be not of the same kind as that professed by Chris Sims (1996) which aims at data reduction or compression, with an explicit analogy to the same kind of stripped-down laws as thought to be true of physics and as exemplified in Mill's *homo economicus*. The difference seems to be that in David Hendry's long-run applied study of inflation, the aim of the modelling is not to reach stripped-down laws, but to represent the world in such a way as to retain its full complexity of contributing causes and circumstances. Of course this probably involves data reduction and compression, but the aim is representation, and via that, explanation, not reduction *per se*.

I want to stress that the two modelling traditions evident in the papers by McCallum and Hendry are associated with different explanatory aims. One characteristic of both kinds of models is that they have a representative role. Such small mathematical models as discussed by McCallum represent, primarily, the theoretical claims of their

---

[2] In contrast, Mitchell did not go in for models. He did produce representations, but these were primarily as measuring devices—his aim with statistics seems to have been description and measurement not explanation. Though his work certainly was not theory-free, the theory did not seep very far into the representations—it is difficult to see them as models.

authors about the stripped-down laws or structure of the economy. Hendry's models are also representations. They provide a statistical representation of the data from the economy, but they are unusual in the extent to which they also represent both a set of theoretical claims about the economy as well as a set of specific historical circumstances which affect the economy. Such representations are critical to the purpose of interpreting or explaining what happens in the world.[3]

2. Econometrics as a science of history

In the traditional philosophical account of scientific explanation, the 'covering law' account, we explain with exceptionless laws which operate under well-defined circumstances. Faced with several such claims, we must choose between them, otherwise we are guilty of overdetermination. In history, though we might locate causes with lawlike features, there are good reasons why we might combine several such causes, as well as incorporating many special circumstances, into our explanations. For example, accounts of the Great Depression based on single-law explanations fail miserably. For a satisfactory explanation, we need to appeal not only to monetary theory, Keynesian theory, and so forth, but also to the specific historical circumstances of 1929–34.

This divide is not purely a difference of explanatory aim between the mathematical models of theorizing and econometrics. Econometrics may itself fall into either camp in this divide. As Hendry suggests (page 96), 'most explanations are either mono-causal (. . .) or mono-sectoral.' That kind of econometrics, which holds to one theoretical device and divorces from historical claims, implicitly relies on the covering law mode of explanation and follows a different explanatory aim from that exemplified in Hendry's paper. Perhaps this difference can be also be interpreted in terms of the clever distinction Kevin Hoover has made between econometrics as testing conducted under 'apriorism' and 'econometrics as observation' (1994). Mono-causal models are more often associated with the former, while David Hendry's paper would come under the latter I suggest. Of course, it must be understood that 'observation' in science is a no less demanding and difficult task than theory testing. As De Marchi notes, quoting from Mill's 1836 essay:

[H]e [Mill] lamented that the particular causes operating in any particular instance (in political economy) are 'not revealed to us by infallible authority'. Instead those causes 'are to be collected by observation; and observation in circumstances of complexity [read: where multiple causes operate] is apt to be imperfect. Some of the causes may lie *beyond* observation; many are apt to escape it, unless we are on the look-out for them; and it is only the habit of long and accurate observation which can give us so correct a preconception what causes we are likely to find as shall induce us to look for them in the right quarter. (De Marchi 1998: 15; quoting from Mill 1836: 332)

---

[3] See Morrison and Morgan (1999) for a discussion of the importance of representation in models and the possibility of learning about both theories and the world from using models.

Hendry's programmatic statement of 1980 quotes Hicks that 'as economics pushes on beyond "statics" it becomes less like science and more like History.' Hendry commented (1980: 402) 'While this correctly highlights both the importance of the historical context and the fact that there is only one realization of any economic time series, it does *not* rule out a scientific approach to dynamic economics.' What kind of science is in this current Hendry paper? I think it makes sense to understand it as a science of history. In Hendry's approach, the description of the theory elements provides a framework and it is assumed that all such general accounts are potentially relevant to the specific historical period at hand. It does not assume, a priori, that any one is sufficient for explanation of the historical record, but rather that, as Mill suggested (and historians would concur), you would need to combine them to get a satisfactory explanation of specific events in political economy. This is effectively how historians set about explaining events (see for example, Hawthorn 1991). But it also resembles Mill's second move in the science of political economy: the inclusion of both generally and occasionally relevant other factors. As we see in Hendry's paper: 'inflation is deemed to be the resultant of all forces of excess demand.... and the empirical evidence below accords a role to many of the potential effects. In particular, the evidence explicitly excludes any single factor being the sole explanation' (page 98). Because of this eclecticism about theory, critics from the tradition of small abstract modelling complain of a very casual use of theory. Of course this is symmetric with the reverse critique from econometricians about the casual use of observations by those working with small abstract models.

The aim of empirical explanation, explanation for the specific case, is not without wider support even if not all share Hendry's eclecticism about theory use. Richard Lipsey (in commenting on another paper at the conference) referred to the example of Douglas North, whom he characterized as having a 'big theory' but who recognized that he must also explain how it fits every case; all the circumstances have to be filled in. Econometrics as a science of history might be characterized as providing more general accounts (or models) within which we can also explain specific events of history. This is surely a definition with which one of the founding fathers of econometrics, Jan Tinbergen, could agree, and one which matches the suggestion of Chris Sims (in a different context at the conference) that 'a good system model should provide a story about each individual historical episode.'

My account of the process of the historical explanation supposed in this view of econometric modelling does not yet incorporate another element, one conceived in Mill's science of history, namely that it would rest on similarity reasoning by which like events would be recognized and built up into a general account of certain kinds of events. In Hendry's paper we see this process of reasoning at work in the way that specific historical circumstances are considered in the form of indicator variables. Hendry's use of these variables is to consider each historical event in terms of similarity with other such events. How similar do two war effects have to be to count as the same? Can we recognize patterns in data from historically similar events, and justify these patterns with statistical measures? As we see from Hendry, the analogical reasoning or similarity argument is used to determine exactly how the historical circumstances are taken into account in the equation.

How far then should we characterize Hendry's econometrics as a science of history? It is well known that it relies on both the development of appropriate statistical technologies (to which he has been an important contributor) and the development of a systematic general-to-specific modelling strategy. As we have seen, in that modelling, 'most extant theories of inflation are given the opportunity to matter—so that no "single cause" explanation is imposed from the outset.' In addition, specific historical circumstances are allowed to play their role. Thus criteria from economic theory, from statistical theory, and from economic history all play their part in suggesting and deciding the contents and process of the modelling.

But it seems that it is also helpful to understand Hendry's modelling strategy as a whole in relation to particular ideas about the history of the economy. The modelling situation is designed for a long-run data period (1874–1993) characterized by Hendry as one in which

both evolutionary and special factors can intrude to confound modelling. Since the economy is a non-stationary process, the entity about which knowledge is acquired changes over time.... While such factors pose serious challenges to empirical models, they also suggest that abstract theories will exclude much of the policy-relevant environment, and anyway have themselves evolved over time.

In other words: the world has been changing, the policy environment has been time-specific and changing, the abstract theory itself has been changing. In this context, 'the emphasis is on a progressive research strategy, not an attempt to find "economic laws"' (page 86). The aim is rather to use all these resources to get at the evolving structures of the economy[4] but at the same time to be able to give accounts of specific events in the history of the economy.

The paper itself provides, in shorthand form, the typical iteration process of modelling in this tradition, in which assumptions of changing structure and circumstances, rather than single constant laws, are the starting points. Although any published paper can not be 'live' econometrics,[5] we gain a sense of exactly how econometrics as observation is a 'learning-through-doing' modelling process rather than a passive acceptance of evidence viewed through a mono-causal theory lens. It is also a process that involves not only learning about theories but also about the specific circumstances of the world.

---

[4] Modelling is not just aimed at a superficial level. We need to go to the programmatic statements of an earlier paper to see this: 'The first set of tools yields only descriptions of the empirical phenomena, using informal models that are consistent with the main data features, but do not go below the phenomenological level to prise apart the underlying structure of driving forces in the economy. As we proceed, deeper features will emerge, as will tools for deciding if indeed we are discerning structure' (Hendry and Doornik 1995: 77–8).

[5] 'Doing econometric studies live is useful in stressing that econometrics is not a mechanistic application of recipes that ensure useful answers, but instead is an iterative gleaning of information from evidence' (Hendry and Doornik 1995: 100).

3. History of monetary policy

My first experience of working as an economist began in February 1973 when I joined Citibank in London as a research assistant on the same day that the foreign exchange markets closed on the final collapse of the Bretton Woods/Smithsonian system. Over the next two and a half years I worked with Citibank's economist in London, Dr John Atkin, whose job was to explain recent events in the economy, particularly in relation to monetary and trade policy, and to predict exchange rates and interest rates. This was a pretty hard task, because, of course, the economic world in March 1973 was different from that in January 1973. No one knew how floating exchange rates without the dollar peg would work; no one had much sense of what it would mean for monetary policy. He was very successful at predicting interest and exchange rates—but he was an economic historian by training not an economist!

Bennett McCallum's paper offers a history of monetary policy analysis in economics since that period which combines elements of the history of theory, the history of central bank thinking, and the role of empirical evidence in the process of changing beliefs in the economics profession about monetary policy.[6] The paper begins with a period of revolution both in empirical circumstances (the collapse of the old order) and with the 'rational expectations and real-business-cycle revolutions'. Thereafter, the history of the period is presented as one of rather normal science (in the Kuhnian sense) in which the main changes are portrayed as theory developments, along with associated tools such as modelling techniques and the development of the kind of 'testing' programme associated with RBC modelling. In this account, scientific ideas change in a rather explainable way in response to theoretical puzzles, empirical evidence both negative and positive, formal and informal. On the whole, the formal (i.e. 'scientific') empirical evidence is given more credence than informal evidence. Perhaps, given the extent of changes in the world of monetary arrangements and the price inflations of the period, it would have helped to recognize explicitly the events of economic history as a separate category of explanatory factors alongside the empirical evidence from scientific economics. Nevertheless, this rather spare history of monetary policy analysis fits together very nicely; history usually presents a somewhat messier story!

4. Targets and measuring rods: the science of monetary policy

One of the particularly interesting aspects of this history is how what constitutes the instruments and what the targets have changed over the period McCallum discusses. It helps to clarify the issues if we recognize that there are three elements in the monetary policy system: the measurement instrument, the control instrument, and the target to

---

[6] One particular problem, pervasive in this literature, is whether we are talking about the economists' view of the central bank responsibility—or the central bankers' view of their responsibility. McCallum's account is mainly concerned with the beliefs of economists working on monetary policy analysis in and out of central banks.

be controlled, not just two: the measurement instrument is usually overlooked. It may be helpful to think of this by analogy with a household heating system, in which the target to be controlled is the air temperatures the operating instrument of control is the furnace or boiler, and the indicator or measuring rod of the target conditions is the thermometer as in Figure 7A.1.

The way these three separate elements fit together shows us that there are certain criteria which determine whether the system works adequately. (Note that it is the relations and general functions of the instruments which are important in the analogy, not the substantive content of the individual parts.) There needs to be a one-way causal link from control to target, and a second one-way link from target conditions to measuring instrument. There should be no causal link from measuring instrument to target: we should not be able to operate on the measurement system to alter the target system (we cannot alter the air temperature by altering the thermometer reading, only by altering the furnace). We can imagine connecting the measuring rod via some switch device (i.e. a thermostat) to the control instrument so that the measurement system automatically links to the control instrument. But we should not be able to alter the measuring instrument directly from the control system without first altering the target. That is, the presence of this additional switch instrument should not blur the required independence of the measurement function from the control function: the measurement system must measure the target conditions independently of the control system.

Using this analogy for the monetary policy system suggests that we have to be sure about the following elements. First, that the causal relationships between the conditions, the measuring system, the control system, and the target system are one way. The measuring rod must be directly affected by the conditions of the target system (register those changes) but not be directly affected by any change in the control

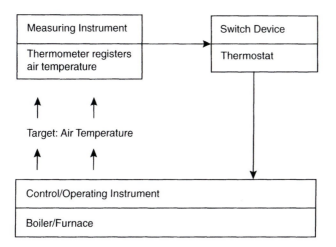

Fig. 7A.1. *Elements in monetary policy system: analogy with household heating system*

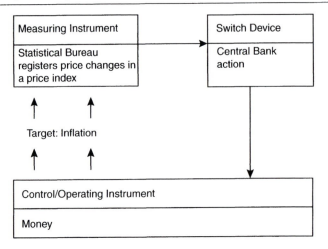

Fɪɢ. 7A.2. *Monetary policy system: analogical example*

system; and the control system must be able to influence the target system in the way we suppose. As an analogical example, in Figure 7A.2, inflation is the target, the control/operating instrument is money, and the target conditions are registered (measured) in a price index calculated by the statistical bureau. Inflation cannot be altered by changing the published price index but only via changes in the control instrument, and only in the way conceived in the workings of the system which relate money changes to price changes. If there is an intervening automatic switch device (like a thermostat that does away with human judgement, which might be equivalent to the central bank following an automatic rule of money control in response to changes registered in the price index), we have to be doubly sure that the measuring apparatus provides an accurate measure of the circumstances and that the operating instrument really works as we assume since it implies that we do not or cannot override the system.

These issues of independence and directions of causal determinacy have important implications which I take up in respect of the methodology of this field. Note that the aim of my analysis here is to be clarificatory of some general issues involved, and to point out what I consider to be oddities about this field, not to be critical of McCallum's excellent and in places deep discussion of the debates and research problems in this field.

To begin with, understanding that there is a measuring device enables us, with the help of McCallum's illuminating discussion, to locate a certain confusion in the conduct and analysis of monetary policy. For example, according to the history given in the paper, in the 1980s in the USA, interest rates became the 'operating target' (that is, the control instrument) but at the same time they were also the 'indicators of monetary conditions' (page 122), while inflation rates became the 'targets' (ibid).[7]

---

[7] As McCallum has argued elsewhere (1997: 11) it would certainly help to clarify these kinds of discussions if the economics literature would stop using 'targets' for both the instruments to operate the control and the thing to be controlled!

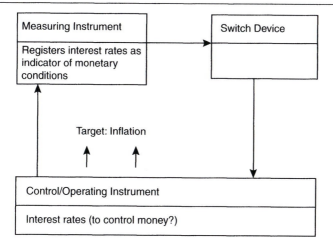

FIG. 7A.3. *Monetary policy system: the 1980s confusion?*

This situation, portrayed in the analogy of Figure 7A.3, easily demonstrates the query—can interest rates be both the measure for monetary conditions (i.e. the thing measured in the thermometer) at the same time as the control variable in the operating system (the furnace)? Only, it seems, if we want to measure the condition of the control instrument, not the target. Otherwise, I think not. The Federal funds rate can be the instrument for control, but if so, it thereby negates an independent measuring role for any interest rate strongly correlated with that rate. Or, interest rates can be a measuring device for monetary conditions, but not at the same time the instrument of control.

In addition, it is striking that if this is a 'science' of monetary policy, what counts as the target, what counts as the control, and what the measuring rod should have been so unstable over a relatively short time and should continue to vary between countries. Science is thought to generate reliable, stable, or generalizable knowledge. Yet, from McCallum's history, it seems that since 1973, we can find monetary policy based on measuring instruments registering R (interest rates), P (prices), or M (money); taking P, M, or Y (income) as the target variable; and taking R or M as the control variable. If this is a science, it does not look much like 'normal' science, but nor does it look like revolutionary change. Rather this evidence suggests a period of more rapid change, uncertainty, or even confusion, than McCallum's 'normal science' history suggests.

I take as a further example, an announcement in the press during the Bergamo meeting that suggested the European Central Bank's monetary policy would be based on an 'explicit inflation target, a monetary reference value and a mix of other indicators' (*Financial Times*, 14/10/98). It is not clear from this report that a distinction is made between the indicators to be measured and the target: is the 'monetary reference value' the target to be controlled or the indicator of conditions? (No doubt because the system has lags, the variables to be measured are likely to include not only recent versions of the target variables, but also other variables which might give indications of the likely future path of the target variable, i.e. 'indicators' of the target variable.) The report went on 'He [Wim Duisenberg] said the monetary pillar would be "thicker", but he made clear that the ECB would not apply its monetary reference range "mechanistically". The ECB's approach marks a distinct departure from the Bundesbank strategy, which has used an explicit monetary target. The Bank of England uses direct inflation targeting' (ibid.). Is the 'monetary pillar' the target? If so, how does a 'thicker pillar' differ from the monetary target of the German tradition? Calls for greater 'transparency' by the ECB during the ensuing year appeared to be a call for clarification of the issue of target versus control variables, as much as the choice of alternative targets.

The opportunity to apply my analogy more directly comes with Section 4 of McCallum's paper, where we have an account of a typical model of three equations employed at two recent conferences and apparently shared between central bank economists and academic economists. This is one of the kind of stripped-down models I referred to earlier in my discussion of Mill's legacy to economics.[8] McCallum's account nicely draws attention to something strange about the model, namely that money does not appear in it. It seems as if any model of this kind without money demand is Hamlet without the ghost.[9] If money were to appear in an additional money-demand equation such as (4), McCallum shows it would be irrelevant to the policy rules and in determining policy actions. Maybe R is the ghost standing in for money? But 'No', R here is the control instrument. The absence of money balances is explained by the assumption of separability, an 'analytical convenience' (page 129) of the model for which 'justification' has not been 'explicitly discussed' (page 130).

In this case, portrayed in Figure 7A.4, we can view the right-hand side of equation (3) as the measuring instrument registering certain changes in inflation and output and the central bank operates merely as the switch device to raise or lower R according to that equation. So equation (3) is interpreted not as a causal claim, but as a registration and a unidirectional rule-setting device equivalent to the thermometer plus thermostat of Figure 7A.1). The level of R set by that equation determines or 'controls' the performance of the economy, whose internal workings are depicted in equations (1) and (2) (the equivalent of the furnace), while in equation (4) we have a description of the inflow required by that system. In other words, we can picture equation (4) as an additional input pipe which draws water (money) into the system to maintain the specified R setting in the furnace (the economy).

It is not clear whether the model discussed here is actually used for policy advice in central banks, but given the closeness of policy analysis to policy advice to policy conduct inside central banks, we might be uneasy, for three reasons. First, while the control equations represented in such small simple models (or even larger ones) can be useful, they can also be potentially dangerous. As we have long understood, and as McCallum notes in his paper, the Lucas critique prefigured in the Marschak critique

---

[8] How far the model is able to explain historical specifics of empirical observations is unclear.

[9] I infer, although it is not explicit in this paper, that McCallum does think money matters.

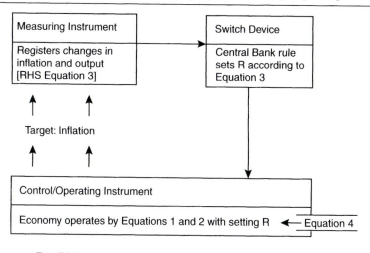

FIG. 7A.4. *Monetary policy system: model from McCallum's paper*

suggests that for policy analysis a structural rather than a reduced form model is required. The status of this model might be open to doubts on this head. McCallum argues (elsewhere)[10] that such an IS equation as shown in equation (1) is structural, meaning that it is one 'in which all the parameters are policy invariant according to the model in hand'. But while it is open to the theorist to define it as structural (rather than as some kind of quasi-reduced form) in the context of a particular model, whether it is genuinely autonomous in all empirical circumstances might be open to doubt. For example, would the model work all right in periods of deflation as well as in periods of inflation? (That is, using our analogy, can we be sure that we can reverse our furnace into an air-conditioner when a different version of the heating problem comes along?) If the conditions assumed in the model are met in practice, then we can use it with confidence, but given the history of the period since 1973 and the variability evident in Hendry's long-run account—who knows?[11]

Second, given that, as McCallum reports, there is not much agreement on the contents of the model, economists suggest that we should, as an alternative, look for a policy rule that is robust to different models. That is, we could have lots of different equations (1) and (2), each of which might have very different theoretical content, or even ignore them altogether, as long as we maintain a viable robust (3). Equivalent in the analogy is the argument that we do not need to know how our furnace works, we do not have to understand or know the theory of a furnace, only how to turn it on and off. This sounds perfectly reasonable, but only because we can locate an engineer who does know the theory and so can fix it when it goes wrong. (The normal critique of this kind of scientific instrumentalism returns us either to the arguments about knowledge of

[10] See e.g. his account with Nelson (1999).
[11] The period since 1973 looks very volatile to an economic historian, but some of Taylor's (1993) findings suggest variance of output and inflation are less under floating rates than under fixed, so maybe in the future we will see these decades as ones of relative calm!

the structure above, or to a despair about the lack of scientific curiosity it portrays.) What would constitute a 'viable robust policy rule'? McCallum's account of the literature suggests that this means one which stands up to lots of different equations (1) and (2) (i.e. stripped down theoretical or abstract models), where the viability and robustness of the policy rule are tested via simulation studies.

But let us look more closely at that policy rule of equation (3). As suggested in the analogy above, we can interpret it as a joint measurement and switching device. It indicates the conditions of the target variable by registering the inflationary pressure in the system and links this to a level of the control variable of interest rates. But if we are to rely on such an equation surely we would want to return to an analysis such as David Hendry's, and have a measuring device to register not just these two pressure points, but all the ones observed to be relevant at various times according to empirical models? That is, we would want to find a measuring device, and thus a policy rule equation, which was robust not just in simulations of small abstract mathematical models, but which had proved its robustness empirically in the science of history sense, robust to dramatic changes and the long-run evolution of the economy as well as for the history of all the pressure points which theorists had dreamt up.

Thirdly, McCallum notes (page 127) the interesting change that monetary policy analysis is 'now typically conducted in terms of a choice between alternative policy rules as contrasted with the choice of policy actions to be taken in a particular episode.' But, presumably, it remains the case that even in the scientific analysis of monetary policy, discretion should never be entirely ruled out in practice or even in theory. The policy rule (such as equation (3)) for setting R should never be entirely mechanical, and not just for technical reasons. The fact that a Taylor-type policy rule like (3) might fit past data is not evidence that the policy rule is like that: is that how R is set by any Central Bank? Nor is it evidence that if we were to start using (3) as our policy rule it would still work or fit (for reasons economists have well rehearsed)! But apart from these points, policy-makers would be irresponsible to choose a policy rule and stick to it without always considering the nature of the here-and-now episodes: the history of the day. Economists don't think much of the non-scientific knowledge base of policy-makers like central bankers, but it often contains immense tacit knowledge about the economy and the banking sector and so forth, just as economists have tacit knowledge about the data, their equations, their models, etc.[12] One of the characteristics of tacit expert knowledge in any field is knowing how far rules will take you, when they can be ignored, and when they should be ignored, for example, when other central bank responsibilities are involved such as the health of the banking sector. Once again, we might return to the Hendry project here. Some historical circumstances are so different, are so important, that judgement and tacit knowledge of all the specific circumstances, that is, the evidence from the science of history, should be incorporated into the policy decisions. In monetary policy particularly, theoretical and empirical analyses of policy which ignore the events of history will remain of limited value.

---

[12] For a discussion of the role of tacit knowledge in using models in economic policy-making, with particular examples from central bank experience, see Den Butter and Morgan, 1998.

5. Epilogue

Mill thought that abstractions were necessary to the scientific pretensions of political economy because they would reveal the true nature of economic activity to us. But he did not think that that was all you needed in order to explain things in the economy. The modern economics equivalent to Mill's abstractions, stripped-down models, are suggestive, insightful perhaps, certainly worth working with, but they are neither sufficient for explanation of particular cases, nor for policy analysis and control. But nor are they necessarily antagonistic to the scientific study of the specific circumstances and contributing causes revealed by empirical work; indeed, for Mill these were complementary activities, two sides of the science of economics. The kind of models discussed by McCallum and those generated by David Hendry are rightly regarded as different species of models, but as I have argued here, following Mill, they are complementary in the sense that stripped-down models are likely to need the help of empirical models to explain the specifics of the world or to be used to intervene in the economy.

REFERENCES

De Marchi, N. (1998) 'Putting evidence in its place: John Mill's early struggles with history', Paper presented at the Leverhulme Conference on 19th Century Historical Political Economy, Cambridge, October 1998.

Den Butter, F. A. G. and M. S. Morgan (1998) 'What makes the models-policy interaction successful?' in *Empirical Models and Policy Making*, Special Issue, *Economic Modelling* 15(3): 443–73.

Hawthorn, G. (1991) *Plausible Worlds* (Cambridge: Cambridge University Press).

Hendry, D. F. (1980) 'Econometrics—Alchemy or Science?' *Economica* 47: 387–406.

—— and J. Doornik (1995) 'A Window on Econometrics', *Cyprus Journal of Economics* 8(2): 77–104.

Hoover, K. D. (1994) 'Econometrics as observation: the Lucas critique and the nature of econometric inference', *Journal of Economic Methodology* 1(1): 65–80.

McCallum, B. T. (1997) 'Issues in the design of monetary policy rules', NBER Working Paper 6016.

—— and E. Nelson (1999) 'An optimising IS-LM specification for monetary policy and business cycle analysis', *Journal of Money, Credit and Banking* 31(3): 296–316.

Mill, J. S. (1836) 'On the definition of Political Economy', repr. in *Methodology of Economics: Nineteenth-Century British Contributions, 1: John Stuart Mill* Introduction by R. E. Backhouse (London: Routledge, 1997)

Morrison, M. and M. S. Morgan (1999) 'Models as mediating instruments', in *Models as Mediators*, ed. by M. S. Morgan and M. Morrison (Cambridge: Cambridge University Press).

Sims, C. A. (1996) 'Macroeconomics and Methodology', *Journal of Economic Perspectives* 10(1): 105–120.

Taylor, J. B. (1993) 'Discretion versus policy rules in practice', *Carnegie-Rochester Conference Series on Public Policy* 39: 195–214.

7B Monetary policy: general discussion

Bennett McCallum: In writing down this little three-equation system I meant at least two of those equations to refer to blocks of equations. One of the studies that I was talking about, the one by Brayton *et al.* (1997), was using as their model the Fed's existing model which has, say, fifty stochastic equations and a bunch of identities, but the logical structure of it was as I was describing. So I did not feel that anything I was saying really hinged on the model being small.

David Hendry: Theories are, of course, a priori creations of the human mind. We invent the names of the concepts. We invent the properties they are going to satisfy. We invent the rules by which they can be manipulated, and economics has got a very big set of tools for doing that. Much of the profession does accept a particular framework for doing this, which McCallum spelt out in terms of intertemporal optimization with rational expectations. My belief is that agents mimic that, but do not do that. That is, the sort of evidence that I am presenting would not fit in with any of these theories, particularly the one-factor theory that McCallum put forward, for example, precisely because if we can't, with every variable we have thought of, and all the theoretical knowledge we have got, come up with models that explain most of the salient periods of history, I fail to see how agents can form rational expectations *ex ante* about these events.

Let's take 1917. It depended on whether tanks were successful on the Western Front, whether the Germans decided to prosecute the war despite America's entry into it, whether France decided to launch a major offensive against Germany. All these are things agents would have had to have formed rational expectations about in 1916 to predict the inflation rate in 1917 and I just regard that as absurd. The same with knowing that the oil crisis is going to happen. To have a formation of expectations one period ahead is very different from this altogether. It was on the slide that Morgan put up that agents have minimal rules for doing this—that they mimic rationality. In this sort of world, $\Delta^2 \log P = 0$ (the assumption that inflation does not persistently accelerate throughout history) works as an unbiased predictor, on average, over the entire period. There is nothing rational about it. It is not even a forecast in a certain sense, although it fits in with the view that you model all these breaks as being an $I(2)$ rather than an $I(1)$ effect, but you do not systematically reject such a trivial little model. Now if agents wanted to have a way of avoiding systematic errors, they would not form rational expectations—they haven't the faintest idea what the data generation process is, they don't know what information to condition on, they don't know the events that would be there to condition on, they don't know even how to begin to tackle that problem—but they could have formed unbiased expectations by using this very simple rule, just predicting inflation one step ahead by looking at what it was last period. That rule mimics rationality. It is rather like Morgan's servo-mechanism. It is rather like the thermometer. It doesn't need to predict the temperature outside but would get much better behaviour out of the system if it did. If the thermometer was intelligent and could look ahead and see, 'The temperature has been going up, the sun is out, it will go even higher. Put on more air-conditioning now and you will get the temperature to what you want it to be rather more quickly.' That is an issue of efficiency rather than unbiasedness or predictability. And these theoretical models that are underlying what I am doing are much more like the hydrologist's theoretical model. I think it is simply unimaginable where hydrology would be today if hydrologists had insisted on working out the theory of turbulence from quantum dynamics. They wouldn't have made one iota of a contribution to understanding it because it is a system property and it is enormously complicated how turbulence behaves, how waves behave, how they propagate, etc. They have theories about all these things that are macrotheories. They are not based on individual agents. I don't work with that kind of model because I simply do not see how one agent trades with itself in the stock market and forms all these expectations and carries out intertemporal optimization, etc., etc. I simply don't see how it is done and I don't know how to do it with a hundred million heterogeneous agents with different endowments, different intelligence, different knowledge stocks, different ways in which they form all their expectations. Many of them make mistakes: many of them buy houses at the top of housing booms—they are clearly not forming any kind of sensible expectations, let alone rational ones. So I just think you need a macrotheory. Morgan calls it casual, and I agree it is not enormously spelt out in the paper. But it is spelt out in some of my earlier papers. I think it is still the programme Morgan put up and I do not back off from any of what I said there, although I had not thought of myself as inventing a science of history, nor was I aware of Mill being an antecedent. It certainly is not an empiricist programme. The aim is to find out, given the welter of non-constancy that we observe, whether we can get somewhere towards a constant understanding of them over the period. I admit that the number of dummies tells you I have failed, but I would be very interested to see what models would actually succeed in doing this given all the variables that I have tried.

Adrian Pagan: I notice that on the right-hand side of one of Hendry's equations there is a variable called 'exchange rate' (EER_t). When I was thinking about how I would try to work this into a system, thinking of a recursive VAR-type system, it seemed rather odd to me that I would have the exchange rate on the right-hand side rather than on the left-hand side in the period of floating exchange rates. In a period of fixed exchange rates that would seem to be a sensible thing. That is a sort of exogeneity question.

Hendry: That is why I pointed out that we fitted this model to data over fixed exchange rates and then gave you the predictions over how it worked over floating exchange rates. It actually gives this wonderful prediction that in 1992, when the UK quit EMU, there wouldn't be any inflation, and that is what happened. It said there wouldn't be because we were devaluing from an enormously overvalued situation in a period of recession. There were lots of people in Britain who were terrified of the inflation that was going to follow from that.

Pagan: McCallum's is quite a nice paper. But like Morgan, I would have liked it to be a little messier. In particular I would have liked it to discuss some of the issues which have come up but are not discussed, such as the role of money. I know it is true that in your simple model, and a lot of the characterizations, money has disappeared, but within central banks there is an enormous amount of discussion about just why money is important and most of it goes under the heading of the asset-price channel. There is much discusssion about whether monetary rules, if they exist, should be based upon looking at asset prices as well. Once you are in the asset-price world, and I think a lot of that is the thinking behind the European Central Bank, then you really do have to think about how you would introduce it into these models. If it doesn't come through the IS curve as a real balance effect, then I think you are looking at some sort of New Keynesian-type mechanism. There has been a lot of discussion about that and I would have liked to have seen a little discussion of this in the paper.

The second thing that I thought was missing was the monetary-conditions index material. I know you don't like the monetary-conditions index but there are enough central banks round the world who do use a monetary-conditions index that some attention needs to be paid to it in a paper that is a survey of what has actually happened. I know central banks love the simple model you describe, because it always makes them look good. John Taylor (1993) took the Henderson rule and showed how well it worked in describing central bank behaviour, but there's an awful lot of fooling around to get that equation to work. It works all right for the American economy after I have fiddled around with the target inflation rate and after I have fiddled around with what the actual output gap is. If I go to a lot of other countries, it doesn't work at all without a tremendous amount of effort. The paper, however, captures very well what has been going on in theory and evidence. The only thing I would say about it is that when you say academics and central bank staff think the same way and do the same sort of analysis, that is because they only invite along to conferences people who think the same way as they do.

Andrew Oswald: I am a labour economist who finds this quite a strange conference to come to because people seem so passionately to oppose each other, not just about economic substance. So it seems sensible to work out the differences and, more importantly, the agreements, between McCallum and Hendry. Let's look at McCallum's equation (2). Are they basically in agreement on this equation except for the expectations term? Is that where the disagreement is coming?

McCallum: Hendry really doesn't like that formulation, in part because a large part of the explanatory power is on the forward-looking expectational variable. Most of what I have said doesn't hinge on this formulation, but in the studies that I am talking about these were typically forward-looking specifications.

Pagan: They have normally got backward-looking terms as well, and the explanation is along the lines that Hendry suggested. In the slowdown of inflation in the early 1990s most people assumed inflation would carry on as before.

McCallum: This is not *my* favourite.

Hendry: I certainly want to treat expectations differently, and it would be rather closer to the expectations model that Adrian has done, which would give you ΔP_{t-1}. You have now picked up two out of the twelve variables. So what else do I want to put in there? McCallum might say that it is the $\bar{y}$ bit—that some of my data were actually determining $\bar{y}$. I doubt that, but some of them might be. My $\bar{y}$ is a very simplistic specification and it could be that other variables like the interest rate are, but you can't rewrite it. If you try to model mine as $\bar{y}$ being close to the sort of thing that might come out of equation (1) as the equilibrium growth rate for real output, you have great difficulty finding interest rates having any effect. One of the reasons I was writing this paper is that recently I have been giving a lot of lectures at the Bank of England and I was really getting very concerned that they are basing everything on the hope that interest rates are a powerful enough tool in shifting aggregate demand and the exchange rate, which also shifts aggregate demand, to bring the economy back again every time inflation goes up. My model finds lots of other things come in there. Past wages come in there. The Bank obviously think that's right. Whenever wage rates went up they upped the interest rate to try to dampen it down. They think the exchange rate comes in there. Again, they look at the exchange rate and say, 'Well, we won't put interest rates up too high because the exchange rate is overvalued.' All these things are in their thinking. Now you may want to argue that you can rewrite the model in terms of $\bar{y}$, but I couldn't. But I am not saying that is impossible.

McCallum: I wouldn't put the exchange rate influences into $\bar{y}$. I would make it an open economy model. Mine in the second session of these conferences is such. A point worth making is that I quite agree that equation (2), the price adjustment formulation, is something about which macroeconomists do not agree. I have a footnote in the paper saying that my own candidate for the weakest component in a macroeconomic model is the price-adjustment sector. By weakest I mean the one on which there is least professional agreement. I could provide a long list of the price-adjustment theories that are current. It is not the case that there is agreement among macroeconomists about the right specification of equation (2).

I am surprised to hear people, including Morgan, saying that there is something funny about this policy rule. It matches exactly the newspaper and television accounts and all our commonsense accounts of what central bankers do. They get in the room and they sit and they argue about which is the bigger problem: inflation or unemployment. Well, those are the two terms on the right-hand side of the rule there and they argue about which of these two terms is quantitatively going to dominate and at the end of all that they raise interest rates if inflation is the bigger problem and they lower them if unemployment is the bigger problem. That is all that equation says.

Carlo Favero: The Bundesbank would not agree.

McCallum: Officially they would not agree, but that is what they do, just like anyone else.

Hendry: May I add one caveat to that. I think they change μ_1 and μ_2 [in McCallum's equation (3)] dramatically and regularly and sometimes in Britain it is the balance of payments deficit that does it and not either of these factors. But otherwise we are pretty much in agreement.

Favero: Moreover this rule explains the result that we do not understand much of inflation. According to this rule, if the central banker is not brave enough to set μ_1 lower than 1, inflation can get anywhere, and this could be an explanation for your inability to get rid of dummies.

Hendry: I will come back to that, but I do not think that is what actually went on.

Huw Dixon: Equation (2) is basically a long-run Phillips curve, as you would find in any standard intermediate macro textbook. But it has gone through an interesting history. There is the original literature in the early 1970s, looking at this sort of equation, but then it flipped round and became the Lucas supply curve so that the $y - \bar{y}$ went on the left side and you had the price expectation on the right. Now that we have this monetary policy stuff, it has suddenly flipped round again and now you have output on the right-hand side explaining inflation. What is also interesting is that a lot of the theory which gave rise to the arguments about central bank independence was based on the Lucas supply curve, the surprise version, where price expectations were on the other side. Equation (1) is also interesting because there is the basic question, 'Do real interest rates affect the economy?' I think they do, and obviously we can think of examples, German unification and so on, but, going back to Friedman, and I agree with Friedman on this, with long and unpredictable lags. I would be very interested to see what the empirical evidence for equation (1) is, where you have quite an instantaneous effect of real interest rates on output.

McCallum: That is very hard to fit. The Fed uses thirty-five equations for equation (1).

Hendry: With post-war quarterly data for Britain, equation (1) works very well. Over the whole sample period I cannot get it to work. There is some irreconcilability there that needs some deeper study than I have been able to do. But Mizon and I (1993) find that equation, not with $g - \bar{g}$, but with basically the first line of (1): a strong cointegrating relationship with the trend in as an approximation to the $\bar{y}$ term that we have in there. It works within a number of studies that we have done.

Dixon: Turning to Hendry's paper, when I looked at the preferred equation, it is explaining inflation basically by world inflation, lagged wages, and so on. To a certain extent, if I were a monetarist I would be thinking that it could still be money that is really driving inflation.

Hendry: That is why I call them proximate determinants throughout the paper, deliberately because underlying it all, something else could be driving it and to do that you have to complete the entire system. Not only wages, but the exchange rate might rise and fall with the money stock. All I am saying is that if you look at the actual inflation equation and give these other things a free chance, that's what turns out.

Christopher Sims: I found the paper interesting, mostly for the graphs. It is worthwhile to look at data over very long periods of time and we don't very often do that. But the paper illustrates many of the things that bother me most about Hendry's methodological approaches. The paper contains no discussion of the economics of this equation. The question is, 'What is this equation meant to be used for?' Hendry has, in the discussion here and also in the paper, mentioned that the equation can be useful only in the context of a larger system, but we don't have an explanation of what that larger system would look like. There is no way we can know that an estimate of a single equation relationship like this is going to be useful in a larger system without some discussion of how that larger system would be identified and how we can know that this equation does not mix together the influences we would like to treat, the relationships that reflect the determination of policy variables, and the relationships that reflect the reaction of the economy to policy variables. This underlies the uneasiness that has already been expressed by various people about having, on the right-hand side, variables that are clearly endogenous from the point of view of thinking about how the private sector reacts and clearly respond directly to policy and are part of a policy reaction function, like exchange rates, interest rates, and money variables. We don't even have a discussion of why P is on the left and not other t-dated variables. In a systems context, the fact that we estimate this equation by least squares is just unsupported in the paper. So I am very mistrustful about the idea that we could use this equation to answer questions about how to control inflation.

I think that the reason Hendry thinks he can proceed this way is that he has a tendency to rely on stability of statistical relationships in place of economic reasoning. I think that is a mistake. Stable statistical relationships can turn out to be trivial, and they can turn out not to be identified once we consider the underlying stochastic economic theory. Worse, this equation is not even structural relative to time shifts. That is, it is not even useful for forecasting. There are two reasons for that. One is the reason Hendry has already mentioned: that to forecast you have to have forecasts of these right-hand side variables that are part of the whole system. It is not really a forecast to push this equation forward in artificial time, where you get to push in the values of these right-hand side variables at their observed values. The equation is not a forecasting equation as it is written.

But more important and fundamental is the strategy of using a sequence of dummy variables. Morgan has already pointed out the fact that this can make one uneasy. Calling these variables deterministic does not make them so. This really reflects a very fundamental difference in methodological approaches between somebody like me who takes a Bayesian, basically subjectivist view of randomness, and Hendry who I am sure does not. But the fact is, having observed the need for a large number of deterministic dummy variables to explain the behaviour of inflation historically in the context of this equation, sensible people, including me and probably Hendry, must assume that more of these will be needed in the future. In order to use this model for forecasting, we have to ask ourselves how long do we think it will be before the next dummy variable is needed, how big it will be, and what its effects are going to be. To be useful, even for forecasting, a model like this must, at least implicitly, better formally, account for the fact that these dummy variables are actually a certain kind of random disturbance term. I think one way to describe what Hendry is finding is something that is actually pervasive in macroeconomics, more pervasive in monthly time-series than in the longer time-units, but maybe it has to do with relatively how long a sample is, that we get large outlier disturbances. People have been spending more time trying to get the linear structure right than trying to go back and do the very difficult job of doing the econometrics right recognizing that we have fat-tailed distributions on the disturbances. But this kind of equation can't even be thought of as part of a forecasting system that is seriously useful until the nature of the randomness that is implicit in these 'deterministic' dummies is clarified.

Hendry: There is probably a very different view of forecasting underlying how we are thinking about these problems. I have actually changed my view in the last six months quite radically on it and agree *slightly* more with Sims than I would have done six months ago. It is basically in terms of 'Are economists in the business of forecasting earthquakes?' Say you are forecasting the US economy. Then strictly, since there is a chance of an enormous earthquake in the mid-West, an enormous earthquake in California, all your models should build in some probability of these earthquakes occurring and you should modify your forecasts accordingly. But just imagine going to a policy-maker and saying, 'I have got this weighted average of my probabilities of Los Angeles and San Francisco disappearing and the mid-West vanishing and that is going to give a fall of 85 per cent in GNP, otherwise it is going up by $2\frac{1}{2}$ per cent so my weighted average means it is going up by 1 per cent. I think that is just not very helpful. What this model can forecast is conditional on there not being another war—the dummies are only in there for wars, not because they are outliers—or another oil crisis. Then the forecasts have the properties I expect them to have. Other than those, I agree I have to forecast these awkward interaction terms, and they are very difficult to forecast.

You asked how I got this equation. This equation is simply the first equation out of a VAR, conditional on world prices and exchange rates. Why is it conditional on exchange rates? Because in almost all the sample in which it was developed, exchange rates were fixed. It was not built over a floating exchange rate period. There was a very small part of it in the 1930s when the exchange rate floated, but for the most part they were fixed. Consequently I think it is perfectly valid to ask the question by conditioning on them, because they are in that sense not stochastic variables of the kind you think of. This is the first equation of the VAR. The money-demand equation uses essentially the same variables at the outset. So does the output equation, the interest rate equation, etc. They just happen to have a little bit of extra conditioning relative to the VAR. So if you think this is lacking identification, unless you think it is purely due to the conditioning on world inflation, then I think you ought to think seriously about all your VARs.

McCallum: From the long-run point of view that your paper is taking, the exchange rate is not fixed. As a sort of quasi-monetarist I want to point out how nicely your evidence conforms with monetarist thinking about these things. Your departure from purchasing power parity is absolutely tiny over this whole sample, despite enormous changes in the price level. A lot of the explanatory power of the year-to-year stuff is coming from temporary deviations from purchasing power parity. Now purchasing power parity is a monetarist proposition—it is the quantity theory applied to an open economy. Both purchasing power parity and the quantity theory are implications of the notion of long-run monetary neutrality. Purchasing power parity is the statement that the real exchange rate is, from a long-run perspective, unaffected by major changes in monetary variables.

Hendry: In fact the original equation was formulated as a *ppp* equation. Then we undid the bits to get it down to inflation.

James Hartley: I would like to return to Oswald's question because I am not sure it was really answered. I would like to rephrase it. Hendry has this long equation (10) which is much like McCallum's equation (2). Is the difference here a theoretical difference, that one of you does not like the theory that the other one is using? Is it an evidence difference? What is the heart of the difference here and how do we locate it?

Hendry: If one took McCallum's equation seriously, then obviously most empirical efforts should go into modelling the expected future price inflation, because that is the key variable in that equation. You would also not put into that equation lots of the other things that I think possibly do matter in that equation. So if you then based your policy advice purely on how agents have formed that expectation—which is a reduced form restriction in a particular sense—and only the deviation of output from its natural growth rate or whatever, then if it happened that past wages were the major determinant and didn't enter the $E(\Delta P_{t+1})$ you would simply get policy wrong. So that is the kind of difference. What worries me a lot about theoretical models is that they don't spell out enough how eclectic one has to be in order to explain the history. I could have dropped the war years, and maybe Sims would have been happier if the war years weren't in there at all, but I think the war years, being the biggest shocks we have had, are the most informative and ought to be looked at. If they can't be fitted with the theory we need to know why, because in wars it is quite important to control inflation, not to have labour doing crazy things, for example, and not to have firms making excess profits and making social disruption.

Katarina Juselius: Hendry's paper is partly graphical and I think that is very useful. I think also that the two major features of your model are that you have the several disequilibrium relations and the unexplained dummies. I then looked at the graphs of the deviations from steady state. The picture was somehow unclear because you have these two effects. It would be clearer if the effects of the dummies could be removed so that you could see the pure disequilibrium effect.

We are here in order to understand why we differ on methodological questions. If you take McCallum's equations (2)–(4), because I did not include government expenditure in the information set I talked about today, and instead of having expectations you say expectations are exactly equal to the actual outcome, getting rid of the expectations operator, then I think what I suggested in the end is very similar to what you have there. The only difference, as far as I can see, is that my approach started from a description using statistical rules, whereas you have economic explanations and economic reasoning. In a sense I think one should be able somehow to get down and ask whether the differences are so large after all, because I don't think they really are when one gets to the end.

McCallum: I would like to agree, but there is one thing that I cannot agree with. Even if you take out the government spending variable, the logic of the kind of system that I am describing makes you use equation (1), not (4). If the central bank is running monetary policy with an interest rate instrument, then it is simply feeding out however much money the system demands, period by period, to make the interest rate prevail. So that all that last equation is doing is telling how much money comes into the system, whereas you haven't got rid of the first equation, which is saving and investment behaviour. That kind of behaviour is still important in the economy and so, even without government spending in the model at all, you still have to, by the logic of central bank operating procedures, stick with the first three equations for the simultaneous determination of those three variables.

Juselius: The reason why I had the money demand in my discussion was that I started off with Romer's treatment. I ended up by saying that it cannot have any impact under very general conditions.

McCallum: I have a disagreement on this with Romer, not with you.

Hendry: I took up modelling money demand because Alan Walters was in the room next to me at LSE and Alan was convinced that money caused everything. It caused output, it caused inflation, it caused the exchange rate, it caused absolutely everything. I took up modelling money demand in order to demonstrate that money was essentially an epiphenomenon in the economy. So we completely agree that equation (4) is right at the bottom there. It is nearly irrelevant, but to persuade government officials of that has taken more than a decade and a half of very hard work. It is still the case that some government officials think that the stock of money is the most important thing in the economy.

McCallum: Whether it is an epiphenomenon or not depends on the central bank operating procedures. If the central bank uses the money stock as its instrument variable, then it would have to be included in the system. Actual central banks today don't.

Oswald: Did you believe it was an epiphenomenon before you started?

Hendry: Yes. I started because Alan was so convinced that you had to control it.

Oswald: Isn't it rather dangerous to have started this big statistical exercise with this?

Hendry: You have to have a reason for starting with things.

Martin Eichenbaum: There is a potential thing that would make the McCallum's paper even nicer than it is and it points to some of the tensions in the desire for simplicity when we model and the desire for richness of detail when we actually go to the data. I want to recommend an article to McCallum, written by one of his best students, Charlie Evans (Evans and Croushore, mimeo) where he actually says 'How does the Taylor rule look in real time?' He makes the enormous effort to actually get the data available to policy-makers at the time they make their decisions, the actual price level and things that they could get. What you see is, sure enough, that qualitatively it looks OK. But there are huge deviations in that ε_t. It displays a great deal of serial correlation. Now the flip side of that equation (3) is one equation in one of these identified VARs. That is just literally one of these equations. I think it would be useful to make that connection—how much is missing from those identified VARs in the list of variables, etc.

REFERENCES

Brayton, F., Levin, A., Tryon, R., and Williams, J. C. (1997) 'The evolution of macro models at the Federal Reserve Board', *Carnegie-Rochester Conference Series on Public Policy* 47: 43–81.
Evans, C. L. and Croushore, D. (mimeo) 'Data revisions and the identification of monetary policy shocks' (Federal Reserve Bank of Chicago).
Hendry, D. F. and Mizon, G. E. (1993) 'Evaluating dynamic econometric models by encompassing the VAR', in P. C. B. Phillips (ed.), *Models, Methods and Applications of Econometrics* (Oxford: Blackwell): 272–300.
Taylor, J. (1993), 'Discretion versus Policy Rules in Practice', *Carnegie-Rochester Conference Series on Public Policy* 39: 195–214.

Part III

THE INFLUENCE OF RECENT DEVELOPMENTS IN ECONOMETRIC TECHNIQUES

8 Models and relations in economics and econometrics

KATARINA JUSELIUS

1. Introduction

Empirical macroeconomic models based on a probability approach (Haavelmo 1943) explicitly start from a stochastic formulation of the chosen data. Because most macro-economic data exhibit strong time dependence, it is natural to formulate the empirical model in terms of time-dependent stochastic processes. Within this family the vector autoregressive (VAR) process based on Gaussian errors has proved to be a popular choice. There are many reasons for this: the VAR model is flexible, easy to estimate, and it usually gives a good fit to macroeconomic data. However, the possibility of combining long-run and short-run information in the data by exploiting the cointegration property is probably the most important reason why the cointegrated VAR model continues to receive the interest of both econometricians and applied economists.

Theoretical economic models, on the other hand, have traditionally been developed as non-stochastic mathematical entities and applied to empirical data by adding a stochastic error process to the mathematical model. As an example of this approach I will use the macroeconomic treatment in 'Inflation and Monetary Policy', ch. 9 in D. Romer (1996): *Advanced Macroeconomics*.

From an econometric point of view the two approaches are fundamentally different: one starting from an explicit stochastic formulation of *all* data and then *reducing* the general statistical (dynamic) model by imposing testable restrictions on the parameters, the other starting from a mathematical (static) formulation of a theoretical model and then *expanding* the model by adding stochastic components. For a detailed methodological discussion of the two approaches, see for example, Gilbert (1986), Hendry (1995), Juselius (1993), and Pagan (1987).

Unfortunately, the two approaches have been shown to produce very different results even when applied to identical data and, hence, different conclusions. From a scientific point of view this is not satisfactory. Therefore, I will attempt to bridge the gap between the two views by starting from some typical questions of theoretical interest and then show how one would answer these questions based on a *statistical* analysis of the VAR model. Because the latter by construction is 'bigger' than the

This paper has benefited from useful comments by Andreas Beyer, Carlo Favero, Hans-Christian Kongsted, Kevin Hoover, Søren Johansen, Adrian Pagan, and the participants at the conference 'Theory and Evidence in Macroeconomics', in Bergamo, Italy. Financial support from the Danish Social Sciences Research Council and the Joint Committee of the Nordic Social Sciences Research Council is gratefully acknowledged.

theory model, the empirical analysis not only answers a specific theoretical question, but also gives additional insight into the macroeconomic problem.

A theory model can be simplified by the *ceteris paribus* assumptions 'everything else unchanged', whereas a statistically well-specified empirical model has to address the theoretical problem in the context of 'everything else changing'. By embedding the theory model in a broader empirical framework, the analysis of the statistically based model can provide evidence of possible pitfalls in macroeconomic reasoning. In this sense the VAR analysis can be useful for generating new hypotheses, or for suggesting modifications of too narrowly specified theoretical models. As a convincing illustration see Hoffman (2000).

All through the paper I will address questions of empirical relevance for the analysis of monetary inflation and for the transmission mechanisms of monetary policy. These questions have been motivated by many empirical VAR analyses of money, prices, income, and interest rates and include questions such as:

- How effective is monetary policy when based on changes in money stock or changes in interest rates?
- What is the effect of expanding money supply on prices in the short run? in the medium run? in the long run?
- Is an empirically stable demand for money relation a prerequisite for monetary policy control to be effective?
- How strong is the direct (indirect) relationship between a monetary policy instrument and price inflation?

Based on the VAR formulation I will demonstrate that every empirical statement can, and should, be checked for its consistency with all previous empirical and theoretical statements. This is in contrast to many empirical investigations, where inference relies on many untested assumptions using test procedures that only make sense in isolation, but not in the full context of the empirical model.

The organization of the paper is as follows: in Section 2 I briefly consider the treatment of inflation and monetary policy in Romer (1996) with special reference to the equilibrium in the money market. I discuss the problem of inverting an equilibrium money-demand relation to get a price relation when the model is stochastic. Section 3 discusses informally some empirical and theoretical implications of unit roots in the data and Section 4 addresses more formally a stochastic formulation based on a decomposition of the data into trends, cycles, and irregular components. Section 5 gives an empirical motivation for treating the stochastic trend in nominal prices as $I(2)$ and Section 6 as $I(1)$. The consequences of either choice is spelt out and the implications for testing long-run and medium-run price homogeneity are discussed. Section 7 introduces the VAR model and defines the $I(2)$, and $I(1)$, models as parameter restrictions on the general model. Section 8 discusses the choice of cointegration rank given a priori economic knowledge. Section 9 discusses just- and over-identifying restrictions on the long-run parameters and gives examples of restrictions which are consistent with (i) real and nominal separation and (ii) real and nominal interactions in the economy. Section 10 discusses identification of common driving trends from a statistical and economic point of view. The possibility of identifying and estimating economic shocks based on estimated residuals is discussed at some length. Section 11 treats identication of the short-run adjustment parameters given an identified long-run structure and discusses some questions relevant for monetary policy. Section 12 summarizes and concludes.

2. Inflation and money growth

A fundamental proposition in macroeconomic theory is that growth in money supply in excess of real productive growth is the cause of inflation, at least in the long run. I will consider briefly some conventional ideas underlying this belief as described by Romer (1996: ch. 9).

The well-known diagram illustrating the intersection of aggregate demand and aggregate supply provides the framework for identifying potential sources of inflation as shocks shifting either aggregate demand upwards or aggregate supply to the left. See the upper panel of Figure 8.1.

As examples of aggregate supply shocks that shift the *AS* curve to the left Romer (1996) mentions: negative technology shocks, downward shifts in labour supply, and upwardly skewed relative-cost shocks. As examples of aggregate demand shocks that shift the *AD* curve to the right he mentions: increases in money stock, downward shifts

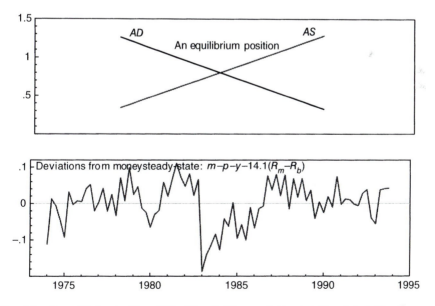

FIG. 8.1. *An equilibrium position of the AD and AS curve (upper panel) and deviations from an estimated money-demand relation for Denmark:* $(m - p - y)_t - 14.1(R_m - R_b)$ *(lower panel)*

in money demand, and increases in government purchases. Since all these types of shocks, and many others, occur quite frequently there are many factors that potentially can affect inflation. Some of these shocks may only influence inflation temporarily and are, therefore, less important than shocks with a permanent effect on inflation. Among the latter economists usually emphasize changes in money supply as the crucial inflationary source. The economic intuition behind this is that other factors are limited in scope, whereas money in principle is unlimited in supply.

More formally the reasoning is based on money demand and supply and the condition for equilibrium in the money market:

$$M/P = L(R, Y), \quad L_R < 0, \quad L_y > 0, \tag{1}$$

where M is the money stock, P the price level, R the nominal interest rate, Y real income, and $L(\cdot)$ the demand for real money balances. Based on the equilibrium condition, i.e. no changes in any of the variables, Romer (1996) concludes that the price level is determined by:

$$P = M/L(R, Y). \tag{2}$$

The equilibrium condition (1) and, hence (2), is a static concept that can be thought of as a hypothetical relation between money and prices for fixed income and interest rate. The underlying comparative static analysis investigates the effect on one variable, say price, when changing another variable, say money supply, with the purpose of deriving the new equilibrium position after the change. Thus, the focus is on the hypothetical effect of a change in one variable (M) on another variable (P), when the additional variables $(R$ and $Y)$ are exogenously given and everything else is taken account of by the *ceteris paribus* assumption.

However, when time is introduced the *ceteris paribus* assumption and the assumption of fixed exogenous variables become much more questionable. Neither interest rates nor real income have been fixed or controlled in most periods subject to empirical analysis. Therefore, in empirical macroeconomic analysis *all variables* (inclusive of the *ceteris paribus* ones) are more or less continuously subject to shocks, some of which permanently change the previous equilibrium condition. In this sense an equilibrium position is an inherently time-dependent concept in empirical modelling. Hence, the static equilibrium concept has to be replaced by a dynamic concept, for instance a steady-state position. For an equilibrium relation time is irrelevant. Discussing a steady-state relation without a time index is meaningless.

In a typical macroeconomic system new disturbances push the variables away from steady-state, but the economic adjustment forces pull them back towards a new steady-state position. The adjustment back to steady-state is disturbed by new shocks and the system essentially never comes to rest. Therefore, we will not be able to observe a steady-state position and the empirical investigation has to account for the stochastic properties of the variables as well as the theoretical equilibrium relationship between them. See the lower panel of Figure 8.1 for an illustration of a stochastic steady-state relation.

In (1) the money-market equilibrium is an exact mathematical expression and it is straightforward to invert it to determine prices as is done in (2). The observations from a typical macroeconomic system is adequately described by a stochastic vector time-series process. But in stochastic systems, inversion of (1) is no longer guaranteed (see for instance, Hendry and Ericsson 1991) and is likely to result in misleading conclusions.

Because the observed money stock is not a measurement of an equilibrium position it can be demand or supply determined or both. This raises the question whether it is possible to empirically identify and estimate the underlying theoretical relations. For instance, if central banks are able to effectively control money stock, then observed money holdings are likely to be supply determined and the demand for money has to adjust to the supplied quantities. This is likely to be the case in trade-and-capital-regulated economies or in economies with flexible exchange rates, whereas in open deregulated economies with fixed exchange rates central banks would not in general be able to control money stock. In the latter case one would expect observed money stock to be demand determined.

Given that the money-demand relation can be *empirically* identified, the statistical estimation problem has to be addressed. Because macroeconomic variables are generally found to be non-stationary, standard regression methods are no longer feasible from an econometric point of view. But since cointegration analysis specifically addresses the non-stationarity problem, it is a feasible solution in this respect. The empirical counterpart of (1) can be written as a cointegrating relation, i.e.:

$$(M/P)_t - L(R_t, Y_t) = v_t, \tag{3}$$

where v_t is a stationary process measuring the deviation from the steady-state position at time t. The stationarity of v_t implies that whenever the system has been shocked it will adjust back to equilibrium. This is illustrated in Figure 8.1 (lower panel) where the deviations from an estimated money-demand relation based on Danish data (Juselius 1998*b*) is graphed. Note the large equilibrium error about 1983, as a result of removing restrictions on capital movements and the consequent adjustment back to steady-state.

However, empirical investigation of (3) based on cointegration analysis poses several additional problems. Although in a theoretical exercise it is straightforward to keep some of the variables fixed (the exogenous variables), in an empirical model none of the variables in (1), i.e. money, prices, income, or interest rates, can be assumed to be fixed (i.e. controlled). The stochastic feature of all variables implies that the equilibrium adjustment can take place in either money, prices, income, or interest rates. Therefore, the equilibrium deviation v_t is not necessarily due to a money supply shock at time t, but can originate from any change in the variables. Hence, it is no longer possible to interpret a coefficient in a cointegrating relation as in the conventional regression context, which is based on the assumption of 'fixed' regressors. In multivariate cointegration analysis all variables are stochastic and a shock to one variable is transmitted to all other variables via the dynamics of the system until the system has found its new equilibrium position.

The empirical investigation of the above questions raises several econometric questions:

What is the meaning of a shock and how do we measure it econometrically? How do we distinguish empirically between the long run, the medium run, and the short run? Given the measurements can the parameter estimates be given an economically meaningful interpretation? These questions will be discussed in more detail in the subsequent sections.

3. The time dependence of macro-data

As advocated above, the strong time-dependence of macroeconomic data suggests a statistical formulation based on stochastic processes. In this context it is useful to distinguish between:

- stationary variables with a short time-dependence and
- non-stationary variables with a long time-dependence.

In practice, we classify variables exhibiting a high degree of time persistence (insignificant mean reversion) as non-stationary and variables exhibiting a significant tendency to mean reversion as stationary. However I will argue that the stationarity/ non-stationarity or, alternatively, the order of integration of a variable, is not in general a *property of an economic variable* but a convenient statistical approximation to distinguish between the short-run, medium-run, and long-run variation in the data. I will illustrate this with a few examples involving money, prices, income, and interest rates.

Most countries have exhibited periods of high and low inflation, lasting sometimes a decade or even more, after which the inflation rate has returned to its mean level. If inflation crosses its mean level, say ten times, the econometric analysis will find significant mean reversion and, hence, conclude that inflation rate is stationary. For this to happen we might need up to hundred years of observations. The time-path of, for example, quarterly European inflation over the last few decades will cover a high inflation period in the 1970s and beginning of the 1980s and a low inflation period from mid-1980s until the present date. Crossing the mean level a few times is not enough to obtain statistically significant mean reversion and the econometric analysis will show that inflation should be treated as non-stationary. This is illustrated in Figure 8.2 where yearly observations of the Danish inflation rate have been graphed for 1901–92 (upper panel), for 1945–92 (middle panel), and 1975–92 (lower panel). The first two time-series of inflation rates look mean-reverting (though not to zero mean inflation), whereas significant mean-reversion would not be found for the last section of the series.

That inflation is considered stationary in one study and non-stationary in another, where the latter is based, say, on a subsample of the former might seem contradictory. This need not be so, unless a unit-root process is given a structural economic

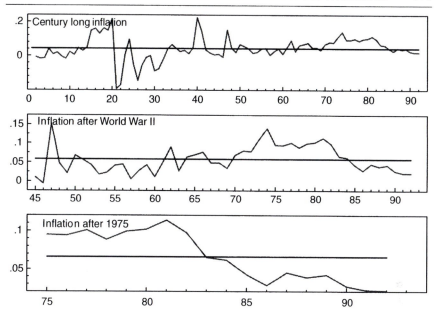

Fɪɢ. 8.2. *Yearly Danish inflation 1901–92 (upper panel), 1945–92 (middle panel), and 1975–92 (lower panel)*

interpretation. There are many arguments in favour of considering a unit root (a stochastic trend) as a convenient econometric approximation rather than as a deep structural parameter. For instance, if the time perspective of our study is the macro-economic behaviour in the medium run, then most macroeconomic variables exhibit considerable inertia, consistent with non-stationary rather than stationary behaviour. Because inflation, for example, would not be statistically different from a non-stationary variable, treating it as a stationary variable would invalidate the statistical analysis and, therefore, lead to wrong economic conclusions. On the other hand, treating inflation as a non-stationary variable gives us the opportunity to find out which other variable(s) have exhibited a similar stochastic trend by exploiting the cointegration property. This will be discussed at some length in Section 4, where I will demonstrate that the unit-root property of economic variables is very useful for the empirical analysis of long- and medium–run macroeconomic behaviour.

When the time perspective of our study is the long historical macroeconomic movements, inflation as well as interest rates are likely to show significant mean reversion and, hence, can be treated as a stationary variable.

Finally, to illustrate that the same type of stochastic processes are able to adequately describe the data, independently of whether one takes a close-up or a long-distance look, I have graphed the Danish bond rate in levels and differences in Figure 8.3 based on a sample of ninety-five quarterly observations (1. 1972–3. 1995), ninety-five

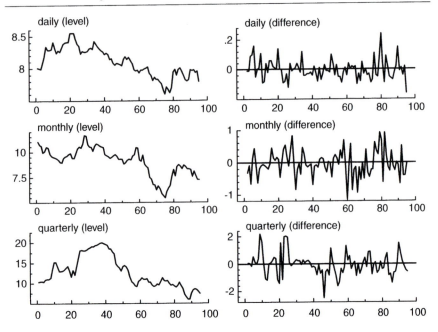

FIG. 8.3. *Average Danish bond rates, based on daily observations, 1 May to 25 Sept. 1995 (upper panel); monthly observations, Nov. 1987 to Sept. 1995 (middle panel); and quarterly observations, 1972: 1 to 1995: 3 (lower panel)*

monthly observations (11. 1987–9. 1995), and ninety-five daily observations (1.5.1995–25.9.1995). The daily sample corresponds to the little hump at the end of the quarterly time series. It would be considered a small stationary blip from a quarterly perspective, whereas from a daily perspective it is non-stationary, showing no significant mean reversion. Altogether, the three time-series look very similar from a stochastic point of view.

Thus, econometrically it is convenient to let the definition of long run or short run, or alternatively the very long run, the medium long run, and the short run, depend on the time perspective of the study. From an economic point of view the question remains in what sense can a 'unit-root' process be given a 'structural' interpretation.

4. A stochastic formulation

To be able to discuss the above questions I will consider a conventional decomposition into trend, T, cycle, C, and irregular component, I, of a typical macroeconomic variable:

$$X = T \times C \times I.$$

Instead of treating the trend component as deterministic, as is usually done in conventional analysis, I will allow the trend to be both deterministic, T_d, and stochastic, T_s, i.e. $T = T_s \times T_d$, and the cyclical component to be of long duration, say six to ten years, C_l, and of shorter duration, say three to five years, C_s, i.e. $C = C_l \times C_s$. The reason for distinguishing between short and long cycles is that a long/short cycle can either be treated as non-stationary or stationary depending on the time-perspective of the study. As an illustration of a long cycle that was found non-stationary in the statistical analysis (Juselius 1998*b*) see the graph of trend-adjusted real income in Figure 8.4, middle panel.

An additive formulation is obtained by taking logarithms:

$$x = (t_s + t_d) + (c_l + c_s) + i, \tag{4}$$

where lower-case letters indicate a logarithmic transformation. Though the stochastic time dependency of the variables is of primary interest in the subsequent discussions, the linear time-trend cannot be left out since it is a measure of average linear growth trends usually present in economic data.

To clarify the meaning of a unit root in the econometric analysis and its economic interpretation I will first assume that the empirical analysis is based on a quarterly model of, say, a few decades and then on a yearly model of, say, a hundred years. In the first case, when the perspective of the study is the medium run, I will argue that prices should generally be treated as $I(2)$, whereas in the latter case, when the perspective is the very long run, prices can sometimes be approximated as a strongly correlated $I(1)$, process.

The definition of a stochastic trend requires a further distinction between:

- an unanticipated shock with a permanent effect (a disturbance to the system with a long lasting effect), and
- an unanticipated shock with a transitory effect (a disturbance to the system with a short duration).

To give the non-expert reader a more intuitive understanding for the meaning of a stochastic trend of first or second order, I will describe inflation π_t as the sum of permanent, ε_{pt}, and transitory, ε_{st}, shocks, starting from an initial time point π_0, i.e.:

$$\pi_t = \varepsilon_{pt} + \varepsilon_{pt-1} + \varepsilon_{pt-2} + \cdots + \varepsilon_{p1} + \varepsilon_{st} + \varepsilon_{st-1} + \varepsilon_{st-2} + \cdots + \varepsilon_{s1} + \pi_0.$$

A permanent shock is by definition a shock that has a lasting effect on the level of inflation, such as a permanent increase in government expenditure, whereas the effect of a transitory shock disappears either during the next period or gradually. An example of a transitory price shock is a value added tax imposed in one period and removed the next. In the latter case prices increase temporarily, but return to their previous level after the removal. Therefore, a transitory shock can be described as a shock that occurs a second time in the series but then with opposite sign. Hence, a transitory shock disappears in cumulation, whereas a permanent shock has a long-lasting effect on the level. In practice we only observe one shock being the sum of the two, i.e. $\varepsilon_t = \varepsilon_{pt} + \varepsilon_{st}$. However, in the summation:

$$\pi_t = \sum_{i=1}^{t} \varepsilon_i + \pi_0 \tag{5}$$

only the permanent shocks will have a lasting effect and we call $\sum_{i=1}^{t} \varepsilon_i$ a stochastic trend. The difference between a linear stochastic and deterministic trend is that the increments of a stochastic trend change randomly, whereas those of a deterministic trend are constant over time.

A representation of prices instead of inflation is obtained by integrating (5) once, i.e.:

$$p_t = \sum \pi_i = \sum_{s=1}^{t}\sum_{i=1}^{s} \varepsilon_i + \pi_0 t + p_0. \tag{6}$$

It appears that inflation being $I(1)$ with a non-zero mean, corresponds to prices being $I(2)$ with linear trends. The stochastic $I(2)$ trend is illustrated in the upper panel of Figure 8.4.

The question whether inflation rates should be treated as $I(1)$ or $I(0)$ has been subject to much debate. Figure 8.2 illustrated that inflation measured over the last decades was probably best approximated by a non-stationary process, whereas measured over a century by a stationary, though strongly autocorrelated, process. For a description of the latter case (5) should be replaced with:

$$\pi_t = \sum_{i=1}^{t} \rho^i \varepsilon_i + \pi_0, \tag{7}$$

where the autoregressive parameter ρ is less than but close to one. In this case prices would be represented by:

$$p_t = \sum \pi_i = \sum_{s=1}^{t}\sum_{i=1}^{s} \rho^i \varepsilon_i + \pi_0 t + p_0, \tag{8}$$

i.e. by a strongly autoregressive first-order stochastic trend and a deterministic linear trend.

The difference between (5) and (7) is only a matter of approximation. In the first case the parameter ρ is approximated with unity, because the sample period is too short for the estimate to be statistically different from one. In the second case the sample period contains enough turning points for ρ to be significantly different from one. Econometrically it is more optimal to treat a long business-cycle component spanning over, say, ten years as an $I(1)$ process when the sample period is less than, say, twenty years. In this sense the difference betweeen the long cyclical component c_l and t_s in (4) is that t_s is a true unit-root process $(\rho = 1)$, whereas c_l is a near unit-root process $(\rho \leq 1)$ that needs a very long sample to distinguish it from a true unit-root process.

I will argue below that, unless a unit root is given a structural interpretation, the choice of one representation or the other is not very important as such, as long as there is consistency between the analysis and the choice. However, from an econometric point

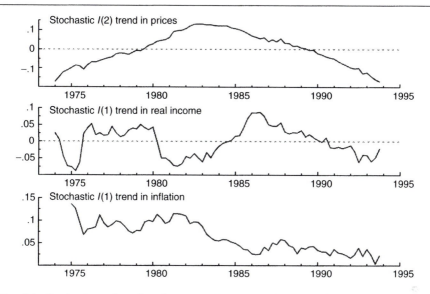

Fig. 8.4. *Stochastic trends in Danish prices, real income, and inflation, based on quarterly data 1975:1 to 1994:4*

of view the choice between the two representations is usually crucial for robust inference and should, therefore, be based on all possible information. See Hendry and Juselius (2000).

To give the economic intuition for the subsequent multivariate cointegration analysis of money-demand–money-supply relations, I will illustrate the above ideas in Section 5 and 6 based on five Danish time-series: $\mathbf{x}_t = [m, p, y, R_m, R_b]_t$, $t = 1, \ldots, T$, where m is a measure of money stock, p the price level, y real income, R_m the own interest on money stock, and R_b the interest rate on bonds. All variables are treated as stochastic and, hence, from a statistical point of view need to be modelled, independently of whether they are considered endogenous or exogenous in the economic model. Figure 8.4 illustrates the different stochastic trends in the Danish data: in the upper panel trend-adjusted prices describe a stochastic $I(2)$, trend, in the middle panel trend-adjusted real income describes a stochastic $I(1)$, trend, and in the lower panel the inflation rate describes another stochastic $I(1)$, trend which corresponds to the differenced $I(2)$, trend.

5. Treating prices as $I(2)$

To illustrate the above ideas I will all through the paper assume two autonomous shocks u_1 and u_2, where for simplicity u_1 is a nominal shock causing a permanent shift in the aggregate demand (AD) curve and u_2 is a real shock causing a permanent shift in the aggregate supply (AS) curve. In this section I will assume that the long-run stochastic trend t_s in (4) can be described by the twice cumulated nominal (AD)

shocks, $\sum\sum u_{1i}$, and the long cyclical component c_l by the once cumulated nominal shocks, $\sum u_{1i}$, and the once cumulated real (AS) shocks, $\sum u_{2i}$. This representation gives us the possibility of distinguishing between the long-run stochastic trend component in prices, $\sum\sum u_{1i}$, the medium-run stochastic trend in price inflation, $\sum u_{1i}$, and the medium-run stochastic trend in real activity, $\sum u_{2i}$.

As an illustration of how the econometric analysis is influenced by the above assumptions I will consider the following decomposition of the data vector:

$$
\begin{bmatrix} m_t \\ p_t \\ y_t \\ R_{mt} \\ R_{bt} \end{bmatrix} = \begin{bmatrix} c_{11} \\ c_{21} \\ 0 \\ 0 \\ 0 \end{bmatrix} \left[\sum\sum u_{1i} \right] + \begin{bmatrix} d_{11} & d_{12} \\ d_{21} & d_{22} \\ d_{31} & d_{32} \\ d_{41} & d_{42} \\ d_{51} & d_{52} \end{bmatrix} \begin{bmatrix} \sum u_{1i} \\ \sum u_{2i} \end{bmatrix} + \begin{bmatrix} g_1 \\ g_2 \\ g_3 \\ 0 \\ 0 \end{bmatrix} [t] + stat.comp. \tag{9}
$$

The deterministic trend component, $t_d = t$, accounts for linear growth in nominal money and prices as well as real income. If $\{g_1 \neq 0, g_2 \neq 0, g_3 \neq 0\}$, then the average growth rates $\{\overline{\Delta p}_t \neq 0, \overline{\Delta m}_t \neq 0, \overline{\Delta y}_t \neq 0\}$, i.e. real and nominal growth is non-zero consistent with stylized facts in most industrialized countries. If $g_3 = 0$ and $d_{31} = 0$ in (9), then $\sum u_{2i}$ is likely to describe the long-run real growth in the economy, i.e. a 'structural' unit-root process as discussed in many papers on stochastic versus deterministic real growth models. See, for instance, King *et al.* (1991). If $g_3 \neq 0$, then the linear time-trend is likely to capture the long-run trend and $\sum u_{2i}$ will describe the medium-run deviations from this trend, i.e. the long business cycles. The trend-adjusted real income variable in the middle panel of Figure 8.4 illustrates such long business cycles. For a further discussion, see Rubin (1998). The first case explicitly assumes that the average real growth rate is zero whereas the latter case does not. Whether one includes a linear trend or not in (9) influences, therefore, the possibility of interpreting the second stochastic trend, $\sum u_{2i}$, as a long-run structural trend or not.

5.1. *Conditions for price homogeneity*

I will take a closer look at the trend components of m_t and p_t in (9):

$$
m_t = c_{11} \sum\sum u_{1i} + d_{11} \sum u_{1i} + d_{12} \sum u_{2i} + g_1 t + stat.comp.,
$$

$$
p_t = c_{21} \sum\sum u_{1i} + d_{21} \sum u_{1i} + d_{22} \sum u_{2i} + g_2 t + stat.comp.
$$

If $(c_{11}, c_{21}) \neq 0$, then $\{m_t, p_t\} \sim I(2)$. If, in addition $c_{11} = c_{21}$ then

$$
m_t - p_t = (d_{11} - d_{21}) \sum u_{1i} + (d_{12} - d_{22}) \sum u_{2i} + (g_1 - g_2)t + stat.comp.,
$$

is at most $I(1)$. If $\{(d_{11} - d_{21}) \neq 0, (d_{12} - d_{22}) \neq 0\}$, then m_t and p_t are cointegrating from $I(2)$ to $I(1)$, i.e. they are $CI(2,1)$. If, in addition $(g_1 - g_2) \neq 0$, then real money stock grows around a linear trend.

The case $(m_t - p_t) \sim I(1)$ implies long-run price homogeneity and is a testable hypothesis. Money stock and prices are moving together in the long run, but not necessarily in the medium run (over the business cycle). Long-run and medium-run price homogeneity requires $\{c_{11} = c_{21}$ and $d_{11} = d_{21}\}$, i.e. the nominal (AD) shocks u_{1t} affect nominal money and prices in the same way both in the long run and in the medium run. Because the real stochastic trend $\sum u_{2i}$ is likely to enter m_t but not necessarily p_t, testing long- and medium-run price homogeneity jointly is not equivalent to testing $(m_t - p_t) \sim I(0)$. Therefore, the joint hypothesis is not as straightforward to test as long-run price homogeneity alone.

Note that $(m_t - p_t) \sim I(1)$ implies $(\Delta m_t - \Delta p_t) \sim I(0)$, i.e. long-run price homogeneity implies cointegration between price inflation and money growth. If this is the case, then the stochastic trend in inflation can equally well be measured by the growth in money stock.

5.2. Assuming long-run price homogeneity

In the following I will assume that $c_{11} = c_{21}$, and discuss various cases where medium-run price homogeneity is either present or absent.

$$
\begin{bmatrix} m_t - p_t \\ \Delta p_t \\ y_t \\ R_{mt} \\ R_{bt} \end{bmatrix} = \begin{bmatrix} d_{11} - d_{21} & d_{12} - d_{22} \\ c_{21} & 0 \\ d_{31} & d_{32} \\ d_{41} & d_{42} \\ d_{51} & d_{52} \end{bmatrix} \begin{bmatrix} \sum u_{1i} \\ \sum u_{2i} \end{bmatrix} + \begin{bmatrix} g_1 - g_2 \\ 0 \\ g_3 \\ 0 \\ 0 \end{bmatrix} [t] + \cdots \quad (10)
$$

In (10) all variables are at most $I(1)$. The inflation rate (measured by Δp_t or Δm_t) is only affected by the once cumulated AD trend, $\sum u_{1i}$, but all the other variables can in principle be affected by both stochastic trends, $\sum u_{1i}$ and $\sum u_{2i}$.

The case trend-adjusted $(m_t - p_t) \sim I(0)$ requires that both $d_{11} = d_{21}$ and $d_{12} = d_{22}$, which is not very likely from an economic point of view. A priori, one would expect the real stochastic trend $\sum u_{2i}$ to influence money stock (by increasing the transactions, precautionary and speculative demands for money) but not the price level, i.e. that $d_{12} \neq 0$ and $d_{22} = 0$.

The case $(m_t - p_t - y_t) \sim I(0)$, i.e. money velocity of circulation is a stationary variable, requires that $d_{11} - d_{21} - d_{31} = 0$, $d_{12} - d_{22} - d_{32} = 0$, and $g_1 - g_2 - g_3 = 0$. If $d_{11} = d_{21}$ (i.e. medium-run price homogeneity), $d_{22} = 0$ (real stochastic growth does not affect prices), $d_{31} = 0$ (medium-run price growth does not affect real income), and $d_{12} = d_{32}$, then $m_t - p_t - y_t \sim I(0)$. In this case real money stock and real aggregate income share one common trend, the real stochastic trend $\sum u_{2i}$. The stationarity of money velocity, implying common movements in money, prices, and income, is then consistent with the conventional monetarist assumption as stated by Friedman (1970) that 'inflation always and everywhere is a monetary problem.' This case, $(m_t - p_t - y_t) \sim I(0)$, has generally found little empirical support (Juselius 1996, 1998b; Juselius and Gennari 2000; Juselius and Toro 1999). As an illustration see the graph of money velocity in the upper panel of Figure 8.5.

I will now turn to the more realistic assumption of money velocity being $I(1)$.

The case $(m_t - p_t - y_t) \sim I(1)$, implies that $\{(d_{11} - d_{21} - d_{31}) \neq 0$, or $(d_{12} - d_{22} - d_{32}) \neq 0\}$. It suggests that the two common stochastic trends affect the level of real money stock and real income differently. A few examples illustrate this:

Example 1: Inflation is cointegrating with velocity, i.e.:

$$m_t - p_t - y_t + b_1 \Delta p_t \sim I(0), \tag{11}$$

or alternatively

$$(m_t - p_t - y_t) + b_2 \Delta m_t \sim I(0).$$

Under the previous assumptions that $d_{31}, d_{22} = 0$, and $d_{12} = d_{32}$, the $I(0)$ assumption of (11) implies that $d_{11} - d_{21} = b_1 c_{21}$. If $b_1 > 0$, then (11) can be interpreted as a money-demand relation, where the opportunity cost of holding money relative to real stock is a determinant of money velocity. On the other hand if $b_1 < 0$ (or $b_2 > 0$), then inflation adjusts to excess money, though if $|b_1| < 1$, with some time lag. In this case (11) cannot be interpreted as a money-demand relation.

Example 2: The interest rate spread and velocity are cointegrating, i.e.:

$$(m_t - p_t - y_t) - b_3(R_m - R_b)_t \sim I(0). \tag{12}$$

Because $(R_m - R_b)_t \sim I(1)$, either $(d_{41} - d_{51}) \neq 0$, or $(d_{42} - d_{52}) \neq 0$, or both. In either case the stochastic trend in the spread has to cointegrate with the stochastic trend in velocity. If $b_3 > 0$, then (12) can be interpreted as a money-demand relation in which the opportunity cost of holding money relative to bonds is a determinant of agent's desired money holdings. On the other hand, if $b_3 < 0$ then the money-demand interpretation is no longer possible, and (12) could instead be a central bank policy rule. Figure 8.5, the middle panel, shows the interest spread between the Danish ten-year bond rate and the deposit rate, and the lower panel the linear combination (12) with $b_3 = 14.1$. It is notable how well the non-stationary behaviour of money velocity and the spread cancels in the linear money-demand relation.

From the perspective of monetary policy a non-stationary spread suggests that the short-term central bank interest rate can be used as an instrument to influence money demand. A stationary spread on the other hand signals fast adjustment between the two interest rates, such that changing the short interest rate only changes the spread in the very short run and, hence, leaves money demand essentially unchanged.

In a model explaining monetary transmission mechanisms, the determination of real interest rates is likely to play an important role. The Fisher parity predicts that real interest rates are constant, i.e;

$$R_t = \mathcal{E}_t \Delta_m p_{t+m}, \tag{13}$$

where $\mathcal{E}_t \Delta_m p_{t+m}$ is the expected value at time t of inflation at the period of maturity $t + m$.

If $(\Delta_m p_{t+m} - \mathcal{E}_t \Delta_m p_{t+m}) \sim I(0)$, then the predictions do not deviate from the actual realization with more than a stationary error. If, in addition $(\Delta p_t - \Delta_m p_{t+m}) \sim I(0)$, then $R_t - \Delta p_t$ is stationary. From (13) it appears that if $(R_m - \Delta p) \sim I(0)$ and $(R_b - \Delta p) \sim I(0)$, then $d_{42} = d_{52} = 0$. Also if $d_{42} = d_{52} = 0$, then R_m and R_b must be cointegrating $(R_m - b_4 R_b)_t \sim I(0)$ with $b_4 = 1$ for $d_{41} = d_{51}$. In this sense stationary real interest rates are both econometrically and economically consistent with the spread and the velocity being stationary. It corresponds to the situation where real income and real money stock share the common AS trend, $\sum u_{2i}$, and inflation and the two nominal interest rates share the AD trend, $\sum u_{1i}$. This case can be formulated as a restricted version of (10):

$$\begin{bmatrix} m_t - p_t \\ \Delta p_t \\ y_t \\ R_{mt} \\ R_{bt} \end{bmatrix} = \begin{bmatrix} 0 & d_{12} \\ c_{21} & 0 \\ 0 & d_{12} \\ c_{21} & 0 \\ c_{21} & 0 \end{bmatrix} \begin{bmatrix} \sum u_{1i} \\ \sum u_{2i} \end{bmatrix} + stat.comp. \tag{14}$$

Though appealing from a theory point of view, (14) has not found much empirical support. Instead, real interest rates, interest rate spreads, and money velocity have frequently been found to be non-stationary. This suggests the presence of real and nominal interaction effects, at least over the horizon of a long business cycle.

By modifying some of the assumptions underlying the Fisher parity, the non-stationarity of real interest rates can be justified. For example, if agents systematically mispredict future inflation, i.e. $(\Delta_m p_{t+m} - \mathcal{E}_t \Delta_m p_{t+m}) \sim I(1)$, or if the inflation differential is non-stationary, i.e. $(\Delta p_t - \Delta_m p_{t+m}) \sim I(1)$, then $R_t - \Delta p_t \sim I(1)$ is consistent with a modified Fisher parity. In this case one would also expect $E_t(\Delta_b p_{t+b} - \Delta_m p_{t+m}) \sim I(1)$, and $(R_m - R_b)_t \sim I(1)$ would be consistent with the predictions from a modified expection's hypothesis (or the Fisher parity).

In Section 9, I will briefly discuss the case where the spread, the real interest rates, and the velocity are non-stationary, but otherwise restrict the discussion to the more straightforward case (14).

6. Treating prices as $I(1)$

In this case $\rho < 1$ in (7) implying that inflation is stationary albeit strongly auto-correlated. The representation of the vector process becomes:

$$\begin{bmatrix} m_t \\ p_t \\ y_t \\ R_{mt} \\ R_{bt} \end{bmatrix} = \begin{bmatrix} c_{11} & d_{12} \\ c_{21} & d_{22} \\ 0 & d_{32} \\ 0 & d_{42} \\ 0 & d_{52} \end{bmatrix} \begin{bmatrix} \sum u_{1i} \\ \sum u_{2i} \end{bmatrix} + \begin{bmatrix} g_1 \\ g_2 \\ g_3 \\ 0 \\ 0 \end{bmatrix} [t] + stat.comp. \tag{15}$$

Money and prices are represented by:

$$m_t = c_{11} \sum u_{1i} + d_{12} \sum u_{2i} + g_1 t + stat.comp.,$$
$$p_t = c_{21} \sum u_{1i} + d_{22} \sum u_{2i} + g_2 t + stat.comp.$$

If $c_{11} = c_{21}$, there is long-run price homogeneity, but $(m_t - p_t) \sim I(1)$ unless $(d_{12} - d_{22}) = 0$. If $d_{12} \neq 0$ and $d_{22} = 0$, then

$$m_t - p_t = d_{12} \sum u_{2i} + (g_1 - g_2)t + stat.comp.$$

If $d_{12} = d_{32}$, then $(m_t - p_t - y_t) \sim I(0)$. From $\{m_t, p_t\} \sim I(1)$ it follows that $\{\Delta p, \Delta m\} \sim I(0)$, and real interest rates cannot be stationary unless $d_{42} = d_{52} = 0$. Hence, a consequence of treating prices as $I(1)$ is that nominal interest rates should be treated as $I(0)$, unless one is prepared a priori to exclude the possibility of stationary real interest rates.

As discussed above, the inflation rate and the interest rates have to cross their mean path fairly frequently to obtain statistically significant mean-reversion. The restricted version of (15) given below is economically as well as econometrically consistent, but is usually only relevant in the analysis of long historical data sets.

$$\begin{bmatrix} m_t \\ p_t \\ y_t \\ R_{mt} \\ R_{bt} \end{bmatrix} = \begin{bmatrix} c_{11} & d_{12} \\ c_{21} & 0 \\ 0 & d_{12} \\ 0 & 0 \\ 0 & 0 \end{bmatrix} \begin{bmatrix} \sum u_{1i} \\ \sum u_{2i} \end{bmatrix} + \begin{bmatrix} g_1 \\ g_2 \\ g_3 \\ 0 \\ 0 \end{bmatrix} [t] + stat.comp.$$

7. Estimation and hypotheses formulation

The economic relations discussed in Section 2 and the stochastic formulation of the macroeconomic variables discussed in Section 4 can be analysed in a formal statistical framework using the cointegrated VAR model given by:

$$\Delta^2 x_t = \Pi_1 \Delta^2 x_{t-1} + \Gamma \Delta x_{t-1} + \Pi x_{t-2} + \mu_0 + \mu_1 t + \varepsilon_t,$$
$$\varepsilon_t \sim N_p(0, \Sigma), \quad t = 1, \ldots, T, \tag{16}$$

where x_t is a $p \times 1$ vector of variables in the system, the lag length has been set to three, and the parameters $\{\Gamma_1, \Pi_1, \Pi, \mu_0, \mu_1, \Sigma\}$ are unrestricted.

The VAR model is essentially based on the assumption of multivariate normal disturbances, i.e. residuals should behave approximately as a multivariate normal process. In the VAR formulation this amounts to:

$$\Delta x_t - E_{t-1}\{\Delta x_t \mid X_{t-1}\} = \varepsilon_t, \tag{17}$$

where $X_{t-1} = [x_{t-1}, x_{t-2}, x_{t-3}]$, and $E_{t-1}\{\Delta x_t \mid X_{t-1}\}$ is the conditional expectation of Δx_t given the information at time $t - 1$. When x_t contains the most important variables needed to explain the variation in the vector process, the multivariate normality assumption has often been shown to work reasonably well. Nevertheless, major reforms, interventions, and extraordinary events, such as joining or leaving the ERM, abolishing restrictions on capital movements, changing wage indexation schemes, and extraordinary increases in the oil price, are likely to violate the normality assumption. In such cases the information set has to be enlarged with additional variables accounting for this effect, usually in the form of dummy variables, $\mathbf{D}_t$, i.e.:

$$\Delta\mathbf{x}_t - E_{t-1}\{\Delta\mathbf{x}_t|\mathbf{D}_t, \mathbf{X}_{t-1}\} = \varepsilon_t. \tag{18}$$

Note that $\mathbf{D}_t$ in (18) enters the information set only at the time the effect was unanticipated. After the intervention has occurred and the effect is known, the adjustment mechanisms of the model should bring the system back to the new steady-state position. For an illustration see the graph in Figure 8.1, lower panel. In some cases, when interventions or reforms change the data-generating mechanism, i.e. the parameters of the VAR model, such an assumption is too simple. But in order to simplify the subsequent discussion I will ignore altogether this important issue and assume no structural breaks and no need for intervention dummies in model (16). The interested reader is referred to the large econometric literature dealing with regime shifts and structural breaks.

The unrestricted VAR model (16) essentially summarizes the first two moments of the data and is, therefore, a statistical description rather than an economic model. By imposing statistically valid and economically interpretable parameter restrictions on the VAR a more interesting model can be found. See, for instance, Hendry and Mizon (1993) and Hendry (1995) for a discussion of the 'general to specific' VAR approach. In Section 7.1 I will discuss restrictions on the VAR parameters that define the $I(2)$ model and in Section 7.2 that define the $I(1)$ model.

7.1. The $I(2)$ model

The empirical justification for nominal money and prices containing a second-order stochastic trend and a first-order deterministic time-trend was discussed in Sections 3 and 5. The hypothesis that $\mathbf{x}_t$ is $I(2)$, can be formulated statistically as two reduced rank hypotheses on Π and Γ (Johansen 1995a), whereas the hypothesis that $\mathbf{x}_t$ contains deterministic linear trends, but no higher-order trends, can be formulated as restrictions on μ_0 and μ_1 (Rahbek, Kongsted, and Jørgensen 1999).

The prior assumption that there are two stochastic trends derived from permanent shocks to the *AD* and the *AS* curve is formulated as the hypothesis that $p - r = 2$, where r is the rank of Π. The hypothesis that the *AD* trend is $I(2)$ is formulated as an additional reduced-rank hypothesis on Γ. Formally this is stated as: $\Pi = \alpha\beta'$ and $\alpha'_\perp\Gamma\beta_\perp = \zeta\eta'$, where α, β are $p \times r$ matrices, $\alpha_\perp$, $\beta_\perp$ are $p \times (p - r)$ matrices orthogonal to α and β, and ζ, η are $p - r \times s_1$ matrices, where s_1 is the number of $I(1)$ trends (Johansen 1992). Hence, the reduced rank of Π is related to the total number of stochastic trends in the data, $p - r$, whereas the reduced rank of Γ, s_1, is related to the number of second-order non-stationary trends in the data, s_2. Hence, $p - r = s_1 + s_2$.

By assuming $\Pi = \alpha\beta'$ and $\alpha'_\perp\Gamma\beta_\perp = \zeta\eta$ and zero restrictions on quadratic or higher-order trends we can solve the VAR with respect to ε_t and deterministic components to derive the model in moving average form:

$$\mathbf{x}_t = \mathcal{B}_2 \mathcal{A}_2' \sum_{s=1}^{t} \sum_{i=1}^{s} \varepsilon_i + \mathcal{B}_1 \mathcal{A}_1' \sum_{s=1}^{t} \varepsilon_s + gt + Y_t + A + Bt, \quad t = 1, \ldots, T,$$

(19)

where $\mathcal{B}_2, \mathcal{A}_2$ are $p \times s_2$ matrices, $\mathcal{B}_1, \mathcal{A}_1$ are $p \times (p - r)$ matrices, g are the linear trends in the data, Y_t defines the stationary part of the process, and A and B are a function of the initial values $x_0, x_{-1}, \ldots, x_{-k+1}$. See Johansen (1995a,c) and Paruolo (1996) for further details. In this form it is straightforward to interpret $\mathcal{A}_2' \varepsilon_t = u_{1t}$ as the norminal (AD), shock leading to the $I(2)$, trend, $\sum \sum \mathcal{A}_2' \varepsilon_i = \sum \sum u_{1i}$, and $\mathcal{A}_1' \varepsilon_t = u_t$, with $u_t' = [u_{1t}, u_{2t}]$ as the nominal and real shocks producing the two $I(1)$ trends, $\sum u_{1i}$ and $\sum u_{2i}$. The derivation of $\{\mathcal{B}_2, \mathcal{A}_2, \mathcal{B}_1, \mathcal{A}_1, g\}$ as a function of the parameters $(\Pi_1, \Gamma, \alpha, \beta, \mu_0, \mu_1, \Sigma)$ can be found in Johansen (1995a).

Hence, the appropriately restricted VAR model can reproduce the decomposition into stochastic trends, cycles, irregular components (9) discussed in Section 5. Because the VAR is a statistically well-specified model, the basic assumptions underlying the empirical problem such as (i) the number and (ii) order of the stochastic trends, (iii) the presence of linear trends or (iv) quadratic trends in the data, can be checked against the data based on strict hypothesis testing. From the outset of the empirical investigation it is, therefore, possible to infer from the data if the basic economic arguments underlying the economic model are statistically acceptable. If they are not, then the empirical results are likely to suggest in which directions the theoretical framework should be modified. In this sense a stringent VAR analysis can be a useful complement to conventional economic analysis, by not having to rely on basic assumptions never tested.

7.2 The $I(1)$ model

Section 5 showed that long-run price homogeneity implies cointegration between nominal money stock m and prices p. In this case a re-formulation of the data vector based on real money and inflation (instead of nominal money and prices) transforms the model to $I(1)$. This can be formulated as the hypothesis that $\mathbf{x}_t = [m - p, y, \Delta p, R_m, R_b]$ is $I(1)$.

The $I(1)$ model is statistically defined by the reduced rank of $\Pi = \alpha \beta'$ and the full rank of $\alpha_\perp' \Gamma \beta_\perp$. Thus, the $I(1)$ model is based on one reduced-rank condition, whereas the $I(2)$ model was based on two. Rewriting (16) in first differences and levels leads to the well-known cointegrated VAR model in error correction form:

$$\Delta \mathbf{x}_t = \Gamma_1 \Delta \mathbf{x}_{t-1} + \alpha \beta' \mathbf{x}_{t-1} + \mu_0 + \varepsilon_t, \quad \varepsilon_t \sim N_p(0, \Sigma), \quad t = 1, \ldots, T, \quad (20)$$

where $\Gamma_1 = I - \Gamma$ and $\Pi_1 = 0$, i.e. we have assumed only two lags in the model. Solving (20) for ε_t and the deterministic terms gives the moving average representation of the $I(1)$ model:

$$\mathbf{x}_t = \mathcal{B}_1 \mathcal{A}_1' \sum_1^t \varepsilon_i + \mathcal{B}_1 \mathcal{A}_1' \mu_0 t + C^*(L)(\varepsilon_t + \mu) + B, \tag{21}$$

where $\mathcal{B}_1 \mathcal{A}_1' = \beta_\perp (\alpha_\perp' \Gamma \beta_\perp)^{-1} \alpha_\perp' = C$, $\mathcal{B}_1 \mathcal{A}_1' \mu_0 = g$, and $C^*(L)\varepsilon_t$ describes the stationary part of the vector process as an infinite polynomial in the lag operator L, and B is a function of the initial values (Johansen 1991). The lag polynomial $C^*(L)\varepsilon_t$ can describe stationary cycles of short duration, whereas (as discussed in Section 4) $\mathcal{A}_1' \sum_1^t \varepsilon_i$ can describe both long-run and medium-run stochastic trends, where the latter would correspond to long business cycles. It appears, therefore, that (21) reproduces the composition into trend, cycle, irregular component as given by (10) in Section 5. By choosing $\mathcal{A}_1 = \alpha_\perp$ an estimate of the common stochastic trends are obtained:

$$u_t = \alpha_\perp' \sum_1^t \varepsilon_i. \tag{22}$$

Although Π and C are uniquely determined, the decomposition into α, β and $\mathcal{B}_1, \mathcal{A}_1$ is not, as demonstrated by:

$$\alpha \beta' = \alpha H H^{-1'} \beta' = \tilde{\alpha} \tilde{\beta}' = \Pi,$$
$$\mathcal{B}_1 \mathcal{A}_1' = \mathcal{B}_1 Q Q^{-1'} \mathcal{A}_1' = \tilde{\mathcal{B}}_1 \tilde{\mathcal{A}}_1' = C,$$

where H is a $r \times r$ and Q a $(p-r) \times (p-r)$ non-singular matrix. In addition, as will be discussed in Section 10 and 11 the short-run adjustment parameters and the residuals ε_t are not invariant to linear transformation of (20). Therefore, after the basic structure of the VAR model has been determined, the actual economic modelling consists of how to impose identifying and overidentifying restrictions on the model parameters. This will be further discussed in Sections 9–11.

8. On the choice of rank

The cointegration rank divides the data into r adjusting and $p-r$ non-adjusting components. The former are often given an interpretation as equilibrium errors (deviations from steady-state) and the latter as common driving trends in the system. Hence, the choice of r is crucial for all subsequent econometric analysis and for inference on economic hypotheses. The Likelihood Ratio trace test for the determination of the number of unit roots (stochastic trends) in the vector process is based on asymptotic distributions that depends on the deterministic terms in the VAR model (Johansen 1995c). Asymptotic distributions have been tabulated for the most frequently used alternatives, such as a constant and a trend in the model, and restricted versions of them. When model (20) contains institutional dummies that cumulate to broken trends in the data-generating process, the available asymptotic tables are no longer valid (Johansen and Nielsen 1993) and each case should be tabulated separately.

As many simulation studies have demonstrated, the asymptotic distributions are often rather poor approximations in small samples, with consequent size and power distortions (Johansen 1999, 2000; Jørgensen 1999). Because empirical macroeconomic models are typically based on sample sizes of fifty to one hundred observations caution is definitely needed.

The trace test procedure consists of testing the hypothesis of 'at least one unit root' and if accepted continues until the first rejection occurs at 'at least $p - r + 1$ unit roots'. This means that the procedure is essentially based on the principle of 'no prior economic knowledge' regarding the rank r. This is in many cases difficult to justify. As demonstrated in Sections 5–6 in the money market example, the case $(r = 3, p - r = 2)$ can be considered plausible for a reasonably deregulated economy. For a more regulated economy we might have slower market adjustment and, hence, the case $(r = 2, p - r = 3)$ might be preferable a priori.

An alternative procedure is, therefore, to test a given prior economic hypothesis, say $p - r = 2$, using the trace test and, if accepted, continue with this assumption unless the data strongly suggest the presence of additional unit roots. This can be investigated for example by testing the significance of the adjustment coefficients $\alpha_{ir}, i = 1, \ldots, p$ to the r'th cointegrating vector. If all α_{ri} coefficients have small t-values, then including the r'th cointegrating relation in the model would not improve the explanatory power of the model, but would in fact invalidate subsequent inference. Additionally, if the choice of r incorrectly includes a non-stationary relation among the cointegrating relations, then one of the roots of the characteristic polynomial of the model is a unit root or a near unit root. If either of these cases occur, then the cointegration rank should be reduced. Note, however, that additional unit roots in the characteristic polynomial can be the result of $I(2)$ components in the data vector. Reducing the rank in this case will not solve the problem.

Contrary to common beliefs the hypothetical cointegration rank is not in general equivalent to the number of theoretical steady-state relations derived from a partial economic model. For instance, in the money market example of Section 2 there was one equilibrium relation (1). As demonstrated in Sections 5 and 6 (with two instead of just one interest rate) this is consistent with $r = 3$ cointegrating relations and not $r = 1$, which has been incorrectly assumed in many empirical applications. Hence, cointegration between variables is a statistical property of the data that only exceptionally can be given a direct interpretation as an economic steady-state relation.

9. Restrictions on the long-run parameters

Given the number of cointegrating relations, r, the Johansen procedure gives the maximum likelihood estimates of the unrestricted cointegrating relations $\beta'x_t$. Although the unrestricted β is uniquely determined based on the chosen normalization of the reduced-rank problem, the latter is not necessarily meaningful from an economic point of view. Therefore, an important part of the empirical analysis is to impose (over-) identifying restrictions on β to achieve economic interpretability. As an example of just-identifying restrictions, consider the following design matrix $Q = [\beta_1]$, where β_1 is a $(r \times r)$ non-singular matrix defined by $\beta' = [\beta_1, \beta_2]$. In this case $\alpha\beta' = \alpha(\beta_1\beta_1^{-1\prime}\beta') = \alpha[I, \tilde{\beta}]$ where I is the $(r \times r)$ unit matrix and $\tilde{\beta} = \beta_1^{-1\prime}\beta_2$ is a $(r \times p - r)$ full-rank matrix. These just-identifying restrictions have transformed β to long-run 'reduced form'. Because just-identifying restrictions do not change the likelihood function, no tests are involved. In general just identification can be achieved by imposing one normalization and $(r-1)$ restrictions on each β_i. Additional restrictions are over-identifying and, therefore, testable. See Johansen (1995b) and Johansen and Juselius (1992, 1994) for a more detailed treatment.

Consistent with the discussion in Section 5, I will assume three cointegrating relations in the money market example and, hence, two autonomous common trends, $\sum u_{1i}$ and $\sum u_{2i}$. Assuming nominal and real separation of the long-run structure as in (14) we would expect the following hypothetical cointegrating relations:

$$(m - p - y) \sim I(0),$$
$$(R_b - R_m) \sim I(0),$$
$$(R_b - \Delta p) \sim I(0).$$

Each imposes two over-identifying restrictions on the cointegrating space, i.e. a total of six testable restrictions. As illustrated below they completely determine the cointegration space:

$$\beta' x_t = \begin{bmatrix} 1 & -1 & 0 & 0 & 0 \\ 0 & 0 & 0 & 1 & -1 \\ 0 & 0 & -1 & 0 & 1 \end{bmatrix} \begin{bmatrix} (m-p)_t \\ y_t \\ \Delta p_t \\ R_{m_t} \\ R_{b_t} \end{bmatrix}.$$

If, however, there are permanent (at least over the business cycle-horizon) interaction effects between the nominal and the real side of the economy, one would expect the above relations to be $I(1)$:

$$(m - p - y) \sim I(1),$$
$$(R_b - R_m) \sim I(1),$$
$$(R_b - \Delta p) \sim I(1).$$

Section 5 demonstrated that when real money stock and real income are not cointegrating, then one of them, or both, must be additionally affected by the stochastic nominal trend. Similarly, when the two interest rates are not cointegrating, then at least one of the interest rates must be affected by both stochastic trends. This might suggest market rigidities or imperfections, as the following example illustrates.

Assume that $R_b - \Delta p \sim I(0)$, but $R_m - \Delta p \sim I(1)$. Moreover, assume that the bond rate is affected only by the stochastic inflation trend, $\sum u_{1i}$, but that the short-term rate is affected by the inflation trend, $\sum u_{1i}$, as well as the real trend, $\sum u_{2i}$. In this case $(R_b - R_m) \sim I(1)$ could be consistent with an economy where the bond rate is determined by $R_b = f(\Delta p)$ and the central bank determines the short rate, based on a policy rule that includes excess inflation as well as excess aggregate demand, i.e. $R_s = f(\Delta p - \pi^*, y - bt)$, where π^* is a fixed target rate.

The following cointegration relations might suggest real and nominal interaction effects in the money market:

$$\{(m - p - y) + \beta_1(R_b - R_m)\} \sim I(0),$$
$$\{R_m - R_b - \beta_2\Delta p\} \sim I(0),$$
$$(y - \beta_3\Delta p - \beta_4 t) \sim I(0).$$

With some minor modifications, the stationarity of the above relations has found surprisingly strong empirical support in many empirical applications. See for example Juselius (1998a,b), Juselius and Gennari (2000), and Juselius and Toro (1999), all of them analysing European money markets based on two decades of quarterly data for Germany, Denmark, Italy, and Spain. The stationarity of the first relation is illustrated by Figure 8.5, where velocity and the interest rate spread are shown to contain the same stochastic trend, so that the linear combination, $(m - p - y)_t - 14.1(R_m - R_b)_t$, becomes a stationary steady-state relation.

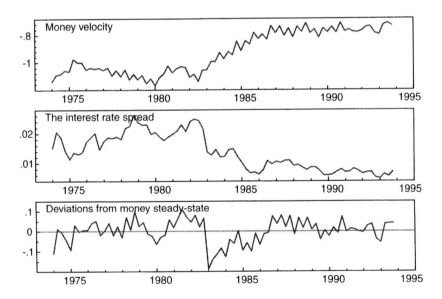

FIG. 8.5. *Money velocity (upper panel), the interest rate spread (middle panel), and money demand (lower panel) for Danish data*

The above examples have shown that a money-demand relation of the type discussed in Romer (1996) can be found empirically either as a linear combination of two stationary cointegration relations $(m - p - y)_t$ and $(R_m - R_b)_t$, or as a cointegration relation between two non-stationary processes, $(m - p - y)t - b_2(R_m - R_b)_t$. The implications of either case for the effectiveness of monetary policy may, however, be quite different.

For this reason, cointegration properties can provide useful information about the relationship between, say, a policy instrument variable and a target or a goal variable. These relationships are quite likely to change as the economy becomes deregulated, thereby allowing market forces to become more effective. Therefore, changes in cointegration properties can contain valuable information about the consequences of shifting from one regime to another. See, for instance, Juselius (1998a).

10. Restrictions on the common trends

As discussed in Section 7, for each α and β describing long-run relations in the data and the adjustment towards them, there is a dual representation in terms of $\alpha_\perp$ and $\beta_\perp$ that describes the common trends and their loadings. The $p \times (p - r)$ matrix $\alpha_\perp$ describing the common stochastic trends, $\alpha'_\perp \sum \varepsilon_i$, is overparametrized in the sense that it is possible to impose one normalization and $(p - r - 1)$ restrictions on each $\alpha_{\perp i}$, without changing the likelihood function. Additional restrictions are over-identifying and, hence, testable.

There are essentially two identification problems in the common stochastic trends model: the first is how to impose restrictions on the residuals $\hat{\varepsilon}_t$; the second is how to impose restrictions on the coefficients of $\alpha_\perp$. The first identification problem arises because the VAR residuals are not invariant to linear transformations. This can be illustrated by pre-multiplying (20) with the non-singular $(p \times p)$ matrix A_0:

$$A_0\Delta\mathbf{x}_t = A_0\Gamma_1\Delta\mathbf{x}_{t-1} + A_0\alpha\beta'\mathbf{x}_{t-1} + A_0\mu + A_0\varepsilon_t, \tag{23}$$

or equivalently:

$$A_0\Delta\mathbf{x}_t = A_1\Delta\mathbf{x}_{t-1} + a\beta'\mathbf{x}_{t-1} + \mu_a + v_t, \tag{24}$$

$$v_t \sim N_p(0, \Omega),$$

where $A_1 = A_0\Gamma_1$, $a = A_0\alpha$, $\mu_a = A_0\mu$, and $v_t = A_0\varepsilon_t$.

Because different choices of A_0 lead to different estimates of the residuals, the question of how to define a shock is important. The theoretical concept of a shock, and its decomposition into an anticipated and unanticipated part, has a straightforward correspondence in the VAR model as a change of a variable, $\Delta\mathbf{x}_t$, and its decomposition into its explained part, the conditional expectation $E_{t-1}\{\Delta\mathbf{x}_t \mid \mathbf{X}_{t-1}\}$, and its unexplained part, the residual ε_t. The requirement for ε_t to be a correct measure of an unanticipated shock is that the conditional expectation $E_{t-1}\{\Delta\mathbf{x}_t \mid \mathbf{x}_{t-1}\}$ correctly describes how agents form their expectations. For example, if agents use model-based rational expectations from a model that is different from the VAR model, then the conditional expectation would no longer be an adequate description of the anticipated part.

Theories also require shocks to be 'structural', usually implying that they are, in some sense, objective, meaningful, or absolute. With the reservation that the word structural has been used to cover a wide variety of meanings, I will here assume that it describes a situation when the effect of a shock is (i) unanticipated (novelty), (ii) unique (a shock hitting money stock alone), and (iii) invariant (no additional explanation by increasing the information set).

As discussed above the argument for a shock to be novel relies on the credibility of the expectations formation, i.e. whether $\varepsilon_t = \Delta x_t - E_{t-1}\{\Delta x_t \mid g(X_{t-1})\}$ is a correct measure of the unanticipated change in x. The uniqueness can be achieved econometrically by choosing A_0 such that the covariance matrix Ω becomes diagonal and, as will be demonstrated below, by appropriately restricting $\alpha_\perp$. For empirical applications see Mellander, Vredin, and Warne (1992) and Hansen and Warne (1995). But whether the resulting estimate of ε_t can be interpreted as economically novel and unique, depends crucially on the plausibility of the underlying assumptions. Some of them cannot be checked against the data, for example the diagonality of Ω, and different schools will claim structurality for differently derived estimates.

The requirement that a structural shock must not change when increasing the information set is probably the most crucial from an empirical point of view. Theoretical models, based on which structural uniqueness is claimed, are always based on many simplifying assumptions inclusive of the *ceteris paribus* assumption. In empirical models the *ceteris paribus* assumption can be met only by conditioning on omitted theory information. Since most (all) macroeconomic systems are stochastic and highly interdependent, the inclusion of additional variables in the model is likely to change the estimated shocks. See also the discussion in Levtchenkova, Pagan, and Robertson (1998).

Although derived from sophisticated theoretical models, structural interpretability of estimated shocks seems hard to justify. In my view, a structural shock is a theoretical concept with little empirical content in macroeconometric modelling. This does not imply that empirical analyses of common trends based on the estimated residuals $\hat{\varepsilon}_t$ from (20) or a $\hat{v}_t$ from (24) and restricted versions of them are uninteresting. Far from useless they can provide valuable insight on the driving forces within the specific system under analysis.

The estimates of the $(p - r)$ common 'autonomous' shocks u_{it} are usually linear functions of the VAR residuals $\hat{\varepsilon}_t$, i.e. $u_{jt} = \omega_j' \hat{\varepsilon}_t, j = 1, \ldots, p - r$. As demonstrated by (21) and (22), $\omega = \alpha_\perp$ gives a straightforward estimate of the 'unrestricted' $p - r$ common stochastic trends:

$$\sum \hat{u}_{ji} = \omega_j' \sum_{i=1}^{t} \hat{\varepsilon}_i = \alpha'_{\perp j} \sum_{i=1}^{t} \hat{\varepsilon}_i, \quad j = 1, \ldots, p - r, \tag{25}$$

where $\hat{\varepsilon}' = [\hat{\varepsilon}_m, \hat{\varepsilon}_y, \hat{\varepsilon}_{\Delta p}, \hat{\varepsilon}_{Rb}, \hat{\varepsilon}_{Rm}]$. The estimates of $\alpha_\perp$ are under-identified in the sense that one can impose $(p - r - 1)$ restrictions and a normalization on each $\alpha'_{\perp i}$ without changing the likelihood function. Assuming $p - r = 2$, just identification of (25) can be achieved by imposing one zero restriction and a normalization on each vector. For example, by assuming that real shocks do not influence the nominal stochastic trend, and that money shocks have no influence on the real stochastic trend we obtain the following just-identified common trends estimates:

$$\sum \tilde{u}_{1i} = [1, 0, \omega_{13}, \omega_{14}, \omega_{15}] \sum_{i=1}^{t} \left[\hat{\varepsilon}_{m_i}, \hat{\varepsilon}_{y_i}, \hat{\varepsilon}_{\Delta p_i}, \hat{\varepsilon}_{Rb_i}, \hat{\varepsilon}_{Rm_i} \right]' = \tilde{\alpha}'_{\perp 1} \sum_{i=1}^{t} \hat{\varepsilon}_i,$$

$$\sum \tilde{u}_{2i} = [0, 1, \omega_{23}, \omega_{24}, \omega_{25}] \sum_{i=1}^{t} \left[\hat{\varepsilon}_{m_i}, \hat{\varepsilon}_{y_i}, \hat{\varepsilon}_{\Delta p_i}, \hat{\varepsilon}_{Rb_i}, \hat{\varepsilon}_{Rm_i} \right]' = \tilde{\alpha}'_{\perp 2} \sum_{i=1}^{t} \hat{\varepsilon}_i.$$

The over-identifying assumption that the nominal stochastic trend derives solely from shocks to money stock and the real stochastic trend derives from shocks to real income is expressed as:

$$\tilde{\tilde{u}}_{1t} = [1, 0, 0, 0, 0] \hat{\varepsilon}_t = \tilde{\tilde{\alpha}}'_{\perp 1} \hat{\varepsilon}_t,$$

$$\tilde{\tilde{u}}_{2t} = [0, 1, 0, 0, 0] \hat{\varepsilon}_t = \tilde{\tilde{\alpha}}'_{\perp 2} \hat{\varepsilon}_t.$$

This hypothesis imposes four zero restrictions on each $\alpha_{\perp i}$ of which one can be obtained by linear manipulations. Hence, there are three over-identifying restrictions on each $\alpha_{\perp i}$, i.e. altogether six testable restrictions.

11. Restrictions on the short-run parameters

Formulation (24) showed that the choice of transformation matrix A_0 does not affect the specification of the long-run parameters β. Hence, one can impose identifying restrictions on the long-run and short-run parameters in two steps. I will, therefore, assume that the β vectors have been fully identified in the first step of the identification scheme. The discussion of how to impose identifying restrictions on the short-run parameters of (24) will be based on a given identified $\beta = \tilde{\beta}$, i.e. for:

$$B_0 \Delta \mathbf{x}_t = B_1 \Delta \mathbf{x}_{t-1} + a \tilde{\beta}' \mathbf{x}_{t-1} + \mu_a + v_t, \quad v_t \sim N_p(0, \Omega). \tag{26}$$

The unrestricted set of parameters $(B_0, B_1, a, \mu_a, \Omega)$ is not uniquely determined in the sense that one can impose $(p - 1)$ restrictions and one normalization on each equation, without changing the likelihood function. Additional restrictions are over-identifying and, hence, testable (see Johansen and Juselius 1994). User-friendly computer programs are readily available for empirical application of the tests, for example the powerful test procedures in PcFiml (Doornik and Hendry 1998).

The VAR model is usually heavily overparametrized. This is particularly so for the short-run parameters. By imposing zero restrictions, other linear restrictions, and non-linear (for example symmetry) restrictions, the number of model parameters can be substantially reduced. The identification problem is essentially about how to satisfy (i) mathematical uniqueness, (ii) statistical significance, and (iii) economic interpretability. In Johansen and Juselius (1994) these three stages are called generic, empirical, and economic identification.

Mathematical uniqueness is related to such restrictions on (26) that give a unique mapping between (20) and (26). Statistical significance is important for two reasons: (i) the coefficients of our empirical model should preferably describe relevant aspects of the investigated economic system, (ii) leaving insignificant coefficients in the model is likely to introduce near singularity in the model. This is particularly so if the insignificant coefficients violate mathematical uniqueness when restricted to zero. The economic interpretability is definitely the most difficult and demanding requirement of the identification process and where cooperation between empirical and theoretical economists is likely to be most rewarding.

It appears from (26) that the VAR model describes the anticipated part of a change from $t - 1$ to t in money, income, inflation, and interest rates by:

- current (anticipated) changes in the system variables,
- short-run adjustment to the lagged changes of the system variables (temporary dynamic effects), and
- short-run adjustment to long-run steady-states (the cointegrating relations).

The representation (26) allows for the possibility that agents react differently on (i) disequilibrium between levels of variables, (ii) lagged changes in the determinants, and (iii) nominal acceleration rates. This very rich empirical structure allows us to ask relevant economic questions within a framework that mimics the actual behaviour in economic systems, such as dynamic adjustment towards long-run and medium-run steady-states, strong interaction effects, etc.

I will end the discussion by first demonstrating how the original question of a money-demand relation raised by Romer (1996) can be addressed within the VAR model. I will then illustrate some extensions of the analysis related to the effectiveness of monetary policy. In doing so I will simplify (26) by assuming that B_0 is upper triangular, Ω is diagonal, and $B_1 = 0$. Generalization to more complicated specifications should be straightforward. A detailed specification of the model is given below:

$$
\begin{bmatrix}
1 & b_{12} & b_{13} & b_{14} & b_{15} \\
0 & 1 & b_{23} & b_{24} & b_{25} \\
0 & 0 & 1 & b_{34} & b_{35} \\
0 & 0 & 0 & 1 & b_{45} \\
0 & 0 & 0 & 0 & 1
\end{bmatrix}
\begin{bmatrix}
\Delta m_t^r \\
\Delta^2 p_t \\
\Delta y_t \\
\Delta R_{mt} \\
\Delta R_{bt}
\end{bmatrix}
$$

$$
=
\begin{bmatrix}
\mu_1 \\
\mu_2 \\
\mu_3 \\
\mu_4 \\
\mu_5
\end{bmatrix}
+
\begin{bmatrix}
a_{11} & a_{12} & a_{13} \\
a_{21} & a_{22} & a_{23} \\
a_{31} & a_{32} & a_{33} \\
a_{41} & a_{42} & a_{43} \\
a_{51} & a_{52} & a_{53}
\end{bmatrix}
\begin{bmatrix}
(m - p - y)_{t-1} \\
(R_b - R_m)_{t-1} \\
(R_b - \Delta p)_{t-1}
\end{bmatrix}
+
\begin{bmatrix}
v_{mt} \\
v_{\Delta pt} \\
v_{yt} \\
v_{R_{mt}} \\
v_{R_{bt}}
\end{bmatrix}
\tag{27}
$$

where $m^r = m - p$ and the cointegration relations are given by the first set of identified relations discussed in Section 9. Within this framework I will address three questions related to the effectiveness of monetary policy. To simplify the discussion I have chosen to focus solely on the money and inflation equations, albeit being aware that a complete answer should be based on an analysis of the full system.

$$\Delta m_t^r = b_{12}\Delta^2 p_t + b_{13}\Delta y_t + b_{14}\Delta R_{mt} + b_{15}\Delta R_{bt}$$
$$+ a_{11}(m - p - y)_{t-1} + a_{12}(R_b - R_m)_{t-1} + a_{13}(R_b - \Delta p)_{t-1} + \varepsilon_{mt},$$

$$\Delta^2 p_t = b_{23}\Delta y_t + b_{24}\Delta R_{mt} + b_{25}\Delta R_{bt}$$
$$+ a_{21}(m - p - y)_{t-1} + a_{22}(R_b - R_m)_{t-1} + a_{23}(R_b - \Delta p)_{t-1} + \varepsilon_{pt},$$

$$\Delta y_t = \ldots$$

$$\Delta R_{mt} = \ldots$$

$$\Delta R_{bt} = \ldots$$

Question 1. Is money stock adjusting to money demand or supply? If $a_{11} < 0$, $a_{12} < 0$, and $a_{13} = 0$, then empirical evidence is in favour of money holdings adjusting to a long-run money-demand relation. The latter can be derived from the money stock equation as follows:

$$(m - p) = y + a_{12}/a_{11}(R_b - R_m)$$
$$= y + \beta_1(R_b - R_m). \tag{28}$$

Relation (28) corresponds to the aggregate demand-for-money relation discussed in a static equilibrium framework by Romer, with the difference that (28) is embedded in a dynamic framework.

If $a_{11} < 0$, $a_{12} = 0$, and $a_{13} = 0$, empirical evidence is more in favour of money holdings adjusting to money supply. This could be consistent with a situation where central banks are able to effectively control money stock and the monetary policy control rule is to keep velocity around a constant level.

Question 2. Is an empirically stable money-demand relation a prerequisite for central banks to be able to control inflation rate? This hypothesis is based on essentially three arguments:

2.1. There exists an empirically stable demand for money relation.
2.2. Central banks can influence the demanded quantity of money.
2.3. Deviations from this relation cause inflation.

First, the empirical requirement for a stable money-demand relation is that $\{a_{11} < 0, a_{12} < 0,$ and $a_{13} = 0\}$, and that the estimates are empirically stable. In this case money stock is endogenously determined by agents' demand for money and it is not obvious that money stock can be used as a monetary instrument by the central bank.

Second, given the previous result (i.e. $a_{11} < 0$, $a_{12} < 0$, and $a_{13} = 0$), central banks cannot *directly* control money stock. Nevertheless, controlling money stock indirectly might still be possible by changing the short-term interest rate. But $a_{12} < 0$ and $(R_b - R_m) \sim I(0)$ imply that a change in the short-term interest rate will transmit through the system in a way that leaves the spread basically unchanged. Therefore, if the data have the property of (14), it seems difficult to justify a claim that central banks can effectively control money stock.

Third, if deviations from a stable money-demand relation do cause inflation (in the short run), then the following condition should be satisfied: $\{a_{21} > 0,\ a_{22} > 0,\ \text{and } a_{23} = 0\}$. Given the assumption that agents can satisfy their desired level of money, it does not seem plausible that agents would deliberately choose to hold excess money (negative or positive). In this case excess money would lead to inflation only if central banks insist on supplying more money than that demanded (which seems to be the opposite of inflation control). Therefore, the frequently used assumption that an empirically stable demand for money relation is needed for central banks to be able to control inflation seems logically flawed.

Question 3. Is money causing prices or prices causing money? When discussing this question one has to distinguish between the case when money stock is (i) demand determined or (ii) supply determined. If money stock is demand determined, then the arguments above suggest that prices are causing money. If money stock is supply determined and central banks can effectively control money stock, for example by keeping money velocity at a stationary level, then $\{a_{11} < 0,\ a_{12} = 0,\ \text{and } a_{13} = 0\}$ should be the case. If inflation is increasing in the short run with excess money supply, then we would expect $\{a_{21} > 0,\ a_{22} = a_{23} = 0\}$. In this case prices are adjusting in the *short run* to the level of nominal money stock. The question whether prices causes money or money causes prices in the *long run* has to be answered based on the estimates of the long-run impact of a shock in money stock on prices, as compared to the impact of a shock in prices on money stock.

Therefore, the question whether money causes prices or prices cause money empirically is a difficult and intricate econometric question. This is in striking contrast to the simplistic argument behind the inverted money-demand relation in Romer (1996).

12. Conclusions

The motivation for writing this paper was to point out the need for research programmes in macroeconomics that mimics that of the present state of research in macroeconometrics, in the sense of developing theoretical models of the macroeconomy that replicates the basic features of macroeconomic data, such as:

- stochastic variables and relations,
- strongly time-dependent data,
- cointegration and integration properties,
- short-run adjustment towards long-run dynamic or static steady-states,
- short-run and long-run feedback effects.

I have tried to illustrate the potential usefulness of the cointegrated VAR model to address important macroeconomic questions. My purpose has been to demonstrate that within this framework:

- conventional macroeconomic questions can be efficiently addressed,
- a large number of additional questions can be empirically investigated,
- new macroeconomic hypotheses are likely to emerge for further theoretical development.

I have primarily addressed questions related to the cointegration property of the data and the corresponding dynamic adjustment processes, thereby demonstrating the potential usefulness of the VAR model for inference on macroeconomic transmission mechanisms. But a large number of additional questions related to the analysis of static and dynamic steady-states, speed of adjustment, long-run and short-run feed-back effects, weak, strong, and super exogeneity, driving forces, expectations formation, etc., have only been briefly touched upon. The interested reader is referred to a large number of published papers that address these issues in more detail.

With the above (admittedly quite simplistic) examples I have tried to demonstrate that careful empirical analyses based on the basic features of the cointegrated VAR model can be useful for asking relevant macroeconomic questions. The requirement that all empirical statements have to be consistent with the information given by the full stochastic model should minimize the risk for 'ad hoc' results. Nevertheless, data do play a dominant role in this approach and the ultimate testing of new hypotheses suggested by the empirical analysis has to be made against new data.

REFERENCES

Doornik, J. A. and Hendry, D. F. (1998) *GiveWin. An interface to empirical modelling*, Timberlake Consultants.

Friedman, M. (1970) 'The counterrevolution in monetary theory', Institute of Economic Affairs, Occasional Paper 33.

Gilbert, C. L. (1986) 'Professor Hendry's methodology', *Oxford Bulletin of Economics and Statistics* 48: 283–307.

Haavelmo, T. (1943) 'The probabilty approach in econometrics', *Econometrica* 12(suppl.): 1–118.

Hansen, H. and Warne, A. (1995) 'A common trends analysis of Danish unemployment', submitted to *Empirical Economies*.

Hendry, D. F. (1995) *Dynamic Econometrics* (Oxford: Oxford University Press).

—— and Ericsson, N. R. (1991) 'An econometric analysis of UK money demand in Monetary trends in the United States and the United Kingdom by Milton Friedman and Anna J. Schwartz', *American Economic Review* 81: 8–38.

—— and Juselius, K. (2000) 'Explaining cointegration analysis: Part 1', *The Energy Journal* 21: 1–42.

—— and Mizon, G. E. (1993) 'Evaluating econometric models by encompassing the VAR' in *Models, Methods and Applications of Econometrics*, ed. P. C. Phillips (Oxford: Blackwell).

Hoffman, M. (2000) 'The relative dynamics of investment and the current account in the G7 economies', University of Southampton discussion paper in Economics and Econometrics 0005/2000.

Johansen, S. (1992) 'A representation of vector autoregressive processes integrated of order 2', *Econometric Theory* 8: 188–202.

—— (1995a) 'A statistical analysis of cointegration for $I(2)$ variables', *Econometric Theory* 11: 25–59.

—— (1995b) 'Identifying restrictions of linear equations: with applications to simultaneous equations and cointegration', *Journal of Econometrics* 69: 111–32.

—— (1995c) *Likelihood Based Inference in Cointegrated Vector Autoregressive Models* (Oxford and New York: Oxford University Press).

—— (1999) 'A Bartlett correction factor for tests on the cointegrating relations', *Econometric Theory*, forthcoming.

—— (2000) 'A small sample correction for tests of hypotheses on the cointegrating vectors', *Journal of Econometrics* forthcoming.

—— and Juselius, K. (1992) 'Testing structural hypotheses in a multivariate cointegration analysis of the *PPP* and the UIP for UK', *Journal of Econometrics* 53: 211–44.

—— and —— (1994) 'Identification of the long-run and the short-run structure, An application to the ISLM model', *Journal of Econometrics* 63: 7–36.

—— and Nielsen, B. (1993) 'Asympotics for cointegration rank tests in the presence of intervention dummies', Manual for the simulation program DisCo, Preprint, University of Copenhagen, http:www.math.ku.dk.

Jørgensen, C. (1998) 'A simulation study of tests in the cointegrated VAR model', Ch. 3 in 'On the I(2) cointegration model', Ph.D. thesis, Institute of Economics, University of Copenhagen.

Juselius, K. (1993) 'VAR models and Haavelmo's probability approach to macroeconomic modelling', *Empirical Economics* 18: 595–622.

—— (1996) 'An empirical analysis of the changing role of the German Bundesbank after 1983', *Oxford Bulletin of Economics and Statistics* 58: 791–819.

—— (1998a) 'Changing monetary transmission mechanisms within the EU', *Empirical Economics* 23: 455–81.

—— (1998b) 'A structured VAR under changing monetary policy', *Journal of Business and Economics Statistics* 16: 400–12.

—— and Gennari, E. (2000) 'European integration and monatary transmission mechanisms: The case of Italy', submitted to *Journal of Applied Econometrics*.

—— and Toro, J. (1999) 'The effect of joining the EMS: Monetary transmission mechanisms in Spain', Working Paper, 22, Institute of Economics, University of Copenhagen.

King, R. G., Plosser, C. I., Stock, J. H., and Watson, M. W. (1991) 'Stochastic trends and economic fluctuations', *American Economic Review* 81: 819–40.

Levtchenkova, S., Pagan, A., and Robertson, J. (1998) 'Shocking stories', *Journal of Economic Surveys* 12, 507–32.

Mellander, E., Vredin, A., and Warne, A. (1992) 'Stochastic trends and economic fluctuations in a small open economy', *Journal of Applied Econometrics* 7: 369–94.

Pagan, A. R. (1987) 'Three econometric methodologies: A critical appraisal', *Journal of Economic Surveys* 1: 3–24.

Paruolo, P. (1996) 'On the determination of integration indices in $I(2)$ systems', *Journal of Econometrics* 72: 313–56.

Rahbek, A., Kongsted, H. C., and Jørgensen, C. (1999) 'Trend-Stationarity in the $I(2)$ Cointegration Model', *Journal of Econometrics* 90: 265–89.

Romer, D. (1996) *Advanced Macroeconomics* (New York: McGraw-Hill).

Rubin, J. (1998) 'On the permanent-transitory decomposition in the cointegrated VAR', in '*Econometric Studies of a European Economic and Monetary Union*', Ph.D. thesis 45, Institute of Economics, University of Copenhagen.

9 Unit roots and all that: the impact of time-series methods on macroeconomics

RON P. SMITH

1. Introduction

Over the past twenty years or so applied macroeconomics has been transformed by the widespread adoption of a set of new statistical techniques. The techniques I shall focus on are: unit-root tests, vector autoregressions (VARs), Granger-causality tests, and cointegration, which I will refer to as 'unit roots etc.'.[1] Although these techniques were invented to answer statistical questions, they diffused very rapidly through applied economics because they were thought to be able to answer important theoretical questions in macroeconomics. I will argue that these techniques have not delivered on the early promises made for economics. They did not deliver on their promises, not because the techniques were not useful (they have proved very useful for a range of purposes), but because the promises were unrealistic. The promise appeared to be that difficult economic questions could be unambiguously answered by the mechanical application of statistical techniques.[2] This is a story about the gullibility of many economists who wanted to believe that 'Yes, Virginia, there really is a free lunch' and were inevitably disappointed. It is not primarily a story about statistical snake-oil salesmen: their claims were usually well qualified, though not always in a language the potential users understood. My impression is that issues that are well known in the technical literature are not always appreciated by applied economists. Therefore I have deliberately kept the exposition in this paper very elementary.[3]

Section 2 examines the statistical motivation for the development of these techniques and provides a brief review to establish terminology and notation. To emphasize conceptual motivation it deliberately abstracts from all the technical statistical issues and uses very simple economic examples for exposition. Section 3 examines the economic motivation for adopting these techniques. Section 4 examines the issues in interpretation that arise in using the techniques for these purposes, trying

Prepared for the conference on 'Theory and Evidence in Macroeconomics', Bergamo, October 1998. I am grateful for the comments of the discussants at the conference. Much of the work on this paper was done while I was visiting the University of Colorado at Boulder.

[1] There are a range of other time-series techniques that might be included, such as GARCH, Markov switching models, non-linear adjustment processes, panel time-series, etc. However, my impression is that these have not yet been as important in macroeconomics as the four I focus on. In addition, the four I have chosen are very closely linked, so it is natural to consider them together.

[2] Of course, earlier techniques were also often used mechanically.

[3] More technical discussions can be found in Pesaran and Smith (1998) and Levtchenkova, Pagan, and Robertson (1998), LPR, on which this paper draws.

to answer the economic questions. I make no claim for originality in identifying these problems; they are all widely known and usually clearly set out in the original literature, though they are often ignored in many applications. As Sims (1996: 109), discussing critiques of statistical methods, points out: 'The popularity of critiques probably arises from the excesses of enthusiasts of statistical methods. Pioneering statistical studies can be followed by mechanical applications. Important formal inference techniques can be elaborated beyond what is useful for, or even at the expense of, their actual application.' Section 5 concludes.

It will be useful to distinguish three stages in empirical work. We begin with some purpose, such as forecasting, explanation, or policy formation. Then we summarize the evidence, which may be either *primarily* quantitative, in which case the summaries tend to take the form of estimates or test statistics, or *primarily* qualitative, in which case we summarize the evidence in narrative description. In either case we can ask how good the summary is of what actually happened and we might construct different summaries for different purposes. In both cases I emphasize *primarily*, because much qualitative judgement goes into statistical models and much quantitative information goes into narrative description. Finally, we interpret the empirical summary in terms of economic concepts.[4] Again this can be done numerically or it can be done verbally. Statements like 'The US depression of the 1930s was caused by monetary contraction which led the economy to stabilize at an underemployment equilibrium' interpret the evidence in terms of unmeasurable economic concepts (caused, stabilized, underemployment, equilibrium), as much as any formal model does. Qualitative and quantitative accounts are usually regarded as substitutes, alternative ways of doing economics; I will treat them as complements. The economic interpretation of statistical summaries can be done in a number of ways. I will emphasize two. The first is translating the statistical summaries into estimates of the economic measures of interest. The second is using the estimates to interpret specific historical events.

To answer many interesting macroeconomic questions, interpretation is central. However, for other purposes, e.g. unconditional forecasting, one does not need to interpret the statistical summary: if the summary model forecasts well it can be used without any interpretation. In empirical sciences, like medicine, this may be the rule: aspirin was used to relieve pain long before anyone could interpret how it worked. In economics, where empirical regularities are rarer, people may have more confidence in an apparent regularity if it can be given some interpretation. Of course physicians usually provided interpretations, e.g. of how aspirin worked, long before there was any basis for them.

In general, collecting and summarizing the evidence does not imply an interpretation. This is an issue that has been extensively discussed by historians and is also relevant to statistics. The 'facts', in themselves, do not provide an answer to the interesting theoretical questions. Much of the problem of the unit root etc. literature

---

[4] These elements—purpose, summary, and interpretation—are closely related to the criteria of relevance, statistical adequacy, and consistency with theory used in Pesaran and Smith (1985). I have adopted the 'summarize' and 'interpret' terminology from LPR (1998).

arises from the belief that estimates or test statistics would provide the answers in themselves. This is a particular case of the confusion of economic importance with statistical significance repeatedly criticized by McCloskey (e.g. 1985: ch. 9). The economic question, 'How large is large?' (e.g. deviations from purchasing power parity), cannot be answered from the statistical question: 'Could this estimate have arisen by chance in a sample of this size?' Much of the unit root etc. literature shows the same type of confusion: the belief that a statistical result could answer an economic question without interpretation.

In trying to provide an idealized history of the interaction between the statistical innovations and their economic adoption in macroeconomics, there are some problems of terminology and historiography. First, although this paper is about econometrics, I have avoided using the term. I want to distinguish between issues of statistical methods and economic theory, and econometrics is about synthesizing statistical methods, economic theory and data, thus combining the elements I want to distinguish. Whenever I use the term 'theory' it applies to economic theory, interpreted widely, not just 'pure theory', rather than econometric or statistical theory. Secondly, the sequence I adopt for conceptual and expositional purposes to analyse the techniques: unit roots, VARs, Granger causality, and cointegration, does not correspond to the historical sequence of the development of these techniques. Of these four techniques historically Granger causality came first and all had their origins in a long tradition of time-series analysis. Thirdly, it should be emphasized that there is no coherent group of 'unit-rooter' statisticians; there are significant disagreements between the people who developed these techniques. For instance, Sims who was central to the adoption of VARs and Granger causality in economics, is highly sceptical of unit-root testing and cointegration. A time-series statistician, Harvey (1997: 200), provides a rousing denunciation of the whole enterprise: 'The recent emphasis on unit roots, vector autoregressions and cointegration has focussed too much attention on tackling uninteresting problems by flawed methods.'

2. Statistical motivation

To begin this section, a metaphor might be useful. The classic image of a random walk (unit-root process) is a drunk farmer[5] staggering out of the bar to find his way home across the fields. He takes a pace forward in the direction of home, then randomly staggers a pace left or right; and goes on doing this. He could end up anywhere, unfortunate runs of leftward staggers are consistent with randomness. Each stagger has a permanent effect. If a sober friend leaves the bar some time later trying to find him, the friend's best guess is to head towards the drunk's farm: on average the left and right staggers should cancel out. But the longer the drunk has been staggering, the more odd sequences of left or right staggers could accumulate and the further from the path he could have got. Cointegration is a story about two drunks leaving the bar

---

[5] In Boulder, an agricultural entrepreneur challenged by alcohol impairment.

together heading for the same house, arranged so they do not knock each other over when they stagger in opposite directions. If they go off independently, they will stagger in different ways and will tend to diverge. If they are going to stay together, one, or other, or both has got to take account of the distance between them and stagger in the direction of the other drunk; there has to be some Granger causality. The question of interpretation is: having measured various farmers' paths, how do you decide whether they were drunk and not merely wandering around checking their cows?

Suppose we have data on an economic variable, y_t; $t = 1, \ldots, T$. In the examples in this section, y_t will be taken as the logarithm of per-capita GDP, measured over a number of years. Economic variables are trended and a central statistical issue is the nature of the trend. There are two popular candidate models. The trend-stationary model is:

$$y_t = \alpha + \rho y_{t-1} + (1 - \rho)gt + \varepsilon_t \tag{1}$$

an autoregressive process, y_t regressed on its own lag, with a deterministic trend t. The process will be stationary around the trend, if: $-1 < \rho < 1$ and ε_t is a mean zero stationary error.[6] Stable, linear difference equations with a deterministic trend have been standard in empirical economic models since the 1930s, given their ability to allow for both growth and cycles. This is a first-order process, a single lag of y_t on the right-hand side, but higher orders, more lags of y, can be included. The long-run growth rate of the variable (assuming it is in logarithms) is g.

The unit-root or difference-stationary model (the variable is stationary having been first differenced) arises when $\rho = 1$,[7] giving

$$\Delta y_t = y_t - y_{t-1} = \alpha + \varepsilon_t. \tag{2}$$

A special case of the difference-stationary model is the random walk, where the error term is not only stationary, but white noise.[8] The growth rate of the difference-stationary series is α, often called the 'drift term'.[9]

If starting from year zero, we substitute back using:

$$y_t = \alpha + y_{t-1} + \varepsilon_t = 2\alpha + y_{t-2} + \varepsilon_t + \varepsilon_{t-1},$$

etc. we get

$$y_t = y_0 + \alpha t + \sum_{i=0}^{t-1} \varepsilon_{t-i}.$$

---

[6] A variable is said to be 'stationary' if its mean, variance, and covariances with its earlier values do not change with time. This is also called 'weak', 'second-order', or 'covariance stationarity'.

[7] The terminology arises because in higher-order equations, more lags, the issue is not whether $\rho = 1$, but whether any roots of the characteristic equation which determines stability equal one.

[8] A white-noise error term has mean zero, constant variance and is independent of its previous values.

[9] To visualize a random walk with drift, just imagine the field is sloping so the drunks have a tendency to drift downhill as they stagger home.

Thus y_t is determined by its initial value, a deterministic trend, and a 'stochastic trend', the sum of the past errors. In a stable autoregression, past errors are multiplied by ρ^t, with $-1 < \rho < 1$, so the effects of the shocks tend quite quickly to zero as time passes; the effects of shocks are transitory, the drunk tends to return to the path. When $\rho = 1$, the effects are permanent, they remain forever embodied in all future values of y_t, the drunk could stagger anywhere.

In economics, the common practice was to take deviations from a deterministic trend; in statistics, under the influence of Box and Jenkins (1970) the practice was to remove the trend by differencing. These two methods of detrending produced series which looked very different: deviations of log income from a linear trend show recognizable long cycles; growth rates (the change in the logarithm) look much more random. The number of times you needed to difference the series to make it stationary (after removing deterministic components, like the trend) is called the 'order of integration'. A variable is integrated of order zero, $I(0)$, if it does not need differencing to make it stationary, like the trend-stationary case above. It is integrated of order one, $I(1)$, if it must be differenced once to make it stationary. Box–Jenkins models differenced the series enough to make it stationary and then modelled the series in terms of its lagged values through either moving average or autoregressive terms.[10] This approach produced very parsimonious models (few estimated parameters) which tended to forecast quite well. Practitioners of this method determined the order of integration by inspecting various graphs. In principle, it is merely a matter of testing whether $\rho = 1$: whether there was a unit root in y_t. In practice, under the null hypothesis that $\rho = 1$, the estimate $\hat{\rho}$ had a non-standard distribution, so devising a test was not straightforward. A test was developed by Dickey and Fuller (1979) and subsequently a range of other tests have been proposed and widely used to test the unit-root hypothesis. The unit-root hypothesis was rarely rejected for economic time-series. This seemed to indicate that most economic variables were $I(1)$ and contained a stochastic trend.

The Box–Jenkins methodology was essentially univariate, but economists were primarily interested in the interactions between variables. The multivariate form of the autoregression is the vector autoregression, VAR.[11] Suppose that we were interested in the interaction between real income and real money, where m_t is the logarithm of real per-capita money stock. The first-order, one-lag, VAR involves regressing each variable on lagged values of itself and the other variable, as well as any deterministic component such as a trend. For instance:

$$y_t = a_{10} + a_{11}y_{t-1} + a_{12}m_{t-1} + \gamma_1 t + \varepsilon_{1t},$$

$$m_t = a_{20} + a_{21}y_{t-1} + a_{22}m_{t-1} + \gamma_2 t + \varepsilon_{2t}. \tag{3}$$

[10] These models are often called ARIMA (autoregressive, integrated, moving average models).
[11] Although VARs (or 'very awful regressions' as they are sometimes known) have been widely adopted by economists there is still considerable debate as to whether they are an appropriate statistical summary of economic time-series, see Harvey (1997).

Notice that the first equation is of the same form as (1), with the addition of lagged money. If lagged values of money help to predict current income, i.e. $a_{12} \neq 0$ in this simple case, or equivalently current values of money help to predict future income, then money is said to be 'Granger-causal' with respect to income. Similarly, if $a_{21} \neq 0$, income is Granger-causal with respect to money (Granger 1969). Granger causality can run in both, either or neither direction.[12]

Economists in the LSE tradition had often treated income as exogenous and estimated 'structural' money-demand equations like:

$$m_t = \alpha_0 + \beta_0 y_t + \beta_1 y_{t-1} + \alpha_1 m_{t-1} + \gamma t + u_t, \tag{4}$$

where the time trend captures, say, financial liberalization. The long-run money-demand function (when $m_t = m_{t-1} = m$; $y_t = y_{t-1} = y$) can be calculated as:

$$m = \frac{\alpha_0}{1 - \alpha_1} + \frac{\beta_0 + \beta_1}{1 - \alpha_1} y + \frac{\gamma}{1 - \alpha_1} t \tag{5}$$

or

$$m = \theta_0 + \theta_1 y + \theta_2 t. \tag{6}$$

One can then test hypotheses like $\theta_1 = 1$; the long-run income elasticity of demand for money is unity. This autoregressive distributed lag (ARDL) model (4) or dynamic linear regression model (see Hendry *et al.* 1984 for a survey) can be rewritten (re-parameterized) in error-correction form:

$$\Delta m_t = a_0 + b_0 \Delta y_t + b_1 y_{t-1} + a_1 m_{t-1} + ct + u_t. \tag{7}$$

This is statistically identical to (4), e.g. identical estimated residuals, but in terms of different parameters, $b_1 = \beta_0 + \beta_1$; $a_1 = -(1 - \alpha_1)$; so $\theta_1 = -b_1/a_1$ and the equation could also be written as

$$\Delta m_t = b_0 \Delta y_t - \lambda(m_{t-1} - \theta_0 - \theta_1 y_{t-1} - \theta_2 t) + u_t, \tag{8}$$

where $\lambda = -a_1$ measures the speed of adjustment and the term in parentheses (the deviation from long-run money-run demand equilibrium) was the error, which was being corrected by the adjustment process. Alogoskoufis and Smith (1991) provide a survey of error-correction models (ECMs). ECMs worked well in many economic applications, being both able to fit the data and to be interpreted in terms of long-run economic theory.

To time-series statisticians within the Box–Jenkins tradition ECMs like (7) did not make any sense. The variables m_t and y_t were clearly $I(1)$: they needed to be differenced once to make them stationary. But if you tried to explain an $I(0)$ variable, Δm_t, by two $I(1)$ variables, lagged m_t and y_t, the two sides of the equation did not

---

[12] Strictly, this is Granger causality in mean; one could also have predictability of higher moments.

balance. The only way that the equation could balance was if $(m_{t-1} - \theta_0 - \theta_1 y_{t-1} - \theta_2 t)$ was in fact $I(0)$. In general, a linear combination of $I(1)$ variables will be $I(1)$, but if there is a linear combination that is $I(0)$, they are said to 'cointegrate' (Engle and Granger 1987). What happens is that the stochastic trends in the two variables exactly cancel out, so the two variables keep close together, making the linear combination (the error or deviation from equilibrium) stationary. As with the drunks, to keep them close requires some feedback between the two variables and this implies that there must be Granger causality in at least one direction.

There is another statistical motivation for cointegration. It has been well known since Yule (1926) that time-series regressions can be misleading, spurious, if the variables are both trended. With trend-stationary variables the problem can be dealt with by including a deterministic trend. Granger and Newbold (1974) re-opened this issue by showing that regressions of two unrelated variables which followed independent random walks (difference-stationary or $I(1)$ variables), would produce significant t-statistics and large R^2. Asymptotically as the length of the time-series increased the R^2 would go to unity, see Phillips (1986). The problem here is that both variables contain stochastic trends. The condition required for a regression of one $I(1)$ variable on another not to be spurious is that the variables cointegrate: there is a common stochastic trend which is cancelled out by the linear combination.

The analysis of cointegration is most conveniently done in a VAR rewritten as a vector error-correction model (VECM). The VAR (3) can be rewritten (re-parameterized) as:

$$\Delta y_t = a_{10} + (a_{11} - 1)y_{t-1} + a_{12}m_{t-1} + \gamma_1 t + \varepsilon_{1t},$$
$$\Delta m_t = a_{20} + a_{21}y_{t-1} + (a_{22} - 1)m_{t-1} + \gamma_2 t + \varepsilon_{2t}. \tag{9}$$

If the levels variables cointegrate, there is a linear combination of them, called the 'cointegrating vector', that is $I(0)$. The changes in each variable are linear functions of this $I(0)$ variable, which is usually interpreted as a deviation from equilibrium:

$$\Delta y_t = \lambda_1(m_{t-1} - \theta_0 - \theta_1 y_{t-1} - \theta_2 t) + u_{t1},$$
$$\Delta m_t = \lambda_2(m_{t-1} - \theta_0 - \theta_1 y_{t-1} - \theta_2 t) + u_{2t}. \tag{10}$$

A re-parameterization does not change the number of parameters estimated ((3) and (9) each involve estimating eight parameters, four in each equation) and the equations are statistically identical. But in moving from (9) to (10) we have imposed restrictions, since the latter only estimates five parameters, $\lambda_1, \lambda_2, \theta_0, \theta_1, \theta_2$. These cross-equation restrictions are of the form that the long-run income elasticity of money demand is the same in the income and money equations. For the variables to cointegrate, either λ_1 or λ_2 or both must be non-zero, there must be feedback from the deviation from equilibrium to keep the variables moving too far apart, i.e. there must be Granger causality in at least one direction. If both λ_1 and λ_2 are zero, and the shocks are white noise, then y_t and m_t are just random walks. Once the basic idea was appreciated a large number of techniques were proposed for testing the null hypothesis of no cointegration and estimating the cointegrating vectors, the θ_i in this case, if the null hypothesis was rejected. Although the statistical properties of the alternative techniques vary, the market leader is the procedure proposed by Johansen (1988). It is very widely used because it was rapidly implemented in popular packages, it handles multiple cointegrating vectors easily, and it integrates testing and estimation within a consistent framework.

3. Economic purpose

The previous section discussed the statistical issues these techniques addressed; this section discusses the economic issues they were hoped to address. I will follow the same sequence as before: unit roots, VARs, Granger causality, and cointegration, although, as noted in the introduction, this was not the historical order in which the techniques were developed. The economic questions that they were designed to answer were the nature of the trend and cycle, the nature of the shocks that caused the cycle, the pattern of causality, and the existence and nature of equilibrium.

The paper that brought the issues of unit-root testing to economists' attention was Nelson and Plosser (1982). The motivation for this paper was explicitly economic. It was suggested that demand shocks were transitory, supply shocks were permanent. Thus one could distinguish whether demand shocks (Keynesian or monetarist) or supply shocks (real business cycle) were a better explanation of fluctuations by determining whether log GDP and other economic variables were $I(0)$ or $I(1)$. If GDP were $I(1)$, difference-stationary, this would suggest that shocks were permanent supply shocks; if it were $I(0)$, this would suggest that shocks were transitory, demand shocks around a deterministic trend. By applying Dickey–Fuller tests, Nelson and Plosser concluded that most economic series were $I(1)$ and thus they interpreted the shocks as supply- rather than demand-determined. 'We conclude that macroeconomic models that focus on monetary disturbances as a source of purely transitory fluctuations may never be successful in explaining a large fraction of output variations and that stochastic variation due to real factors is an essential element of any model of macroeconomic fluctuations' Nelson and Posser (1982: 39). Their results also killed the previously fashionable model which explained GDP variations by money-supply surprises; there was no way this could be true since money-supply surprises were white noise by construction and GDP variations were highly persistent. The Lucas supply curve, found in most theoretical models at that time, just could not provide an interpretation of the summary statistics of the time-series properties.

Beveridge and Nelson (1981) provided a new way of separating the permanent, trend, components from the transitory shocks. This literature was a continuation of a much older economic research programme, distinguishing between shocks and transmission mechanisms. It was continued by, among others, Blanchard and Quah (1989) and King *et al.* (1991). The economic question was whether these statistical techniques would allow one to separate trend and cycle, shocks and transmission mechanism. King *et al.* (1991: 819) summarize the economic issues:

A central, suprising and controversial result of some current research on real business cycles is the claim that a common stochastic trend—the cumulative effect of permanent shocks to productivity—underlies the bulk of economic fluctuations. If confirmed this finding would imply that many other forces have been relatively unimportant over historical business cycles, including monetary and fiscal policy shocks stressed in traditional macroeconomic analysis.

Further, while it had long been known that certain theories, in particular the efficient market hypothesis, implied that asset prices should be random walks, Hall (1978) showed that under certain assumptions the permanent income theory implied that consumption should also be a random walk. Thus the order of integration had implications for macroeconomics as well as finance. Testing the permanent income hypothesis seemed merely a matter of testing whether consumption was a random walk, a matter of testing whether any past information could predict changes in consumption.

The adoption of VARs was also a response to a set of economic problems. The first was practical: the traditional structural macroeconometric models had appeared to forecast poorly relative to simple Box–Jenkins models in the early 1970s. The second was theoretical: there was increasing dissatisfaction with the arbitrary division of variables into endogenous and exogenous[13] and the 'incredible' identifying assumptions, particularly the exclusion restrictions, required to identify traditional macroeconomic models. The classic paper is Sims (1980). VARs, by treating all variables symmetrically as endogenous, avoided the need to distinguish a priori between endogenous and exogenous and being purely statistical reduced forms did not require identifying assumptions. VARs also appeared to provide a framework within which the exogeneity assumptions could be tested. Contrast (4) with (3). The first assumes income is exogenous and that money demand equals money supply, both potentially questionable assumptions. The second allows the interaction between the two variables to be determined purely by the data. There had been a substantial dispute about whether money caused income or income caused money and Granger-causality tests appeared to provide a way to answer a central economic question (Sims 1972). It seemed that money could be treated as exogenous if it was not Granger-caused by income and this was a testable proposition.

VARs need not be atheoretical: if agents face linear constraints and quadratic objective functions, their optimal decision rules can be written as VARs and rational expectations impose cross-equation restrictions on these VARs. Subject to these restrictions, the coefficients estimated from these VARs can be used to estimate the 'deep parameters' of technology and tastes; Hansen and Sargent (1991, which was written much earlier) and Sargent (1978) emphasize this promise of the VAR.

Cointegration offered an empirical way of dealing with two fundamental economic issues. First, it provided a way of testing the stability of the great ratios (Kosobud and

---

[13] Liu (1960) is an early expression of this dissatisfaction.

Klein 1961). These included purchasing power parity, constant real exchange rate, stable money demand, constant velocity of circulation, consumption function proportionality, constant consumption (saving) income ratios, etc. Theorists tended to take them as empirical (if stylized) facts; empirical economists tended to take them as theoretical predictions. If the logarithms of the original variables were $I(1)$, the logarithms of these ratios should be $I(0)$, and this was testable. The second possibility cointegration appeared to offer was to operationalize the fundamental economic concept of equilibrium as meaning that some linear combination of non-stationary variables should be stationary. Under this definition, one could test for the existence of equilibrium, estimate the equilibrium relationship, and measure the adjustment processes that returned the economy to equilibrium.

4. Issues in interpretation

The statistical problem is to obtain summaries of the data: estimates, test statistics, residuals, etc., with known properties. The economic problem is to relate these estimates and test statistics to the economic concepts, parameters, or other measures of economic interest. This raises issues of identification, which is discussed first. Then the difficulties in interpreting the summaries are considered for four sets of economic measures: trend and cycle, shocks, causality, and equilibrium. Then the issue of inference, judging the quality of the statistical summary, is discussed, and finally the consequences of these issues are discussed.

4.1. Observational equivalence and identification

Observational equivalence is, as Hansen and Heckman (1996: 87) point out, pervasive in economics: alternative interpretations, with quite different theoretical or policy implications, are equally consistent with the same data. Again, a metaphor might help. You are on the bridge of a ship, and you can observe the helmsman wildly swinging the wheel and frantically adjusting the engines while the ship continues on a steady course. These observations are consistent with either the hypothesis that the controls are having no effect or that the helmsman is effectively offsetting the effects of wind and tide to maintain a steady course. No analysis of the data would allow one to decide between the explanations, they are observationally equivalent. Other information is needed to identify which is the correct interpretation of the data. Once this extra information, e.g. a belief that the controls do work, has been used to identify the interpretation, the observations can be used to answer other questions, e.g. how good a job the helmsman is doing, a question that makes no sense if the controls do not work.

While in principle the identification issue is straightforward, in practice very effective aversion therapy—traumatic early exposure to rank and order conditions—encourages most economists to treat identification as a complex technical issue rather than a question about how to interpret data. The basic issue is how our observations, or summaries of them in estimates and test statistics calculated from the associations or correlations in the data, can be interpreted in economic terms. This is just as much a problem for narrative accounts. After 1979 the UK observed a massive drop in manufacturing output; at the same time it also became an oil producer and experimented with rather different fiscal and monetary policy rules. How you tell an economic story about those observations, and there are a number of different stories that could be told, is an identification problem.

To illustrate the formal story of identification, let us return to the money–income example. An unrestricted 'structural form', which allows for both simultaneous and lagged feedback between the two variables is:

$$m_t = c_{10} + c_{11}m_{t-1} + c_{12}y_{t-1} + c_{13}t + b_{11}y_t + v_{1t},$$
$$y_t = c_{20} + c_{21}m_{t-1} + c_{22}y_{t-1} + c_{23}t + b_{21}m_t + v_{2t}. \tag{11}$$

If the right-hand-side endogenous variables are solved out, one gets the 'reduced form':

$$m_t = (1 - b_{11}b_{21})^{-1}[(c_{10} + b_{11}c_{20}) + (c_{11} + b_{11}c_{21})m_{t-1}$$
$$+ (c_{12} + b_{11}c_{22})y_{t-1} + (c_{13} + b_{11}c_{23})t + (v_{1t} + b_{11}v_{2t})],$$
$$y_t = (1 - b_{11}b_{21})^{-1}[(c_{20} + b_{21}c_{10}) + (c_{21} + b_{21}c_{11})m_{t-1}$$
$$+ (c_{22} + b_{21}c_{12})y_{t-1} + (c_{23} + b_{21}c_{13})t + (v_{2t} + b_{21}v_{1t})] \tag{12}$$

which in this case is the VAR (3):

$$y_t = a_{10} + a_{11}y_{t-1} + a_{12}m_{t-1} + \gamma_1 t + \varepsilon_{1t},$$
$$m_t = a_{20} + a_{21}y_{t-1} + a_{22}m_{t-1} + \gamma_2 t + \varepsilon_{2t},$$

the eight regression parameters of which can be consistently estimated by ordinary least squares. The structural form has ten parameters, so we cannot estimate these from the eight reduced-form parameters without some extra information: two restrictions to reduce the number of unknown parameters in the structural form to eight. Notice also that, as is clear from (12), the reduced-form errors will be complicated mixtures of the structural errors and cannot be interpreted as pure money and income shocks.

To interpret the summary statistics, the estimated parameters and errors from the VAR, one has to supplement the data with an untestable economic story. The plausibility of the interpretation then depends on the plausibility of that economic story. There are many such stories all implying different interpretations. One possibility is to assume that lagged income does not influence money and lagged money does not influence income, $c_{12} = c_{21} = 0$. However, one might have little confidence in these restrictions, since if current money influences income, there is no strong reason to believe that lagged money does not influence income. Another possibility is to impose a causal ordering, such as that money does not influence current income, $b_{12} = 0$, and the two structural errors are uncorrelated $E(v_{1t}v_{2t}) = 0$. With these two restrictions, the system becomes recursive and each equation can be consistently estimated by least squares. Orthogonalized impulse response functions impose this recursive identifying assumption through the choice of order of the variables. Again there may be no very strong theoretical justifications for these particular restrictions. Ideally we would like 'weak' just-identifying assumptions on which everybody could agree, but these may not be available.

4.2. Trend and cycle

For various purposes economists wish to decompose an observed time-series into a trend component and a cyclical component:[14]

$$y_t = \tau_t + v_t, \quad t = 1, 2, \ldots, T.$$

There are obviously an infinite number of ways that this could be done in addition to the ways considered in Section 2, though many of these ways would be very silly. But they would all have the property that the sum of the two components 'explained' the observed series exactly. If one were purely interested in forecasting, one could choose a decomposition such that the predicted value for h periods ahead, $\hat{\tau}_{T+h}$, was likely to have the smallest forecasting error,[15] but this estimate may not look like a trend as it is usually interpreted in economics. Even if we agree on some broad characterization of what trend and cycle should look like, e.g. the trend should account for as much of the variance of y_t as possible while being fairly smooth (e.g. as in the Hodrik–Prescott filter), we would still have to choose what we mean by 'fairly smooth'. Getting this wrong can give us silly decompositions.[16] It is noticeable that when people propose new methods for decomposing trend and cycle on US data, they evaluate them by how well they replicate the NBER reference cycles, based on explicit economic judgements. For series in other countries there is rarely a sensible reference point to evaluate the statistical procedure. As Canova (1998: 500) comments 'Different detrending methods imply different sets of economic relations because they generate different economic concepts of the business cycle.'

4.3. Shocks

Having decomposed the series into trend and cyclical component, we may then wish to interpret the shocks that cause the variation in trend and cycle, e.g. in terms of demand and supply shocks. Two common and statistically convenient identifying assumptions are either that demand shocks are transitory and supply shocks permanent, or that

---

[14] This simplifies the problem because after detrending the residual will contain not just the cycle but other components such as seasonal and irregular factors which have to be filtered out.

[15] This would usually imply that v_t should be an unforecastable innovation and τ_t a function of past information and some parameters that were constant over time.

[16] The value of the smoothing parameter of 1600 for the Hodrik–Prescott filter gives sensible results for the logarithm of quarterly US GNP, but silly results for other time-series; again the silly/sensible interpretation is an economic, not a statistical judgement.

demand and supply shocks are independent. Neither may be economically plausible. The Depression of the 1930s is usually interpreted as an international demand shock but it had very long-lasting effects. Natural disasters—hurricanes, tornadoes, etc.— are usually interpreted as supply shocks destroying physical and human capital, but tend to have transitory effects. Major wars, supply shocks which destroy large amounts of physical and human capital, tend to have transitory effects, as German and Japanese recovery indicated. This 'phoenix effect' of wars was extensively discussed by economists in the nineteenth century. The interpretation of the Korean and Vietnam Wars shocks to the US economy is more complicated but both involved demand and supply effects. Whatever their interpretation, such major shocks have implications for unit-root testing. An $I(0)$ series with a step change can also be described as $I(1)$ since shocks, such as step changes like the 1930s Depression, have permanent effects (Perron 1989). The decomposition has to be interpreted in terms of the underlying narrative, which will determine whether it is more useful to describe it as $I(1)$ or $I(0)$ plus a step change.

Nor is orthogonality of the demand and supply shocks very plausible. In the textbook, just-identified, demand and supply model, there is no reason to expect the observed demand and supply shocks (typically labelled 'income' and 'the weather') to be uncorrelated. Imagine a major supply shock, a hurricane that destroyed a large part of the capital stock; governments would almost immediately respond with demand-management measures unpredicted on past patterns, thus the net effect of both would be difficult to determine. Automatic stabilizers like the tax system and unemployment benefit do the same for smaller shocks.

The order of integration is a summary of the sample property of the series; there is no reason to believe that it is an inherent property of the variable. Under one monetary regime inflation may be stable, prices are $I(1)$; under another regime, inflation may be accelerating, prices are $I(2)$. What is the best summary often depends on the span of the data (the length of time covered, not the number of observations). The post-Second World War UK unemployment rate is dominated by the strong upward trend from the mid-1960s, so it is best described as $I(1)$; longer spans of the unemployment rate, e.g. from the mid-nineteenth century, show a number of long cycles, but appear mean-reverting in the very long run, best described as $I(0)$. Again, to say that the UK post-war unemployment rate is best described as $I(1)$ does not mean that it really is $I(1)$. An $I(1)$ series can go anywhere, the unemployment rate, bounded by zero and unity, cannot. The tendency to think that the order of integration of the series is an inherent property is an example of the tendency to confuse useful summaries of the data with economic interpretations.

Within the US literature, dominated by the one-good closed-economy macroeconomic model, the emphasis has been on unobserved demand and supply shocks. For most of the rest of the world, multi-sector small open economies, the main shocks are observable: foreign variables like oil prices or world real interest rates, development of North Sea oil in the UK, German reunification. Trying to interpret the effects of these observable shocks, while not easy, is easier than interpreting unobservable shocks since the foreign variables may be regarded as exogenous and there may be natural exclusion restrictions. Analysis of such observable shocks indicates the difficulty of separating shocks into uncorrelated demand and supply components. While the discovery of North Sea oil in the UK was a supply shock, many of its important consequences were the product of the demand responses to it.

People also wanted to use VARs to examine the effect of shocks, in particular policy shocks to money. The problem is that, as is clear from (12), the reduced-form errors in the VAR are not structural errors and they will be correlated, because they are functions of both structural errors. Nor is the reduced-form money shock well defined, since, if ε_{1t} changes, ε_{2t} will also change, since they are correlated. Sims (1980) suggested creating new orthogonal errors to estimate the impulse response functions. These are not unique; they depend on the ordering of variables. As pointed out by Cooley and Leroy (1985), the choice of ordering was an implicit identification assumption that was equivalent to the assumption that the system was recursive, as discussed above. Again the just-identifying assumption is an a priori economic judgement, the plausibility of which can only be discussed in economic terms.

Quite apart from how one handles the identification of the shocks, it is not always clear that the estimated residuals can be interpreted as monetary policy shocks. They may not look like historical descriptions of actual monetary policy shocks and it may be implausible to assume that the information sets of monetary authorities or economic agents correspond to the variables the econometrician puts on the right-hand side of the VAR. The interpretation has to be evaluated in terms of a historical economic story.

4.4. Causality

Granger causality measures the incremental predictability that one variable provides for another. This is a useful measure in many circumstances, but, as noted very early on by economists such as Tobin and Kaldor and statisticians such as Zellner, it rarely corresponds to economic causality. However, the distinction, while well known, seems to be ignored in much of the applied literature. One of the major problems is that in terms of engineering usage, the economy is 'non-causal': the future can influence the past through expectations. Hence 'reverse causality' is common. Kaldor commented that the money supply began to increase in late November and four weeks later Christmas happened, so the money supply Granger-caused Christmas. In terms of the metaphor above the helmsman's actions are Granger non-causal with respect to the course of the ship; but, if the controls really do work, they do determine the course of the ship; Buiter (1984) and Granger (1988) discuss Granger causality and control. Another familiar example is the permanent income hypothesis, under which expected future income determines consumption but income is Granger non-causal with respect to consumption, while consumption is Granger causal with respect to income.

4.5. Equilibrium

Within the LSE tradition, the practice of using economic theory to specify the long-run equilibrium was already well established in a single-equation context. The short-run dynamics, which might be complicated mixtures of adjustment and expectations processes were left unrestricted. Even though the economy was never in equilibrium, the long run could be inferred from the attractor that the short-run adjustments were tending towards.[17] Cointegration, as noted above, was partly a response to these formulations, it extended them by allowing for multiple long-run relationships. In both contexts, the operational definition of equilibrium (e.g. Engle and Granger 1987: 252), was that a linear combination of economic variables equals zero, and that the equilibrium error, the deviation of this linear combination from zero, is stationary. This is a natural definition in the cases of the Great Ratios, where a linear combination of the logarithms of the variables should be constant, but was a very narrow version of the contested economic concept of equilibrium.[18] Equilibrium is an elusive notion in applied economics as the earlier literature on estimating disequilibrium models had shown.

Cointegrating vectors are not uniquely determined, since any linear combination of cointegrating vectors will also be a cointegrating vector. To identify a single cointegrating vector is relatively easy, we need one restriction, which is typically the normalization condition of choosing a 'dependent variable' and giving it a unit coefficient. With two cointegrating vectors, e.g. a demand equation and a supply equation, we need two restrictions on each equation; with r cointegrating vectors we need r restrictions on each equation, one of which will be provided by normalization. These restrictions can be provided by Cowles Commission-type exclusion restrictions (e.g. income does not appear in the supply equation and the weather does not appear in the demand equation), though with the difference that they apply only to the long-run relations. Johansen (1988) provided the restrictions, by treating the cointegrating vectors as eigenvectors, orthogonal with unit length. While mathematically natural, given the statistical structure of the problem, it was almost impossible to give the Johansen estimates of multiple cointegrating vectors any economic interpretation.

4.6. Inference

Even if one's objective is merely to summarize the data in a statistical test, there are difficulties and the answers to many of the empirical questions tested (Is US GDP $I(1)$? Is the real exchange rate $I(0)$? Does money Granger-cause income?) remain contested. Tests may not be useful summaries, since they provide an answer to a very specific question: what is the probability assuming the experiment was repeated many times of getting a test statistic this large if the null hypothesis and model were true? Often this is not an interesting economic question. The statistically convenient null may not be the appropriate economic one (initially the nulls were unit root and no cointegration, though tests for the nulls of stationarity or cointegration have been

---

[17] Identifying the equilibrium, adjustment, and expectations components of the conventional long-run solution (5) also presented problems which attracted a lot of attention. See the discussion in Alogoskoufis and Smith (1991).

[18] This is one reason that I am reluctant to follow Hendry in renaming ECMs as 'equilibrium correction mechanisms'.

developed). Conventional significance levels may not capture the costs of type I error (rejecting the null when it is true) or type II error (accepting the null when it is false); economic importance is not the same as statistical significance. This is a particular problem with tests of unit roots and non-cointegration, since these tests tend to have low power (probability of rejecting the null when it is false) or high probabilities of type II error. It is very difficult to distinguish unit-root processes from stationary cases where the root is close to 1. The asymptotic probability of type I error for the tests may be very misleading indications of the small sample probabilities. Usually for any hypothesis there are a number of tests available (augmented Dickey–Fuller or Phillips–Perron for unit roots) with different properties. The tests are sensitive to the sample used (the observation window); the span of the data; the number of lags; the treatment of deterministic elements such as intercepts, trends, and dummy variables; and the number of variables in the VAR. Thus even for the series most studied, US GDP, there is still no consensus as to whether it is $I(0)$ or $I(1)$, e.g. Diebold and Senhadji (1996) argue that it is $I(0)$.

4.7. Consequences

The consequence of these issues is that the statistical techniques do not give sharp answers to the questions of economic interest. Of course it was unrealistic to expect them to be able to do so. However, my impression is that much of the diffusion of these techniques was driven by such unrealistic expectations. It seems better to recognize that the statistical summaries have to be discussed in a context which asks the questions typical of any conference discussions,[19] such as:

- Why are you doing this?
- What is the quality of the data? How well do they match the theoretical concepts? Is the sample atypical or heterogeneous?
- How good are the statistical summaries? Are they sensitive to specification, structural instability, non-linearities, etc?
- How are the economic parameters of interest identified? And are the just-identifying assumptions economically plausible?
- Are the assumptions about expectations and information sets plausible? And do they give rise to problems of reverse causation?
- Does the implied economic story (e.g. about the time-pattern of monetary shocks) match wider historical evidence?

5. Conclusion

Sections 2 and 3 are deliberately positive: they try to explain why people thought these techniques would solve statistical and economic problems. Section 4 is deliberately

---

[19] These points all occur in the reports of the discussion at conferences on international business cycles and empirical macroeconomics in CEPR (1998).

negative: it tries to explain why these techniques, however useful they were in sum-marizing the data, could not answer the economic questions. The negative tone may suggest to some that I am being nihilistic, arguing that econometrics is useless. This is not the case: I believe that we have learned a lot from the exercise and that it is better to be realistic about the difficulties involved in the measurement and testing of economic theories than to assume we know the answers a priori as theorists and calibrators are prone to do. Ironically, the natural home for these techniques may be within the paradigm they were supposed to replace: structural simultaneous equations econo-metric modelling where there is a long tradition of combining the statistics with an economic interpretation. While there are many ways to do economics, if we cannot explain, at least *ex post*, how the main macroeconomic aggregates move, currently the realm of the time-series econometrican, we cannot claim either understanding or policy credibility. Not doing econometrics does not remove the difficulties. Theorists tend to use qualitative empirical information to establish stylized facts on which to base their models; Summers (1991) is a good exposition of the arguments for this approach. The qualitative information comes from 'case studies', such as the Great Depression and the reunification of Germany. In principle, these natural experiments are infor-mative; in practice, informal examination of historical incidents is liable to all the problems that plague econometrics: omitted-variable bias, identification problems, exogeneity assumptions, etc.[20] Just because there are no econometrics does not mean there are no problems of inference.

REFERENCES

Alogoskoufis, George, and Smith, Ron P. (1991) 'On error correction models: specification, interpretation and estimation', *Journal of Economic Surveys* 5(1): 97–127.

Beveridge, Stephen, and Nelson, Charles R. (1981) 'A new approach to decomposition of economic time series into permanent and transitory components with particular attention to measurement of the "business cycle"', *Journal of Monetary Economics* 7 (March): 151–74.

Blanchard, Olivier, and Quah, Danny (1989) 'The dynamic effects of aggregate demand and supply disturbances', *American Economic Review* 79: 655–73.

Box, G. E. P. and Jenkins, G. M. (1970) *Time Series Analysis, Forecasting and Control* (San Francisco, Calif.: Holden Day).

Buiter, Willem H. (1984) 'Granger causality and policy ineffectiveness', *Economica* 51: 151–62.

Canova, Fabio (1998) 'Detrending and business cycle facts', *Journal of Monetary Economics* 41: 475–512.

CEPR (1998) *CEPR Bulletin*, 70 Winter/Spring, Centre for Economic Policy Research.

Cooley, Thomas F. and Leroy, Stephen F. (1985) 'Atheoretical macroeconomics: a critique', *Journal of Monetary Economics* 16: 283–308.

Dickey, David A. and Fuller, Wayne A. (1979) 'Distribution of the estimators for autoregressive time series with a unit root', *Journal of the American Statistical Association* 74: 427–31.

---

[20] King *et al.* (1994) examine this issue in detail in the context of political science, where methodological basis for narrative stories, of the sort economic theorists often weave, has been extensively examined.

Diebold, F. X. and Senhadji, A. S. (1996) 'The uncertain unit root in real GNP: Comment', *American Economic Review* 86(5): 1291–8.

Engle, Robert F. and Granger, Clive W. J. (1987) 'Cointegration and error correction: representation, estimation and testing', *Econometrica* 55: 251–76.

Granger, Clive W. J. (1969) 'Investigating causal relations by econometric models and cross-spectral methods', *Econometrica* 37: 424–38.

—— (1988) 'Causality, cointegration and control', *Journal of Economic Dynamics and Control* 12: 275–93.

—— and Newbold, Paul (1974) 'Spurious regressions in econometrics', *Journal of Econometrics* 2: 111–20.

Hall, Robert E. (1978) 'Stochastic implications of the life cycle–permanent income hypothesis: theory and evidence', *Journal of Political Economy* 86(6): 971–88.

Hansen, Lars Peter, and Heckman, James (1996) 'The empirical foundations of calibration', *Journal of Economic Perspectives* 10(1): 87–104.

—— and Sargent, Thomas J. (1991) *Rational Expectations Econometrics* (Boulder, Colo.: Westfield Press).

Harvey, Andrew (1997) 'Trends, cycles and autoregressions', *Economic Journal* 107 (January): 192–201.

Hendry, David F., Pagan, Adrian R. and Sargan, J. Dennis (1984) 'Dynamic specification', in *Handbook of Econometrics*, ii, ed. Z. Griliches and M. D. Intriligator (Amsterdam: Elsevier): 1023–1100.

Johansen, Soren (1988) 'Statistical analysis of cointegrating vectors', *Journal of Economic Dynamics and Control* 12: 231–54.

King, Gary, Keohane, Robert, and Verba, Sidney (1994) *Designing Social Inquiry* (Princeton, NJ: Princeton University Press).

King, R. G., Plosser, C. I., Stock, J. H., and Watson, M. W. (1991) 'Stochastic trends and economic fluctuations', *American Economic Review* 81: 819–40.

Kosobud, Robert, and Klein, Lawrence (1961) 'Some econometrics of growth: great ratios of economics', *Quarterly Journal of Economics* 25 (May): 173–98.

Levtchenkova, S., Pagan, A. R., and Robertson, J. C. (1998) 'Shocking stories', *Journal of Economic Surveys* 5(12): 507–32.

Liu, T. C. (1960) 'Underidentification, structural estimation and forecasting', *Econometrica* 28: 855–65.

McCloskey, Donald N. (1985) *The Rhetoric of Economics* (Madison, Wis.: University of Wisconsin Press).

Nelson, C. R. and Plosser, C. I. (1982) 'Trends and random walks in macroeconomic time series: some evidence and implications', *Journal of Monetary Economics* 10(2): 139–62.

Perron, P. (1989) 'The Great Crash, the oil price shock and the unit root hypothesis', *Econometrica* 57(6): 1361–401.

Pesaran, M. H. and Smith, R. P. (1985) 'Evaluation of macroeconometric models', *Economic Modelling* 2: 125–34.

—— (1998) 'Structural analysis of cointegrating VARs', *Journal of Economic Surveys* 5(12): 471–505.

Phillips, P. C. B. (1986) 'Understanding spurious regression in econometrics', *Journal of Econometrics* 33: 311–40.

Sargent, Thomas J. (1978) 'Estimation of dynamic labour demand schedules under rational expectations', *Journal of Political Economy* 86(6): 1009–44.

Sims, Christopher A. (1972) 'Money, income and causality', *American Economic Review* 62: 540–52.

—— (1980) 'Macroeconomics and reality', *Econometrica* 48: 1–48.

—— (1996) 'Macroeconomics and methodology', *Journal of Economic Perspectives* 10(1): 105–20.

Summers, L. (1991) 'The scientific illusion in empirical macroeconomics', *Scandinavian Journal of Economics* 93: 129–48.

Yule, G. U. (1926) 'Why do we sometimes get nonsense correlations between time-series', *Journal of the Royal Statistical Society*, repr. in D. F. Hendry and M. S. Morgan, *The Foundations of Econometric Analysis*. (Cambridge University Press, 1995).

10A Models all the way down: comments on Smith and Juselius

KEVIN D. HOOVER

1. Econometrics in different keys

Before the Bergamo Conference, I had never met Katarina Juselius or Ron Smith. So, when I was reading their papers for this volume, I amused myself trying to guess from the tone and style of their papers something about their ages, temperaments, and life experiences. For though their papers are in many ways similar and derive from what I imagine to be a common intellectual background, their tone and ambitions are different. I found much to admire in both papers and, indeed, much to agree with.

Both papers are too rich for me to react to all that I found notable. Smith is to be congratulated for the way in which he lays bare the connections in the development of unit roots, vector autoregressions (VARs), Granger-causality, and cointegration. His account, as he notes, is ahistorical—but no less useful for that. Equally, I admire the intricately detailed account that Juselius gives of the formulation and interpretation of cointegrating VARs. It is a model of thoughtful conceptual preparation for empirical investigations that could be profitably studied by any applied macroeconomist.

The central message of Smith's paper is that there is a mismatch between statistics and economic theory. The result is a glib appropriation of statistical results to support economic conclusions, even when the statistical tests do not adequately map onto the economic notions. Smith rightly stresses the importance of developing sensible economic interpretations of statistics and of using a variety of sources of information (qualitative, historical, institutional), while noting that the more qualitative sources may suffer from parallel interpretive problems. But, aside from the passing suggestion that we might all be better off to think hard about the structural econometrics of Haavelmo and the Cowles Commission, he offers little practical guidance on how to get the interpretive project going. While he says that he is optimistic, there is a note of world-weariness in Smith's tale.

Juselius's tone is the opposite of Smith's. She too sees the gap between theory and statistics and argues that statistics must enter in at the ground level and be developed into a set of constraints on theorizing. She then proceeds to give detailed examples of what she has in mind. There is a cheerful optimism in her tale.

2. The theory–data gap

One common feature of their papers is the focus on the gap between theory and data. The problem is that econometrics packages and describes data, but descriptions, in themselves, are not useful. Economics needs and seeks—directly or surreptitiously—structure, where *structure* can be defined broadly as those enduring features of the economy that stay put in the face of interventions, manipulations, shocks, and so forth. It is the yearning for structure that recommends to Smith the econometrics of the 1940s (Haavelmo and the Cowles Commission). As Mary Morgan's (1990) history of econometrics or David Hendry and Morgan's (1995) more recent anthology of essential original works in econometrics (mostly from before 1950) demonstrate, these issues have an even longer history in econometrics than Smith suggests.

Juselius despairs of defining structure adequately and retreats to the claim that, even taken descriptively, a statistical analysis of common trends is useful. Similarly, Smith states that unidentified VARs are good enough for unconditional forecasts. This does not seem right in either case. The only use these descriptions could have is based on the notion that the future will be like the past. Even if our descriptions do not permit the articulation of structures, we must appeal to the notion of structure to warrant any *use* of the statistics economically. Take a trivial example. We can always generate a descriptive statistic such as the mean age of the people in a conference room. But to what use can we put that statistic if we are unable to relate the occupants of the room to larger groups of people. If the people are all economists and, we believe, randomly chosen, then we might extrapolate to the mean age of all economists. If they are all adult men and randomly chosen, then we might extrapolate to the mean age of all adult men. It is the extra-statistical information that makes the statistic interpretable and useful. Without it, it is just a number.

3. Structure and the problem of induction

When stripped down to its barest form, the problem has a much older history, having been formulated at the dawn of modern economics by David Hume. It is important to recall that Hume was both an economist and a philosopher (as well as a historian and general man of letters). Both his philosophy and his economic essays ought to be read (Hume 1739, 1742, 1777). The economic essays, indeed, would help to temper the more radical readings of Hume as a sceptical philosopher (see Hoover 2001: ch. 1).

Hume took data (i.e. sense data) to be fundamental (the foundation of knowledge). As actors, however, we seek necessary connections, causes, and effects—that is to say, *structure*. Hume is famous for his attack on induction. In this context, his attack can be reformulated simply: data do not wear their structure on their faces. In one sense, this is the end of the story: Hume is right, data alone do not reveal the economic structures that generated them. His own solution was to locate necessary connection in the customary regard that we feel for sequences that are repeated frequently enough. We expect that the glass *must* fall to the floor when tipped off the table because it has done so every time we can recall in the past. Hume has no doubt that we reason this way. But he believes that it is irrational and that the 'must' indicates nothing more than our familiarity with glasses and other objects falling in particular circumstances.

Hume's problem is still with us. And in economics we have adopted something like Hume's solution to it. In order to estimate and test structural models we make a priori identifying assumptions, which are grounded in a kind of professional custom about what is reasonable or what is derivable from theory. That custom itself has a customary basis. Is this a solution? Or is it standing naked whistling in the dark? Christopher Sims underlined the problem in his 'Macroeconomics and Reality' (1980): the identifying assumptions typically employed are literally incredible.

The first thought twenty years ago was that we could get everything we needed out of the unrestricted VAR. But it was soon shown (as both Juselius and Smith recount) that anything useful in a VAR required, at a minimum, an identifying assumption for the Wold-causal ordering of the contemporaneous variables. The data really do not wear their own structure. But which causal order? There were endless debates. Another possibility is discussed by both Juselius and Smith—namely, that cointegration relations provide identifying assumptions. Even though zero or other exact restrictions on parameters are unlikely to be credible, coarser restrictions might be plausible. Again, which can be taken as acceptable a priori is disputed. Juselius implicitly endorses the typical assumption that shocks to nominal things do not have long-run effects, although they may have short-run effects, on real things. (This is another assumption shared with Hume, a long-run quantity theorist who recognized short-run exceptions.) Juselius renders this assumption in the form of independence of aggregate-supply shocks from aggregate-demand shocks. Smith, however, attacks this independence assumption as implausible. The emperor has no clothes. Do we have any to give to him?

4. The role of models

Both Juselius and Smith highlight a gap between data and theory. The central methodological problems that they pose are why that gap exists? And what would one do to fill it? The answer, I suggest, to both questions is, *models*. There is a gap because we deal not with the structure of reality but with models of it, and the only way to fill it is to take modelling seriously.

Morgan's (1990) *History of Econometric Ideas* identifies two distinct streams of development. The business-cycle stream started with the business-cycle barometers and other atheoretic descriptions of macroeconomic aggregates and developed over the century into time-series analysis in the Box–Jenkins or unrestricted-VAR tradition. The demand–analysis stream started with a maintained demand theory and attempted to measure the actual demand elasticities. These streams partly merged in the 1930s and 1940s in the work of Frisch, Tinbergen, Haavelmo, and the Cowles Commission, and redivided to form various schools of econometric practice. One of these streams is the standard textbook view in which theory proposes and estimation tests and disposes. This apriorist approach has not been a great success since the theories are rarely rich enough to do justice to the complexities of the data.

I once suggested that we should oppose this 'econometrics-as-measurement approach' to an 'econometrics-as-observation approach' in which econometrics would be regarded as generating observations, through its various ways of filtering the data, that it was the job of theory to explain. Just as with photographs through telescopes, some observations would be informative, others less so. Juselius's paper convinces me that econometrics too deals exclusively in models. Perhaps this should not have been a revelation, since the phrase 'econometric model' just trips off the tongue, but her paper brings out clearly how much even characterizing the data depends upon untested and untestable assumptions.

I am reminded of the famous tale of the cosmologist who is challenged by an old woman. She pooh-poohs his explanation of the structure of the universe. Everyone knows, she says, that the world sits on the back of giant turtle. The scientist replies, 'But, Madam, on what does the turtle stand?' To which the old lady says, 'Young man, you think that you are very clever, but the turtle stands upon the back of another turtle. It's turtles all the way down.' So too in empirical macroeconomics. It is not just that we have theoretical models; it's models all the way down.

Even the 'raw data' themselves are models in the sense that substantive choices are made that are not inherent in the data. For example, Juselius cites the well-known fact that velocity is $I(1)$; but in the USA this appears to be true for M1-velocity, while M2-velocity appears to be $I(0)$. The choice is part of the econometric model of money.

Where does our confidence in models come from? This is a vexed question. Smith laments the use of statistics, say, Granger-causality tests even when the needed sense of causality is not Granger's sense of incremental predictability. I suggest that the practice of using them this way is in fact a disguised appeal to authority—a fallacy, but one with strong psychological appeal to those whom doubt might otherwise immobilize. The difficulty goes right back to Hume and needs to be nipped in the bud. Hume is wrong to regard sense data as foundational. The eyes do not see and ears do not hear and then interpret the data; they see and hear interpreted data. We can be brought to doubt the evidence of our own eyes and ears, to doubt the natural interpretations that thrust themselves on us, but it is self-defeating to start with the premiss that they are misleading.

En route to the Bergamo Conference, I saw 'The Truman Show' in which Jim Carrey's character is brought up without his knowledge in a completely staged environment, complete with artificial weather and actors for friends and parents. Though he comes to doubt the reality of his world, it would not have been sensible for him to have doubted such a perfect fraud from the beginning. He discovers the truth by noticing incongruities and attempting to bring a reasonable order to his model of how the world works. So too in economics. There are always assumptions that we do not really doubt and that others share. We start from them and use them to place limits on the possible classes of acceptable economic models and acceptable statistical models of the data. There is an interplay on these margins, and it may force us sometimes to abandon a class of models. Smith credits Nelson and Plosser's time-series models and unit-root tests of US macroeconomic data as having forced macroeconomists to abandon the Lucas surprise-only aggregate supply function. (I do not think that Nelson and Plosser did this single-handedly. It does not, however, change the story to recognize that the cumulative weight of incongruities isolated by Barro and others, as well as Nelson and Plosser, finally led the mainstream opinion in macroeconomics to drift away from, rather than decisively reject, the Lucas supply function.)

The process through which statistical evidence affects theoretical commitments does not look much like the textbook pattern: deduce testable conclusions from a theory and then test them. That notion is not so much wrong as limited, itself requiring a large number of unsupported assumptions to make it work in special cases. The model is not so much testing and disposal as it is one of relentless criticism and mutual adjustment. And to demonstrate that these are not merely empty slogans, one need only look at Juselius's careful attempts to work out the relationships between non-stationary characterizations of data and the possible theoretical models that might be consistent with them.

REFERENCES

Hendry, David F. and Mary S. Morgan (eds.) (1995) *The Foundations of Econometric Analysis* (Cambridge: Cambridge University Press).
Hoover, Kevin D. (1994) 'Econometrics as observation: the Lucas critique and the nature of econometric inference', *Journal of Economic Methodology* 1(1): 65–80.
—— (2001) *Causality in Macroeconomics* (Cambridge: Cambridge University Press): forthcoming.
Hume, David (1739) *A Treatise of Human Nature*. Page numbers refer to the edition edited by L. A. Selby-Bigge (Oxford: Clarendon Press, 1888).
—— (1742) (a) 'Of money', (b) 'Of interest', (c) 'Of the balance of trade', in *Essays: Moral, Political, and Literary*. Page references to the edition edited by Eugene F. Miller (Indianapolis: Liberty *Classics*, 1885).
—— (1777) *An Enquiry Concerning Human Understanding*. Page numbers refer to L. A. Selby-Bigge (ed.). *Enquiries Concerning Human Understanding and Concerning the Principles of Morals*, 2nd edn. (Oxford: Clarendon Press, 1902).
Morgan, Mary S. (1990) *The History of Econometric Ideas* (Cambridge: Cambridge University Press).
Sims, Christopher A. (1980) 'Macroeconomics and reality,' *Econometrica* 48(1): 1–48.

10B New econometric techniques and macroeconomics: a discussion of Smith and Juselius

CARLO A. FAVERO

1. Introduction

The two papers by Ron Smith (Chapter 9) and Katarina Juselius (Chapter 8) analyse developments in macroeconometrics related to vector autoregressive models of time-series and reach different conclusions. Smith is rather negative and concludes that such techniques, however useful they were in summarizing the data, could not answer economic questions because they have not solved satisfactorily the identification problem. Juselius is positive and claims that empirical analyses based on the basic feature of the cointegrated VAR model can be useful for asking relevant economic questions.

The controversy between Smith and Juselius seems to be mainly focused on the identification of the long-run structure of the economy. Some references appear to a parallel ongoing debate, centred on the short-run structure of the economy. To my judgement such debate reflects the main differences between how macroeconometrics is done on the different sides of the Atlantic ocean: structural VARs in level on the one side and small structural cointegrated models on the other side. I think these two papers are very useful also to illustrate the second debate, and I shall concentrate my discussion on both aspects of the identification problem. In the first section I shall briefly clarify what I intend for short-run and long-run identification. I shall then consider in turn the VAR approach and the LSE approach, based on the estimation of structural cointegrated models.

2. Short-run and long-run identification: two separate issues

To illustrate the importance of the identification problem, consider a model of the monetary transmission mechanism, which involves a vector of macroeconomic variables Y_t and a vector of monetary variables M_t, a total of m variables is included in the VAR. The VAR approach and the LSE approach to modelling time-series are based on a common statistical model, which, for the sake of simplicity, we represent as follows:

$$\begin{pmatrix} \mathbf{Y}_t \\ \mathbf{M}_t \end{pmatrix} = \mathbf{D} \begin{pmatrix} \mathbf{Y}_{t-1} \\ \mathbf{M}_{t-1} \end{pmatrix} + \mathbf{u}_t, \tag{1}$$

$$\mathbf{u}_t = \begin{pmatrix} \mathbf{u}_t^Y \\ \mathbf{u}_t^M \end{pmatrix},$$

$$u_t \mid I_{t-1} \sim n.i.d.(\mathbf{0}, \Sigma),$$

$$\begin{pmatrix} \mathbf{Y}_t \\ \mathbf{M}_t \end{pmatrix} \mid I_{t-1} \sim \left(\mathbf{D} \begin{pmatrix} \mathbf{Y}_{t-1} \\ \mathbf{M}_{t-1} \end{pmatrix}, \Sigma \right),$$

where $\mathbf{D}$ is a matrix of coefficients, and $\mathbf{u}_t$ is a vector of innovations. We have used first-order autoregressive representations, this is general in that vector autoregressive processes of any higher order can be re-parameterized as first-order processes.

Moving from the statistical model to the structural model involves two separate identification problems.

2.1. Long-run identification

The reduced form (1) can be rewritten as:

$$\begin{pmatrix} \Delta \mathbf{Y}_t \\ \Delta \mathbf{M}_t \end{pmatrix} = \Pi \begin{pmatrix} \mathbf{Y}_{t-1} \\ \mathbf{M}_{t-1} \end{pmatrix} + \begin{pmatrix} \mathbf{u}_t^Y \\ \mathbf{u}_t^M \end{pmatrix},$$

$$\Pi = \mathbf{D} - \mathbf{I} \tag{2}$$

Johansen shows that, in case the vector $(\mathbf{Y}_t \ \mathbf{M}_t)$ is non-stationary but admits k cointegrating relationships, then Π is of reduced rank k and we have

$$\Pi = \alpha\beta',$$

where α is an $(m \times k)$ matrix of weights and β is an $(m \times k)$ matrix of parameters determining the cointegrating relationships. In the case of existence of multiple cointegrating vectors, an interesting identification problem arises. In fact, α and β, are only determined up to the space spanned by them and, for any non-singular matrix ξ conformable by product, we have:

$$\Pi = \alpha\beta' = \alpha\xi^{-1}\xi\beta'.$$

In other words β and $\beta'\xi$ are two observationally equivalent bases of the co-integrating space. The obvious implication is that, before solving such identification problem, no meaningful economic interpretation of coefficients in cointegrating vectors can be proposed. The solution to such problems is achieved by imposing a sufficient number of restrictions on parameters such that the matrix satisfying such constraints in the cointegrating space is unique. Such a criterion is derived in Johansen (1995) and discussed in the work of Johansen and Juselius (1999), Giannini (1992), and

Hamilton (1994). Note Smith (1999) considers only identification of cointegrating vectors by imposing that there are orthogonal eigenvectors with unit length. In fact, much more general restrictions can be implemented within the Johansen procedure.

2.2. Short-run identification

We face an identification problem in that there is more than one structure of economic interest which delivers the same statistical model for our vector of variables.

In fact for any given structure,

$$A\begin{pmatrix} \Delta \mathbf{Y}_t \\ \Delta \mathbf{M}_t \end{pmatrix} = \mathbf{C}_1 \alpha \beta' \begin{pmatrix} \mathbf{Y}_{t-1} \\ \mathbf{M}_{t-1} \end{pmatrix} + \mathbf{B} \begin{pmatrix} \mathbf{v}_t^Y \\ \mathbf{v}_t^M \end{pmatrix}, \tag{3}$$

$$\begin{pmatrix} \mathbf{v}_t^Y \\ \mathbf{v}_t^M \end{pmatrix} \mid I_{t-1} \end{pmatrix} \sim (\mathbf{0}, \mathbf{I}), \tag{4}$$

which gives rise to the observed reduced form (2) when the following restrictions are satisfied

$$A^{-1}\mathbf{C}_1 = I, \quad A\begin{pmatrix} \mathbf{u}_t^Y \\ \mathbf{u}_t^M \end{pmatrix} = \mathbf{B}\begin{pmatrix} \mathbf{v}_t^Y \\ \mathbf{v}_t^M \end{pmatrix},$$

there exists a whole class of structures which give rise to the same statistical model (2) under the same class of restrictions:

$$FA\begin{pmatrix} \mathbf{Y}_t \\ \mathbf{M}_t \end{pmatrix} = F\mathbf{C}_1\alpha\beta'\begin{pmatrix} \mathbf{Y}_{t-1} \\ \mathbf{M}_{t-1} \end{pmatrix} + F\mathbf{B}\begin{pmatrix} \mathbf{v}_t^Y \\ \mathbf{v}_t^M \end{pmatrix}, \tag{5}$$

where F is an admissible matrix in the sense it is conformable by product with $A, \mathbf{C}_1, \mathbf{B}$ and $FA, F\mathbf{C}_1, F\mathbf{B}$ feature the same restriction with $A, \mathbf{C}_1, \mathbf{B}$.

The parameters describing the short-run structure of the model are identified if the only admissible matrix is the identity matrix. Note that the short-run identification issue is totally separated from the long-run identification issue.

Having illustrated the fundamentals, we now analyse in turn the two different approaches to macroeconometric modelling by considering in turn motivation, identification, short-run identification, long-run identification, and results.

3. The VAR approach

3.1. Motivation

VAR models differ from structural LSE models as to the purpose of their specification and estimation. In the traditional approach the typical question asked within a macroeconometric framework is 'What is the optimal response by the monetary authority to movement in macroeconomic variables in order to achieve given targets for the same variables?' After the Lucas critique (1976), questions like 'How should a central bank respond to shocks in macroeconomic variables?' are to be answered within the framework of quantitative monetary general equilibrium models of the business cycle. So the answer has to be based on a theoretical model rather than on an empirical *ad hoc* macroeconometric model. Within this framework there is a new role for empirical analysis, i.e. to provide the evidence on the stylized facts to be included in the theoretical model adopted for policy analysis and to decide between competing general equilibrium monetary models. The operationalization of this research programme is very well described in a recent paper by Christiano *et al.* (1998). Three are the relevant steps:

- monetary policy shocks are identified in actual economies,
- the response of relevant economic variables to monetary shocks is then described,
- the same experiment is then performed in the model economies to compare actual and model-based responses as an evaluation tool and a selection criterion for theoretical models.

Traditional Cowles Commission structural models are designed to identify the impact of policy variables on macroeconomic quantities in order to determine the value to be assigned to the monetary instruments (M) to achieve a given target for the macroeconomic variables (Y), assuming exogeneity of the policy variables in M on the ground that these are the instruments controlled by the policy-maker. Identification in traditional structural models is obtained without assuming the orthogonality of structural disturbances. As a consequence, impulse response analysis cannot be implemented within this framework, dynamic multipliers being computed instead. Dynamic multipliers describe the impact of monetary policy variables on macroeconomic quantities without separating changes in the monetary variable into the expected and unexpected components.

VAR modelling would reject the Cowles Commission identifying restrictions as 'incredible'; however VAR models of the transmission mechanism are not estimated to yield advice on the best monetary policy; they are rather estimated to provide empirical evidence on the response of macroeconomic variables to monetary policy impulses in order to discriminate between alternative theoretical models of the economy. Monetary policy actions should be identified using restrictions independent from the competing models of the transmission mechanism under empirical investigation, taking into account the potential endogeneity of policy instruments.

3.2. Identification

Monetary policy shocks are not readily observable: given a statistical model for the vector of variables of interest, some structure has to be assumed to identify the monetary shocks, i.e. to impose restrictions on the elements of matrices A and B. Given the purpose of VAR models, such structure must be independent from the specific predictions of competing macroeconomic theories.

The recent literature on the Monetary Transmission Mechanism (see Christiano *et al.* 1998) offers good examples on how this kind of restriction can be derived. VAR of the MTM are specified on six variables, with the vector of macroeconomic non-policy variables including gross domestic product (GDP), the consumer price index (P) and the commodity price level (Pcm), the vector of policy variables which includes the federal funds rate (FF), the quantity of total bank reserves (TR), and the amount of non-borrowed reserves (NBR). Given the estimation of the reduced form VAR for the six macro and monetary variables a structural model is then identified by: (i) assuming orthogonality of the structural disturbances; (ii) imposing that macroeconomic variables do not simultaneously react to monetary variables, while the simultaneous feedback in the other direction is allowed, and (iii) imposing restrictions on the monetary block of the model reflecting the operational procedures implemented by the monetary policy-maker. All identifying restrictions satisfy the criterion of independence from specific theoretical models, in fact, within the class of models estimated on monthly data, restrictions (ii) are consistent with a wide spectrum of alternative theoretical structures and imply a minimal assumption on the lag of the impact of monetary policy on macroeconomic variables, whereas restrictions (iii) are based on institutional analysis. Note that, having identified the 'monetary rule' by proposing an explicit solution to the problem of the endogeneity of money, the VAR approach concentrates on *deviations* from the rule. In fact, such deviations provide researchers with the best opportunity to detect the response of macroeconomic variables to monetary impulses that are not expected by the market. The VAR approach to the monetary transmission mechanism has been criticized on the basis that it views Central Banks as 'random number generators'. This does not seem to be correct: in fact, monetary policy rules are explicitly estimated in structural VAR models. However, the focus is not on rules but on deviations from rules, since only when central banks deviate from their rules it becomes possible to collect interesting information on the response of macroeconomic variables to monetary policy impulses, to be compared with the predictions of the alternative theoretical models.

The VAR approach concentrates on short-run identification. In a famous paper Sims *et al.* (1990), and argue that a VAR model in levels in the presence of cointegration is overparameterized and therefore leads to inefficient but consistent estimates of the parameters of interest. The loss of efficiency has to be weighted against the risk of inconsistency of estimates which occurs when the 'wrong' cointegrating restrictions are imposed. Imposing the 'wrong' cointegrating parameters will make the system converge to the 'wrong' long-run equilibria but it will also bias the short-run dynamics as the system is pulled in the wrong direction. For this reason VAR in levels rather than cointegrated VARs are used when the issue of economic interest is not related to the short run rather than to the long run. The analysis of the monetary transmission mechanism is a standard example of such instance.

3.3. Results

In a series of recent papers, Christiano *et al.* (1998) apply the VAR approach to derive 'stylized facts' on the effect of a contractionary policy shock, and conclude that plausible models of the monetary transmission mechanism should be consistent at least with the following evidence on price, output and interest rates: (i) the aggregate price level initially responds very little; (ii) interest rates initially rise, and (iii) aggregate output initially falls, with a *j*-shaped response, with a zero long-run effect of the monetary impulse. Such evidence leads to the dismissal of traditional real business cycle models, which are not compatible with the liquidity effect of monetary policy on interest rates, and of the Lucas model of money, in which the effect of monetary policy on output depends on price misperceptions. The evidence seems to be more in line with alternative interpretations of the monetary transmission mechanism based on sticky prices models (Goodfriend and King 1997), limited participation models (Christiano and Eichenbaum 1992), or models with indeterminacy-sunspot equilibria (Farmer 1992).

3.4. Problems

Although the VAR approach has been successful in establishing a number of stylized facts on the monetary transmission mechanism, the methodology is not completely uncontrovertible. As VAR models are the natural empirical counterparts of dynamic general equilibrium monetary models, their statistical adequacy is not as closely scrutinized as the adequacy of reduced-form specification within the LSE approach. In particular, in many of the applications outliers are not removed and non-normality is not an uncommon feature. Parameter stability is also an issue in the debate. As far as identification is concerned, the idea of using restrictions neutral with respect to the theories under scrutiny is nice but not always implementable. In fact, VAR models of the monetary transmission in open economies have not been as successful in establishing stylized facts, probably because of the difficulties in generating a 'neutral' identification scheme. Last, the issue of shocks. We have already noted that the role of shocks in VAR has been overemphasized, however Cochrane (1998) has noted that the response of macrovariables to expected monetary policy seems to have more sensible properties than the response to shocks, and the contribution of Ben McCallum (Chapter 6) to this conference seems to go along with this view. Moreover, Rudebusch has criticized VAR-based monetary policy shocks on the argument that they are very little correlated with direct measures of monetary shocks derived from financial markets. Such a view has been questioned by Sims (1996) and by some empirical results showing that the responses of macrovariables to monetary shocks derived from financial markets are not statistically different from their responses to VAR-based shocks (see Bagliano-Favero 1998), but the issue is still open to some debate.

4. The LSE-cointegration-based approach

4.1. Motivation

This approach to macroeconometric modelling explains the ineffectiveness of the traditional Cowles Commission models for practical purposes of forecasting and policy in terms of their incapability of representing the data. The root of the failure of the traditional approach lies in the little attention paid to the statistical model implicit in the estimated structure. There are several possible causes for the inadequacy of statistical models implicit in structural econometric models: omission of relevant variables, omission of the relevant dynamics for the included variables, and invalid assumptions of exogeneity. The LSE solution to the specification problem is the theory of reduction. Any econometric model is interpreted as a simplified representation of the unobservable Data Generating Process (DGP). For the representation to be valid or 'congruent', to use Hendry's own terminology, the information lost in moving from the DGP to its representation, given by the adopted specification, must be irrelevant to the problem at hand. Adequacy of the statistical model is evaluated by analysing the reduced form. Therefore, the prominence of the structural model with respect to reduced-form representation in the Cowles Commission approach to identification and specification is reversed. The LSE approach starts its specification and identification procedure by specifying a general dynamic reduced-form model. The congruency of such a model cannot be directly assessed against the true DGP, which is not observable. However, a series of diagnostic tests are proposed as criteria for evaluating the congruency of the baseline model. The general principle guiding the application of such criteria is that congruent models should feature true random residuals, hence any departure of the vector of residuals from a random normal multivariate distribution should be taken as a symptom of misspecification. Once the base-line model has been validated, the reduction process begins by simplifying the dynamics and by reducing the dimensionality of the model by omitting equations for those variables for which the null hypothesis of exogeneity is not rejected. In fact the concept of exogeneity is refined within the LSE approach and is broken down in different categories, determined by the purpose of the estimation of the econometric model. A further stage in the simplification process could be the imposition of the rank reduction restrictions in the matrix determining the long-run equilibria of the system and the identification of cointegrating vectors. The product of this stage is a statistical model for the data, possibly discriminating between short-run dynamics and long-run equilibria. Only after this validation procedure structural models are identified and estimated. Just-identified specifications do not require any further testing, as their implicit reduced form does not impose any further restrictions on the base-line statistical model. The validity of overidentified specification is instead tested by evaluating the validity of the restrictions implicitly imposed on the general reduced form. After this last diagnostics for the validity of the reduction process have been performed, structural models are used for the practical purposes of forecasting and policy evaluation.

The paper by Juselius (Chapter 8) features all the ingredients of such strategy. The counterpart of the careful control of congruency in the model specification is that at the end of the process answers to macroeconomic questions of interest are provided without referring to a specific theoretical model. In Juselius's contribution, questions on efficiency of monetary policy are asked without discussing at all a theoretical macroeconomic model of reference. The theoretical baseline is a money-demand equation, which includes five variables and therefore leads to specification of a multivariate system for money, prices, output, and interest rates with the only theoretical back ground of an LM curve.

4.2. Identification

The long-run structure of the system is identified after having found the number of cointegrating vectors. In the case of Juselius we have three cointegrating vectors identified respectively as a velocity equation, an interest rate spread, and a Fisher relation. The short-run identification is achieved by imposing a recursive structure with is taken as illustration. In fact, the question of interests is answered by testing hypothesis on the parameters describing the speed of adjustments in presence of disequilibria which are determined by the lagged and not by the contemporaneous responses of the system.

4.3. Problems

Cointegrated VARs are mainly data-driven specifications; the macromodel for the relevant DGP is not fully specified, as is clearly the case with the contribution of Juselius. Therefore it is not easy to interpret the results from a simultaneous model, when we have (loose) theories generating only a subset of the equations. Moreover, there are difficulties with an approach aimed at discriminating between theories on the basis of the outcome of test statistics, based on a number of joint hypotheses, some of which are clearly independent from the theories tested. There is also an issue with the critical values for the testing procedures in the Johansen framework. First, they depend crucially on the specification of the deterministic nucleus of the VAR, so the inclusion of dummies for outliers introduces modifications in the relevant critical values. A solution to this problem is available, see Johansen and Nielsen (1993). Second, recent work by Johansen (1999), has shown that it is important to implement small sample corrections for the asymptotic critical values, when applicable. Taking these two aspects together, it is likely that a re-assessment of all the empirical evidence proposed in the nineties without implementing the appropriate corrections is necessary. So what do we make of all the judgements issued on theories using the wrong critical values?

Note also that the analysis proposed by Katarina Juselius is based on a multi-step framework: specification of the VAR and its deterministic component, identification of the number of cointegrating vectors, identification of the parameters in cointegrating vectors, and tests on the speed of adjustment with respect to disequilibria. The results of the final test depend on the outcome of the previous stages in the empirical analysis, but the outcome of each step is not so easily and uniquely established empirically. Evidently this statement of mine is questionable, but it has not been questioned in the paper by Juselius where no empirical application of the suggested procedure has been implemented. Lastly, earlier research within the LSE tradition raises doubts on the capability of cointegrated VARs to deliver a congruent representation of money demand. We know from the work of Baba, Hendry, and Starr (1992) as reported by Faust and Whiteman (1997) that a much richer specification than the one implicitly contained in the standard VAR approach, including moving averages and moving standard deviations of interest rates, is necessary in order to achieve congruency. The BHS specification for US money demand, estimated on quarterly data covering the period 1960–88, takes the following form:

$$\Delta(m-p)_t = \underset{[0.097]}{-0.334}\,\Delta_4(m-p)_{t-1} - \underset{[0.039]}{0.156}\,\Delta^2(m-p)_{t-4}$$

$$- \underset{[0.015]}{0.249}\left(m-p-\tfrac{1}{2}y\right)_{t-2}$$

$$- \underset{[0.046]}{0.33}\,\Delta\hat{p} - \underset{[0.132]}{1.097}\,\Delta_4 p_{t-1} + \underset{[0.079]}{0.859}\,V_t + \underset{[1.49]}{11.68}\,\Delta SV_{t-1}$$

$$- \underset{[0.104]}{1.409}\,AS_t - \underset{[0.063]}{0.973}\,AR_{1t} - \underset{[0.049]}{0.255}\,\Delta R_{ma,t} + \underset{[0.055]}{0.435}\,R_{nsa,t}$$

$$+ \underset{[0.07]}{0.395}\,\Delta Ay_t + \underset{[0.003]}{0.013}\,D_t + \underset{[0.02]}{0.352} + \hat{u}_t, \tag{6}$$

where heteroscedasticity consistent estimators are reported in brackets; m is the log of M1; y is the log of real GNP using 1982 as base year; p is the log of the deflator; Δ^2 is the square of the difference operator Δ; $\Delta_{\hat{p}} = \Delta(1+\Delta)p_t$; $\Delta_4(m-p)_{t-1} = 0.25((m-p)_{t-1} - (m-p)_{t-5})$; V_t is a nine-quarter moving-average of quarterly averages of twelve-month moving standard deviations of 20-year bond yields; $SV_t = \max(0, S_t) * V_t$ where S is the spread between the 20-year Treasury bond yield and the coupon equivalent yield on a one-month TBill; $AS_t = 0.5(S_t + S_{t-1})$; AR_{1t} is a two-quarter moving-average of the one-month T-bill yield; $R_{ma,t}$ is the maximum of a passbook savings rate, a weighted certificate of deposit rate and a weighted money market mutual fund rate; $R_{nsa,t}$ is the average of weighted NOW and SuperNow rates; $Ay_t = 0.5(y_t + y_{t-1})$ and D_t is a credit control dummy which is -1 in 1980(2), 1 in 1980(3), and zero everywhere else. BHS report 11 diagnostics, all passed. The achievement of data congruency implies some evident cost in terms of parsimony of the specification and economic interpretability of the results. I am somewhat sceptical that such specification could be produced by a VAR approach to cointegration, or by any VAR analysis.

5. Conclusions

I very much agree with Smith in stating that the fundamental problem of macro-econometrics is identification, I hope that my discussion has shown that the tension between the different solutions adopted on two sides of the Atlantic is naturally driven by the different starting points of the two approaches: empirical models are theory driven on the one side and data driven on the other side. I strongly believe that there is something to be said for collaborative efforts, and more communication. This conference has offered a good opportunity, and a rare one so far; I hope there will be more in the future.

REFERENCES

Baba, Y., D. F. Hendry, and R. Starr (1992) 'The demand for M1 in the USA, 1960–1988', *Review of Economic Studies* 59: 25–61.

Bagliano, F.-C. and C. A. Favero (1998) 'Measuring monetary policy with VAR models: an evaluation', *European Economic Review* 1069–112.

Bernanke, B. S. and I. Mihov (1995) 'Measuring monetary policy', NBER Working Paper 5145.

Christiano, L. J. and M. Eichenbaum (1992) 'Liquidity effects and the monetary transmission mechanism', *American Economic Review* 82(2): 346–53.

Christano, L. J., M. Eichenbaum, and C. Evans (1998) 'Monetary Policy shocks: what have we learned and to what end?' NBER Working Paper 6400.

Cochrane, J. (1998) 'What do the VARs mean? Measuring the output effects of monetary policy', *Journal of Monetary Economics* 41(2): 277–300.

Cushman, D.O. and T. Zha (1997) 'Identifying monetary policy in a small open economy under flexible exchange rates', *Journal of Monetary Economics* 39: 433–48.

Farmer, R. E. A. (1992) 'Money in a real business cycle model', Dept. of Economics, UCLA.

Faust, J. and C. H. Whiteman (1997) 'General-to-Specific procedures for fitting a data-admissible, theory inspired, congruent, parsimonious, encompassing, weakly exogenous, identified, structural model to the DGP: A translation and critique', Board of Governors of the Federal System, International Finance Discussion Paper 576.

Giannini, C. (1992) *Topics in structural VAR econometrics, Lecture Notes in Economics and Mathematical Systems* (Springer-Verlag).

Goodfriend, M. and R. King (1997) 'The new neoclassical synthesis and the role of monetary policy', *NBER Macroeconomics Annual 1997* (Cambridge, Mass.: MIT Press).

Hamilton, J. (1994) *Time-Series Analysis* (Princeton, Princeton University Press).

Hendry, D. F. (1995) *Dynamic Econometrics* (Oxford: Oxford University Press).

Johansen, S. (1995) *Likelihood Based Inference on Cointegration in the Vector Autoregressive Model* (Oxford: Oxford University Press).

—— (1999) 'A Bartlett correction factor for tests on the cointegrating relationships', downloadable from http://www.iue.it/Personal/Johansen/Welcome.html.

—— and Nielsen, B. G. (1993) Asymptotics for the cointegration rank tests in the presence of intervantion dummies, Manual for the simulation program DisCo, manual and program are available at the URL http://www.nuff.ox.ac.uk/users/nielsen/disco.html.

Leeper, E. M., C. A. Sims, and T. Zha (1996) 'What does monetary policy do?', available at ftp://ftp.econ.yale.edu/pub/sims/mpolicy.

Lucas Jr., R. E. (1972) 'Expectations and the Neutrality of Money', *Journal of Economic Theory* 4 (April): 103–24.

—— (1976) 'Econometric policy evaluation: a critique', in K. Brunner and A. Meltzer (eds.), *The Phillips Curve and Labor Markets* (Amsterdam: North-Holland).

Rudebusch, G. D. (1996) 'Do measures of monetary policy in a VAR make sense?', Temi di Discussione 269, Bank of Italy.

Sims, C. A. (1996) 'Comment on Glenn Rudebusch's "Do measures of monetary policy in a VAR make sense?"' mimeo, available at ftp://ftp.econ.yale.edu/pub/sims/mpolicy.

——, J. H. Stock, and M. Watson (1990) 'Inference in linear time-series models with some unit roots', *Econometrica* 58: 113–44.

—— and Tao Zha (1996) 'Does monetary policy generate recessions ?', mimeo, available at ftp://ftp.econ.yale.edu/pub/sims/mpolicy.

10C Econometric techniques: general discussion

Christopher Sims: When I first started writing down my comments on the two papers I wrote that we can see how big a barrier the Atlantic Ocean still is, but then Favero's comments made me scratch that out!

The first point I would like to make concerns Juselius's paper where she writes that there does not seem to exist a research programme in macroeconomics that mimics the present state of the art in macroeconometrics in the sense of developing theoretical models of the macroeconomy that replicate the basic features of macroeconomic data, such as stochastic variables and relations, strongly time-dependent data, cointegration and integration properties, short-run adjustment towards long-run dynamics or static steady-states and short-run and long-run feedback effects. Now in fact, on the other side of the Atlantic there are two research programmes that do all these things and have done so for a long time. They are the real business cycle school of analysis and the identified VAR group. On this side of the Atlantic people may think that these programmes do not handle strongly time-dependent data, cointegration and integration properties, and short-run adjustment to long-run dynamics, but this is based on fundamental differences about statistical methodology.

My second main point also concerns Juselius's paper where she says 'because macroeconomic variables are generally found to be non-stationary, standard regression methods are no longer feasible from an econometric point of view and cointegration analysis is therefore the most obvious choice.' This is based, in my view, on a naïve sticking with Neymann–Pearson testing in circumstances where it is clearly no longer appropriate. As far as I can see, the only consistent way to think about inference in scientific reporting is to think that what we are doing is creating information about likelihood functions. Likelihood functions are what is necessary for decision-making and when we do statistical reporting we ought, even when we do supply coefficients and standard errors or hypothesis tests, to be helping our readers understand the shape of the likelihood function. From the point of view of the likelihood principle, there is no sharp distinction between models containing integration and cointegration and models that do not. The likelihood function does not have a shape that jumps when one of these things is present or is not present. In fact the asymptotics of the shape of the likelihood, in the sense of the asymptotic approximations that are justified in analysing the shape of the likelihood, even work in the presence of unit roots, so that you get Gaussian likelihood in large samples despite the presence of unit roots, even though distributions of estimators do jump.

So the reason the North American side of econometrics pays so little attention to unit roots and cointegration is that, in the view of many of us, these are side issues. It is not necessary to pre-process our models and data and decide how much integration and cointegration there is before we proceed, and there are great disadvantages in doing so. I think these come out in Juselius's paper. We are told, both here and in

Smith's paper, that integration or the lack of it and cointegration are not to be thought of as deep fundamental properties of series but as things that are tested for statistical significance and used to characterize a particular sample. But it is also suggested that doing this is a preliminary step. We do this first to build a foundation and then start thinking about theory and the testing. But this is very dangerous. In fact, when we look at the shapes of likelihood functions we see that, despite the fact that asymptotic theory tells us that integration and cointegration are pinned down at a much higher rate as t goes to infinity than the short-run coefficients, so that asymptotically it is OK to treat cointegration and integration results as if they were fixed and known, it doesn't affect the asymptotic distribution of the rest of the inference.

If we look at the actual shape of likelihoods we find in economics, there is a lot of uncertainty about which variables are integrated and which are not and how much cointegration there is. This reflects the well-known fact that the power of unit-root tests is low. So that even in situations where we can accept lots of unit roots and cointegrations it may be true that we could also easily contemplate models with much less of this. And it turns out that if we, on top of maintained hypotheses of integration or cointegration start imposing additional restrictions based on intuition or a priori theory, it often turn out that there is a strong interaction between what we get out of this preliminary cointegration analysis and what we get from the second stage, and we never discover how uncertain our results are unless we go back and ask, 'Well suppose that instead of accepting the null of integration or accepting the null of cointegration I had not accepted it, even though the statistical tests told me I could, but since it is a weak power test let's ask what would have happened in the alternative.' And often the substantive results can come out quite different. But in a multivariate model, the programme of doing this with every possibility of imposing or relaxing unit roots or relaxing or imposing cointegration is just mind-boggling. And it is unnecessary because a single descriptive problem—the problem of describing the likelihood—can take care of all this jointly. We can analyse the uncertainty about unit roots and cointegration jointly with the remaining uncertainty in the model and that is what we ought to be doing. And it is easy. It is easier technically, but it lets us get closer to what is really the hard problem (and I agree with Smith on this): the hard problem is identification and it is pervasive. But by getting ourselves away from being tied up in the difficult technical complexities of Neymann–Pearson testing for unit roots, we can get ourselves to what are really the hard problems—identification.

The approach of bringing in theory in a casual and naïve way, that we see in Juselius's paper, is really a bad approach. We see, for example, a cointegrating relationship between M, P, Y, and r, presented and then the possibilities discussed of treating it as a money-demand relation or, if the sign on the coefficient on r is wrong, as a money supply relation. This is really no different from saying, 'We are going to regress p on q or q on p and if the coefficient comes out negative we will call it a demand curve and if it turns out positive we will call it a supply curve.' If somebody did that, we would all recognize that this is a fallacy, a naïve way to proceed. There is an identification problem, and once there is an identification problem probably a regression of q on p is neither demand nor supply, and if there is a situation where you have a doubt you cannot solve it just by looking at the sign of a coefficient. This is just as true in a cointegration relationship as in an ordinary regression. Cointegration analysis is of no help in identification. That is my view.

Bennett McCallum: I want to add a bit of substantive discussion to Juselius's claim about monetary theory of the conventional type as applying that the excess demand for money is an $I(0)$ variable. This exact case is discussed in Section 5 of my paper. I contend that there is no reason at all to claim that traditional money-demand theory implies a cointegrating relationship among real money balances, income, and the interest rate. The reason is that a traditional money-demand relationship is certainly going to have some stochastic disturbance term and this is going to include the effects of changes in payments technology, which are not observable. But technological changes in the payments industry, as with technological changes of other types, are ones that no one would expect to be reversed. This suggests that the stochastic process generating the disturbance term includes a unit-root component and that implies that money demand does not imply a cointegrating relationship among these variables. I would add that none of this is disturbing to most traditional monetary analysts, for one of the things these people believe in is long-run monetary neutrality which implies that monetary shocks have no long-run effects on real variables but does not imply that there are no real shocks that have effects on the price level. Even the most extreme monetarists estimate money-demand functions under the assumption that the disturbance terms are $I(1)$. My colleague Allan Meltzer handed me an example of this a few days ago, and they are about as traditional as you can get.

I happen to think, moreover, that this argument carries over to all sorts of relationships. All the sorts of things that people seem to think should be cointegrating relationships, all interesting behavioural relationships, are going to have disturbance terms and these will have in them the effects of omitted variables, which will include technology and taste shocks. I would expect all of those things to be approximately permanent. At least, I have no reason to believe that there would be an absence of any permanent component in those disturbance processes, so I would not expect to find cointegration anywhere. If you find it, OK, but I see absolutely nothing in economic theory to suggest that there are cointegrating relations all over the place.

Tom Mayer: There is another problem with the usual use of cointegration tests. We use a 5 per cent significant level, and say if we cannot reject at 5 per cent we assume it is not there. If you think about it, along the lines of Smith's paper, this is awfully difficult to defend. I want to comment briefly on a comment Friedman once made, that inflation is always a monetary phenomenon. You can interpret this along the line of a natural law like the law of gravitation, or you could interpret it as a rule of thumb about what is true in a capitalist economy. You judge the statement very differently depending on which interpretation you place on it.

David Hendry: I do not see RBC and identified VARs as achieving anything like the programme Juselius spells out. RBCs gradually moved over the last decade from models that had no attachment to reality to the kind of models we saw yesterday that are beginning to look like the European kind of models, where they talk about involuntary unemployment, where they talk about trying to get the data, where they talk about shocks that have occurred in a large measure, where it is recognized that the data are non-stationary, etc. I also have incredible difficulty with this North American view that it is hard to identify things. This is also reflected in Smith's paper. I would just suggest to the Captain that we turn the wheel to the left for five minutes and see if the ship turns. If the ship turns or if we see another ship coming towards it and we see the Captain turn to avoid it, we are well aware of what the identification is. The moral of that is, in a world of large structural breaks that we have seen over the last century and a quarter, the difficulty is not to identify uniquely one out of a hundred billion observationally equivalent relationships. It is to find anything that is even vaguely constant and invariant to the shocks that have occurred. I think the problem is completely different.

I also think the word identification is misused appallingly by the different people this morning. It has three attributes. There is a rather trivial mathematical uniqueness attribute. Is it the case that, given the class of invariants under which you are willing to operate, the thing that you are dealing with is invariant? That is the old-fashioned Cowles rank-and-order condition for uniqueness for linear systems. It is not even correct if there are variance restrictions, but it is one way of characterizing a trivial class of 'Is it unique under the class of transformations?' Now it can also happen that there exist several other specifications that are unique under those transformations, given that specification. So it tells you that it had got nothing to do with reality. You can identify models by arbitrary, stupid restrictions that happen to be unique. The interesting question is the correspondence to reality of the entities with which we are dealing. Then there is a third attribute of identification, which is interpretability. Can you interpret the thing that corresponds to reality? Is it indeed a supply curve, a demand curve, or something else?

Where this gets to its most ludicrous, in my view, is using identified VARs trying to interpret shocks. You could have a completely structural model of the economy and the shocks not be structural and never interpretable. I think identification problems occur in that literature because you are trying to identify the unidentifiable. Shocks are made up of everything that is missing from the model. They are derived from the properties of the specification, from the measurement structure of the data, from the information you have used and the restrictions you have put on, and in my view will never be structural and never identifiable. We can nevertheless identify structural equations in many senses. I also think that Smith's lack of historical context leads to some very misleading interpretations in the sociology. I am not sure this matters because how we got here does not matter. We are here now and lets deal with it. This applies to Favero's paper.

I find the idea that narrow money does not have demand shocks just mind-boggling. Narrow money has as many demand shocks as broad money has, and in Britain probably more. I also find it mind-boggling to think that only shocks to policy rules have any impact and that's something that is common on the other side of the Atlantic.

Let's set up a very simple policy rule: the Bank of England does not change interest rates till inflation goes above $2\frac{1}{2}$ per cent, but then it will put them to a million per cent per annum. It is an announced rule, so it is not a shock when it goes to a million per cent per annum, but I would be staggered if the economy did not crash when that happened. It is not the shock that matters—it is the levels of things that matter.

Now let's get on to Sims's idea that the Sims *et al.* (1990) theorem allows one only to throw all the garbage into a model and leave it hanging around like that and then make inference. Now we know that these things do indeed converge a bit faster, so sometimes it is not so serious. But in fact, multicollinearity, in the old-fashioned sense, occurs appallingly in models in which you have eight or nine levels-cointegrated variables. You just get uninterpretable effects. Now one of the beauties of cointegration is that certain restrictions on certain parts of the cointegration space, as Juselius points out, can have very profound implications for restrictions that you are trying to put on elsewhere, and sometimes you simply cannot put them on at all.

I think the historical record is as follows. When I started as a student there was a certain approach to econometrics. The theorists sat in an armchair. They dictated the way the equation should look and the econometricians decorated them with a few parameters. They did all that in the context of the model representing stationary data. All the theory was about stationary data. Everything I learned as a student was stationary. You might get to stationarity by differencing, but you only dealt with stationary data. The unit-root literature caught on in large measure because it was the first significant model of non-stationarity. I think it caught on in Britain long before it caught on in North America because Box and Jenkins hammered at you unless you thought about the whole problem of non-stationarity. Sims will remember a conference in Minnesota in the mid-1970s at which I was very antagonistic and which he wrote up in his review of the conference 'all Hendry's acerbic comments on other people's work' because I said there are many ways of removing non-stationarity other than differencing. I actually thought cointegration was so blindingly obvious that it was not even worth formalizing it. You could get the mortgage stock going off to infinity, the deposits of the building societies going off to infinity, but the ratio between them would stay essentially constant at 90 per cent. I still think, in that sense, it is completely trivial but it is very, very interesting because these are the things that, notwithstanding Smith's difficulties, are equilibria in the sense that (a) they are the targets agents are trying to achieve and (b) when they get there they will stay there and when they are not there they will try to move there. They are certainly not error-correction mechanisms, as they are still often called in the literature. They have the property that, in forecasting models, for example, if you have built them in, and if the equilibrium shifts, your forecasts are appalling for ever.

Many of the decisions the profession has made about the roles of these things lack one ingredient, and I was really waiting for Kevin to bring it into his talk but it never appeared. He went back to Hume and Hume's criticisms. Absolutely wonderful. Let's apply Hume's criticisms to Newton. Newton wrote about absolute time and absolute space. He made these enormous assumptions—complete rubbish as we now know.

They don't exist. There is no meaning to attach to them. Did it matter? No, it turned out it didn't matter at all. The planets behaved pretty much according to his gravitational rules. It would have looked a bit different if we had had a much bigger sun—we might have got to relativity more quickly—but the whole idea is that this needs to take place in a progressive research strategy. Eichenbaum's paper really embodies that. He is doing things today that he would not have dreamed of doing ten years ago. There is a vast amount of progress and this progress is what is lacking in all the discussion. We rule out certain attributes of reality. The wars come along and they rule out that defence expenditure does not have certain effects on the economy. They rule out that certain relationships are cointegrated. If you know they are not cointegrated, that is very important information, I believe, in understanding how policy will rule.

McCallum comes along and says everything has got a unit root in it. Well, in that case you would simply not find cointegrating relations. It is not a theoretical issue. If we go back to the period of the 1880s, Alfred Marshall and Francis Edgworth were both giving evidence to the House of Commons on technological change in money-demand equations. Edgeworth was extremely concerned about the introduction of the telegraph. It was going to allow people to have just one bank account in London and they could just telegraph money to people when they needed it. What an enormous effect this was going to have on money-demand equations. Edgeworth was even more concerned about the cheque book. This newfangled gadget had just been invented, and people could write cheques—they did not even need to telegraph it to Manchester. Has it changed the money-demand structure of the British economy? In my view, not at all. Nor have money machines, for you still need the money at the end of the month to pay the credit card. There have been detailed studies of the impact of technological change on money demand. We have measurements of it, of numbers of machines, of the number of transactions on credit cards, and the Bank of England finds essentially nothing out of that kind of approach. So let's let empirical evidence come in and alter the theorists' view of these things. Let's build models and if they do find cointegration it is an important restriction and it will let us build what is really crucial—a progressive research strategy that is looking for regularities that turn out to persist for long periods.

Adrian Pagan: I think when one observes both schools, one is struck by the fact there is a difference between them. If you think about the impulse–response functions that you see in Sims's articles, all the shocks are regarded as transitory and the effects all go to zero in the end. If you think about the impulse–response functions you get out of Hendry's articles, with the cointegration imposed, that is not true. That is a very big difference between them. Real business-cycle models when they began looked just like Sims's VARs, but increasingly they have moved to having a unit root in the technology shock and that produces impulse–response functions that look more like Hendry's. So I think we are seeing some convergence along those lines. People do think that there are some permanent shocks and they are imposing them. To some extent that comes from the interpretation of the data.

Sims: If you look at the last few papers I have done, the shocks, the impulse–responses, do not come back to zero.

Pagan: Actually that is not true. If I use my data, which I assume is very similar to yours, and I run them out for three to four hundred periods they go back to zero, with the exception of exchange rates. Well—quicker than that. This is a difference between whether you think shocks are permanent or whether you think shocks are transitory. It is very important in a model. We would like to impose a restriction that a shock is persistent, but we do not know how to do that very well, so we have to make a decision about whether we say it is transitory or whether we say it is permanent and that has enormous implications at the end. Juselius's paper was like trying to say 'I am only half pregnant'—that is these things persist but they are not permanent. You were saying that these are just statistical approximations but I think there is a fundamental difference between these two things. When you come down to thinking about how models interact with data, you get forced to think about what might be a permanent shock and if there is a permanent shock how it might be imposed. That turns out to be a very difficult thing to do. I have written about this in the 'Shocking Stories' paper (1998) that Smith referred to and it is one of the things that drove us mad—trying to select a permanent shock that would actually produce what we saw in the data. I think it is a big challenge for all modellers.

Martin Eichenbaum: There appears to be this misconception that because people in the identified VAR group look at unexpected shocks, or seek to identify unexpected shocks, that somehow we have the view that only unexpected shocks matter, say with respect to monetary policy. But in fact nothing could be farther from the truth. The only reason that I look for unexpected shocks, and I may differ here from Sims, is that I am looking for various experiments to test my models against. I then want to construct a model which passes some variety of test—to confront it with the kind of experiment that Hendry has in mind. What if Alan Greenspan adopted a completely different rule? So there is absolutely no presumption in my mind that only unexpected monetary policy matters and I don't think that Sims thinks this either. If anything, to the extent that monetary policy matters a lot, it is only because of the expected component.

That raises a general issue, and here I want to go back to Minnesota, that in the end we are not going to convince people's minds about anything unless the models we work with have economic agents in them, market institutions, constraints—things that we recognize. All the cointegration stuff in the world may or may not be useful but it has none of that. There is nothing in it that looks like economics. It can be useful as a data summary but it is not going to convince anyone about anything substantial about the way the world works. Larry Christiano and I wrote a paper called 'Unit roots and real GNP: do we know and do we care?' (1990) in which the abstract was no. It does not matter from a model perspective if you put 0.998 in or 1.01. It just doesn't matter. Except in the very, very long run, except with respect to beta. The reason is that nothing sharp happens at one. Now, there is an issue about whether you can get cointegration with systems effects about the long run. Hendry criticized the model that

I wrote yesterday because we don't have cointegrating relationships but that is not true. There is a portion of that model called $X(t)$, the technology shock, and every variable that Hendry wants to be cointegrated in that model is. It is a balanced growth path and if I put in a unit root there I have all the cointegrating relations that you want. So that is, in the context of that specific paper, a statement that is not true. It is the least interesting, least important part of those models.

Katarina Juselius: I think I should first respond to Sims's long critisicm. I had the impression that he was criticizing a paper I had not written. Take, for instance, the low power of unit-root tests. I have never reported the results of a unit-root test in any of my papers for just that reason and I argued very strongly that, instead of *exclusively* using statistical tests for saying how many common stochastic trends there could be in the data, one should use economic knowledge *as a first prior*.

I took a very simple question, as illustrated by Romer (1996), because I thought that was the simplest possible one, it suggests some data and he had estimated the relation based on time-series data. Then I said, 'Now let's consider the consequence of the data being stochastic and let's do a likelihood inference on those data', meaning that we have to say something about the time-dependence, its stochastic properties, and so on. Because most macroeconomic data can be described by its first two moments, I started with what I would say was a minimal set of assumptions and instead of using the covariances, I tried to reformulate the covariances in a way that can be interpreted. This was all to illustrate the procedure of taking data seriously whilst having some prior questions. One of those prior questions was 'Is nominal growth a monetary problem in the long run and in the short run?' I tried to show we can have different outcomes (stationary or non-stationary velocity) and that we get different implications for inference in both these cases. I tried to say that, whatever we do, it is very important that we check the internal consistency of the results. I fully agree on sensitivity analysis. It is necessary always to do a sensitivity analysis when you do empirical analysis to see how sensitive your conclusions are to, say, how you choose to represent the model. I would like to ask Eichenbaum what criteria he would use if he does not accept the information in the data? I use the statistical analysis to find out when I am wrong.

Eichenbaum: The fact that I don't particularly use cointegration tests does not mean that I don't use statistical analysis. Yesterday the whole first half of the paper was attempting to use statistical analysis to identify some interesting experiments and then one can use sampling uncertainty, etc. Subject to a variety of issues about using small-sample statistics or large-sample statistics, the issue is not whether one looks at the data or not. The cointegration guys can't seize the high road of being the only ones who look at the data.

Juselius: I talked about the first two moments, more or less, in the data.

Ron Smith: Having been described as a world-weary pessimist, I should emphasize I am an applied economist. I do statistics and am not being nihilistic. It just seems to me that what we should be arguing about is 'What is the right way to summarize the data? How do we interpret it?' and it is clear that those are very difficult questions. What I want to try to get across is that the idea that there is a simple way to do it, to churn it out like a sausage machine, is just wrong. The sort of issues which are getting discussed here are exactly right. There are quite complicated issues about how you actually do interpret the data. Just to throw in something else, which Juselius and Sims would agree on, though I have my doubts, is a VAR a good way to summarize the data? There are a lot of people who say that it is not: it is massively overparameterized, it leaves out most of the variables Hendry would want to put into the whole system, and that is another question. We then say, 'Is this a good data summary?' and then we just have to agree on what those things are. Again, it comes up regularly, constant parameters. I happen to be someone who believes that parameters change quite regularly, and that they change in systematic ways that we can model in certain circumstances. What makes it interesting is that these are very difficult questions. Going back to my observational equivalence story, of getting the captain to do something different, Britain had the advantage of Mrs Thatcher who did go off in that sort of way and we are still arguing about how to interpret that particular story. Did she really miss the iceberg or not?

REFERENCES

Eichenbaum, M. and Christiano, L. (1990) 'Unit roots in real GNP: do we know and do we care?', *Carnegie-Rochester Conference Series on Public Policy* 32(0): 7–61.
Levtchenkova, S., Pagan, A., and Robertson, J. (1998) 'Shocking Stories', *Journal of Economic Surveys* 12: 507–32.
Romer, D. (1996) *Advanced Macroeconomics* (New York: McGraw Hill).
Sims, C.A., Stock J.H., and Watson, M. (1990) 'Inference in linear time series models with some unit roots', *Econometrica* 58: 113–44.

Part IV
GROWTH

11 Econometric analysis and the study of economic growth: a sceptical perspective

STEVEN N. DURLAUF

1. Introduction

This essay has an explicitly provocative purpose—namely, to argue that the econometric component of the new economic growth literature has done little to adjudicate leading growth questions. While I believe this empirical literature has identified a number of interesting data patterns and led to the development of a number of important new econometric methods (both achievements exemplified in the work of Quah (1996a,b, 1997)), the vast body of empirical studies has shed remarkably little light on the main theoretical issues which have emerged since the seminal papers of Romer and Lucas. While largely a critique of existing empirical practice, my hope is that the essay will prove to be suggestive of alternative ways to think about growth data.

The empirical growth literature with which I am concerned consists of cross-section (and sometimes panel regressions) of aggregate growth rates on various country level variables.[1] A generic form of this type of regression is

$$g_i = X_i\gamma + y_{i,0}\beta + \epsilon_i, \tag{1}$$

where g_i is real per capita growth in economy i over a given time period, X_i is a vector of country-specific controls, $y_{i,0}$ is the real per capita income of the country at the beginning of the period over which growth is measured, and ϵ_i an unexplained residual. The singling out of initial income as a determinant of growth is done in order to allow testing for the convergence hypothesis, which we describe below. This type of regression has been employed to study an immense range of growth theories.

In its initial incarnations, the equation was employed to determine whether the neoclassical Solow–Swan growth model well describes cross-country growth dynamics; the most persuasive paper of this type is Mankiw *et al.* (1992) which limited the variables in X_i to those which are directly implied by the Solow model—namely, population growth and human and physical capital savings rates. A fair description of this early literature is that it showed that observed growth dynamics for the

I thank the National Science Foundation, John D. and Catherine T. MacArthur Foundation, and Romnes Trust for financial support. I also thank William Brock and Rodolfo Manuelli for useful conversations on the issues in this paper. Andros Kourtellos and Artur Minkin have provided excellent research assistance. All errors are mine.

[1] The use of panel regressions has been motivated primarily by a desire to permit the researcher to eliminate country-specific fixed effects by differencing. Durlauf and Quah (1998) criticize this approach. The arguments made in this paper apply equally well to cross-sections and panels.

time-period of approximately 1950–90 are in a number of respects qualitatively consistent with the predictions of the neoclassical model.

Perhaps the most important claim of this literature is the consistency of observed data with the convergence hypothesis. By convergence, this literature refers to the hypothesis that β is less than zero. A negative β in the standard cross-country growth regression implies, after controlling for various country-specific factors, that countries with lower initial incomes grow, on average, faster than those with higher initial incomes. The convergence hypothesis has been treated as a critical test of neoclassical versus endogenous growth theories, since the Solow model predicts a negative β. In turn, some endogenous growth theories, which typically are based on global increasing returns to scale, imply that β should be positive. Further, the idea that, other things equal, rich countries grow more slowly than poor ones, has the substantive implication that current per capita income differences across nations can be expected to narrow.[2]

The second stage of the empirical growth literature has been less concerned with convergence and tests of the validity of the neoclassical model. Rather, this literature has been interested in which variables should be included in X_i. As theories have proliferated as to why factors ranging from democracy to trade openness to geography should influence cross-country growth patterns, evidence in support of these theories has been sought by the determination that empirical proxies for these theories, when included as elements of X_i, are statistically significant; Durlauf and Quah (1999) survey the range of candidate explanations.

2. Basic problems

While generating a range of interesting findings on patterns in the cross-country data, there are strong reasons to question whether the empirical growth literature has done much to adjudicate causal explanations of growth. This is a sweeping claim, of course, and can only be fully defended through a detailed study of the various empirical papers which purport to argue for a particular explanation. However, there do seem to be a set of general problems with the empirical growth literature which imply that attempts at structural or causal inference have not been successful.

2.1. Causality versus correlation

The many candidate variables in the growth literature are typically endogenous. It is hard to think of reasons why savings rates, political characteristics, inequality and the like would *not* be determined jointly with growth rates. Therefore, any movement from the observation of statistical significance of a variable coefficient in a regression to claims about causality is not warranted. This criticism has the status of a 'folk' objection in the growth literature, in that it has been made so many times that it is not clear to whom it can be first attributed. However, frequency of complaint does not invalidate

---

[2] See Bernard and Durlauf (1996) for a discussion of different statistical notions of convergence and Galor (1996) for a discussion of the convergence-related implications of different growth theories.

the basic point. While there have been some very limited efforts to deal with endogeneity, it seems fair to say the literature has largely ignored this question, relying on vague suggestions (e.g. Barro (1999: 12) that timing can uncover the difference between causality and correlation. This of course, is nothing more than the *post hoc ergo propter hoc* fallacy which periodically reappears in economic debates (cf. the monetarist–Keynesian debates between James Tobin and Milton Friedman, Tobin (1970)).

At first glance, it might seem that there is an obvious solution to the simultaneity problem I have described—namely, the use of instrumental variables to proxy for the various regressors X_i. Such a solution is more problematic than one might think. Suppose that there exists a set of instruments which are strictly exogenous, in the sense that they are determined outside of the system which determines growth and the other regressors in equation (1), and that these instruments causally determine those regressors. Formally, what I mean is that suppose for a given choice of regressors X_i and equation (1) we could identify an additional set of regressors Z_i such that

$$X_i = Z_i A + \eta_i, \tag{2}$$

where Z_i is a deterministic function $F(\cdot)$ of some underlying factors ξ which are determined outside the socio-economic system as constituted over the period of study.

$$Z_i = F(\xi). \tag{3}$$

The components of Z_i can be thought of as variables such as longitude or latitude, land area of country i, or language. This system would seem well designed for using Z_i to instrument for some or all of the elements of X_i. However, even in this 'ideal case' it is unclear that the Z_i's are valid instruments for the regressors in the context of equation (1).

The reason that Z_i's may not be valid instruments is that growth theories are 'open-ended', by which I mean that the claim that one variable influences growth does not typically imply that other variables do not. So, a theory which says that democracy positively influences growth will usually have no implication for whether or not geography influences growth. The regressor error ϵ_i is the cumulation of these unmodelled factors, and cannot be given any further interpretation. Even if Z_i is determined outside the socio-economic system, this does not imply it is uncorrelated with ϵ_i. Therefore, for an instrument to be valid for equation (1), one has to assume that it is uncorrelated with ϵ_i, which would require the very strong assumption that it is uncorrelated with all the omitted growth determinants.

To see how this may be problematic, consider the paper by Frankel and Romer (1996) on trade and growth. (I single this paper out as it well illustrates the pitfalls of instrumental variables use in the context of thoughtful study.) Frankel and Romer argue that since trade openness is clearly endogenous, it is necessary to instrument such a variable in the standard cross-country regression if one is to consistently estimate the trade coefficient. In order to do this, they use a geographic variable, i.e. area, as an instrument. However, is it plausible that country land-size is uncorrelated with the omitted growth factors in their regression? The history and geography literatures are replete with theories of how geography affects political regime, development, etc. For example, larger countries may be more likely to be ethnically heterogeneous, leading to attendant social problems. Alternatively, larger countries may have higher per capita military expenditures, which means relatively greater levels of unproductive government investment and/or higher distortionary taxes. My point is not that any of these links is necessarily salient, but that the use of land area as an instrument presupposes the assumption that the correlations between land size and all omitted growth determinants are in total negligible. It is difficult to see how one can defend such an assumption when these omitted growth determinants are not specified.

Notice that this openendedness is different from what one found in rational expectations models, at least with respect to instrumental variables. In the rational expectations literature, econometric implementation of a model is typically done by constructing a variable which equals the difference between some quantity realized at date t and the optimal forecast of that quantity at $t - 1$, under the assumption that the model is true, since an optimal forecast error must be orthogonal to all information available at the time the forecast is made. Hence any variables which are realized before t are available instruments.

Now, one might argue that the distinction I have drawn between the logic of growth regressions and the logic of rational expectations econometrics is unfair, in that in each case one is actually using instruments under the assumption that the model under analysis is correctly specified, which means that the instruments are uncorrelated with some error-ϵ_i in the case of growth regressions and a forecast error in the case of rational expectations. However, the key difference is that the rational expectations specification contains the total economic reasoning of a model in a way which the growth regressions do not, given the open-endedness of growth theories.

2.2. Model specification

A second problem with the empirical growth literature has been a lack of attention to the implications of various growth theories for the specification of the empirical models used to compare growth theories. The use of linear cross-country regressions is usually justified by appealing to a linearization of the Solow growth model, or by the assumption that the aggregate production function is Cobb–Douglas. Rather than direct testing of neoclassical versus endogenous growth alternatives, the literature has used the results of this linear regression to argue in favour of one or the other theory. Hence the interest in the sign of β.

The relevant issue in assessing growth theories using such regressions is whether alternatives to the Solow model will be revealed using such a functional form. The problem is that for many endogenous growth theories, the linear regression (1) is a misspecification of the growth process. Therefore, in assessing growth theories via the regression, one needs to ask how data generated by an endogenous growth model will appear when passed through a misspecified linear model. It is far from clear that the salient statistical implications of a given endogenous growth model will be preserved in such an exercise. Bernard and Durlauf (1996) give the following example of what might happen. For models of multiple steady-states such as Azariadis and Drazen (1990), assume that all countries within a sample have identical characteristics X_i, which means that growth dynamics can be approximated as

$$g_i = (y_{i,0} - y_i^*)\beta' + \epsilon_i, \tag{4}$$

where y_i^* is the steady-state for country i and $\beta' < 0$. This model exhibits local convergence, in the sense that countries associated with the same steady-state will exhibit Solow-type dynamics. Assume further that there are a discrete number of these steady-states and that some countries are associated with each. This is a case where there is no economically interesting form of convergence as different initial incomes can produce different limiting income levels.

If one runs a regression of the form (1), then there is an omitted variable, $-y_i^*$, when the data are in fact generated by (4). To see how this affects interpretations of convergence, consider the value of the β coefficient in the regression

$$g_i = c + y_{i,0}\beta + \epsilon_i \tag{5}$$

(which is a special case of (4) when all countries have the same steady-state). Expressed in terms of population moments, when equation (4) is the correct specification, β equals

$$\beta = \frac{\beta' cov(y_{i,0} - y_i^*, y_{i,0})}{var(y_{i,0})} = \beta'\left(1 - \frac{cov(y_i^*, y_{i,0})}{var(y_{i,0})}\right). \tag{6}$$

This expression illustrates two things. First, $\beta < 0$ in the standard cross-country growth regression is compatible with a model with multiple steady-states, since one can easily identify joint distributions y_i^* and $y_{i,0}$ where this is so (recall that β' was assumed to be negative). Second, the degree of global convergence observed via the misspecified regression can exceed that which occurs locally, if $cov(y_i^*, y_{i,0}) < 0$. Intuitively, if countries with higher steady-state incomes tend to have lower initial incomes, this will create spurious evidence of convergence.[3]

What this example is meant to illustrate is that by failing to consider the properties of cross-country regressions when estimating using data from non-neoclassical models, one can easily draw spurious inferences concerning the validity of the neoclassical model. Endogenous growth theories, as a corollary of their capacity to produce multiple steady-states or explosive growth trajectories, embody deep non-linearities in their structures. Regressions such as (1) which do not explicitly model these non-linearities are capable of producing results which appear supportive of the neoclassical model.

2.3. Discrimination between growth theories

A third problem with the empirical growth literature is the multiplicity of theories. In their 1998 survey of the empirical growth literature, Durlauf and Quah (1999) found

---

[3] This example was chosen for algebraic simplicity; it can easily be generalized to allow for countries with different initial conditions to converge to different steady-state growth rates.

over ninety different variables that have been proposed for cross-country growth regressions of approximately 100 observations; since that survey a number of new variables have appeared. Each of these variables is, in my judgement, at least somewhat plausible *ex ante* as at least a partial determinant of growth.

This large number of candidate variables relative to available data is naturally a worry. Unfortunately, there do not exist any satisfactory ways to let the data determine which variables are selected. At one level, this is a statement about the statistics literature, and not about empirical economics *per se*. While there are a plethora of procedures which have been proposed for variable selection (see Miller (1990) for a survey of classical methods and Beauchamp and Mitchell (1988) and George and McCulloch (1993) for Bayesian approaches), it is fair to say that no consensus exists as to appropriate procedures.

This being said, the empirical growth literature has not even approached this level of sophistication. There are two well-known efforts which attempt to determine which variables robustly 'matter' in growth regressions: Levine and Renelt (1992) and Sala-i-Martin (1997). Each of these papers in essence attempts to identify which possible growth determinants, as defined as a fixed universe of variables, is robustly statistically significant, where robustness is defined as remaining significant in the presence of various other possible variables. Specifically, a large set of regressions are run with different combinations of variables; robustness of a given variable is evaluated relative to the distribution of coefficients and standard errors generated for the variable. In the case of Levine and Renelt, Leamer's (1983) extreme bounds analysis is employed, which identifies variable significance as fragile if the range of different point estimates is too great across the different regressions which are run. In the case of Sala-i-Martin, a variable is robust if the estimate of its associated coefficient is statistically significant for at least 95 per cent of the regressions.

While these papers both represent useful exercises, there are clear limitations to each. One problem is the sensitivity of the robustness criteria to which alternative variables are included; see Durlauf and Quah (1999) for an extensive discussion. To give one example, suppose I augment the regressor set in Sala-i-Martin's original analysis with a number of silly (from the perspective of a growth regression) variables. Suppose further that after adding these variables, the percentage of regressions where a given variable coefficient is statistically significant is increased. Does this increased percentage of significant coefficients mean that the variable is more robust than before? It would given Sala-i-Martin's evaluative criterion for robustness, although for the thought experiment just described it clearly should not.

More generally, these procedures are based upon the assumption that the statistical significance of individual variables should be used to determine model selection—an assumption that is hard to justify (and is at odds with most of the model selection literature in statistics). These types of procedure make it possible for one to reject a set of variables as non-robust, due to high collinearity, even though the exclusion of all of them substantially degrades the explanatory power of the regression.

However, even accepting these exercises at face value, there is the more general question of whether robustness is a desirable criterion for assessing growth explanations. To see why this may well not be true, notice that robustness in these two papers ultimately means that a variable is statistically significant in the presence of combinations of other variables. For this to be true, it must be the case that the variable is not too highly correlated with others in the variable set under study. But why would one expect this lack of correlatedness to hold for the sorts of variables which are candidate growth theories? Among the candidate explanations for growth differences, various authors have studied democracy (e.g. Barro 1996), inequality (e.g. Alesina and Rodrik 1994), corruption (e.g. Mauro 1995), trade policy (e.g. Levine and Renelt 1992) and a large number of alternative measures of a society's social, political, and economic status. What is important about such variables is that none of them can be thought of as being determined independently of aggregate growth. In other words, the same processes which determine growth also will determine the social and political landscape of a country. Hence one would expect these various measures both to correlate with growth in a bivariate or regression sense, but also to correlate with each other and hence not be robust in the sense which we have described. Notice that this last point is independent of whether there is simultaneity bias in a cross-country growth regression. Each of these variables can causally determine growth, yet be highly correlated with one another. Therefore, for many of the candidate growth explanations, robustness is an implausible property.

2.4. Heterogeneity

A final conceptual difficulty concerns the assumption of an invariant statistical model in cross-country growth analysis. As conventionally specified, cross-country regressions pre-suppose that the analyst believes that the coefficients of the exercise are interpretable as country invariant relationships between some control variable and growth. The existence of such a relationship is far from obvious. What does it mean to say that one expects a 1 per cent change in school enrolment to have the same effect on the growth rate in the USA as Botswana? I realize that at some level, one can criticize any empirical exercise in social science for this reason. The interpretability of any statistical exercise will always be a matter of degree. However, when one is dealing with aggregates as complex as entire countries, it is difficult to see what in terms of causal structure it is that one learns from the standard cross-country exercises which fail to treat parameter heterogeneity as fundamental.[4]

---

[4] Periodically, one finds a cross-country study in which the basic regression (1) is modified so that the coefficient for a particular variable is allowed to take on one of a small set of different values; this is done by sorting countries into groups so that the coefficient is required to be constant within groups. For example, countries with per capita incomes above the median are allowed to have one coefficient for some regressor and countries with per capita incomes below the median are allowed to have another. These analyses are generally quite unsatisfactory. For one thing, the reported country groupings are typically *ad hoc* with few (if any) alternative groupings explored, leaving one worried that the reported results are not robust. Further, allowing for different coefficients for different groups of countries for one variable seems question-begging. Why one variable and not others? Logically, evidence of parameter heterogeneity for one variable has implications for how one analyses all the parameters. What is lacking in the literature are systematic analyses of parameter heterogeneity.

This failure to control for parameter heterogeneity makes any predictive inference from the standard regression models problematic. Does one really think that a marginal change in the level of democracy (assuming a meaningful scale even exists) on growth in a country is independent of its level of education? Unless one understands how individual countries differ from the average behaviours described by the standard cross-country regression, it is impossible to make sensible claims about the effects of political and social change on growth.

This type of worry is more than a theoretical concern, as a number of analyses have demonstrated that there is a deep form of heterogeneity in the data. For example, Durlauf and Johnson (1995) employed a classification algorithm known as a regression tree to divide the countries in the Heston–Summers data set into groups, each of which obeys a common statistical model. The idea of a regression tree (see Breiman *et al.* (1984) for an exhaustive treatment) is that one treats a data set as consisting of observations drawn from a set of linear models. The algorithm is designed to sort the data into groups of observations each of which obeys the same model. This sorting is done on the basis of a set of control variables. The supports of these variables are partitioned into intervals, these intervals define the groupings of observations. For example, Durlauf and Johnson use initial literacy and income as controls, so that country groupings are made on the basis of finding observations which fall into common intervals for these two variables.

Further evidence has been adduced by Canova (1999) in an important recent paper.[5] In this analysis, the logic of the regression tree is preserved in that one seeks to identify groups of countries obeying a common statistical model. However, unlike Durlauf and Johnson, Canova allows the model coefficients to be random for each country within a grouping. This randomness permits intragroup as well as intergroup heterogeneity in the growth process and is particularly appealing in cross-country contexts.

Papers such as Durlauf and Johnson and Canova as well as historical studies such as Landes lead to a common conclusion. Heterogeneity is a key feature of national experiences, so that even if one is willing to consider a common model for uniting these experiences, the parameters of the model are very likely to differ across countries.

It is worth noting that concern over heterogeneity need not lead to agnosticism about empirical work. Much of James Heckman's fundamental contributions to empirical microeconomics (see Cameron and Heckman (1998) and Heckman *et al.* (1998) for recent examples) has been based on the development of constructive ways of dealing with observed and unobserved heterogeneity. The plausibility and importance of heterogeneity is no less in the case of aggregate economies.

3. What is to be done?

These basic concerns about growth empirics touch on many foundational issues concerning the use of statistical analysis in economics. These criticisms come from

[5] As will be seen in the next section, Canova (1999) is very much in the spirit of the directions I recommend for future empirical research.

very different bases, and therefore have very different implications for econometric practice.

For some of the problems with current econometric practice in growth, the implications seem obvious. If the goal of an empirical exercise is to establish causality, then it is necessary to do two things. First, one can consider statistical solutions for regression endogeneity through the use of instruments, model transformation, or any of many well-established techniques. Second, and harder, one must make a plausible argument that the instruments employed do not, through omitted growth explanations, correlate with the regression error in the growth equation. This may be facilitated if the number of instruments available exceeds the number of variables which need to be instrumented, since one can then construct tests of instrument validity (i.e. lack of correlation of the instruments with the growth regression error). Even in this case, the plausibility of a claim of instrument validity based upon a statistical test needs to be assessed in light of the openendedness of growth theories. If the goal of an econometric exercise is to assess the neoclassical growth model relative to an endogenous growth competitor, then the exercise must include the endogenous growth specification if the comparison is to be interpretable.

For other problems, there is no obvious solution. For example, my reading of the statistics literature is that variable selection continues to be a very problematic area of analysis. Further, there also needs to be a recognition that there are limits to what econometric analyses can do in contexts as complicated as growth. With approximately forty annual observations on approximately 100 countries, the high covariance of plausible growth explanations means that statistical analysis alone is very unlikely to be able to fully discriminate across the plethora of growth explanations.

In addition, two modifications in current econometric methodology warrant exploration.

3.1. Greater eclecticism in empirical work

Growth is an obvious area where econometric analysis should be supplemented by historical work to a much greater extent than has been done. Studies such as Landes (1998) contain an immense amount of information, one should also say wisdom, albeit not in the form of formal statistical statements. My belief is that historical analyses of this type can provide strong priors for issues such as variable selection and the parameterization of cross-country parameter heterogeneity. In order to do this formally, it might well make sense to employ Bayesian estimation methods whereby evidence from history is modelled as restrictions on a prior. Even if this integration of qualitative and quantitative analysis does not prove to be workable, there is no question that qualitative studies can supplement econometric analyses when it comes to the assessment of growth theories, which is after all the purpose of the empirical exercises.

3.2. Greater reliance on modern statistical methods

At the same time, it seems clear that the empirical growth literature can be augmented by greater attention to modern developments in statistics. To give the example to which my current thinking is devoted, the issue of parameter heterogeneity is an active area of research in statistics. The literature on non-parametrics has proposed ways to explicitly model regression parameters which smoothly depend on data. Hastie and Tibshirani (1993), for example, explicitly consider ways to analyse regression models of the type

$$g_i = \gamma_1(Z_1)x_{i,1} + \cdots + \gamma_K(Z_K)x_{i,K} + \beta(Z_{K+1})y_{i,0} + \epsilon_i, \tag{7}$$

where Z_k is a regressor specific set of variables and $\gamma_i(\cdot)$'s and $\beta(\cdot)$ are arbitrary (subject to smoothness restrictions) variable-specific functions. By choosing initial conditions such as per capita income and the literacy rate among adults as elements of Z_i, one can in principle estimate how stages of development influence growth determinants through their influence on the effects of other growth variables.

A related approach of this type is known as empirical Bayes estimation (cf. Maritz and Lwin 1989). In the empirical Bayes approach, one conceptualizes the observables R_i and model parameters θ_i as draws from a joint probability measure $\mu(R, \theta)$. The goal of the data analysis is the determination of the posterior probability measure for the model's parameters given the data, i.e. $\mu(\theta|R)$. This posterior probability can be written, using the definition of conditional probability as

$$\mu(\theta|R) = \frac{\mu(R|\theta)\mu(\theta)}{\mu(R)}. \tag{8}$$

From the perspective of most econometric practice, the difficulty with Bayesian analysis is how to specify $\mu(\theta)$, which is the prior distribution of the model parameters.

In empirical Bayes, the key assumption is that each of the θ_i's is assumed to represent a separate draw from the marginal distribution $\mu(\theta)$. This means that one can think about recovering $\mu(\theta)$ from the data. Hence, empirical Bayes methods do not need to rely on the specification of a subjective prior, but rather on the idea that each observation embeds a draw of the parameters from the prior. To see how this recovery can work, notice that the relationship between the prior and the other probabilities in this model can be written as

$$\mu(R) = \int_0 \mu(R|\theta)\mu(\theta). \tag{9}$$

Since $\mu(R)$ and $\mu(R|\theta)$ (this latter being the likelihood function) are estimable, one can see that it is reasonable to ask whether $\mu(\theta)$ (which in principle can be conditioned on data as well) can be recovered from this functional equation. One key question in empirical Bayes analysis is the determination of conditions under which this can be done.

I do not know whether either of these approaches will prove to be particularly useful in studying growth (although my current research is involved with investigating both). The point for the growth literature, however, is that statistical tools exist for constructively dealing with heterogeneity in national growth experiences—tools which have yet to be adequately exploited.

4. Conclusions

The theoretical and empirical growth literature has experienced a remarkable renaissance over the last fifteen years. Yet it appears that few of the substantive economic differences between theories have been adjudicated by growth empirics. Greater attention to issues of model specification, heterogeneity, and non-formal sources of information all seem essential if progress is to be made in this direction.

Many of the criticisms which have been made may seem to be generic problems with empirical work in economics as well as other social sciences. Questions of functional form specification, legitimacy of instruments, and parameter heterogeneity can be raised for virtually any study. In fact, the eminent statistician and probability theorist David Freedman has written a number of very strong attacks on empirical social science research through a careful study of the unjustified assumptions which I believe he would say generically underlie social science studies (e.g. Freedman 1981, 1991). My own criticisms are certainly examples of the sorts of objections he has made. Where we differ is that I do not believe that empirical work should be assessed in black-and-white terms. Assumptions are more or less plausible, not either justified or unjustified. Hence, criticisms of empirical work need to do more than simply identify assumptions. What I believe to be true, and hope has been illustrated in this discussion, is that in the case of the growth empirics, is that issues such as the employment of instrumental variables and heterogeneity are likely to be particularly serious.

This essay has also suggested that Bayesian approaches might well prove to be especially useful in growth contexts. The justifications given for this have not followed traditional Bayesian concerns about coherence and the like, but have rather been based on a pragmatic interest in uncovering more information about the growth process.[6] And to be fair, some of the discussion may reflect my own limited knowledge of Bayesian ideas. Nevertheless, methodological eclecticism seems more than warranted when dealing with issues as complicated as growth.

REFERENCES

Alesina, A. and D. Rodrik (1994) 'Distributive politics and growth', *Quarterly Journal of Economics* 109: 465–90.
Azariadis, C. and A. Drazen (1990) 'Threshold externalities in economic development', *Quarterly Journal of Economics* 105: 501–26.
Barro, R. (1996) 'Democracy and growth', *Journal of Economic Growth* 1: 1–27.
—— (1999) 'Inequality, growth, and investment', NBER Working Paper 7038.
Bernard, A. and S. Durlauf (1996) 'Interpreting tests of the convergence hypothesis', *Journal of Econometrics* 71: 161–72.

---

[6] Indeed, many orthodox Bayesians object to the name 'empirical Bayesian'.

Breiman, L., J. Friedman, R. Olshen, and C. Stone (1984) *Classification and Regression Trees* (New York: Chapman & Hall).

Cameron, S. and J. Heckman (1998) 'Life cycle schooling and educational selectivity: models and evidence', *Journal of Political Economy* 108.

Canova, F. (1999) 'Testing for convergence clubs in income per-capita: a predictive density approach, mimeo (University of Pompeu Fabra, Spain).

Durlauf, S. and P. Johnson (1995), 'Multiple regimes and cross-country growth behavior', *Journal of Applied Econometrics* 10: 365–84.

—— and D. Quah (1999) 'The new empirics of economic growth', *Handbook of Macroeconomics*, J. Taylor and M. Woodford (eds.) (Amsterdam: North-Holland).

Frankel, J. and D. Romer (1996) 'Trade and growth: an empirical investigation', NBER Working Paper 5476.

Freedman, D. (1981) 'Some pitfalls in large econometric models: a case study', *Journal of Business* 54: 479–500.

Freedman, D. (1991) 'Statistical models and shoe leather', in P. Marsden (ed.), *Sociological Methodology* (Cambridge: Blackwell).

Galor, O. (1996) 'Convergence? Inferences from theoretical models', *Economic Journal* 106: 1056–69.

George, E. and R. McCulloch (1993) 'Variable selection via Gibbs sampling', *Journal of the American Statistical Association* 88: 881–9.

Hastie, T. and R. Tibshirani (1993) 'Varying—coefficient models', *Journal of the Royal Statistical Society*, Series B 55: 757–96.

Heckman, J., L. Lochner, and C. Taber (1998) 'Explaining rising wage inequality: explorations with a dynamic general equilibrium model of labor earnings with heterogeneous agents', *Review of Economic Dynamics*: 1.

Landes, D. (1998) *The Wealth and Poverty of Nations* (New York: W. W. Norton & Co.).

Leamer, E. (1983) 'Let's take the con out of econometrics', *American Economic Review* 73: 31–43.

Levine, R. and D. Renelt (1992) 'A sensitivity analysis of cross-country growth regressions', *American Economic Review* 82: 942–63.

Lucas, R. (1988) 'On the mechanics of economic development', *Journal of Monetary Economics* 22: 3–42.

Mankiw, N. G., D. Romer, and D. Weil (1992) 'A contribution to the empirics of economic growth', *Quarterly Journal of Economics* 107: 407–37.

Maritz, J. and T. Lwin (1989) *Empirical Bayes Methods* (New York: Chapman & Hall).

Mauro, P. (1995) 'Corruption and growth', *Quarterly Journal of Economics*, 110: 681–713.

Mitchell, T. and J. Beauchamp (1988) 'Bayesian variable selection in linear regression (with discussion)', *Journal of the American Statistical Association* 83: 1023–36.

Miller, A. (1990) *Subset Selection in Regression* (New York: Chapman & Hall).

Quah, D. (1996a) 'Convergence empirics across economies with (some) capital mobility', *Journal of Economic Growth* 1: 95–124.

Quah, D. (1996b) 'Empirics for growth and economic convergence', *European Economic Review* 40: 1353–75.

Quah, D. (1997) 'Empirics for growth and distribution: polarization, stratification, and convergence clubs', *Journal of Economic Growth* 2: 27–59.

Romer, P. (1986) 'Increasing returns and long-run growth', *Journal of Political Economy* 94: 1002–37.

Sala-i-Martin, X. (1997) 'I just ran two million regression', *American Economic Review, Papers and Proceedings* 87: 178–83.

Tobin, J. (1970) 'Money and income: post hoc ergo propter hoc?' *Quarterly Journal of Economics* 84: 301–17.

12 Growth models and the explanation of the forces behind development processes

PAOLO SYLOS LABINI

1. Preliminary remarks

Modern economic theory was born little more than two centuries ago with Adam Smith as a science concerning the economic development of nations; today we have a formal science based on an essentially static framework; only after the Second World War we have had a number of growth models, most of which share the serious shortcomings of neoclassical economics, whose foundations are static. We have a particular growth model that is based not on neoclassical but on a Keynesian framework: it is the Harrod–Domar model, which has got genuinely dynamic features but ignores the main force of economic growth, namely, technical progress. Neoclassical economists, instead, claim to take into account technical progress in their models, but they do this in a logically untenable way, often by assuming shifts, supposedly due to technical progress, of static curves.

More generally, neoclassical growth models represent attempts to use static theoretical tools for interpreting dynamic processes. These attempts have brought in full light some of the internal inconsistencies of those models. Anticipating part of a synthesis that I will shortly present in a monograph on underdevelopment, here I consider a list of such inconsistencies by referring to five of the most important propositions of neoclassical theory, that is:

  (i) the principle of increasing returns;
 (ii) the principle of diminishing of returns;
(iii) impulses determining productivity growth;
(iv) the rate of interest as the price of capital;
 (v) the static substitution between capital and labour as the basis for explaining income distribution and economic growth.

2. The principle of increasing returns

This principle represents the backbone of Adam Smith's inquiry on the wealth of nations. In Smith's conception this principle is inherently dynamic: the gradual expansion, taking place in the course of time, of the extent of the markets stimulates or makes possible changes in technique or in the organization of production; often changes in techniques are embodied in new machines, introduced by common workmen or by scientists ('philosophers'); the consequence is the increase of productivity ('the productive power') of labour. The progressive division of labour can take place either within each firm—this is the case of the famous example of the pin factory—or among different firms. The latter process, in its turn, implies either an increasing variety of intermediate goods for the production of a given final good or an increasing differentiation of similar but not identical final goods, or both. When the division of labour occurs within individual firms, then the dimension of such firm tends to increase, large firms become more and more frequent and a process of concentration takes place; when it occurs among different firms, then we observe a process of differentiation. In the various stages of industrial capitalism we observe first the prevalence of a process of differentiation, mainly of intermediate goods, then a process of concentration, and then again a process of differentiation, prevailingly of similar but not identical final goods. This is a relatively modern phenomenon occurring after per capita income had amply surpassed the subsistence threshold for increasing masses of people, so that goods of different varieties and qualities capable of satisfying basically the same needs have been produced.

The division of labour occurring within individual firms is at the origin of the economies of scale and, more generally, of what Alfred Marshall called internal economies, whereas the division of labour occurring among different firms is at the origin of what Marshall defined as external economies, emphasizing the importance of localization of productive units to multiply the occasions of the spread of this type of economies and thus the formation end growth of industrial districts.

The main consequence of the division of labour in its various forms is the increase in the productivity of labour due to technical and organizational progress originating by that process. Thus Marshall, in analysing internal and external economies, was compelled to recognize the importance of technical progress; but such a progress was logically incompatible with the static theoretical apparatus that Marshall, like most economists of his time, had accepted; he could relatively easily avoid the contradiction in considering the short-run supply curve of a firm, since in this case plant and technology can be assumed to be given without departing too much from reality. Such an assumption, however, was clearly untenable in the case of the long-run supply curve. Here is the way that Marshall suggested to avoid the difficulty: 'We exclude from view any economies that may result from substantive new inventions; but we may include those which may be expected to arise naturally out of adaptations of existing ideas.' Marshall was aware of the unsatisfactory character of his solution and remarks: 'such notions must be taken broadly. The attempt to make them precise over-reaches our strength' (Marshall 1949: 381).

While recognizing Marshall's intellectual honesty, we have to point out that the valid answer was not the one that he gave but would admit quite clearly that a static apparatus is intrinsically inadequate to analyse dynamic problems. For logical reasons time does not and cannot enter into static curves that are snapshots, whereas the analysis of dynamic processes requires a motion picture: snapshots cannot depict movements, even if these are very small. Given the prestige of Marshall and thus the great influence on economists of his time, he would have been better advised had he clearly recognized that the introduction of dynamic phenomena into a static system was an impossible task and that the economists willing to analyse technical progress and growth would have to follow another route. To be sure, such a recognition would have implied a drastic departure of Marshall from the dominating paradigm of economic theory of his time.

3. The principle of diminishing returns

If the origin of the principle of increasing returns is to be found in Adam Smith's analysis of the division of labour. The principle of diminishing returns originates in David Ricardo's analysis of the distribution of income among rents, profits, and wages. In fact, in preparing that analysis Ricardo worked out the principle of diminishing returns with reference to the agriculture of a given country by taking as his starting point Malthus's principle of population. Neoclassical economists claim that this principle can be generalized and applied to individual firms in all sorts of activities: it can be formulated in the following way: 'when a given quantity of a certain factor of production is combined with increasing amounts of other factors, production increases, first, at a rising rate and, after a point, at a declining rate.'

More than seventy years ago Sraffa demonstrated that the generalization does not hold (Sraffa 1926): the principle of diminishing returns had to be referred, as Ricardo correctly did, only to agriculture as whole, not to individual firms in that and in other activity; in a certain country land can be regarded as given, with the proviso that agricultural products of other countries do not enter easily into the country considered owing to transportation costs and, even more (in England of that time), to protective tariffs. It is true that Ricardo recognized that technical progress in agriculture can counteract the tendency towards diminishing returns; but he thought that in practice that tendency would have had the upper hand. We know that historically, in the countries that have experienced a vigorous overall process of growth, this has not been the case: due to technical progress, returns have been increasing in all activities, including agriculture. But the principle as such remains valid. In fact, as we will see, in particularly backward countries such as those of Central Africa, technical progress in agriculture either does not take place or has not been and still is not vigorous enough to offset Ricardo's tendency. If Sraffa is right, then the principle of diminishing returns cannot be applied to individual firms, neither in agriculture nor in the other activities and neither in the long nor in the short run; it follows that the marginal cost curve as a rule is to be seen as constant and therefore that it coincides with the direct or variable cost both in the short and in the long run.

This has been confirmed by a huge amount of empirical enquiries. Yet, in spite of this and in spite of the devastating critique set out by Sraffa, mainstream economists go on assuming that, as a rule, individual firms marginal cost curves are U-shaped. In my view the reason for this irrational stubborness is not difficult to find: only marginal costs that, at least after a point, are increasing are compatible with the assumption of perfect competition, an assumption that is still at the foundation of mainstream economic theory.

The marginal cost curve first decreasing and then increasing is the counterpart of the marginal productivity curve, referred to both individual firms and the economy as a whole. Such a curve implies a production that up to a point is increasing at an increasing rate and after that point it is increasing at a decreasing rate. The production curve, too, is open to the radical objections that I worked out elsewhere (Sylos Labini 1988) and that are relevant in the critique of another pillar of mainstream economic theory, that is, the Cobb–Douglas production function.

The static interpretation of Ricardo's diminishing returns is an aberration, since they arise only when the population is increasing in the course of time and therefore requires the cultivation of lands of decreasing fertility. Smith's increasing returns, too, are inherently dynamic, since they depend on the expansion in the size of the markets. Ricardo accepted, but did not develop, Smith's proposition. However, he gave an important contribution to the understanding of productivity increases in ch. 31 that he added to the third edition of his Principles: he had in mind manufacturing and established a relation between wages and the price of machinery. Like that of Smith, this proposition, too, is inherently dynamic and, as we will see, can be formalized in a relation including both Smith's and Ricardo's propositions, to explain productivity changes.

4. Impulses determining the growth of productivity

Neoclassical economists take productivity as an exogenous variable, that is, determined by extra-economic impulses, like the development of science and research, seen as external to the economy; they conceive them as impulses giving rise to shifts of the production function or as the consequence on investment in research—this, to my knowledge, being the only case in which there is an attempt to consider a variable (investment in research for profit) that can be seen as an endogenous variable (Romer 1990). Even in this case, however, the basic theoretical framework remains static.

The distinction between major and minor inventions is analytically important. Major inventions that give rise to major innovations often are produced in laboratories of non-profit organizations, like research institutes and universities. These innovations can have important economic consequences, but they are not determined by profit motives and therefore can be treated as exogenous with respect to the economic system. Major inventions can give rise, discontinuously, to major innovations, that according to Schumpeter originate the business cycles and create the conditions for the process of economic growth, which has a cyclical behaviour. This process is continuously fed by minor innovations that are stimulated by the Smith effect (increase of income) and by investment in research by firms: these three impulses are unmistakenly endogenous impulses, since they arise out of the economic system itself.

Productivity growth depends then on minor innovations that are endogenous and are indirectly conditioned by major innovations. These are endogenous when coming from inventions produced in laboratories of non-profit institutions; then the innovations can well be considered as exogenous. (Major innovations of this type have made plausible the conviction that all innovations can be considered as exogenous.) However originated, major innovations are discontinuous; if we intend to explain yearly productivity growth—the year being the typical time-unit relevant in the study of the behaviour of economic variables—we can limit ourselves to consider only minor innovations that are pushed by the impulses described by Smith and by Ricardo. We refer only to manufacturing: that is the most dynamic sector of the economy not only from the standpoint of productivity growth, but also because it supplies all sorts of machinery and appliances to other sectors.

To explain the yearly labour productivity growth in manufacturing by means of an equation, we single out two variables embodying the Smith and the Ricardo effects. In the case of Smith, we take the variations of national income as an index of those of the extent of the market. In the case of Ricardo, we may start with his proposition 'Machinery and labour are in constant competition and the former can frequently not be employed until labour rises' (Ricardo 1951: 315); the simplest thing to do is to consider the variations of the ratio between wages and the price of machines: an increase in this ratio stimulates the substitution between labour and machines. In a first approximation, then, the productivity equation can be written:

$$\pi^* = a + bY^* + c(W/P_{ma}),$$

where the asterisk represents a yearly rate of change.

We may enlarge our analysis and consider other impulses determining the growth of productivity. Thus wage increases can not only stimulate the introduction of labour-saving machinery (the Ricardo effect) a process that requires time; they can also stimulate the growth of productivity in the short run, quite apart the introduction of machinery. In fact, when the rate of the current increase of wages exceeds the rate of productivity growth already under way, that is, when the cost of labour per unit of output tends to rise, managers are induced to save labour by redistributing jobs among workers within individual firms and reorganizing the production process in a more efficient way. If the wage increase is expected to continue at the same speed, managers will be stimulated to introduce labour-saving machines; and here the Ricardo effect becomes relevant. (Alternatively, managers will import intermediate goods produced more cheaply abroad or will transfer their firms, or certain productive operations, to underdeveloped countries, where wages are much lower and increase more slowly. In extreme cases those firms go bankrupt, so that the country considered will begin to import the goods that those firms were producing.)

The third variable of the productivity equation is the current value of the cost of the productivity, given by the ratio between the wage rate and productivity, whereas the second variable, i.e. the ratio W/P_{ma}, should be lagged, since time is necessary before the increase in that ratio can affect labour productivity via the introduction of new machines. Such machines enter into the aggregate investment that can be included in the productivity equation as a fourth variable, recognizing, however, that, when demand increases, investment has principally the role of expanding productive capacity; investment tends always to increase both productivity and productive capacity, though in different proportions, depending on the relative variations of wages and of total demand. Strictly speaking, aggregate investment also includes the expenses in research laboratories, as a rule organized by large firms, not by small ones, by taking into account that, for yearly productivity increases, only minor innovations arising out of those investments are to be considered. In any case, aggregate investment, too, is to be lagged. Thus, the full productivity equation is as follows:

$$\pi^* = a + bY^* + c(W/P_{ma-m})^* + \mathrm{d}L^* + eI_{-n},$$

where m and n indicate lags and where $m > n$, at least when the productivity component of investment tends to prevail over the other, due to a relatively rapid increase of wages.

The Ricardo effect, embodied in the second variable (W/P_{ma}), has not been discussed in recent times. Yet, it is curious to notice that four American economists, Romer, Delong, Bradford, and Summers, leaving, at least for this problem, the neoclassical paradigm, have partially rediscovered the Ricardian proposition, Romer, concentrating his attention on wages, the other two economists, in a paper written together, concentrating their attention on the prices of machines (Romer 1987; Delong *et al.* 1991). I say 'partially' since these economists consider either the behaviour of wages or that of the prices of machines and not, as one should, the two variables together. I say 'partially' also because the Ricardian variable is only one of the four variables that, in my judgement, are to be used in trying to explain productivity change. I remind the reader that Romer considers not nominal but real wages (W/P) and Delong *et al.* consider the real price of machines, that is the ratio between the nominal price and the deflator of the gross domestic product. Romer considers the long-run behaviour of real wages to interpret the long-run behaviour of productivity and, in particular, to explain the slowdown of productivity growth occurring in the USA between 1973 and 1984. It is worth observing that the behaviour of real wages largely corresponds to behaviour of the third variable of my productivity equation, where I consider, not wages, but the cost of labour per unit of output. On the other hand, the behaviour of the real wages has a certain correspondence also with that of the second variable of my equation (W/P_{ma}), that, however, is lagged. The correspondence is the greater, the closer is the behaviour of the prices in general, or of the cost of living, and that of the prices of machines. Often, however, the correspondence is not close. It is more logically correct to compare the behaviour of the wages with that of the prices of machines rather than with the behaviour of the cost of living or prices in general. After a painstaking cross-section analysis, Delong *et al.* conclude that the relative price of machines, conceived as the ratio between nominal prices and the GDP deflator, can greatly contribute to explain the different levels of productivity in a considerable number of countries, including several underdeveloped ones.

The basic idea of these economists is well founded, but wages should be related to the prices of machines and not to the cost of living, and the prices of goods should be related to wages and not to the GNP deflator; moreover, the explanatory variables are not one but at least four. In particular, Romer intends to present a 'crazy explanation' of the productivity slowdown in the USA; if we take into account the proposition put forth by David Ricardo, all the 'craziness' disappears; in its place we find crass ignorance of the classical economists.

5. The 'price of capital'

Neoclassical economists consider 'capital' as an aggregate quantity that can be measured independently from income distribution and the rate of interest as its 'price'. This is wrong: 'capital'—a term by which neoclassical economists mean fixed capital—cannot be measured in that way (see the summary of a long debate prepared by Harcourt 1972) and the rate of interest—as Schumpeter pointed out long ago (1912)—is the price of the loans needed by firms to buy all the means of production, both durable and non-durable capital goods and the goods constituting the so-called circulating capital—not only intermediate goods, raw materials, energy, but also the services of labour. It is true that durable capital goods, say machines, require a long period—several years—before the sums of money that have been anticipated can be recouped, whereas those spent for non-durable capital goods and for wages will be recouped in a short period—a year; it is also true that the interest rate for long-term loans seldom coincides with the short-term rate. As a consequence, a variation of the rate of interest is likely to modify the profitability of the use of the different factors of production and therefore modify the composition of demand of the factors. But we cannot predict whether an increase in the interest rate will reduce the demand for machines relatively to that of labour. Instead, we can certainly state that the demand for machines will increase and that of labour will relatively decrease if wages rise with respect to the prices of machines—which is exactly what Ricardo was pointing out. Moreover, we can state that an increase in the rate of interest will depress the demand for all sorts of factors of production. But we can say nothing about the change of techniques, becoming more or less capital-intensive depending on the variations of the interest rate, in full contradiction with the neoclassical thesis, according to which there is an inverted relation between the interest rate and the intensity of capital.

The above considerations are fully consistent with the critical arguments worked out, originally developing a view to be found in Piero *Sraffa's Production of Commodities by means of Commodities*, mainly by Luigi Pasinetti and Pierangelo Garegnani, in a symposium promoted by Paul Samuelson, that has entered in the history of economic ideas with the label 'debate on reswitching' (Sraffa 1960; Samuelson 1966). From the standpoint of logic, the victory was of the 'heretics', but the economists of the tradition have been able to relegate the conclusions into the area of paradoxes in order to save the dominating paradigm. Up to now, this operation has been successful, since the debate on reswitching has been ignored.

Neoclassical economists consider the substitution between labour and 'capital' that is supposed to occur when, given technology, the rate of interest—the 'price of capital'—varies. Very different indeed is the substitution determined by a change occurring in the course of time in the prices of machines with respect to labour; thus, if wages rise, new machines will be produced capable of saving labour and these machines will substitute a number of workers. Then, the change in the ratio wages/ prices of machines determines the adoption of new techniques. It is fitting to call 'static' the neoclassical substitution (changes in relative prices, constant technology, conceived as the system of available technologies) and 'dynamic' the latter type of substitution. This distinction plays an important role in the critical discussion of another pillar of mainstream economics, that is, the Cobb–Douglas production function.

6. Dynamic and static substitution: a critique of the Cobb–Douglas production function

This function, first worked out by Wicksell and subsequently rediscovered by Douglas in collaboration with Cobb (Wicksell 1934; Douglas 1934), originally was intended to explain the distribution of income based on the marginal productivity of the so-called factors of production—as an extreme simplification: labour and capital. Empirically this function seemed to work well; thus it was widely adopted and then has been extended to explain, in a first approximation, the growth process, both in advanced and in underdeveloped countries. I have criticized the very foundation of this function either as a theory of distribution or as a starting point to explain both income distribution and economic growth (Sylos Labini 1995). Here I briefly recall the essential lines of my critique.

The Cobb–Douglas function is based on the following assumptions.

 (i) Conditions of atomistic competition obtain in all markets, so that prices are parameters.
 (ii) Cost curves are U-shaped, but all firms are at the point of minimum cost, where, for an instant, returns are constant: only with constant returns the sum of the two well-known exponents for labour and for capital is equal to one and Euler's theorem can be applied.
 (iii) The aggregate capital can be treated as though it were a single capital good—the various capitals are malleable and adaptable at will.
 (iv) The notion of marginal elasticity of substitution, based on the marginal productivity of each factor and often assumed to be constant, allows us to use the exponents of the two factors, L and K, to explain the two main distributive shares.
 (v) The isoquant, expressing the static substitution between labour and capital in a given moment, is pushed to the right by technical and organizational progress, that is assumed to be 'neutral', so that the shape of the isoquant does not change.
 (vi) The value of aggregate capital can be measured independently of its returns.

It is possible to maintain that the above assumptions are completely divorced from reality; as for assumption (vi), it is logically unacceptable.

In my paper I show that the success of empirical testing of the Cobb–Douglas function is an illusion. Cross-section testing, as Phelps Brown pointed out (1957), does not count; instead, the tests on time-series are relevant, on condition that the constraint $\alpha + \beta = 1$ be not introduced; but only in very few cases these tests give favourable results. Recently, the list of the unfavourable results, representing the overwelming majority of the items, has been enlarged by Romer, who found that 'the exponent relating to labour can be substantially inferior to its share in income, possibly 0.1 or 0.2' (Romer 1987). It is interesting to point out that the conviction that the Cobb–Douglas function is valid is so deeply rooted that he speaks of a 'puzzle': it does not occur to him that the finding simply depends on the fact that there is something radically wrong in the very conception of that function—dogmas cannot be put in question. Thus, nobody prepared a census of the empirical tests of the Cobb–Douglas function and, as it has been the case with the proposition, theoretical criticisms have been simply ignored.

Already Mendershausen (1938), before Phelps Brown, correctly maintained that 'each exponent simply explains the relation between two different rates of growth.' I accept this point of view and try to explain the forces that condition the evolution of the different quantities.

My interpretation is strictly related to my productivity equation. The ratio Y/L is a way to consider the productivity of labour of the whole system or of manufacturing, if we restrict our analysis to this important sector; the ratio K/L is what Pasinetti (1981) defines as the degree of mechanization. The variation in the two ratios is similar, but they do not coincide. The comparison between the two variations can be made with the following formula:

$$Y/L = \gamma K/L.$$

That formally corresponds to the Cobb–Douglas function, under certain assumptions. Indeed, the original function

$$Y = AL^\alpha K^\beta$$

becomes

$$Y/L = (K/L)^\gamma$$

if we put $A = 1$ and introduce the constraint $\alpha + \beta = 1$. We call the exponent γ and not β to avoid confusions, since the economic meaning of γ has nothing to do with β and with the theory of income distribution. The exponent γ varies over time and its variations are governed by the two main impulses included in the productivity equation, that is, the Smith and Ricardo effects:

$$\gamma = a + bY + cW/P_{ma}.$$

My interpretation of the radically revised Cobb–Douglas function has been tested by a distinguished Italian economic statistician, Franco Giusti (1995), who considered a series of individual Italian industries; the results of his inquiry came out decidedly favourable to the model.

I devoted a considerable attention to the Cobb–Douglas production function since it continues to be accepted as a sort of dogma in recent works both concerning advanced and underdeveloped countries, often attributing to the exponents more meanings than original ones—to try and take into account the concept—today very fashionable—of human capital. If the function here discussed is wrong, as I believe, then it can have not only negative effects in the interpretation of the growth process, but it can divert the analytical efforts of the economist into wrong directions.

A final remark. The Cobb–Douglas production function, originally intended, as we have seen, to explain income distribution and subsequently extended by Robert Solow to explain, in a first approximation, the process of growth, recently has been used more and more in growth models: the question of income distribution has been put aside, in the conviction, however, that the explanation of income distribution provided by the Cobb–Douglas, again, in a first approximation, is undoubtedly valid, as shown by the naïve comments put forth by Romer. Thus, the theory of income distribution is in a very bad shape indeed. All the other models intended to explain income distribution have been neglected; in my view, the most promising model was the one proposed by Michal Kalecki, highly praised by Keynes (Kalecki 1938; Keynes 1939), a model that I developed subsequently both from the theoretical and the empirical point of view (Sylos Labini 1979). It is interesting to point out that this model allows us to take into account in the theory of income distribution that particular but important type of technical progress that gives rise to the increase in labour productivity. Kalecki's model has had, up to now, the same criticisms of the dominating paradigm—such as the behaviour of the cost curves, the reswitching debate, and the neoclassical theory of income distribution: they have been marginalized and then ignored, without demonstrating that those criticisms are wrong.

7. Conclusion

The logical inconsistencies of the neoclassical propositions just mentioned, revealed by the attempts at adapting static models to interpret essentially dynamic processes, show that we have to work out new growth models that are genuinely dynamic in their character and thus free from those inconsistencies. To do this, we have to try to study the forces behind development processes. I believe that we have to reconsider, with modern eyes, the views of the classical economists, mainly Smith and Ricardo. The productivity equation presented above, that I worked out several years ago, embodying what I called the Smith and the Ricardo effects, is an example showing that the efforts to use the analyses of the classical economists, that are inherently dynamic, to try and understand certain fundamental problems of economic growth of our time can be fruitful.

But, just considering the classical economists and particularly Adam Smith, the founder of our science that he conceived as the science of the economic development of nations, we realize that we have to enlarge the scope of our inquires concerning development processes, especially if we intend to analyse not only countries that today are advanced, but also underdeveloped countries. In fact, if we want to go deep into the interpretation of development processes, then we cannot limit ourselves to the purely quantitative aspects of such processes but we have also to study the institutional and cultural evolution behind them. True, such an ambitious research programme implies very serious difficulties and risk. The difficulties depend on the vastness of the said programme that necessarily implies a non-superficial knowledge of the history and of institutions of the countries considered, as the great inquiry worked out by Smith has rendered very clearly. The risks refer mainly to the study of the cultural evolution of the countries under examination, since it is easier to be rigorous in working out a quantitative rather than a qualitative analysis. But there are no alternatives.

REFERENCES

Delong, J. B., Bradford, T., and Summers, L. H. (1991) 'Equipment, investment and economic growth', *Quarterly Journal of Economics*, 106: 445–502.

Domar, E. (1957) *Essays in the Theory of Economic Growth* (Oxford: Oxford University Press).

Douglas, P. H. (1934) *The Theory of Wages* (New York: Macmillan).

Garegnani, P. (1966) 'Switching of techniques', *Quarterly Journal of Economics*, 80: 554–67.

Giusti, F. (1995) 'Sostituibilità' dinamica dei fattori capitale e lavoro. Settore industria e branche industriali, in *Modelli di produzione*, Dipartimento di teoria economica e metodi quantitativi per le scelte politiche dell' Universita' di Roma La Sapienza.

Harcourt, G. C. (1972) *Some Cambridge Controversies in the Theory of Capital* (Cambridge: Cambridge University Press).

Harrod, R. (1948) *Towards a Dynamic Economics* (London: Macmillan).

Kalecki, M. (1938) 'The determinants of the Distribution of National Income', *Econometrica* 6: 97–112.

Keynes, J. M. (1939) 'Relative movements of real wages and output', *Economic Journal*, 49: 34–51.

Krugman, P. (1995) *Development, Geography and Economic Theory* (Cambridge, Mass.: MIT Press).

Malthus, T. M. (1976) *An Essay on the Principle of Population* (New York: Kelley).

Marshall, A. (1949) *Principles of Economics*, 8th edn. (London: Macmillan).

Menderhausen, H. (1938) 'On the significance of Professor Douglas's production function', *Econometrica* 6: 143–53.

Pasinetti, L. L. (1966) 'Changes in the rate of profit and switches of techniques', *Quarterly Journal of Economics* 80: 503–17.

——(1981) *Structural Changes and Economic Growth* (Cambridge: Cambridge University Press).

Phelps Brown, E. H. (1957) 'The meaning of the fitted Cobb–Douglas function', *Quarterly Journal of Economics* 71: 546–60.

Ricardo, D. (1951) *On the Principles of Political Economy and Taxation*, P. Sraffa (ed.) (Cambridge: Cambridge University Press).

Romer, P. M. (1987) 'Crazy Explanations of the productivity slowdown', in *Macroeconomics Annual* (Cambridge, Mass.: MIT Press).

—— (1990) 'Endogenous technological change', *Journal of Political Economy* 98/2: S71–102.

Samuelson, P. (1966) 'A Summing up, in "Paradoxes in Capital Theory: A Symposium"', *Quarterly Journal of Economics* 80: 568–83.

Schumpeter, J. A. (1912) *Theory der wirtschaftlichen Entwicklung* (Berlin: Dunker & Humblot).

Smith, A. (1961) *Wealth of Nations*, E. Cannan (ed.) (London: Methuen).

Solow, R. (1957) 'Technical change and the aggregate production function', *Review of Economics and Statistics* 39: 312–20.

Sraffa, P. (1926) 'The laws of returns under competitive conditions', *Economic Journal* 36: 535–50.

—— (1960) *Production of Commodities by Means of Commodities* (Cambridge: Cambridge University Press).

Sylos Labini, P. (1979) 'Prices and income distribution in the manufacturing industry', *Journal of Post-Keynesian Economics* 2: 3–25.

—— (1988) 'The great debates on the laws on returns and the value of capital: when will economists finally accept their own logic?' *Banca Nazionale del Lavoro Quarterly Review* 166: 263–91.

—— (1983) 'Factors affecting changes in productivity', *Journal of Post-Keynesian Economics* 6: 161–79.

—— (1995) 'Why the interpretation of the Cobb–Douglas production function must be radically changed', *Structural Change and Economic Dynamics* 6: 485–504.

Wicksell, K. (1934) *Lectures on Political Economy* (London: Routledge).

13 Why so much scepticism about growth theory? Comment on Durlauf and Sylos Labini

ANDREA SALANTI

The two papers on which I am commenting[1] start from two very different perspectives on how to approach the problems of economic development and growth. Steven Durlauf is clearly at his ease within the current mainstream perspective. In contrast, Paolo Sylos Labini is highly suspicious, to say the least, of what nowadays is popular under the label of new growth theory (NGT), as well as of its neoclassical antecedents of the 1950s and 1960s. He warmly recommends us to pay the due attention to the classical approach—in particular, to Smith's 'old' theory of growth.[2] Despite this difference, and indeed for quite different reasons, both authors exhibit a good dose of scepticism and dissatisfaction about the answers that modern growth theory has to offer to one of the oldest and most fascinating questions in economics. This is, to put it as plainly as possible, 'What causes growth?'.

Sylos Labini's critical attitude stems from two strongly held and repeatedly disclosed (see, for instance, Sylos Labini 1984 and 1993) beliefs: (i) that the analytical skeleton of neoclassical economics is intrinsically static and therefore ill-suited to deal with an inherently dynamic phenomenon like economic growth; (ii) that in order to understand the fundamental mechanisms behind economic growth we should (re)start from what Schumpeter named the 'magnificent dynamics' of classical economists. Consequently, he focuses on:

- a dynamic interpretation of the two principles of increasing and decreasing returns embracing Sraffa's critiques of Marshall and pointing at the original classical version of such principles;
- the endogenous character of 'minor' innovations, which implies that the increase in labour productivity can be explained by four independent variables (the increase of national income as a proxy of the Smithian 'extent of the market', the rate of

---

[1] Steven Durlauf was prevented from participating in the conference and sent his promised paper for the volume after it. Paolo Sylos Labini, in his turn, sent for publication a revised version somewhat different from his delivered speech. This is why this section, differently from the previous ones, is not followed by a report of the subsequent discussion.

[2] Sylos Labini makes a distinction between the 'old' growth theory of classical economists (Smith, Ricardo and, in some respects, Marx) and the 'modern' growth theory (without any further distinction) subsequent to Harrod, Domar, and Solow's pioneering works. In this comment, if only for the sake of mutual understanding, I follow the nowadays more conventional distinction between classical economics, 'old' growth theory from Harrod-Domar until the early 1970s (cf., e.g. Burmeister and Dobell 1970 or Wan 1971) and 'new' growth theory (as is now summarized e.g. in Barro and Sala-i-Martin 1995 or in Aghion and Howitt 1998).

change of the ratio between wages and the price of machines, the unit cost of labour, and, finally, aggregate investment including R&D expenses);
- a critique of the neoclassical production functions and the associated notion of 'price of capital'.

Durlauf, on the other hand, laments the inconclusiveness of much recent empirical work intended to exploit some of the insights provided by NGT.[3] He goes well beyond some criticisms previously set forth in Durlauf and Quah (1988) with an admittedly 'provocative purpose—namely, to argue that the econometric component of the new growth literature has done little to adjudicate leading growth questions.' His claim is based on a number of arguments no one of which is completely new,[4] but whose persuasive power, when taken together, amounts to more than the sum of their individual persuasive powers. They can be summarized as follows:

- because almost all variables employed to explain real per capita income growth are likely to be endogenous (and possible instrumental variables are, due to the open-endedness of growth theories, likely to be correlated with the error term), we cannot easily jump from finding statistical correlations to claiming stable causal links;[5]
- for models with multiple steady-states the usual specification of empirical models based upon linearization may lead to misleading conclusions about convergence issues;
- discriminating between competing explanations of growth would require reliable criteria for sorting out the relevant variables, but statistical robustness does not seem to be attainable through the currently available procedures of variable selection;
- both econometrics and historical analyses lead us to regard heterogeneity as a key feature of country-specific patterns of growth;
- assuming an invariant statistical model when performing cross-section analyses of growth amounts to completely disregarding the important question of parameter cross-country heterogeneity.[6]

Given the wide range of questions raised by the two contributors, instead of discussing every single issue I will point out a number of methodological points that are relevant to the modern development of growth theory in its various forms.

Let me start by observing that, as stressed in the title of this comment, the two authors share a good dose of dissatisfaction about the findings of NGT (and evidence, for that matter). I think that all this is by no means fortuitous. Sylos Labini, according

[3] For a recent survey of such a 'new growth evidence', see also Temple (1999).

[4] In a sense one could say that some of them have been raised ever since the famous 'Tinbergen debate' (now collected in Hendry and Morgan, 1995: p. VI).

[5] Note, by the way, that even the 'productivity equation' proposed by Sylos Labini in his contribution, though emerging from quite different theoretical intuitions, does not escape this kind of critique.

[6] This is the objection that Durlauf seems to regard as the most fundamental one. Indeed, the last sections of his paper are devoted to suggesting possible ways of dealing with instrumental variables and heterogeneity.

to the common wisdom, is to be regarded as an unorthodox economist and he is not alone in the recent history of growth theory to show such a critical attitude.[7] As both critics and advocates of mainstream economics know even too well, in those fields where mainstream theory appears less satisfactory or somewhat incomplete, it is quite easy to find heterodox approaches which seem better equipped than orthodoxy to deal with some of the issues at stake. A much more difficult task, however, is combining such different insights to form a complete and coherent puzzle to be opposed to orthodoxy as a challenging theoretical alternative. All this prevents paradigmatic shifts or new research programmes supplanting the traditional one, but it cannot impede endless debates.

During such debates, the orthodox school may well be tempted, if only in order to react to some of the most troublesome critiques, to change its research strategy. When this happens, and NGT has been a clear case in point, some old questions are (usually) simply begged (even if new interesting issues are nonetheless raised). This gives critics an opportunity to reiterate their previous critiques. Sylos Labini seems to do exactly this in that he redirects some well known critiques, already raised against the old neoclassical growth theory, towards the 'new' one. The problem, however, is that the old critiques, when directed at the new theory, lose some of their original force, because they necessarily overlook the differences between the two potential targets of criticism.

Consider, for instance, his references to the famous debate on the reswitching and the neoclassical theory of income distribution. In that context a critique aimed at pointing out the 'logical inconsistency' of aggregate production functions could make some sense (even if further reflection suggests that it was not a matter of logic alone).[8] However, it loses much of its impetus when, as is the case with NGT, aggregate production functions cannot but be interpreted as an argument based upon 'as if' reasoning rather than a more or less rigorous attempt to deal with the problem of aggregation in capital theory. Admittedly, 'as if' reasoning is somehow necessary for every macroeconomic argument. The problem, however, is that the inner logic of 'as if' arguments is extremely ambiguous and incomplete, so that we cannot have generally agreed rules for choosing among different assumptions of this kind. I would argue that one reason people speak of 'stylized facts' is simply because they are unwilling to explicitly cope with counterfactual justifications. Nobody would deny, I suspect, that within the empiricist tradition speaking about facts, however stylized they may be, is more palatable than openly advocating 'as if' arguments.

Apart from reswitching and capital reversal, old growth theory was accompanied at the time by fierce and passionate controversies between the two Cambridges over a number of other points. The issues at stake in such a debate are so well known that I can avoid summarizing them here.[9] From the vantage point of the three decades that

---

[7] A number of unorthodox approaches to the theory of growth flourished during the 1960s and 1970s. Cf., e.g. Harris (1978), Marglin (1984), and Walsh and Gram (1980).

[8] On closer scrutiny, as discussed in Salanti (1989), challenging the logical consistency of neoclassical production functions involved not so much a purely logical argument in the ordinary sense of the word as some 'correspondence rules' pertaining to the realm of the (economic) interpretation of the model.

[9] For an (explicitly partisan) account of the whole debate, see Harcourt (1972).

have elapsed since then, the two sides in that debate may now be seen to have had, at least from a methodological point of view, much more in common than was perceived at the time by the participants themselves. On a number of such issues, we may also observe that NGT markedly differs from older approaches.[10] For example:

- A lot of attention was devoted to the study of steady-state equilibria in order to provide an explanation for some stylized facts (which subsequently proved to be much less firm than originally expected). With the advent of NGT the facts to be explained (stylized or not) have undoubtedly changed. This does not, in itself, raise any particular problem. That the subject matter of any economic inquiry changes over time is an obvious fact of historical experience, and that the utility of any scientific theory ultimately consists in its capacity to explain (and, when possible, predict) facts ought to be equally plain. There remains, however, the problem of understanding whether the facts have actually changed over time or whether what has changed is simply our (theory-laden) perception of them.

- Both schools had to resort to some form of what we may now recognize as piecemeal theorizing, due to theorists' reliance on a number of *ad hoc* assumptions about exogenous variables whose explanation was deferred to other pieces of theory. According to such a methodological perspective, each model is built to deal with a specific problem, or a few specific problems, so that the assumptions, or the formal structure, of each particular model cannot be automatically extended to models intended to highlight other problems. This is an approach quite different from the one generally adopted by neoclassical economists. The neoclassical view on theory-making, in fact, may be summarized by saying that all economic models must be built on the common basis of a few basic premises, individual maximizing rationality and subjectivistic equilibrium being the most well known. NGT supports a different choice of what is to be regarded as exogenous, probably more coherent with its own methodological premises. The price to be paid, however, is twofold: (i) the old distinction between 'development' and 'growth' virtually vanishes, but the underlying problem reappears, as Durlauf forcefully reminds us, in the form of the heterogeneity of structural parameters; (ii) the usual economists' list of 'fundamentals' does not seem sufficient for an adequate explanation of growth and a rapidly growing number of other exogenous variables seems relevant. Because some of these do not fall within the traditional boundaries of the discipline, in addition to the problem of their selection, we have to face the even bigger question of the demarcation of 'economic' phenomena.

- Empirical applications were scarce and almost limited to estimating Solow's residual, and/or total factor productivity, while cross-country data were regarded as highly suspicious if not totally useless. Somehow in the same tradition of classical economics, both schools were trying to focus on what were perceived as the fundamental mechanisms capable of fostering growth (that is, in other words,

---

[10] The same could be said, with some caveats, of the associated short-run macrotheories (that is, early Keynesianism for Harrod–Domar, the neoclassical synthesis for Solow, and new classical economics for NGT).

on the fundamental laws of motion of industrialized economies). With NGT the number of relevant variables has enormously increased, so we may wonder whether it is still appropriate to regard it as an inquiry about the fundamental mechanisms lying behind economic growth. When I see studies on the relation between, say, personal distributions of income, levels of democracy, or different tax systems and growth, I think that we cannot speak anymore of 'fundamental' laws.

Above all, NGT seems to differ from its 'old' predecessor in the emphasis placed upon its descriptive adequacy. The literature of 1960s and 1970s contained plenty of caveats about the limitations of growth theory. It was usually maintained that its content was neither a satisfactory description of actual growth processes or development experiences, nor a useful starting point for policy recommendation, but simply a first step towards a better understanding of some fundamental mechanisms (primarily the accumulation of capital) affecting economic growth. As Frank Hahn puts it:

The theory of growth is not a theory of economic history. It is of no help in answering Max Weber's famous question and only of marginal use in understanding, say, Industrial Revolution. Where the theory is to be taken descriptively, it takes the institutional setting for granted and highly idealises it. The parts of the theory which are to be understood as prescriptive have hardly anything to say on either the actual problems of 'control' or on the society to be controlled. (Hahn 1971: p. vii)[11]

In this respect new growth theorists share a different and more ambitious attitude. Consider, for instance, the following passages taken from a recent and widely acclaimed advanced textbook on NGT:

Because of its explicit emphasis on structural aspects of the innovation process, endogenous growth theory makes it possible to bridge the gap between theory and various strands of empirical and historical literature. ... Thus one of our primary motivations in developing the model of Chapter 3 with capital accumulation and population growth is to show that when these other important aspects of growth are taken into account, our approach becomes broadly consistent with the empirical observations that have been adduced to refute it. (Aghion and Howitt 1998: 6–7)

Behind this sharp change of perspective we may easily detect a firm belief in the possibility of deriving from growth theory some reliable prescriptions of policy designed to rise the rate of growth of actual economies.[12] If this goal could actually be achieved, its importance could be hardly underestimated. Indeed, when we dwell upon the arithmetic of compound rates in the long run, it is very difficult to remain

---

[11] The same warnings are reiterated at the end of the same introduction in the following terms: 'It would be as philistine and silly to write off modern growth theory as it would be to take it as a completed theory of the world. When an economist shows that all warranted paths seek the steady-state ... [h]e is aware of all that has been left out; he does this exercise in the hope that it will eventually help in more ambitious undertakings. The student, therefore, should approach the literature not in the expectation that he will learn all about economic change and growth, but rather that he will see rather good minds struggling with the most elementary aspects of what may become such a theory. (Hahn 1971: p. xv).

[12] Cf., e.g. Shaw (1992) and Crafts (1996).

unimpressed by its astounding implications. A 3 per cent yearly growth rate makes the magnitude involved more than four times higher after half a century and a yearly rate of 2 per cent implies a final level more than seven times the initial one over a century. Figures like these suggest that in the long run it is not so much the optimal allocation of given resources (or the effectiveness of counter-cyclical policies) as the rate of growth of per capita magnitudes, that (given an acceptable degree of inequality of the distribution of individual incomes) determines people's standard of life.

Commenting on such figures at a time when even old growth theory had still to be worked out, John Maynard Keynes (1972) did not resist the temptation to predict that within a century or so the economic problem would have ceased to be the main worry of humankind. Now we would perhaps be better advised to say that the realization of such a kind of prophecy will be postponed to some other century. In the meantime, of course, we will continue to look for sound explanations of the determinants of economic growth. The ultimate scope of this research, as in other fields of economics, should be to discover some effective set of policy recommendations suited to promote economic growth. Common experience, however, seems to suggest that in the last decades macroeconomics has achieved somewhat better results in dealing with short-run theories and policies than in dealing with the corresponding extensions to the long run. Indeed, it could be hardly denied that, say, controlling inflation has been easier than targeting a desired rate of growth. Perhaps this is so because development and growth are matters that involve too many things outside the domain of economics as usually perceived. I suspect that this is precisely the ultimate reason for so much worry about the present state of growth theory and policy.

REFERENCES

Aghion, Ph. and P. Howitt (1998) *Endogenous Growth Theory* (Cambridge, Mass.: MIT Press).
Barro, R. J. and X. Sala-i-Martin (1995) *Economic Growth* (New York: McGraw-Hill).
Burmeister, E. and A. R. Dobell (1970) *Mathematical Theories of Economic Growth* (London: Macmillan).
Crafts, N. (1996) 'Post-neoclassical endogenous growth theory: what are its implications?', *Oxford Review of Economic Policy* 12: 30–47.
Durlauf, S. and D. Quah (1998) 'The new empirics of economic growth', NBER Working Paper 6422, and forthcoming in J. Taylor and M. Woodford (eds.), *Handbook of Macroeconomics* (Amsterdam: North-Holland).
Hahn, F. H. (ed.) (1971) *Readings in the Theory of Growth* (London: Macmillan).
Harcourt, G. C. (1972) *Some Cambridges Controversies in the Theory of Capital* (Cambridge: Cambridge University Press).
Harris, D. J. (1978) *Capital Accumulation and Income Distribution* (London: Routledge & Kegan Paul).
Hendry, D. F. and M. Morgan (1995) *The Foundations of Econometric Analysis* (Cambridge: Cambridge University Press).

Keynes, J. M. (1972) 'Economic possibilities for our grandchildren' [1930]; in D. Moggridge (ed.), *The Collected Writings of John Maynard Keynes, IX—Essays in Persuasion* (London: Macmillan): 321–32.

Marglin, S. A. (1984) *Growth, Distribution, and Prices* (Cambridge, Mass.: Harvard University Press).

Salanti, A. (1989) ' "Internal" criticisms in economic theory: are they really conclusive?', *Economic Notes* 19: 1–14.

Shaw, G. K. (1992) 'Policy implications of endogenous growth theories', *Economic Journal* 102: 611–21.

Sylos Labini, P. (1984) *The Forces of Economic Growth and Decline* (Cambridge, Mass.: MIT Press).

——(1993) *Economic Growth and Business Cycles. Prices and Process of Cyclical Development* (Aldershot: E. Elgar).

Temple, J. (1999) 'The new growth evidence', *Journal of Economic Literature* 37: 112–56.

Walsh, W. and H. Gram (1980) *Classical and Neoclassical Theories of General Equilibrium* (New York and Oxford: Oxford University Press).

Wan Jun., H. Y. (1971) *Economic Growth* (New York: Harcourt Brace Jovanovich).

Index

acceleration rates 192
Adelman, I. F. L. 72, 78
ad hoc conditions 1, 6, 13, 228, 278
adjustment processes 208, 213, 232
  coefficients 186
  cost 125
  money demand 171, 193
  portfolio 95
  price 36, 118, 127, 128, 132, 158
  real income 175
  real wages 96
  short-run 237
  structural 73
AER (American Economic Review) 69
agents 56, 118, 155, 181, 189–90
  choices of 26
  demand for money 193, 194
  forward-looking 31
  heterogeneous 156
  motivations 6
  risk perceptions 93
  see also representative agents
aggregation 1, 3, 4–5, 14, 37, 62, 66, 91
  conditions required for 6
  equilibrium 97
  see also capital; demand; growth; hours worked;
    investment; models; output; prices; supply;
    time-series; variables
Aghion, P. 275 n., 279
agriculture 265
Alesina, A. 255
Alexopoulos, M. 44, 50, 51 n., 53, 54, 64
algorithms 15, 26–7
  Bry-Boschan 27 n.
  classification 256
Alogoskoufis, G. L. 126 n., 204, 213 n.
Altug, S. 120
amplification 37
amplitude 28, 38, 62
analogical reasoning 142, 144
Andrews, D. W. K. 90
approximation 28–9, 64, 86, 89, 130, 159, 186, 270
  asymptotic 237
  price 175, 176
  statistical 172
  superneutrality 134
AR(1) process 37, 38 n., 89, 134
ARCH effect 101, 109
ARDL (autoregressive distributed lag) model 204
ARIMA (autoregressive, integrated, moving
  average) model 36, 203 n.
Arrow-Debreu market 69

'as if' arguments 277
Asia 75
asset prices 38, 39, 157, 207
assets financial demands 96, 109
assumptions 9, 11, 47, 51, 95, 129, 144,
  179–80, 241–2, 270
  ad hoc 13, 278
  auxiliary 8
  ceteris paribus 168, 170, 190
  compromising 14
  Dixit–Stiglitz 6 n., 13 n.
  exogeneity 207
  identifying 207, 210, 212, 221
  independence 221
  inflation 155
  linearity 48
  normality 182, 183
  overidentifying 191
  perfect competition 265
  rational expectations 127
  theoretical 12
  untestable 222
  untested 168, 222
asymmetry 35, 101, 109
asymptotic theory 185, 186, 214, 237, 238
Atkin, J. 146
Attfield, C. L. F. 90
Auerbach, A. 30
Australia 39
autocorrelation 120
autocovariance 125
autoregression 110, 176, 202
  first-order 101, 226
  second-order 101, 105, 108
  stable 203
  see also ARDL; ARIMA
Axilrod, S. H. 124 n.
Azariadis, C. 253

Baba, Y. 91 n., 233
Backhouse, R. E. 4 n., 10 n., 73, 79
backward countries 265
Bagliano, F.-C. 230
balance of payments 159
Ball, L. 117
Banerjee, A. 85, 90, 97, 98
Bank of England 90, 150, 158, 241
bank reserves 229
bankruptcy 267
Barro, R. J. 45, 118 n., 119 n., 121 n., 127,
  222, 251, 255, 275 n.
Basu, S. 120

Batini, N.   117
Bayesian approaches   161, 254, 257, 258, 259
Beauchamp, J. J.   254
Benassy, J.-P.   119 n.
Bentham, Jeremy   141
Berg, C.   117, 123
Bernanke, B. S.   122 n.
Bernard, A.   250 n., 252–3
Beveridge, S.   206
Beyer, A.   167 n.
bivariates   88, 110
Blanchard, O. J.   2, 30, 206
Blaug, M.   1
Blinder, A. S.   12, 80, 117, 124 n., 132
'blips'   88, 90, 111, 174
Boehm, E.   23 n.
Boer War   94
Boldin, M.   23 n.
bonds   173, 177, 180
   long-dated   101
   Treasury, yields   233
booms   61, 156
Boschan, C.   27 n.
bounded rationality   7
Box–Jenkins models   203, 204, 207, 221, 241
Brash, D.   117
Brayton, F.   129 n., 155
breaks   109
   structural   85, 95, 183
   see also co-breaking
Breiman, L.   256
Bretton Woods   86, 93, 115, 116, 120–1, 146
Britain, *see* United Kingdom
Broaddus, A.   122
Brock, W.   249 n.
Bronfenrenner, M.   61
Brunner, K.   124 n.
Bry, G.   27 n.
Bryant, R. C.   131
budget constraint   50
Building Societies Act (1986)   107
Buiter, W. H.   212
Bundesbank   121, 150, 159
Burmeister, E.   275 n.
Burns, A. F.   23–4, 24–5, 29, 61, 62, 63, 78, 121 n.
Burnside, C.   5, 6, 15, 16, 43–9 *passim*, 54, 63–7
   passim, 69, 70, 71, 75, 76, 78–9, 80
business cycles   9, 11, 14–15, 16, 23–81, 207, 221
   innovations and   266
   Mitchell's statistical programme   142
   real, emergence of theory   12
   trends and   210
   see also duration; growth; peaks and troughs;
      phases; RBCs; turning points

Caldwell, B.   1
calibration   54, 65, 125, 215
   versus estimation   120

Calvo, G. A.   128, 130 n.
Cameron, G.   91 n.
Cameron, S.   256
Canova, F.   25, 62, 63, 210, 256
capacity   131, 267–8
capacity utilization   37, 73
capital   51, 96, 109, 211, 249
   accumulation of   279
   aggregate   270
   excess demand for   97
   household's incentive to invest in   56
   price of   269–70
   rental rate of   50
capital movements   93, 171, 182
capital stocks   3, 50, 131
capitalism   264
Carter, Jimmy   45, 73, 74
Cartwright, N.   4 n.
causality   104, 108, 143, 147, 148, 163, 221
   establishing   257
   versus correlation   250–2
   see also Granger causality
Cecchetti, S.   117
censoring rules   27
central banks   16, 170, 188, 228, 229
   monetary policy   115, 116, 120, 123, 129, 131,
      132, 157–9 *passim*, 193, 194
   operating procedures   4, 163, 164
   short-term interest rates   180
   see also Bank of England; Bundesbank; ECB;
      Federal Reserve; Riksbank
CEPR (Centre for Economic Policy Research)
   214 n.
ceteris paribus conditions   8, 88, 168, 170, 190
Chari, V. V.   36
cheques   242
chi-square distribution/test   49, 101
Cho, J. O.   119 n.
choices   26, 31, 66, 69, 176–7, 278
   consumption   36
   dynamic   129
Christiano, L.   23, 24, 26 n., 31, 35, 36 n., 43 n., 54,
      117, 132, 228, 229, 230, 243
Chu, C. S.   90
Citibank   146
Clarida, R.   117
Clements, M. P.   85, 87
Cobb–Douglas production function   252, 266,
      270–2
co-breaking   87, 109, 111
Cochrane, J.   230
coefficients   45, 46, 48, 49, 90, 111, 207,
      226, 253
   adjustment   186
   correlation   32
   dummy variable   70
   in forecasting   125, 126
   insignificant   192

negative 238
recursive 101
restrictions on 189
risk aversion 38
significant 254
Cogley, T. 35, 37, 120
cointegration 17, 87, 88, 91, 92, 98, 109, 111,
    188, 193, 201–2, 207–8, 213, 242, 243
  analysis no help in identification 239
  bivariate 110
  determining 226
  deviations from 97
  equilibria and 103, 104, 108
  exploiting 173
  hypothetical 187
  identifying assumptions and 221
  indicators can distort determination of 86
  inflation with velocity 180
  introducing dummy variables into 90
  long-run price homogeneity and 179–81,
    184
  monetary analysis and 133–4
  multivariate 171, 177
  non-stationarity and 171, 186
  one of the beauties of 241
  preliminary analysis 238
  rank 185–6
  stationary 189
  statistical motivations for 205
  unrestricted 186
  VAR 167, 182, 184, 219, 229, 232
Collard, F. 35–6, 37
collateral 39
commodities 71, 87, 97, 100, 109, 229
  aggregation over 3
co-movements 15, 16, 24, 29, 61, 62, 71, 75,
    76, 78
  aggregate 67
  different kinds of episodes 72
  matching 63
competition 267
  atomistic 270
  imperfect 5, 6, 13
  international 97
  monopolistic 6, 13
  perfect 6, 7, 53, 265
Competition and Credit Control (UK) 107
competitiveness 92
concentration 264
conditioning 161, 162
  valid 106
confidence intervals 46
confirmation 1, 3
consequences 214, 266
  factor-demand 108, 109
constancy 101, 106
  extended 87
constraints 51, 64, 66, 226, 270

inequality 53
linear 207
no-bonding 50
consol rate 90
consumer price index 229
consumption 27, 36, 37, 51–2, 55, 65, 71, 74,
    118, 120
  co-movements of 29
  constant 208
  cycles 75
  lowered 54
  marginal utility of 130
  should be random walk 207
consumption function proportionality 208
contractions 24, 33, 38, 39
  too long 36
  see also CTS
contracts 50, 51, 53, 71
control instruments 146–9, 150
convergence 249, 250, 252, 276
  spurious evidence of 253
convergence criteria (Euro) 122
Cooley, T. F. 29, 62, 119 n., 212
correlation 8, 93, 100, 120, 175, 209
  statistical 276
  see also serial correlation
correlation coefficients 32
corroboration 71
cost curves 270, 272
cost of living 268
cost-plus-pricing rules 7
'cost-push' effect 96, 98, 101, 108
costs 97
  adjustment 125
  capital 109
  fixed 52, 54
  labour 267, 268, 276
  marginal 265, 266
  minimum 270
  opportunity 90, 95, 180
  productivity 267
  relative 169
  transportation 265
coupons 233
covariance 125, 190
co-variation 75
Cowles Commission 213, 219, 220, 221, 228,
    230–1, 240
Crafts, N. 279 n.
crash (1921) 99
credit 96, 233
  rationing 70, 107
  selective controls 122
critical values 232
cross-section studies 4, 8, 18
Croushore, D. 164
CRRA utility function 38
CTS (contraction terminating sequences) 27

currency pegs 86, 116, 121, 146
Cuthbertson, K. 133

dampening effects 56, 108, 123, 158
Danish data 171, 172, 173, 177, 180, 188
Darnell, A. C. 1 n.
data series 90–2
dating process 27, 30
debt 90, 94, 95, 98
  prices determined by 104
decision rules 66
decomposition 174, 184, 185, 189
  silly 210
deduction 1, 10
defence spending 45, 63, 64, 69, 70
deflation 92, 97, 109, 151
deflators 90, 233, 268
degrees of freedom 49
Delli Gatti, D. 5
Delong, J. B. 268
demand 98, 267, 268, 269
  aggregate 158, 169, 177, 179, 183, 193
  capital 97
  factor 88
  goods and services 88, 94, 97, 101, 108, 109
  labour 50, 52, 54, 108
  shocks 206, 210–12
  see also excess demand; money demand
De Marchi, N. 141, 142, 143
democracy 250, 251, 256
Den Butter, F. 152 n.
deposit rates 233
depreciation rate 50, 103
deregulation 86, 107, 171, 189
deterministic function 251
deterministic shifts 85, 87, 88, 90, 109
deterministic trends 25, 175, 178, 202, 205
  deviations from 203
  forcing processes with 26, 34
  linear 176
  removal of 134
devaluations 96, 98, 101, 108–9, 121, 156
Devereux, M. B. 43
deviations 73, 92, 95, 97, 98, 164, 178, 203,
    204, 229
  ppp 101, 109, 162
  real-income 104
  salient 86
  stable money demand 193, 194
  steady-state 163, 171, 185
  see also standard deviation
DGP (data generation process) 88–9, 231
diagnostics 105, 106, 231
Dickey, D. A. 85, 203, 206, 214
Dicks–Mireaux, L. A. 96
Diebold, F. X. 214
differenced data 88, 203
difference-stationary process 134

differentiation 264
Dimitri, N. 1 n.
discount 5
disequilibrium 94, 97, 101, 108, 109, 163, 192, 232
distribution 90, 253, 270
  asymptotic 185, 186, 238
  chi-squared 49
  fat-tailed 161
  limiting, non-degenerate 89
  marginal 258
  non-standard 203
  normal, cumulative 27
  prior 258
  random normal multivariate 231
'disturbing causes' 141–2
Divisia price indices 91
division of labour 15, 264, 265
Dixit–Stiglitz assumption 6 n., 13 n.
Dixon, H. D. 5, 7, 13, 70, 75, 159–60
Dobell, A. R. 275 n.
dollar (US) 116, 121, 146
Domar, E. D. 275 n.
  see also Harrod–Domar
Doornik, J. A. 85, 86, 87, 90, 91 n., 97, 101,
    145 n., 191
Douglas, P. H., *see* Cobb–Douglas
Dow, J. C. R. 96
Dow, S. C. 1 n.
Drazen, A. 253
drift 27, 35, 37
  random walk with 71
DSGE literature 37
Duhem–Quine problem 1, 8
Duisenberg, W. 150
dummy variables 45, 86–90 *passim*, 98, 103,
    109, 156, 214
  coefficients 70
  credit control 233
  credit derationing 107
  deterministic 160, 161
  dropping 104–5
  inability to get rid of 159
  institutional 186
  intervention 183
  restriction of 100, 101
  unexplained 163
Dungey, M. 39
durables 62, 70, 269
duration of cycle 28, 29, 33, 175, 176, 181,
    203, 211
  getting it correct 34
  short, stationary 185
Durlauf, S. N. 13, 18, 249 n., 250, 252–3, 253–4,
    256, 275–6, 278

ECB (European Central Bank) 122, 149,
    150, 157
'eclectic' model 107

ECMs (error-correction models) 204, 213 n.
econometrics 2, 4, 8, 69, 87, 119, 120, 133,
    167–245
  as a science of history 143–5
  macroeconomics and 16–18
economic purpose 206–8
Economic Review 124
economies of scale 264
Edelberg, W. 46, 70
Edgeworth, F. 242
efficiency 156
  labour market 77
  loss of 229
effort 53
  imperfectly observable 50
  non-zero 52, 54
Eichenbaum, M. 5, 6, 7, 15, 16, 35, 43–5 nn.,
    46–9 *passim*, 54, 63–70 *passim*, 74–80 *passim*,
    119, 132, 164, 230, 242, 243–4
eigenvalue 90
elasticity:
  demand for money, long-run 204, 205
  labour supply 36
  substitution 270
empiricism 45–7, 48, 74, 87, 89, 90, 97, 177, 184,
    187, 222, 276
  Bayesian estimation 258
  cointegration 207–8
  computer programs for tests 191
  consistency with previous statements 168
  eclecticism 257
  growth literature 249, 250, 253, 257
  long- and medium-run behaviour 173
  nominal money 183
  RBC 119, 120
  scientific progress 133
  UK inflation 98–106
  VAR analysis 168
  see also evidence; explanations; identification;
      microeconomics; models; money demand;
      research; testing
employment 2, 3, 50, 51, 53, 73, 122
  high inflation with no enhancement in 123
  monetary shocks and 119
  upward pressure on 56
EMU (European Monetary Union) 122, 156
ENDO model 35
endogeneity 228, 229, 251
  regression 257
  see also variables
endowments 93
  time 52, 54
England 265
Engle, R. F. 71, 101, 107, 133, 205, 213
Epstein, P. 29 n.
equality 53, 55
equilibrium 53, 55, 57, 67, 73, 87, 97, 208
  cointegration and 103, 104, 108

competitive 13, 54
  devaluations out of 108–9
  errors 171, 185, 205
  general 5, 50–4, 120, 228, 230
  growth rate for real output 158
  important departures from 88
  indeterminacy-sunspot 230
  long-run 110, 111, 204, 212, 231
  money demand 168, 193, 204
  money market 170, 171
  non-linear correction 107
  operational definition of 213
  partial 5
  short-run 212–13
  steady-state 278
  see also disequilibrium
equilibrium law of motion 47
Erceg, C. 117, 125 n.
Ericsson, N. 71, 85, 87, 88, 90, 91, 95, 96, 97,
    101, 107, 109, 126, 171
ERM (Exchange Rate Mechanism) 109, 182
errors 9, 91, 99, 184, 203, 214
  equilibrium 171, 185
  expectational 118, 119, 127
  forecast 89, 101, 105, 210, 252
  reduced-form 209
  regressor 251
  standard 100, 101, 107–8, 109, 237
  stationary 180, 202
  structural 209, 212
  technical 134
  see also ECMs; VECMs
estimates/estimation 49, 126, 167, 172,
    182–5, 203–5 *passim*, 207, 278
  Bayesian 257, 258
  inconsistency of 229
  maximum likelihood 186
  observations in 208
  recursive coefficient 101
  structurality for 190
  underidentified 190
  see also calibration; least-squares estimation
Estrella, A. 117
ETS (expansion terminating sequences) 27
Euler equations/theorem 126, 270
evaluation 8, 15, 75, 78, 254
Evans, C. L. 120, 132, 164
Evans, J. L. 1 n.
evidence 3–4, 6, 9, 11–12, 24, 39, 109, 125,
    133, 162, 228
  anomalous 13
  assumptions contradicted by 13
  business–cycle research 66–7
  convergence, spurious 253
  econometric 16, 123
  empirical 13, 98, 115, 127, 132, 144, 232, 242
  growth 250
  historical 214, 257

evidence (*Cont.*)
  interest rates   230
  juridical   141
  microeconomic   5, 7
  output   230
  price   230
  quantitative   36
  unambiguous   14
excess demand:
  capital   97
  inflation deemed to be resultant of all
    forces of   144
  money   86, 91, 98, 99
  negative   109
exchange controls   86
exchange rates   90, 91, 93, 98, 101, 158,
  160, 243
  agreements disintegrated   116
  constant   208
  depreciation   103
  external shocks affecting   96, 97
  fixed   156, 161, 171
  flexible   171
  floating   86, 146, 156, 161
  predicting   146
  real   92, 162
  see also EMU; ERM
exogeneity   228, 231
  see also variables
exogenous forcing processes   36
expansions   24, 25, 33, 35, 39, 61
  getting the length correct   34
  much too short   36
  prediction and actual duration   37–8
  see also ETS
expectations   6, 156, 157, 158, 162, 213
  conditional   182, 189
  exactly equal to outcome   163
  forward-looking   12
  price   126, 159
  unbiased   7, 155
  unconditional   87, 127–8
  unrealistic   214
  see also rational expectations
explanations   24, 143, 255, 276, 278
  causal   11, 250
  empirical   109, 144
exports   96, 97
external economies   264
extreme bounds analysis   254

factor-demand consequences   108, 109
factors of production   96, 97, 265, 269, 270
facts   9, 133
  analysis applied to   1
  business cycle   26, 62, 76, 80;
    one-dimensional   78
  see also stylized facts

falsification   1, 3
Farmer, R.   230
Faust, J. C.   233
Favero, C. A.   159, 167 n., 230, 237, 240
federal funds   229
Federal Reserve   121, 122, 123 n., 124,
  129 n., 155
  equations   159
  see also FOMC
feedbacks   39
  short- and long-run   17, 237
Feldstein, M.   117, 130
Ferri, P.   7
final goods   264
financial crises   2
financial liberalization   204
Finn, M.   63
firms   51, 56, 265, 267, 270
  competitive   50, 53
  identical   6
  large   264
  price of loans needed by   269
Fischer, S.   30, 130 n.
Fisher, J. D. M.   5, 6, 15, 16, 44–9 *passim*, 54,
  63-7 *passim*, 69, 70
Fisher, L.   30 n.
Fisher, S.   2
Fisher parity/relation   180, 181, 232
Fitzgerald, T.   23, 24, 26 n.
Florida   123
fluctuations   25, 26, 29, 61, 79
  asset price   38, 39
  cyclical   118, 119, 123
  inflation   122
  interest rate   93
  modern approach to analyzing   31
  transitory   206
  unemployment   73
FOMC (Federal Open Market Committee,
  US)   15, 80, 115
forcing processes   26, 34, 36
forecasts   2, 7, 14, 17, 125, 160, 161, 203
  confidence interval   109
  errors   89, 101, 105, 210, 252
  ineffectiveness of Cowles Commission
    models   230-1
  optimal   252
  unconditional   220
France   155
Frankel, J.   251
Freedman, D.   259
Friedman, B.   117
Friedman, M.   90, 96, 127, 159, 179, 239, 251
Frisch, R.   96, 97, 221
F-test   101
Fuhrer, J. C.   126, 127, 128, 130 n.
Fuller, W. A.   85, 203, 206, 214
fundamental mechanisms   278-9

Gagnon, J.   124 n.
gains   35
Gali, J.   120
Galor, O.   250 n.
Garegnani, P.   269
Gaussian conditions:
  errors   167
  likelihood   237
GDP (gross domestic product)   12, 27, 33, 62 n.,
    214, 229
  deflator   268
  growth in   35, 78–9
  highly persistent variations   206
  per capita   32, 202
  real   15, 45
Generalized Method of Moments   54
Gennari, E.   179, 188
geography   250, 251–2
George, E.   254
Gerlach, S.   117
Germany   61, 121, 123 n., 155, 188
  reunification   159, 211, 215
  see also Bundesbank
Giannini, C.   226
Gibbard, A.   5
Gilbert, C. L.   167
Giusti, F.   271
GNP (gross national product)   73, 77, 103, 161, 210 n.
  real   233, 243
  surprises   12, 206
Godfrey, L. G.   101
Godley, W. A. H.   96
gold   96, 116
gold standard   86, 93, 121
Goldberger, A. S.   72
  see also Klein–Goldberger
Goodfriend, M.   115 n., 121 n., 122, 126, 230
Goodhart, C.   117
goods and services   70, 88, 94, 97, 101, 108, 109
Gordon, D. B.   121 n.
Gordon, R. J.   127
Gordon, S.   38
government   65
  deficits   94, 96, 97, 159
  demand-management measures   211
  fiscal variables   119
  interest rate differential   104
  profligate   98
  unproductive investment   252
  see also budget constraint; policy
government expenditure   35, 73–4, 163, 175
  permanent shock to   63
government purchases   44, 46, 50, 54, 55, 57, 58
  exogenous movements   45
  increase in   74, 170
  log of   128
  persistent rise   56
Gram, H.   277 n.

Granger, C. W. J.   1, 8 n., 133, 213
Granger causality   17, 202, 204, 205, 207, 212, 222
  development of   219
Great Depression (1930s)   4, 61, 72, 143, 211, 215
Great Ratios   213
Greenspan, A.   243
Group of Seven nations   121
growth   4, 61–2, 73, 202, 244, 247–81
  aggregate   122, 249, 255
  consumption   38
  cross-section studies of   18
  endogenous   35, 37, 250, 252, 253
  GDP   35, 78–9
  linear   178
  money   98, 108, 109, 121, 122, 134, 169, 178, 179
  NBER-type cycles   25
  negative   27, 70, 75
  nominal   178
  output   75, 77, 78, 103, 123, 162
  per capita   249
  policy-makers and   74
  positive   27
  price   179
  productive   169
  real   169, 178
  steady-state   34, 253
  trend   37, 94
  volatility in   32, 35, 36, 37, 38
  see also NGT
Gruber, J.   54, 65
Gulf crisis/war (1990–1)   74, 122

Haavelmo, T.   167, 219, 220, 221
Hagen, J. von   117
Hahn, F.   279
Hairault, J.-O.   119 n.
Haldane, A.   117, 122 n.
Hall, R. E.   117, 118, 207
Hamilton, J. D.   85, 226–7
Hands, D. W.   1 n., 13 n.
Hansen, B. E.   101
Hansen, G.   50, 69
Hansen, H.   101, 190
Hansen, L. P.   118, 119 n., 120 n., 207, 208
Harcourt, G. C.   269, 277 n.
Harding, D.   9, 14–16 *passim*, 27 n., 61–3 *passim*,
    69, 72
Harris, D. J.   277 n.
Harrison, S.   36 n.
Harrod, R.   275
Harrod–Domar model   263, 278 n.
Hartley, J. E.   9, 36, 77, 78, 79, 115 n., 162
Harvey, A.   203 n.
Hastie, T.   258
Hatanaka, M.   85
Hausman, D. M.   8
Hawthorn, G.   144
Heckman, J.   120, 208, 256

Henderson, D.   117, 125 n., 157
Hendry, D. F.   5–9 *passim*, 13 n., 16–17, 70–1, 73, 75, 85–7 *passim*, 91, 94, 95, 97, 101, 107, 109, 126, 142–5 *passim*, 151–64 *passim*, 167, 171, 183, 191, 204, 213 n., 220, 231, 233, 239–44 *passim*, 276 n.
Heston–Summers data set   256
heterogeneity   31, 156, 255–6, 257, 258, 276, 278
    ethnic   252
heteroscedasticity   101, 233
Hetzel, R.   115 n.
Hicks, J. R.   1, 144
historical studies   18, 72, 74, 256
history   141–5, 152, 251
    evidence from   214, 257
Hoffman, M.   168
homogeneity   86, 178–81, 184
Hoover, K. D.   1 n., 86, 120 n., 132, 143, 167 n., 220, 241
hours worked   54, 57, 58
    aggregate   45, 47
households   51–3, 56
    maximization of utility   64
    risk-sharing   50
Howitt, P.   275 n., 279
H–P (Hodrick–Prescott) filter   25, 26, 32, 63, 72, 74, 76, 77, 79, 210
Huang, K. X. D.   36
Hume, David   96, 220–1, 222, 241
Humphrey–Hawkins Act (US, 1975)   122
hydrology   7, 156
hypotheses   58, 74, 101, 111, 118, 133, 179, 182–5, 208, 250
    convergent   249
    efficient market   207
    expectational   125, 126, 127, 181
    joint   232
    life-cycle   62
    maintained   238
    null   203, 206, 231
    permanent income   207
    reduced-rank   183
    testing   184, 186, 203, 204, 205, 214, 249
    VAR analysis useful for   168
    see also NRH
identification   8, 17, 133, 162, 189, 190–1, 228, 230, 238
    cointegration analysis no help in   239
    Cowles Commission approach to   231
    economic/empirical/generic   192
    misuse of the word   240
    observational equivalence and   208–10
    short-run/long-run   225–7, 229, 232
    specification and   9–10
IMF (International Monetary Fund)   31, 123 n.
imports   73–4, 96, 97, 108, 267
impulse response functions   47, 54–7, 74, 110, 210, 212, 242, 243

income   3, 95, 168, 203, 205, 208
    common   51, 52–3
    distribution of   265, 269, 270, 271, 272, 277
    exogenous   204, 207
    fixed   170
    future   204
    gross   45
    increase of   266
    initial   249, 250, 253
    labour   96, 271
    lagged   209
    money and   207
    national   3, 90, 267
    per capita   250, 258, 264, 276
    permanent   207
    ratio of debt to   94, 98
    rental   50–1
    see also real income
income taxes   54
    distortionary   50
indeterminacies   36
indicators   87, 89–90, 97, 98, 100, 106–11 *passim*
    monetary   122, 144, 148, 149
    unrestricted   86
indices   267
    price   3, 45, 91, 148, 229
    trade-weighted   92
    wage   182
induction   1, 4, 10
inferences   9, 49, 95, 109, 168, 186, 213–14, 241
    causal   250
    predictive   256
inflation   2, 16, 71, 91–111, 121–8 *passim*, 142, 175, 241
    accelerating   211
    agents mispredict   181
    assumption about   155
    cointegrating with velocity   180
    control of   160, 193, 280
    deemed to be resultant of all forces of excess demand   144
    direct targeting   150
    driven by money   160
    expected   131
    explaining historically   161
    explicit target   149
    future   181
    money growth and   134, 169–72
    non-stationary   172
    output and   123, 127, 128, 159
    peak   86
    price   168, 176, 178, 179
    short-run   194
    slowdown of   158
    stable   211
    stationary   172
    stochastic trends   188
    theories of   145

wage   98, 103, 109
world   159, 162
see also deflation; stagflation
innovations   90, 109, 226
  exogenous   267
  financial   86
  major   266–7
  measurement   132
  minor   268, 275
  normally distributed   27
  variances   88, 134
instrument rules   131
instruments   257
  control   146–9, 150
  monetary   180, 228
integration   17, 133–4, 172, 176, 238
  order of   203, 207, 211
  quantitative and qualitative analysis   257
  see also ARIMA
intercepts   89, 100, 101, 214
interest rates   12, 90, 91, 95, 108, 122, 158,
    162, 241, 269
  affected by stochastic trends   188
  bond   177
  control instrument   148–9, 152
  differentials   104, 109
  estimated policy rule   132
  evidence on   230
  international   93
  liquidity effect of monetary policy on   230
  long-run/short-run   93, 98, 101, 180
  monetary policy and   168
  nominal   133, 170, 181, 182; one-period   128
  predicting   146, 155
  real   128, 159, 180, 181, 182, 211
  setting   129
  short-term   180, 194
  'smoothing' terms   130
  spread   180, 181, 188, 194
  standard deviations of   233
  world   211
intermediate goods   264, 267
internal economies   264
interpretability   187, 192, 233, 240
  structural   190
interpretation   208–14, 242, 266
  dynamic   275
interventions   17, 88, 182, 183
  policy   15, 78
invariance   17, 89, 151, 185, 189, 190, 240, 276
inventions   266
inventories   3
investment   38, 55, 120, 163
  aggregate   267, 268, 276
  co-movements of   29
  consequences of, in research   266
  dampening effect on   56
  falling   56–7

government, unproductive   252
highly volatile   27
household induced to increase   56
improved opportunities   96
inhibited   39
net   3
time   50
Iraq   61
Irons, J.   126
irrational behaviour   7
IS equation/curve   128, 129, 151, 157
IS–LM model   10–11, 12–13, 129
IS–type relation   124
Issing, O.   117
Italy   188, 271

Jacobs, J.   23 n., 25
Japan   121, 211
Jenkins, G. M.   241
  see also Box–Jenkins
Johansen, S.   85, 98, 167 n., 183–7 *passim*, 191,
    192, 206, 213, 226, 227, 232
Johnson, P.   256
Jonung, L.   117
Journal of Economic Perspectives   127
Juselius, K.   5, 9–10, 12, 17, 72–3, 98, 163,
    167, 171, 175, 179, 187–9 *passim*, 191,
    192, 219–23 *passim*, 225–34, 237–9 *passim*,
    241, 244
Jörgensen, C.   183, 186

Kaldor, N.   212
Kalecki, M.   272
Kerr, W.   129
Keynes, J. M.   272, 280
Keynesian economics   2, 6, 13 n., 63, 65, 72,
    73, 93, 143, 278 n.
  demand shocks   206
  growth model based on   263
  monetarist–Keynesian controversy   1, 251
  new   11, 79, 157
Kiley, M.   36
Kimball, M.   119 n.
King, G.   215 n.
King, M.   117
King, R. E.   115 n., 117, 118 n., 119 n., 230
King, R. G.   34, 37, 38 n., 78, 129, 178, 206, 207
Kiyotaki, N.   39
Klein, F. A.   61
Klein, L. R.   72, 77, 208
Klein–Goldberger model   78
knowledge   220, 244
  a priori   9, 186
  tacit   152
Kohn, D.   117
Kongsted, H.-C.   167 n., 183
Koopmans, T. C.   63
Korean War   44, 64, 69–70, 211

Kosobud, R. 207–8
Kotlikoff, L. 30
Kourtellos, A. 249 n.
Kreps, D. M. 10 n.
Kuhn, T. S. 3, 10, 13, 146
Kuwait 61
Kydland, F. E. 62, 63, 78, 118, 120

labour 51, 131, 264, 269, 272, 275
   costs of 267, 268, 276
   machines capable of saving 270
   share in income 271
   see also division of labour
labour demand 50, 52, 98, 108
labour markets 7, 11, 14, 50, 76, 90, 96
   efficiency 77
   policies aimed at reform 108
labour supply 36, 54, 118
   downward shifts 169
   elasticity of 36
lag operators 45, 48, 185
lags 149, 184, 192, 202, 214
   fixed 125, 126
   income 209
   inflation 101
   information 130
   money 108, 203, 204, 209, 229
   productivity 267, 268
   wage 159, 267, 268
Lakatos, I. 10, 11
Landes, D. 257
Landon–Lane, J. 23 n.
Larrain, F. 30, 39
Laxton, D. 31
Layard, R. 96
Leamer, E. 254
least-squares estimation 45, 89, 209, 210
Leroy, S. F. 212
Levin, A. 117, 124 n., 125 n.
Levine, R. 254, 255
Levtchenkova, S. 190, 199 n.
Liederman, L. 117, 122 n.
likelihood functions 17, 90, 187, 189, 190,
   191, 237, 258
   shapes of 238
Likelihood Ratio trace test 185
linear conditions:
   combinations 188, 205, 208, 213
   constraints 207
   cross-country regressions 252
   difference equations 47
   functions 190
   restrictions 191
   transformations 189
   trends 74, 94, 175, 176, 178, 184, 203
linearity 48, 74, 106
Lipsey, R. G. 6 n., 144
liquidity 93, 230

Litterman, R. B. 119
Liu, Z. 36, 207 n.
LM curve 232
loans 269
localization 264
log linearization procedure 54
logarithms 91, 96, 175, 203, 208, 213
Long, J. B. 118 n.
long-run factors 145, 167, 172, 173, 187, 265
   cointegration 86
   equilibrium 110, 111, 212, 231
   feedbacks 17, 237
   identification 226–7, 232
   inflation 16, 101, 103–4, 142
   money 107, 133, 134, 162, 168, 178, 204,
      205, 230
   Phillips curve 127, 159
   price homogeneity 179–81, 184
   productivity 268
   real wages 268
   restrictions on parameters 186–9, 191–4
   steady-state 73, 192
   stochastic trends 178, 185
   structural trends 178
   supply curve 264
losses 28, 39
LSE approach 17, 204, 212, 225, 227, 230–3
Lucas, R. E. 23, 29, 62, 116, 118 n., 119, 125,
      126, 127, 130 n., 135, 150–1, 228, 230, 249
Lucas supply curve 12, 159, 206, 222
Lwin, T. 258

McCallum, B. T. 7, 9, 11–12, 13, 16–17, 69, 74–5,
      117, 118, 126–9 *passim*, 130–2 nn., 142, 146,
      148–53 *passim*, 155, 157–8, 159, 162–4 *passim*,
      230, 239, 242
Maccini, L. 23 n.
McCloskey, D. N. 201
McConnell, M. 35 n.
McCulloch, R. 254
machines 266, 267, 268, 269, 276
   capable of saving labour 270
macrotheories 1, 5, 7, 156
Maes, I. 16
Major, John 94
Malthus, T. R. 265
Mankiw, N. G. 118, 249
Manuelli, R. 249 n.
manufacturing 47, 266, 271
   labour productivity growth in 267
mapping 32, 192
marginal cost curve 265, 266
marginal productivity curve 266
Marglin, S. A. 277 n.
Maritz, J. 258
mark-ups 108
   equilibrium 97
market clearing 12, 74, 118, 127

markets 98
  competitive 12, 119; perfectly 7
  efficient 207
  foreign exchange 146
  money 170, 171, 186, 187, 233
  oligopolistic 6
Markov process 199 n.
  two-state 38
MARs (moving average representations) 47, 48,
    78–9, 93, 111, 184–5, 203, 233
Marschak, J. 126, 150–1
Marshall, A. 242, 264, 265, 275
Marx, K. 275
mathematical uniqueness 191, 192, 240
matrices 9, 183, 184, 226
  covariance 190
  non-singular 185, 187
Mauro, P. 255
maximization problem 64
Mayer, T. 1 n., 15, 69–70, 73, 239
means 104, 172
  unconditional 87
measurement 28–9, 44, 77, 85, 91, 109, 130,
    132, 146–52, 240, 242
  making sense of 133
  without theory 8, 63
mechanization 271
Mellander, E. 190
Meltzer, A. H. 124 n., 239
Menderhausen, H. 271
Merz, M. 62 n.
methodology 2–5, 8, 13, 148, 160, 161, 167,
    221, 237, 278
  dating 30
  modifications in 257
  univariate 203
  VAR 230
Metin, K. 96, 98
microeconomics 1–8, 118
  empirical 256
military build-ups/expenditures 44, 252
Mill, J. S. 141–3, 144, 150, 153, 156
Miller, A. 254
Miller, R. 11
Minkin, A. 249 n.
Mintz, I. 25 n.
Mishkin, F. S. 117, 122 n., 124 n.
Mitchell, T. J. 254
Mitchell, W. C. 23–4, 24–5, 29, 61, 62, 63, 77,
    78, 142
Mizon, G. E. 159, 183
models 1, 2, 3, 7, 11, 71, 76, 101, 105, 142,
    158, 219–23
  aggregate 67
  business cycle 15, 16, 63, 67, 76–8 *passim*
  comparison of 107–8
  confidence in 222
  deterministic 9

difference-stationary 202
dynamic linear regression 204
  econometric 144, 167–95, 222, 231
  efficiency wage 43–60, 64
  empirical 8, 86, 88, 144, 153, 170, 186, 190,
    202, 228, 276
  equilibrium 73, 228
  evaluation of 8, 15
  Fed 123 n., 124
  growth 257, 263; endogenous 35,
    37, 252
  Keynesian 6, 63, 72, 73
  limited participation 230
  linear, misspecified 252
  LSE approach 225
  mathematical 143
  monetary 228, 230
  money demand 126, 163
  MPS-style 130 n.
  multivariate 238
  neoclassical 253, 257
  optimization-based 6, 131
  parametric 31
  policy 31
  price adjustment 128
  price stickiness in 12, 36, 119, 230
  pricing to market 108
  quantitative 125
  random walk 33
  rational expectations 252
  RBC 78, 79, 118–20 *passim*, 132, 146, 230,
    239–40, 242
  regression 256, 258
  representative agent 64, 65, 66, 67
  rigorous aggregation in 6
  selection literature 254
  specification 8, 9, 10, 131
  staggered price 36
  static 90
  stationary dynamic 88
  statistical 9, 35, 145, 184, 225, 226, 227,
    231, 276
  steady-state 253, 276
  stochastic 10, 168, 189
  stripped-down 150
  structural 221, 226
  theoretical 9, 10, 32, 34, 35, 48, 190, 222,
    223, 229
  time-series 14
  trend-stationary 202
  very unrestricted 109
  Walrasian 13
  see also ARDL; ARIMA; Box–Jenkins;
    ECMs; ENDO; Harrod–Domar;
    IS–LM; Klein–Goldberger; MULTIMOD;
    Schmitt–Grohe; Solow–Swan; VAR models
moments 54
  conditional 49, 57

moments (*Cont.*)
  population 253
  second 77, 120
monetarist–Keynesian controversy 1, 251
monetary policy 11, 12, 16, 71, 76, 83–164,
  179, 209
  eased and tightened 39
  effectiveness/efficiency of 189, 192, 193, 231
  liquidity effect on interest rates 230
  VAR models and 228
money demand 5, 104, 107, 108, 128, 129,
  150, 162, 192, 238
  adjusted to supply quantities 171
  aggregate 158, 169, 177, 179, 183, 193
  congruent representation of 232–3
  downward shifts 169–70
  empirically stable/identifiable 168, 171, 193
  equals money supply 207
  excess 86, 91, 98, 99
  higher in wartime 88
  instrument to influence 180
  long-run, elasticity for 204, 205
  modelling 126, 163
  money stock adjusting to 193
  precautionary and speculative 179
  stable 193, 194
  structural equations 204
  technological change and 242
money demand functions 5, 126, 129, 134, 239
  long-run 133, 204
money growth and inflation 134, 169–72
  see also real money
money markets 170, 171, 186, 187, 233
  interaction rates 188
money stock 187, 190, 191
  controlling 193–4
money supply 168, 170, 177, 193, 212, 238
  money demand equals 207
  surprises 12, 206
monopoly 6, 13, 119
Monte Carlo study 86, 87
Moore, G. R. 128, 130 n.
Moore, J. 39
Morgan, M. S. 1 n., 6, 8 n., 15, 16, 62 n., 77,
  79, 115 n., 143 n., 152 n., 155, 156, 158,
  160, 220, 221, 276 n.
Morrison, M. 143 n.
motivation 227–8, 230–2
movements 48, 49, 54–5, 56, 58
  asset price 39
  common 179
  cumulative 28–9
  cyclical 77
  exogenous 44, 47
  see also co-movements
moving average, see ARIMA; MARs
MTM (Monetary Transmission
  Mechanism) 228–9

Muellbauer, J. 85 n., 107
multicollinearity 123, 241
MULTIMOD model 31
multipliers 228
multivariate forms 203, 232, 238
  analysis 79
  cointegration 171, 177
  distribution 231
  normal process 182
Muth, R. F. 116 n.

NAIRU (non-accelerating-inflation rate of
  unemployment) 127, 128, 130 n.
Napoleonic Wars 94 n.
narrative approach 44
Nason, J. 23 n., 35, 37, 120
national debt 90, 94, 98
nationalization 86
NBER (National Bureau of Economic Research,
  US) 25, 26, 30, 74, 117, 123, 124, 128, 130
  reference cycles 210
Neale, A. J. 95
Neilsen, B. 186
Nelson, C. R. 206
Nelson, E. 12, 115 n., 117, 118 n., 119, 129,
  151 n., 206, 222
neoclassical economics 56, 115, 125, 132
  growth theory 249, 250, 253, 263, 265,
  266, 275, 277, 278
New Zealand 122
Newbold, P. 205
Newey, W. 49
Newton, Sir Isaac 241–2
Neymann–Pearson testing 238
NGT (new growth theory) 13, 275, 276, 277,
  278, 279
Nickell, S. 96
nominal money 183, 184
non-durables 62, 269
non-linear mechanisms 72, 98, 107, 253
non-profit organizations 266
non-stationarity 75, 85, 86, 97, 109, 134, 174–6
  passim, 183, 226
  cointegration and 171, 186, 189
  many ways of removing 241
  money velocity 180, 181
  variables 171, 172, 173, 208, 237
Nordhaus, W. D. 96
normalization 187, 189, 190, 191, 213
North, D. 144
NOW rates 233
NRH (natural rate hypothesis) 127, 128
nuisance parameters 90
nulls 203, 206, 213, 231, 238

objective function 66
observational equivalence 8, 208–10,
  240, 245

observations 144, 145, 171–4 *passim*, 186, 214, 254, 256
  econometrics as 221–2
oil crises 86, 87, 92–3, 98, 105, 122, 161
Okun's rule 27, 32, 33
oligopoly 6
OPEC (Organization of Petroleum Exporting Countries) 61
optimal decisions 31
optimization 6, 7, 119, 120, 131
  intertemporal 156
Oswald, A. J. 7, 13–14, 80, 157, 162, 164
'outliers' 88, 89, 90, 161
output 13, 29, 36, 53, 62, 69, 122, 268
  aggregate 230
  cumulated gains in 35
  deviations from 98
  evidence on 230
  growth rate 75, 77, 78, 103, 123, 158, 162
  inflation and 123, 127, 128, 159
  input and 97
  lead and lag correlations with 120
  losses in 28, 39
  manufacturing 209
  market-clearing 74
  measuring changes in 150
  monetary policy and 133
  monetary shocks and 119
  national 94
  natural-rate 130
  nominal 91
  per capita 34
  persistence in 79
  real 132, 158
  shocks to 71, 95
  trend growth in 37
  variability of 131
  variations not perfect 79
overheating economy 73
overidentification 187, 191, 231
overvaluation 109, 116

Pagan, A. 1 n., 6, 9, 14, 15, 16, 27 n., 36, 39, 61–3 *passim*, 69–80 *passim*, 156–8 *passim*, 167, 190, 199 n., 242, 243
panic 70
par values 116
parameter changes 87
parameter values 9, 125
Paruolo, P. 184
Pasinetti, L. 269, 271
'pass through' effects 97
Patinkin, D. 129 n.
pattern recognition techniques 26
PcFiml test procedures 191
peaks and troughs 26–7, 28, 79
Perez, S. J. 86, 132

performance 15
  inflation rate 123
  utility-based 125
periodicity 24
'perpetual countermotives' 141
Perron, B. 85, 90, 95, 211, 214
persistence 78–9
  GDP 206
  inflation 128
  output 79
  shocks 34, 35, 36, 39
  time 172
  unemployment 13
perturbations 105
Pesaran, M. H. 199 n., 200 n.
phase-averaging method 25
phases 28–9
Phelps, E. S. 127
Phelps Brown, E. H. 270
Phillips, A. W. H. 90, 96, 121
  see also Phillips curve
Phillips, P. C. B. 85, 205, 214
Phillips curve 13, 36, 126, 130 n.
  long-run 127, 159
  seen as a system relationship 7
plate-stacking 105–6
Ploberger, W. 90
Plosser, C. I. 12, 38 n., 78, 118 n., 119, 206, 222, 223
policy 23, 26, 31, 69, 74–8 *passim*, 80
  'deeper' answers to questions 110
  fiscal 48, 50, 209
  ineffectiveness proposition 118
  labour market reform 108
  macroeconomics and 14–16
  major regime changes 86
  trade 146
  see also monetary policy
politics 39
polynomials 48, 186
  finite-ordered matrix 45, 47
  infinite 185
population 90, 253, 265
  growth 249
  increasing 24, 266
portfolios 95, 96
Portier, F. 119 n.
post hoc ergo propter hoc fallacy 251
ppp (purchasing power parity) 92, 98, 100, 104, 106, 208
  deviations 101, 109, 162
  disequilibrium effect on inflation 108
  slow swings 109
precautionary measures 88
predictions 32, 37–8, 146, 155, 156, 180, 181
  competing 228
  counterfactual 79
  false 76

predictions (*Cont.*)
  future income   204
  theoretical   208
preferences   48, 119, 131
Prescott, E. C.   29, 62, 63, 78, 118, 120
price adjustment behaviour   118, 127, 128, 158
price controls   86, 88, 97, 98, 99
price-cost cycle   36
price deflators   90
price rigidity   36
price stickiness   7, 12, 36, 119–20, 132, 230
  ad hoc assumptions of   13
prices   71, 95, 149, 164, 170, 176
  adjustment   36, 118, 127, 128, 132, 158
  aggregate   87
  approximated   175
  asset   38, 39, 157, 207
  capital   269–70
  changes in   148, 162
  commodity   87, 97, 100, 109, 229
  debt determines   104
  determining   171
  evidence on   230
  external   90
  factor   73
  final-demand   96
  future   126, 162
  gold   121
  homogeneity of   178–81, 184
  $I(1)$ 181–2
  $I(2)$ 177–81
  machinery   266, 267, 268, 269, 270, 276
  money and   168, 194
  nominal   183, 184, 268
  oil   211
  relative   92
  shocks to   95
  stochastic trends in   178
  world   91, 93, 98, 104, 109, 161
private sector   47, 96, 97, 108
privatization   86
probability   27, 34, 51, 52, 213
  asymptotic   214
  conditional   258
  exogenous   53, 69
  joint   258
  posterior   258
  weighted average of   161
production   62, 263, 264, 265
  see also factors of production
production curve   266
production function   120, 131
  aggregate   252, 277
  Cobb–Douglas   252, 266, 270–2
  neoclassical   276
  shifts of   266
productivity   36, 96, 97, 120, 264, 271, 272, 275
  growth of, impulses determining   266–9

long-run behaviour   268
marginal   266, 270
permanent shocks to   207
slowdowns   2, 268, 269
profitability   269
profits   265
  excess   162
  margins   97
  maximizing   5, 53
propagation mechanism   96, 97
prosperity   24
proxies   97, 250, 251
proximate determinants   160

Quah, D.   206, 249, 250, 253–4, 276
quantitative properties   54–9
quantitative theory   31, 162
quantity theory   96
Quiros, G. P.   35 n.

Rahbeck, A.   183
Ramey, G.   33
Ramey, V.   43
Ramey–Shapiro episodes   44–7, 48, 57, 58, 74
Ramsey, J. B.   101
random walks   32, 33, 37, 38, 78, 202
  asset prices/consumptions should be   207
  classic image of   201
  drift with   71
  pure   134
  regressions of unrelated variables following   205
randomness   4, 24, 25, 176, 201, 203, 220, 229, 256
  Bayesian view of   161
  residuals   231
rank-and-order conditions   208, 240
Rappaport, S.   11
rational expectations   5, 12, 116, 119, 127, 128, 146, 252
  ex ante   155
  incorporation of   125, 126
  model-based   189–90
  resistance to   118
  significance of   17
rationality   1, 4, 6–7
rationalization   14
rationing   5, 86, 88, 99
  credit   70, 107
raw materials   71, 269
RBCs (real business cycles)   7, 12, 17, 34–8
  passim, 43, 50, 54, 64, 70, 76, 80, 237
  models   78, 79, 118–20 *passim*, 132, 146, 230, 239–40, 242
Reagan, Ronald   45, 73, 74
real income   104, 133, 177–80 *passim*, 187
  real money and   203
  shocks to   191
  trend-adjusted   175

real money 184, 187, 203
  balances 129, 130, 133, 157, 239
real wages 50, 57, 71, 75
  after-tax 47, 55, 56, 58
  before-tax 54
  downward pressure on 56
  long-run behaviour 268
  productivity-adjusted 96
Rebelo, S. T. 37, 63, 118 n.
recessions 27, 61, 62, 157
  definition of 70, 75
  mild but lengthy 122
recovery 33, 61
reduced-rank conditions 183, 184, 186, 187
reduction theory 231
re-estimation 107
reforms 182, 183
  labour market 108
regressions 87, 95, 98, 105, 171, 209, 238
  growth 249–56 *passim*
  linear 252; bivariate 88; dynamic 204
  static 88
  unrelated variables 205
Renelt, D. 254, 255
rents 50, 265
representative agents 4, 5, 6, 64–7 *passim*
  utility level for 125
research 15, 23, 86, 125, 130, 131, 228
  business-cycle 61, 62, 66
  consequences of investment in 266
  empirical 24
  expenses in 268
  medical 72
  progressive 242
RESET test 101
residuals 88, 98, 101, 109, 185, 278
  estimated 204, 212
  identical 204
  non-zero 86
  random 231
  scaled 105
  unexplained 249
  VAR 189, 190
resources 96
response functions 48
  dynamic 46, 56, 57
  see also impulse response functions
restrictions 184, 186–9, 191–4, 213, 221, 227–30
  passim, 241, 257
  capital movements 171, 182
  coefficients 189
  dummy variables 100, 101
  just-identifying 187
  smoothness 258
  variance 240
returns:
  constant 270
  diminishing 265–6

increasing 263–5, 266
  to scale 250
Ricardo, D. 265, 266, 267, 268, 269, 271, 275 n.
Riksbank–IIES Conference (Stockholm,
    1998) 117, 123, 124, 128, 130
risk 56, 88
  exchange rate 93
risk aversion 38
risk-sharing:
  imperfect 50
  optimal 69
  perfect 69
Robertson, J. 190, 199 n.
robustness 152, 254, 255, 276
Rodrik, D. 255
Rogerson, R. 69
Romer, C. D. 132
Romer, D. 30, 132, 163, 167–70 *passim*, 189, 192–4
    passim, 244, 249, 251, 266, 268–9, 271, 272
Rotemberg, J. 43, 117, 119 n., 128, 129, 130 n.
Rubin, J. 178
Rudebusch, G. 117, 230

Sachs, J. F. 30, 39
Sahasakul, C. 45
St-Amour, P. 38
Sala-i-Martin, X. 254, 275 n.
Salanti, A. 18, 277 n.
salaries 73
Salkever, D. S. 86
Samuelson, P. 269
Sargan, J. D. 96
Sargent, T. J. 64, 65, 66, 116, 117, 118 n.,
    125 n., 127, 207
savings 96, 118, 163, 208, 233, 249
scarcity 70
Schmitt–Grohe, S. 35, 36, 75, 76
Schumpeter, J. A. 266, 269, 275
Schwartz, A. J. 90
science 8, 13, 141–5, 146–52
Seater, J. 45 n.
Senhadji, A. S. 214
sense data 220, 222
sentiment 38
separability 129
serial correlation 32–7 *passim*, 71, 79, 164
  sixth-order 101
  strong positive, in inflation rates 128
Shadman–Mehta, F. 90
Shapiro, M. D. 43
  see also Ramey–Shapiro
Shaw, G. K. 279 n.
shift factors 85, 87, 88, 90, 109, 111, 263
  production function 266
  time 160
  wealth ownership 94
shocks 14, 30, 73, 74, 85, 88, 90, 119, 134
  autonomous 177, 190

shocks (*Cont.*)
  belief   36, 76
  defence spending   63
  deflationary   97
  demand   206, 210–12, 240; aggregate
    169–70, 179
  estimated   190
  exogenous   15, 44, 48, 76
  external   96, 97
  fiscal   6, 16, 43–60, 64, 207
  government expenditure   35
  important   39–40
  income   209
  inflationary   92, 169
  invariant   190
  'large-' and 'medium-size'   86
  major   96, 211
  monetary   12–13, 39, 71, 119, 191, 207, 209,
    212, 228–30 *passim*
  nominal   177–8, 184
  observable   211–12
  permanent   32, 175, 176, 183, 206, 207, 210, 243
  persistent   34, 35, 39
  policy   39, 49, 54, 56, 57, 58, 64
  post-World War I   94–5
  price   71, 97
  productivity   36, 207
  random   4
  real   177, 178, 184, 191
  relationships invariant to   17
  relative-cost   169
  response of variables to   79, 171–2
  stochastic   31
  structural   190
  supply   206, 210–12; aggregate   221
  taste   239
  temporary   63, 64
  transitory   175, 203, 206, 210, 242
  unanticipated   175, 189, 190
  unexpected   243
  unique   190
  VAR-based   230
  volatility of   39
  white noise   205
  see also technology shocks
short-run conditions   191–4, 265
  adjustment   237
  equilibrium   212–13
  feedbacks   17
  identification   227, 229, 232
  inflation   194
  interest rates   93, 98, 101, 180
  supply curve   264
shortages   71
Sichel, D. E.   33
significance   58, 100, 191, 192, 214, 238, 254
significant mean reversion   172, 173, 182
silver   121

simplification   86
  sequential   100
Sims, C. A.   6, 15, 17, 72, 73, 75, 77–80 *passim*,
  119, 120 n., 142, 144, 160–2 *passim*, 200,
  207, 212, 221, 229, 230, 237–9, 241–3 *passim*
simulations   33, 34, 35, 36, 37, 119
  computer   39
  stochastic   125
simultaneity problem   251
single-currency Euro scheme   122
Singleton, K. J.   118, 119, 132
Smith, Adam   263, 265, 266, 267, 271, 275
Smith, R. P.   9, 12, 17, 126 n., 199 n., 200 n., 204,
  213 n., 219–22 *passim*, 225, 227, 233, 238–41
  passim, 243, 244–5
social disruption/problems   162, 252
social science   3
sociology   6, 240
Solow, R. M.   1, 36, 127, 272, 275 n., 278
Solow–Swan growth model   249, 250, 252, 253
Spain   188
special effects   104
specification   17, 18, 50, 126, 131, 158, 192–3, 253
  ad hoc   6
  correct'   133
  forward-looking   157
  identification and   9–10
  LSE solution to   231
  rational expectations   252
spectral density   79
Sraffa, P.   265, 269, 275
stabilizers   211
stagflation   109
standard deviation   27, 34, 37, 58, 90
  moving   233
  residual   105
  unconditional   104
Starr, R.   233
state of emergency   88
stationarity   70, 74, 171–5 *passim*, 179, 203, 241
  cointegration   188, 189
  errors   180, 202, 205
  real interest rates   181, 182
  steady-state   188
  tests for nulls of   213
  vector process   185
  velocity   194
statistics   1, 3, 4, 14, 17, 63, 75, 80, 163, 182,
  183, 201–6, 244
  classical cycle   33
  diagnostic   105
  duration   33
  economic theory and   219
  evaluating   210
  interpretable and useful   220
  model selection literature in   254
  modern techniques/methods   18, 257–8
  observable regularities   8

output series 79
representations 143
significance 191, 192
Smith's lament of use of 222
stable relationships 160
summary 12, 206
techniques 206–7
test 57–9, 208
see also under various headings. e.g.
approximation; business cycles; hypotheses; models; technology
steady-state factors 34, 101, 103, 104, 170
deviations 163, 171, 185
equilibrium 278
long-run 73, 192
multiple 253, 276
static 237
stationary 188
stochastic 171
theoretical 186
Stephenson, E. F. 45
sterling overvaluation 109
Stiglitz, J. E. 5 n.
see also Dixit–Stiglitz
stochastic properties 9, 17, 45, 120, 125, 160, 170–1, 174, 190
disturbance terms 239
statistical formulation based on 172
time-dependent 167, 175
see also models; shocks; stochastic trends; variables
stochastic trends 25, 34, 35, 173, 177, 184, 203
common 180, 185, 189, 190, 205, 207, 244
forcing processes with 26
inflation 188
linear 176
long-run 178, 185
medium-run 185
nominal 191
real 179
second-order 175, 183
Stock, J. H. 61, 62, 63, 117, 130
structural adjustment/change 73, 75, 86
stylized facts 14, 178, 208, 229, 277
evidence on 228
explanation for some 278
VARs and 230
substitution 269
marginal elasticity of 270
Summers, L. H. 12 n., 215, 268
SuperNow rates 233
supply 206, 210–12
aggregate 169, 177, 183, 222
see also labour supply; money supply
supply curve 264
surplus 94
surprises 12, 206
see also shocks

Svensson, L. E. O. 117, 122 n., 123, 130, 131
Sylos Labini, P. 18, 266, 270, 272, 275–7
symmetry 191

Tabellini, G. 117
Tamborini, R. 5
target rules 131
targets 146–52
taxes/tax rates 46, 54, 57, 108, 211
distortionary 50, 56, 252
lump-sum 50, 51, 55, 56
marginal 45, 47, 50, 56
see also income taxes
Taylor, J. B. 117, 118, 121, 123, 124, 128, 130, 131, 151 n., 152, 157, 164
Taylor, M. P. 133
technical progress 97, 131, 134, 263, 264, 270
economists willing to analyze 265
technology 48, 64, 75, 134, 207
business cycle model driven by 76
econometric 86
output using 53
payments 239
statistical 145
technology shocks 15, 34–5, 36, 37, 78, 118, 119, 120, 239, 244
negative 169
Temple, J. 276 n.
temporal behaviour 32
testing 8, 10, 12, 57–9, 184, 244
cointegration 239
cross-section 270–1
diagnostic 231
Dickey–Fuller 206
empirical 191, 270, 271
hypothesis 184, 186, 203, 204, 205
Neyman–Pearson procedures 17
unit-root 85, 185, 186, 206, 214, 222, 238
Thatcher, Margaret 245
time 3, 50, 52, 54, 86, 160, 249, 250
absolute 241
time-dependence 17, 170
macro-data 172–4
stochastic 167, 175
time-series 3, 8, 12, 14, 18, 91, 96, 172, 177, 221
aggregate 29
LSE approach to modelling 225
model parameter values consistent with 125
monthly 161
observed 210
only one realization of 144
stochastic 171, 174
tests on 271
unit-roots and 199–217
Tinbergen, J. 105–6, 144, 221, 276 n.
Tobin, J. 10 n., 127, 212, 251
Toro, J. 179, 188

trade:
  balance of 92
  openness 251
  policy 146
trade regulated economies 171
trade union power 108
transactions 134, 135, 179, 242
transfers 51–2, 64–5
transformations 240
  linear 189
  model 257
'transparency' 150
Treasury bills 45, 90
trends 24, 37, 62, 94, 96, 116–20, 122, 174, 211
  aggregate demand 179
  common 179, 181, 185, 187, 189–91, 220
  cycles and 210
  deviations from 98, 104, 178
  linear 74, 94, 175, 176, 178, 184, 203
  non-stationary 183
  quadratic 183, 184
  stationary 202
  structural 178
  time 183
  unconditional 87
  see also deterministic trends; stochastic trends
Trostel, P. A. 7, 13–14
turbulence 86, 88, 97, 156
turning points 25, 32
  essence of 75
  false 26
  finding 26–7
  measuring the cycle using 28–9

Uhligo, H. 115 n.
unbiasedness 7, 155, 156
uncertainty 48–9, 109
underdeveloped countries 267, 268, 270, 272
undervaluations 101, 109
unemployment 2, 50–2 *passim*, 54, 90, 98, 158, 211
  changes in 70, 101, 108
  cointegration relations 104
  cycles 75, 96
  equilibrium 54
  fluctuations 73
  involuntary 66
  persistence of 13
  see also NAIRU
unemployment insurance 51, 65
unit-roots 172–3, 174, 176, 178, 199–217, 237, 239
  development of 219
  testing 85, 185, 186, 206, 222, 238
United Kingdom 39, 209, 241
  balance of payments 159
  devaluation 156
  inflation 16, 85–114, 157

North Sea oil 211, 212
  see also Bank of England
United States 25, 35, 44–5, 49, 54, 61, 222
  defence spending shock 63
  economic fluctuations 79
  GDP 32, 33, 214
  monetary policy/inflation 76, 121, 122, 132, 148
  money demand 233
  nominal wages 71
  position in world power 86
  productivity growth slowdown 268, 269
  velocity 222
  see also Bretton Woods; Federal Reserve; NBER
Usabiaga, C. 31
utility 125
  ex post 50, 51
  expected 5, 53
  instantaneous 52
  marginal 130
  maximizing 5, 64, 65
utility function 69, 129, 131

value 92, 267
  future 56
  market clearing 127
  mean 104
  monetary reference 149
  natural rate 128
  predicted 210
VAR models 14, 39, 185, 190, 191, 192, 228, 230
  cointegrated 17
  restricted 184
  structural 229
  unrestricted 183
variability 92, 131, 132, 151
variables 27, 29, 72, 85, 92, 134, 174, 204, 249, 254, 275–6
  aggregate 61
  choice 66
  commodity-price 100
  control 150, 152
  disequilibrium between levels of 192
  EER 156
  endogenous 129, 207, 209, 250, 266, 276
  exogenous 48, 49, 170, 171, 211, 266, 278
  expectational 126
  explanatory 13
  fiscal 47, 119
  foreign 211
  goal 189
  growth 258
  indicator 86–90 *passim*, 97, 98, 108, 109, 144, 149–50
  instrumental 251, 257, 276
  interrelations among 78
  levels-cointegrated 241

monetary 129, 144, 149–50, 160, 162, 164, 225, 228, 229
nominal 70, 119
non-fiscal 48
non-stationary 171, 172, 173, 208, 237
omitted 87, 231
policy 228
random 24, 25
real 3, 91, 118, 119, 120, 123, 132, 239
response to shocks 79
Ricardian 268
stationary 172, 173, 179, 202, 203, 205
statistically significant 255
stochastic 161–2, 171–2, 177, 182
target 150, 189
Wold-causal-ordering of 221
see also dummy variables
Varian, H. 5
variance 34–5, 37, 38, 90, 108, 120, 210
disturbance-term 125
error 89, 99
inflation 109
innovation 88, 134
restrictions 240
variates 104
VARs (vector autoregressions) 45, 47, 49, 63, 70, 132–3, 161–2, 168, 209, 225–6, 242, 245
adoption of 207
based on Gaussian errors 167
basic structure determined 185
cointegrated 167, 182, 184, 219, 229, 232
conditional on world prices 98
examining the effect of shocks 212
first-order, one-lag 203
identified 72, 164, 237, 240, 243
initially structural 74
linear functions of residuals 190
linearity assumptions 48
motivation 227–8
number of variables in 214
problems 230
recursive 156
restricted 184
results 229–30
rewritten as VECM 205
standard approach 233
unidentified 220
unrestricted 183, 221
see also VAR models
VECMs (vector error-correction models) 205
vectors 47, 49, 70, 178, 181, 182, 185, 186
cointegrating 111, 213, 226, 227, 230, 231
velocity of circulation 179–80, 181, 188, 193, 222
constant 208
stationary 194

Vercelli, A. 1 n., 10, 11, 12
Vietnam War 45, 61, 70, 211
Vredin, A. 190

wage rigidity 36
wages 66, 73, 88, 90, 95, 104, 158, 265, 270
bidding up 96
efficiency 43–60, 64
inflated 98, 103, 109
lagged 159
nominal 71
price of machinery and 266, 267, 276
variations 268
see also real wages
Walras, M. E. L. 5, 13
Walsh, C. E. 126
Walsh, W. 277 n.
Walters, A. 116, 163, 164
Wan Jun, H. Y. 275 n.
Warne, A. 190
wars 71, 86, 96, 105, 144
'phoenix effect' of 211
see also Boer; Gulf; Korean; Napoleonic; Vietnam; World Wars
Watson, J. 33
Watson, M. W. 61, 62, 63, 119 n., 120, 123 n.
wealth 94
Weber, M. 279
Wecker, W. 27
Weiss, L. 119
welfare 13, 78
state creation and partial destruction 86
Wells, G. 23 n.
West, K. 49
White, H. 101
white noise 12, 202, 205, 206
Whiteman, C. H. 233
Wicksell, K. 270
Wieland, V. 117, 124 n.
Williams, J. 117, 124 n.
Wolman, A. 117, 125 n.
Woodford, M. 43, 50 n., 117, 126, 129
workers 54, 267
shirking 50, 51, 52, 53, 55–6, 65, 66, 69
see also hours worked
World Wars:
First 91, 94 n., 98, 99, 107
Second 4, 25 n., 88, 91, 98, 99, 107
World Wide Web 124

Yule, G. U. 205
Yun, T. 119 n.

Zellner, A. 212

Printed in the United States of America/BNB